To
Julia Haskell Nixon
Sarah Nixon Esslinger
John Haskell Nixon

PREFACE

Physical education today, in a turbulent, rapidly changing cultural milieu, faces unprecedented problems, challenges, and opportunities. Professional students, teachers, coaches, and administrators have a clear need and a heavy responsibility to keep themselves abreast of the most recent developments which change the countenance of this area of scholarly study, research and professional service.

In recent years there has been an almost exponential increase in the number and types of publications concerning physical education, emanating from a wide variety of sources both within and outside of this field. It is beyond the power of the individual physical educator to peruse even one major sector of this plethora of research and professional literature. One can only hope the instructor is astute enough to select and study the priority items which will help him to carry out his responsibilities most effectively.

Another major trend in physical education is the rapid development and extension of specializations, or branches of particular emphasis, and the subsequent pledging of allegiance of the individual physical educator to one or to only a few of these areas of concentration. The era of the specialist has brought forth an accompanying surge in specialized literature. Now more young people than ever before seek highly specialized graduate preparation in specific areas of physical education. Others, both neophyte majors and experienced physical educators, choose to remain in roles requiring widespread generalized interests and competences—in teacher education or administration—or foundations and principles in the broad sense.

The young college student who is deciding whether or not to embark on a career in physical education and those who have definitely committed themselves to it are faced with a major challenge in attempting to gain a general understanding of the field of physical education, both as an area of scholarly study and research and as a profession. They want to know what are its dimensions, it roles, its challenges, its priority concerns, its body of knowledge, its school programs, its philosophical rationale, its value structure, and similar critical questions.

This text, in its eighth edition, intends to serve the main purpose which prompted its inception in 1934, namely, to provide interested and concerned individuals with a straightforward, succinct account of the nature and scope of physical education in today's world. Arguments, evidence, and citations to the works of well known authorities, both in and outside of physical education, support the concepts, the principles, the generalizations, and the philosophical views expressed. The book introduces the novice to the study of physical education. It also provides a foundational overview for subsequent study, in depth, of specialized areas in physical education for the more mature student. It can serve as an appropriate reference in beginning generalized foundations and principles of physical education courses.

The book has been thoroughly revised and updated in every respect. Many changes have occurred in the past five years, in programs and other practical aspects of physical education, in the growth of knowledge and theory in physical education, and in the several foundational disciplines which undergird physical education. Therefore, the major topics covered in the past editions have been brought up-to-date and expanded. Entirely new sections have been added to present recent material in foundational fields not formerly treated in this book, as well as current information and ideas about many programmatic thrusts made by education in the last three to five years. Over all, the eighth edition is much more complete and has greater depth and breadth than previous editions.

This text continues to provide the reference service for which it has been known since its first edition. Each chapter includes numerous references to the latest articles and books on the major themes presented so that the interested reader can easily locate corroborating evidence, or more detailed information, or alternative viewpoints about controversial topics. The Selected Reference list at the end of each chapter has been completely renovated to make it both current and wide in scope so that a much larger number of highly relevant citations to the literature are immediately available to the interested reader. Also, obsolete references have been culled out of the lists.

For many years, the authors have worked together on mutual

projects in various phases of physical education—both disciplinary and professional in nature. We both are generalists and regard ourselves as analysts and synthesizers who strive to produce clear and rigorous interpretations and observations about major topics, problems, and concerns which permeate physical education. We have discussed our individual views, beliefs, and perspectives on many occasions. Although we are in general agreement on the personal philosophical stance from which we view physical education, we do have our differences and our special convictions. Perhaps these idiosyncrasies are visible on occasion—which is just as well! We take equal responsibility for the content of all of the chapters. We assert a general professional accord with the major propositions in the entire book.

We believe, with the utmost personal conviction, that physical education as a subject in the school and college curriculum is an essential educational experience to which all students are entitled full opportunity and exposure on a regular basis. It should be available as an instructional, curricular experience for all boys and girls from kindergarten through the senior year of college for academic credit. We also view physical education as a fundamental disciplinary field with its own unique body of knowledge, a full-fledged member of the family of scholarly disciplines concerned with the discovery and interpretation of human knowledge.

Chapter organization and presentation have been altered significantly to accommodate an expanded discussion of the foundational fields of knowledge which undergird the discipline of physical education. The latest knowledge and theory in each field have been capsulized and directly applied to representative physical education interests and concerns. Also, foundational fields which were not represented in previous editions have been introduced into this book: philosophy, social psychology, comparative education, neurology, anthropology, and growth and development. Chapters have been enlarged through the combination of closely related disciplinary fields and are identified by these expressions—"The Normative Foundations," "The Socio-cultural Foundations," "The Biological Foundations," and "The Psychological Foundations."

The professional-educational phase of physical education constitutes the other half of the book and is concerned with purposes, nature and scope, curriculum, leisure and recreation, competitive sport, evaluation, employment opportunities, and professional leadership. All propositions and warranted information are representative of current thought and most recent evidence.

The general tenor of the book is hopeful and optimistic, while giving full recognition to the realistic problems and difficulties faced by the practitioners of physical education in their everyday assignments. We believe this philosophical stance will best stimulate young professional students and teachers to dream of innovations and to hold a conviction that desirable changes can and should be put into practice as a continuing professional commitment to provide the finest educational experience possible through the medium of physical education.

Chapters 1 and 2 describe the local, national and world situations and rapidly changing forces which hold great significance for the preparation, selection, and in-service education of physical education teachers and specialists in a wide variety of careers. A realistic portrayal of opportunities for professional employment and advancement, and challenges to be faced, is of particular importance to the neophyte major. The opening chapter is followed by a discussion of elements in programs of professional preparation which will most effectively select and prepare young people for a variety of professional roles in different types of public and private settings. Emphasis is placed upon recent evidence from research and experience about how to prepare "effective teachers" by identifying crucial factors in the pre-service and in-service education of physical education personnel.

Chapters 3 and 4 have been completely rewritten and expanded to provide more detailed analysis about the nature, scope, and purposes of physical education. We believe these chapters have wide applicability to interests and problems faced by any physical educator no matter what his local situation.

Chapter 5, the "Normative Foundations," discusses the major philosophical tenets, the historical influences, and the more recent comparative studies of physical education.

Chapter 6, the "Socio-cultural Foundations" of physical education, draws upon the disciplines of anthropology, sociology, and social psychology and relates the current relevant generalizations and constructs from these fields to the interpretation and practice of physical education.

In Chapter 7, the "Psychological Foundations," there is an intertwining of recent research and theory from growth and development, neurology, kinesiology, psychological learning theories, perceptual-motor learning, motor learning, and social psychology as related to the applied phase of physical education as well as its theoretical and knowledge-based disciplinary framework.

Genetics, biomechanics of human movement, physiology of exercise, and special attention to the vast area of physical fitness, constitute the major elements of Chapter 8, the "Biological Foundations."

The impact of changing concepts of schooling and of recent curriculum innovations, newly proposed curriculum models, varying organizational patterns, the movement toward more individualized and personalized curricula based on the specific needs of each pupil, and contemporary physical education responses to these challenges are treated in depth in Chapter 9, "The Physical Education Curriculum." School programs at each unit level are discussed.

"Competitive Sports," the title of Chapter 10, indicates the general boundaries of the discussion contained in this chapter. Special attention is devoted to the many recent dramatic changes occurring in girls' and women's sports. The latest developments in sports for young children and, at the other end of the sports spectrum, the problems and trends in international sports, including a discernible and troubling trend toward the politicizing of sport for national gain, are analyzed. Sports in schools and colleges, as well as in amateur (nonschool) settings, and professional sports, are scrutinized.

Chapter 11, "Leisure and Physical Education," continues and expands upon the fundamental discussions found in past editions relative to these crucial areas of human concern in a rapidly changing world. Emphasized are the responsibilities of educational institutions and, more particularly, the appropriate roles of physical education in the overall context of leisure and recreation domains.

The book concludes with a "new look" at recent developments of significance to practitioners and researchers alike in the areas of evaluation and research. Special emphasis is devoted to an understanding of the appropriate purposes and uses of formative evaluation by teachers and administrators alike to improve their instructional effectiveness and their program quality. Chapter 12 summarizes the most recent developments in evaluation and research.

Striking pictures of youth in action, enjoying and learning from exciting physical education experiences, are again strategically located throughout the text. For pictorial contributions, the authors express indebtedness and appreciation to:

Gwen R. Waters, Instructional Specialist, Physical Education Depart-
     ment, Los Angeles City Unified School District;

James Walsh, Supervisor of Elementary Physical Education, Bellevue
     Public Schools, Bellevue, Washington;

Robert Murphy, Director of Publicity, Department of Physical Educa-
     tion and Athletics for Men, Stanford University, Stanford, Cali-
     fornia;

Robert L. Paulson, Director, Audiovisual Center, Malcolm Price Lab-
     oratory School, University of Northern Iowa, Cedar Falls, Iowa;
     and

Greyson Daughtrey, Director, Health, Physical Education and Safety,
     Norfolk Public Schools, Norfolk, Virginia.

An aesthetic and meaningful dimension has been added to the
eighth edition through unusual illustrations of women in sport. We
thank La Ferne E. Price for making this possible.

The generous and able assistance of Ester McClellan, Dorothy
Farana, Julie Nixon and John H. Nixon of the Stanford University
Community and of Marie R. Mullan, Sheryl L. Gotts and Janet
Whelan of Madison, Wisconsin, in the preparation of the current
revision is gratefully acknowledged.

Appreciation is also expressed to the Physical Education Division of the American Association for Health, Physical Education and
Recreation for support of the Curriculum Project through which clarification and elaboration of the curriculum theory basic to much of the
material presented in Chapter 9 was encouraged during the past
decade.

In summary, we are pleased to have the opportunity and the challenge to again contribute another edition to the professional life of one
of physical education's most influential books, an influence spanning
a time period of forty years. We pay tribute to its founders, Professor
Eugene W. Nixon and Professor Frederick W. Cozens. We recognize
the invaluable contributions made in the past by the late Florence S.
Frederickson and by Lance Flanagan, both of the Department of
Physical Education, University of California at Berkeley.

JOHN E. NIXON
ANN E. JEWETT

CONTENTS

An Introduction to

PHYSICAL
EDUCATION

(Courtesy of the Los Angeles City Board of Education.)

Chapter One

CAREERS AND PROFESSIONAL LEADERSHIP IN PHYSICAL EDUCATION

Physical education has traditionally been considered a professional field appropriate only for those interested in teaching careers. While teaching is still the career choice of most persons prepared with bachelor's degrees in physical education, the field includes an increasingly wide range of occupational specializations. Physical education is now an appropriate undergraduate major for any college or university student interested in any one of a broad spectrum of professions focusing upon the study of human movement phenomena or the use of movement activities in serving others.

TEACHING OPPORTUNITIES

Much concern has been expressed over the impact of rising educational costs and increasing demands for accountability upon the opportunities for professional employment in education. The supply and demand picture for teachers of physical education is not as advantageous today as it was during the 1950's and 1960's. However, the development of new kinds of positions, the expansion of physical education as a discipline and service profession, and the upgrading of standards for teacher certification and local employment have maintained a high level of opportunity for qualified individuals seeking teaching positions.

According to the Census Bureau's October, 1971 survey, there were over sixty-one million persons enrolled in the schools of this nation. The 200,000 beginning teachers produced annually in the approximately one thousand higher education institutions in the United States will continue to find a need for their talents and preparation as a third of the teaching force consists of entrants new to the profession within a five-year period.[41] Added to this is the fact that, in the United States, physical education ordinarily begins in the elementary school, is typically a required subject in the secondary school, and is almost universally offered on an elective or required basis in colleges and universities.

Economic pressures have affected job opportunities in teaching as in many other occupational fields. At the same time, it is encouraging to observe that financial support of public education continues to be a high priority at all levels of government. Total expenditures for public and nonpublic schools at all levels of education from kindergarten through the graduate school amounted to an estimated 83.8 billion dollars during the 1971-72 school year; this amount represented eight percent of the gross national product.[8] The average of salaries paid classroom teachers rose from $7630 in 1967-68 to $10,608 in 1972-73.[41] Professional negotiation legislation and collective bargaining laws have resulted in extensive improvements in fringe benefits for teachers in such areas as sick leaves, maternity leaves, sabbaticals, life insurance, health and disability insurance, salary continuance plans, grievance procedures, and retirement benefits. It should not surprise those entering the profession that continuing professional improvement will be an expectation of employers. Competition for good positions almost eliminated nondegree teachers from the profession during the 1960's. An increasing percentage of public school teachers now earn advanced degrees (27.5% in 1970-71)[41] and almost two-thirds are actively engaged in earning additional college credits after graduation.[41]

The prejudice which once existed against the employment of married women teachers has largely disappeared. In recent years, the proportion of single women teachers has been reduced from seven in ten to slightly over two in ten. Women beginning teaching careers may now think of teaching *and* marriage, rather than teaching *or* marriage, or teaching *until* marriage. In 1970–71, 71.9% of all public school teachers, men and women, were married; over half of all teachers had husbands or wives who worked.[41]

The possibility of shifting jobs from one locality to another has been affected favorably by many changes in regulations in recent years, since such changes have been, for the most part, in the direction of greater uniformity and less specificity in qualification. There is some hope that the National Council for Accreditation of Teacher Education may, with appropriate support, eventually provide the recognized basis for reciprocity in teacher certification among all states.

The new teacher must be willing to begin his professional experience as necessity dictates. The rate of turnover in the favored suburban systems is often low, and it may be necessary to accept a position in a small town, a rural or semirural community, or a community of lower socio-economic status. Here will be found experience not normally offered in larger systems—the opportunity to organize one's own program, a broader variety of duties and responsibilities, and a chance to become acquainted with the administration of the school as a whole. Under such circumstances the new teacher must be qualified and willing to assume teaching assignments in areas other than physical education, in states where this practice is permitted. The young teacher who seeks his first position where the need is greatest may wish to qualify for service in the inner core areas of the large city systems or in other special programs for culturally disadvantaged youth.

As in any field of endeavor, advancement depends to a large extent upon the quality of leadership displayed and the willingness to maintain professional growth through continuing study and self-improvement. Teachers of physical education have exactly the same opportunities for advancement as do teachers in general. Leadership in education for the teacher should not be measured solely in terms of personal advancement from one type of teaching position to another, from the elementary level to the college level, or from teaching to supervision to administration. Leadership in the finest sense may be the day-by-day contribution to the growth of students, to the advancement of the profession, and to the development of the culture of the community as a whole.

Since the school as a center of community living is becoming more of a reality and less of a dream, greater opportunities for advancement and for true community service have become available to many teachers of physical education. Very often, by reason of his particular background of preparation, the physical education teacher is found to be best suited among a given group of teachers to take the lead and to assume greater responsibility in plans to make the school the real center of the community. This is particularly true in smaller communities, where many teachers are apt to begin their professional careers.

Increased interest in improving instruction in the public schools has led to considerable upgrading in standards for teacher qualification in the current decade. Career teachers are now expected to accept personal responsibility for continuing professional growth. School systems encourage and support the professional growth and development of teachers in service by sponsoring inservice education programs; by rewarding professional growth through salary advancement, recognition, and status; and by granting leaves of absence for professional reasons.[32] The individual teacher must, on his own initiative, seek self-improvement through graduate study, workshops, institutes, educational travel, professional conferences, committee projects, research, and professional writing.

Elementary School

It is well recognized that, to be most successful, physical education must lay its foundations in the elementary school. Basic skills and attitudes are learned in this period, and hence it is important that those in charge of the physical education program secure special preparation to enable them to assist in building these essential attitudes and skills. Educators have agreed to the necessity of fundamental training in physical education at the elementary school level, but school administrators have not always insisted upon expert knowledge on the part of teachers. The teacher shortage, and particularly the dearth of physical educators qualified to work with elementary school children, has been such that administrators could not always be insistent in this regard.

Increasingly, job opportunities for physical education teachers have become available in the elementary schools. Elementary school physical educators are employed either as members of a single school faculty teaching children on a full-time basis, or as central office consultants, guiding classroom teachers in the improvement of physical education instruction. As educators have become convinced that movement education in the elementary school years is basic to sound developmental experiences for all children, and not just useful in learning athletic skills early in life, or in facilitating the release of emotional tension, or even in establishing sound habits of play, more school systems are allotting adequate funds for elementary school facilities and competent instruction.

The research reported by the developmental psychologists adds increasing weight to the evidence that motor as well as sensory experiences of children are extremely important in the development of intelligence.[16,23,30] Recognition of the importance of perceptual-motor learning in the child's total development must certainly have an impact on the conduct of elementary school physical education and on the willingness of boards of education to employ qualified experts to give leadership toward more effective physical education programs. The work of Piaget[30] and others suggests that the most crucial period of sensorimotor activity in promoting perceptual development is probably during the child's preschool experiences through the first grade. Acceptance of this conclusion could lead to the creation of many new teaching positions with preschool-age children.

Middle School

Plans for school organization vary in different systems; but the majority of plans include a middle or junior high school unit of two to four years. The middle school concept is growing in popularity. Educators and child development specialists have come to recognize that children in the pre-adolescent age group have unique needs which suggest groupings which are neither elementary nor high school oriented.

The middle school offers particular job satisfactions for teachers. In the large cities, physical education specialists are engaged to teach only physical education. In smaller communities they are often required to teach other subjects, and must qualify for an appropriate certificate. Many middle school physical educators also meet coaching and intramural assignments. In most middle schools, physical education positions are available for both men and women.

Secondary School

It is a general practice in the larger cities throughout the country to engage special teachers of physical education in secondary schools; and, as can readily be seen, this practice opens up a large field of employment. In small and rural high schools, it is still common to select teachers of academic subjects who can coach athletic teams or who are skilled in handling class work in physical education activities. In most cases of this type, the academic schedule of the teacher is lightened. One may teach any combination of classes which the principal sees fit to give him. In recent years, there has been a clear national trend toward the establishment of the centralized or comprehensive high school. In these schools, the teacher of physical education normally carries a full program of teaching physical education classes and coaching or other cocurricular responsibility.

Positions open to beginning teachers are frequently located in the smaller schools. It should be remembered that the smaller the school, the greater the variety of subjects the individual teacher may be required to teach. In many ways this assignment is of distinct advantage to the beginning teacher, since it gives him an understanding of the entire school atmosphere which he would not otherwise obtain. The beginning teacher should welcome an opportunity for service in a small school as an experience of the utmost value to his career.

Community College

It is well recognized that the community college offers a partial solution to our problem of higher education. Increasingly, terminal education at the community college level is replacing that at the high school level; and there appears to be little doubt of the continued growth of the community college as an integral part of our educational system. This educational level, therefore, will present a wide variety of school positions in physical education. The professional education required in most instances will be above that demanded for teaching in junior or senior high school. The trend is toward the master's degree as a prerequisite for teaching in the community college, and in many cases the doctorate is required. Frequently, teaching experience at the secondary level is also a prerequisite for such an appointment.

College and University

Positions in colleges and universities are usually of five types: (1) activity class work; (2) teacher education courses in those institutions offering a major in physical education; (3) administration of intramural programs; (4) the coaching of athletic teams; and (5) conduct of the graduate program for higher degrees. Ideally, teachers of physical education at the college and university level should seek a combination of assignments. Possession of the doctor's degree, or work toward it, is required in a number of institutions to teach undergraduate theory courses. A master's degree and a teaching credential are recommended for activity teaching and coaching assignments. Published books, research, and teaching experience, as well as a doctoral degree, usually are required to guide advanced degree candidates in their work.

Fluctuating enrollments in colleges and universities, along with a critical examination of the quality of programs, are issues facing the profession today. No longer may a teacher achieve advancement and success on the strength of athletic performance as an undergraduate. Rather, he must be a dedicated, educated teacher with knowledge, vision, and professional skills. The college or university physical educator is a scholar, an adviser, a coach, an artist, a researcher, an administrator, an evaluator, an author; yet he is always a teacher, "because that is his essence, that is his commitment, that is his love."[45]

Alternative Schools

Private schools have consistently offered excellent opportunities for the student specially prepared in physical education. The typical private preparatory school gives physical education a prominent place in its curriculum.

Individuals who take positions in private schools primarily on account of their preparation in physical education must be ready to accept assignments outside the field of their specialized professional education. As a rule, not only must the physical educator in the private school teach classes in physical education and coach athletic teams, but he must teach one of several subjects, such as science, history, a language, or mathematics. He must be able to act as a director of a dormitory or take charge of a study hall. He may have to act as instructor in military science and tactics and to organize a group of boys or girls for a recreation trip away from the school. In the summer he may be asked to provide enrichment programs for his pupils in a camp setting.

Nonpublic schools historically represent the right of the individual citizen to provide for the education of his children in ways not accommodated by the local public schools. Many private schools have been established by individuals or groups of citizens to develop programs directed toward particular philosophies of education or specific needs of selected learners as viewed by those establishing the school. In contrast to the private preparatory school, which operates as a small, independent, autonomous unit, parochial schools, in many U.S. cities, provide an extensive parallel educational system. Nationwide, nonpublic school enrollment is now in excess of five million students. Schools operated by the Roman Catholic Church are attended by more than 4,300,000 boys and girls;[43] in some of our largest cities—Philadelphia, St. Louis, Chicago, Boston, New York, and Pittsburgh among them—the nonpublic schools educate as many as a third of all youngsters at the elementary and secondary levels.

Traditional constitutional barriers have limited public support of nonpublic schools. The "child benefit" principle is changing this practice. More and more, Americans are accepting the concept that, given the importance of education to our society, public funds appropriated for educational purposes should be spent for the benefit of children on the basis of their need, irrespective of what kind of school they attend. During Fiscal Year 1970, federally supported educational programs embraced more than two million students from nonpublic schools; the estimated dollar-equivalents of services provided for nonpublic school children were over $77,750,000.[42] While federal funds are seldom appropriated specifically for physical education, programs for the disadvantaged and handicapped frequently include movement-based activity programs. Further, the improved fiscal position of many of the nonpublic schools permits extension of their normal academic programs in ways which strengthen physical education curricula and physical recreation offerings and increase their ability to employ competent individuals prepared as physical education specialists.

Growing acceptance of the child benefit principle has also led to the establishment of alternative public schools. Citizen protests and criticisms of the public schools have been expressed in many communities through the establishment of "free" schools or "open" schools, which differ from other local schools primarily in the lack of curriculum requirements, greater flexibility of organization, and degree of student responsibility for academic decision making. Some of these schools offer exciting options in physical education, while many have completely ignored the potential of this curricular area for innovative education. The alternative school currently offers a great challenge for knowledgeable, experimental physical educators.

Special Education for Exceptional Children

Democracy values individual differences. In recent years the concern for meeting individual needs in education has extended to the development of a wide range of special education programs. As of February, 1965, 1,550,050 pupils were enrolled in special education programs for exceptional children in local public schools.[11] Thirteen thousand nine hundred and sixty of these children were in classes for the visually handicapped; 28,450 for the deaf and hard of hearing; 786,590 for the speech impaired; 64,830 for the crippled and those with special health problems; 30,940 for the emotionally and socially maladjusted; 393,430 for the mentally retarded; 22,090 for other handicapping conditions; and 214,670 for the gifted. While these programs represented dramatic progress in special education, it is estimated that less than 40 percent of the handicapped children in the nation were receiving the appropriate services they needed prior to 1970.[3]

The Education of the Handicapped Act (EHA), signed into law by President Nixon April 13, 1970, provides substantial federal funding for every aspect of educating the handicapped. EHA grants to states for Fiscal Year 1972 totalled $37,499,378; nearly another 115 million dollars was granted to the states for education of the handicapped under Title I and Title III of the Elementary and Secondary Education Act and the Vocational Education Act.[3] These appropriations are part of the strategy to bring about full opportunity for the handicapped and include programs for "mainstreaming" handicapped children into regular education programs, training of professional personnel, instructional media, and research and development programs.

All physical educators should be prepared to adapt instruction to the needs of exceptional children enrolled in regular classes. Physical educators with unique talents and skills are needed in special schools and for special education classes to provide physical education programs for children grouped according to specific areas of exceptionality.

Approximately 8 percent of the population is physically handicapped. Physical educators qualified for work with the physically handicapped are especially in demand. Types of provisions made for the handicapped tend to vary according to size of enrollments. Instruction in special classes is much more common in the larger school systems. The reduction in the past decade in the number of school systems, accompanied by the rise in public school enrollment, has resulted in a dramatic shift in the size of school systems. The United States Office of Education reports that there were only 17,200 school systems in the country at the beginning of the 1971-72 school year, as compared with 35,700 systems in 1961-62, and that the average operating school system had 2,750 pupils in the fall of 1971, in contrast to 1,200 pupils in the fall of 1961.[44] The increase in large school systems supported by federal funds for programs for the handicapped has significantly expanded educational opportunities for the handicapped and increased the demand for physical educators qualified to give leadership in working with the physically handicapped.

CAREERS IN ATHLETICS

Coaching

Historically, many young men have been attracted to the physical education profession by the desire for careers as interscholastic athletics coaches. Since the 1920's, the accepted preparation for coaching has been an undergraduate major in physical education. Since the number of sports and teams increased to a point where the demand for coaches exceeded the supply of physical education teachers, efforts of the professional associations have been directed toward specialized preparation for coaching aspirants and state certification of high school coaches. This trend has opened up realistic options for physical educators to include or to minimize coaching preparation in bachelor's and master's degree curricula as well as encouraging teachers in other academic fields to become qualified and certified coaches if they so desire. Recommendations for strengthening the coaching profession through certification standards, have been provided by the AAHPER Task Force on Certification of High School Coaches and endorsed by the National Council of Secondary School Athletic Directors.[2]

The movement toward equal opportunity for girls and women in sport has concurrently opened up opportunities for women in the coaching field. Coaching now represents a realistic career option for men and women at secondary, community college, college and university levels. Full-time positions in coaching are increasingly available in colleges and universities, in public agencies and in private enterprise.

Officiating

Sports officiating is either a part-time or full-time occupation for thousands of U.S. citizens. Undergraduate college students and even a few secondary school students earn substantial income by officiating in various types of competitive sports events. Many former amateur athletes turn to officiating as a full-time professional career after concluding an athletic career in competitive sports. Women athletes and coaches are finding increasing opportunities in the provision of officiating services as competitive sports programs for girls and women expand. Typically, preparation consists of sport participation experience and qualification to meet exacting standards set by the particular sports organization; this organization usually controls rules, establishes policies, and sets fee schedules for officials as well.

Athletic Training

The significant role of the athletic trainer is abundantly recognized by national associations concerned with health, physical education and athletics, sports medicine organizations, and medical societies and associations. It is increasingly well understood that the athletic trainer is crucial in preventing injuries, in recognizing and evaluating injuries, and in providing appropriate paramedical services when injuries occur. In 1959 the National Athletic Trainers Association approved an educational program for trainers which included provisions for a major study in physical education, preparation for a teaching license, and prerequisites for entry to schools of physical therapy.[40]

The demand for qualified athletic trainers is evident in that every major league professional sports team and every major university athletic program employs at least one full-time athletic trainer on its staff. Future opportunities are indicated in the number of these specialists hired each year by high schools, colleges, and universities. Regrettably, the fewest are working at the level where they are most needed—at the secondary school level. Of approximately 25,000 high schools in the United States, of which at least 60% participate in interscholastic football programs, only about 100 schools have employed a full-time teacher-athletic trainer.[40]

The need for more women to become involved in athletic training is obvious. The practice of athletic training is no longer taboo in women's physical education programs. Qualification of women in this field can help to meet the increasing demands. Presently most training work for women's competitive teams is being performed by men.[17] Athletic training should be incorporated into present professional preparation curricula to further enhance and enrich the qualitative resources of all women in physical education.[17]

Athletic Performance

Athletic excellence is a primary goal of many young Americans. Many who are truly superior performers work toward the peak of Olympic participation and maintain amateur status through the young adult years. Numerous others earn college and university athletic scholarships. Those who are most successful in competition often seek athletic careers. Such careers may be short; but for many athletes in such sports as baseball, football, basketball, hockey, track, golf, and tennis, earnings in a decade of employment exceed those of the average worker during a lifetime vocation.

Although the top women athletes do not presently have equal opportunity with men for large earnings, this situation is changing. Bil Gilbert and Nancy Williamson pointed out in a *Sports Illustrated* feature that in 1971 when Billie Jean King became the first woman athlete to win $100,000 in a year, Rod Laver, the leading winner on the men's tennis circuit, collected $290,000; in 1972 the leading money-winners in golf were Kathy Whitworth among women, collecting $65,063 in 29 tournaments, and Jack Nicklaus among men, winning $320,542 in 19 tournaments.[14] But, as these reporters state, "many parents are becoming exercised, schools are growing increasingly concerned and big changes are in the offing."

SUPERVISORY AND ADMINISTRATIVE POSITIONS

School district organization and arrangements for staff leadership and supervision vary greatly from district to district and state to state. Departments of physical education with three or more faculty members generally appoint a member of the staff as a department chairman; this position may be filled by released time from teaching responsibilities or as a full-time position depending upon the size of the program and the number of faculty members to be supervised. Larger districts usually plan for supervision of instruction and curriculum development in physical education through the appointment of one or more individuals to the central office staff; these positions carry such titles as curriculum associate, curriculum consultant, supervisor, or director of physical education. In some states county supervisors are appointed. There are also a limited number of positions in state departments of public instruction.

School administration also offers opportunities for advancement to qualified physical educators. In fact, a disproportionately large number of school principals are educators whose initial preparation

was in physical education. Administrative positions on the college
and university level include department and division chairmanships,
deanships, and various top-level assignments from assistants to
college deans and vice-presidents to college presidencies. All such
positions in educational supervision and administration clearly require considerable teaching and appropriate staff experience as well
as advanced graduate study in related specializations.

Athletic administration is combined with educational administration in many secondary school and some college and university
positions. However, the trend is toward separating the administration
of athletics from the supervision and administration of physical
education. Athletic directors require practical experience in coaching; but a successful coaching record is not in itself sufficient recom-
mendation for appointment to a position as an administrator of
athletics. An approved program of professional preparation at the
graduate level for those who plan to go into administration of
athletics at the secondary school or college level has been developed
by a Joint Committee on Physical Education and Athletics of the
AAHPER, the NCAA, and the National College Physical Education
Association for Men.[18]

RECREATION LEADERSHIP

The insistent demand for recreation in modern American life
has brought with it the realization of the responsibility of the community to provide not only space and facilities, but trained leadership. During recent years, many curricula in colleges and universities
have been set up to aid in the professional preparation of recreation
workers, and steps have been taken to standardize educational qualifications for positions. These curricula emphasize a broad liberal arts
background pointed toward an understanding of the needs and aspirations of individuals and groups in a democratic society, an understanding of the significance of leisure in our culture, and skill in and
an appreciation of a wide variety of leisure-time activities.

In the past few years, many men and women entering the field
of physical education have given some thought to the possibilities of
the recreational phase of our profession. As a matter of fact, until
recently, many of the recreational positions were occupied not only

by persons with collegiate training in physical education, but also by men and women trained through practical knowledge gained on the playground. More and more, these positions are being filled by professionally prepared recreation personnel.

The major student in physical education should realize that, if he wishes to enter recreation as a profession, he will be competing with persons who are now prepared specifically for this field. He must see to it that his basic preparation in physical education is supplemented by knowledge and appreciation in arts, crafts, dramatics, music, nature study, and the like.

Many part-time positions in community recreation are available during after-school hours and in the summer months, and it is in these positions that the major student in physical education should seek experience. Such positions include playground leader, special activity leader, camp counselor, assistant camp director, waterfront director and lifeguard.

POSITIONS IN PUBLIC, SEMIPUBLIC, AND PRIVATE AGENCIES

Programs of physical activity have become prominent in the over-all plans of almost every type of social agency serving the needs of youth and adults. Thus, there is a reasonable demand for both men and women trained in physical education and allied fields to accept responsibility in connection with such programs. It is impossible to list here all such positions which might be available; a sampling follows.

YMCA, YWCA, YMHA, YWHA, JCC, CYO.   There are full-time as well as part-time positions available in these organizations. In addition, many large individual congregations of organized religious groups have full-time leaders who coordinate the work of volunteer and part-time leaders.

American Red Cross.   A limited number of paid positions for qualified men and women in the teaching and supervising of programs of first aid, water safety, and aquatics are available.

Boy and Girl Scouts, Campfire Girls, 4-H Clubs.   Current membership of the Boy Scouts and the Girl Scouts of America totals over 10,000,000 boys, girls, and adults. 4-H programs serve nearly five million young people 9 to 19 years of age. Organizations such as these offer opportunities for leadership in full- and part-time positions.

Boys' Clubs of America and Girls' Clubs of America. Unusual opportunities for leadership are open in these national federations. Boys' Clubs now enroll one million in 1000 clubs. Membership in Girls' Clubs is more than 130,000 in 200 club centers.

Organized Camping and Youth Hostels. Many positions are available during the summer months for persons already trained or seeking further training and experience in physical education and recreation. It has been estimated that there are in excess of 100,000 camp counselors employed during summer months in the United States. Youth hostel programs require experienced group leaders. Both public and private agencies operating large organized camping programs employ year-round camping directors; such positions are normally open only to experienced professionals.

GOVERNMENT SERVICES

The extension of government services, especially increased federal funding for social welfare and international participation programs, has increased employment opportunities for qualified physical educators.

State Institutions. All the states and the District of Columbia maintain institutions for the treatment of juvenile delinquents. The demand is increasing for adequate provision of both facilities and trained leadership for physical education, athletics, and development of leisure-time activity skills and habits for residents.

Indian Service. Some positions are available in the Indian Service, particularly in school work. Here the necessary training corresponds closely to that required for public school work.

National Park Service. At the end of 1972 there were 38 national parks, eight national seashores, four national lakeshores, and one national scenic riverway in the United States. Over two billion persons now visit these national parklands annually. The federal government maintains at the parks recreation directors whose duties are similar to those of a director at a resort hotel. Need is also growing for personnel to administer camping facilities and programs provided in national parks and park system areas.

Armed Services.   All branches of the military provide fitness and physical recreation programs for service personnel. Physical educators may receive primary or secondary classification in these and other health-related specializations. In addition to teaching positions in schools for dependents of servicemen, a few very challenging opportunities exist for civilian employees to serve as athletic directors, particularly in overseas assignments.

Peace Corps.   The Peace Corps was established by an Executive Order of President John F. Kennedy in 1961. In 1971 it became part of ACTION, a federal agency composed of seven volunteer service programs designed to aid all who need and want help both in the U.S. and abroad. The Peace Corps, designed to provide such aid abroad, was serving 57 nations through 7,500 volunteers at the end of 1972.

Since its inception, the Peace Corps has utilized volunteers competent in the area of physical education. The AAHPER contracts with the Peace Corps to administer physical education and athletics projects in the participating countries. A full-time project director is at work in the recruitment of well prepared volunteers in health, physical education, recreation, and athletics; in the selection of training centers in American colleges and universities; and in serving as an official advisory source to the Peace Corps.

Major assignments for volunteers include assistance with the coaching of university athletic teams and regional and national sports teams. Other responsibilities include the teaching of physical education at training schools, technical colleges, and universities. The Peace Corps presents an opportunity, for those who can qualify, to develop new understanding and knowledge of the world, and to participate personally and directly in the struggle of aspiring nations to build a better life for their people.

Vista.   Volunteers in Service to America is another of the volunteer service programs which make up ACTION. VISTA was organized to parallel Peace Corps opportunities within the United States. Volunteers are trained to work with the poor in many American communities and rural areas.

Teacher Corps. Training programs have been established for those who wish to qualify as physical education specialists for work with culturally disadvantaged children and youth. Recruitment emphasizes employment of minority group persons. Physical educators are also in demand to serve on the staffs conducting these programs.

THERAPY

Many opportunities are open to men and women with undergraduate preparation in physical education to prepare themselves as therapists in several professional specializations. The major student who has a special interest in the therapeutic aspect of physical education will find an ever-widening field of employment opportunities. Those who are ambitious to become fully qualified to carry on the developmental and remedial functions in hospitals and rehabilitation centers will need postgraduate study at an institution providing specialized programs.

Physical Therapy. The undergraduate major training in physical education provides a desirable background (though not the only one) from which to enter physical therapy. Substantial additional training and experience is required. The physical therapist works under the direction of the physician, using such methods of treatment as massage, exercise, mechanical apparatus, heat and cold, light radiation, water, and various forms of electricity.

Corrective Therapy. Since World War II there have been significant developments and a marked expansion in the area of physical and mental rehabilitation. The corrective therapist forms a part of the team responsible for the excellent results obtained. Corrective therapy has been defined as the application of medically prescribed therapeutic exercises and activities in the treatment of the mentally and physically ill. The therapy is aimed not only at the physical disability, but is also aimed at improvement of the psychological and sociological aspects of disease and illness. The teaching methods and activities of physical education are applied in working *with* the patient rather than *on* him in solving his physical or mental problems. Detailed information may be obtained from the American Corrective Therapy Association.

(Courtesy of the Los Angeles City Board of Education.)

Occupational Therapy. Persons with undergraduate physical education preparation may, after further training, enter the health-serving profession of occupational therapy. Physical education preparation is especially helpful to therapists who work with emotionally disturbed children and with adults and patients with perceptual motor disabilities. Therapists working in this area of rehabilitation have found that they can use physical education activities as a medium of communication and restoration. Standards for graduate programs and professional certification requirements are established by the American Occupational Therapy Association, whose headquarters are in New York City.

Dance Therapy. One of the fastest growing of the movement professions is the field of dance therapy. The dance therapist works with children and adults, using dance and expressive movement as another medium for communication and guidance. The dance therapist needs a background in individual and social psychology as well as intensive movement and dance study and experience.

21

EMERGING SERVICE OCCUPATIONS

Physical education professional preparation leaders can expand the job market for graduates by introducing the challenge of developing new positions in teaching movement activities to the full age range of our population.

Preschool Programs. Day care centers are springing up in many communities. Both public and private preschool programs are growing in popularity. In 1971, 4.3 million children were enrolled in nursery schools and kindergartens.[36] Programs for young children should draw heavily upon the educational potential of movement experiences. Yet many of these programs are not staffed with qualified physical educators. Here lies a real opportunity for the enterprising professional.

Health Clubs. In many cities health clubs are exceedingly popular with business men and women, with housewives, and with both young and middleaged adults. Much individual attention is given to members in their physical activity programs through a wide variety of exercise, swimming, and sport facilities. Although such positions call for leadership knowledgeable in exercise physiology, often they have not been filled by qualified personnel. The opportunities for service as well as employment are obvious.

Industrial Programs. Employee recreation programs in industry serve millions of individuals and their families. Such programs form an important part of the total recreational life of the nation. Employment opportunities for college-trained physical educators are increasing.

Continuing Education. Adults in all communities, but especially those in large metropolitan and suburban areas, are finding new interests in physical activities of all kinds. Possibilities for learning new sports and exploring newly developing recreational activities are no longer limited to formal evening programs in the city schools. Creative physical educators can help to develop both club and recreational programs of all kinds which can be supported by voluntary enrollment and participant fees or public subsidies. Ski clubs, archery clubs, curling programs, tennis clubs, and scuba classes are examples.

Retirement Homes. Senior citizens have important exercise, fitness, and recreation needs which have too long been ignored. A tremendous potential for service and employment exists for the physical educator who specializes in working with older persons in retirement homes or villages or public facilities readily accessible to senior citizens able to maintain independent residences. An example of a pioneer project in this field is that reported by Leslie and McLure at the University of Iowa.[21]

RESEARCH

Professional workers within the field of physical education are evidencing increasing interest in physical education as an area of study and research.[26] It is probable that future developments will include increased opportunities for investigating, organizing, and developing knowledge within the field, in addition to the extensive opportunities for applying such knowledge in educational, recreational, and therapeutic settings. Many graduate degree programs in colleges and universities currently emphasize preparation for contributions to research; a few undergraduate curricula are already offering options which permit the student to build a strong background for a career in research. Most higher education institutions now encourage graduate professors to devote a significant part of their time and creative effort to personal research interests. It is anticipated that greater opportunities will become available for primary contributions in physical education research in university, private foundation, commercial industry, and government contexts.

ORGANIZATIONS PROMOTING
PROFESSIONAL LEADERSHIP

Progress in any field is closely tied to the quality of professional leadership available. There are always a number of influences at work which tend to promote in the teacher, or prospective teacher, a better attitude toward his profession and a deeper appreciation of its worth and significance. Quite naturally, the first of these is the environment of the institution in which he receives his professional education. There must be an educational atmosphere, and a faculty which recognizes varied principles, purposes, and philosophies of education and makes provision for adequate facilities, stimulating programs, and competent personalized guidance. These influences will unquestionably shape the student's thought and action and form the foundation upon which his professional life will be built, but these early influences must be considered only a foundation. There must be a continuing awareness of forces outside the institution.

The student should become acquainted, early in his career, with the organizations concerned with the various aspects of the profession, and with the contributions of individual leaders in these organizations. He will appreciate that active membership in organizations concerned with the promotion of his profession, with the establishment of better standards of teaching, and with employment conditions, will be distinctly to his advantage. Progress does not come about by chance or by accident, but through the concerted efforts of interested and alert individuals. Each teacher has the personal responsibility of striving constantly to improve conditions in the particular school or situation in which he finds himself. Cooperation in a professional organization operating on a national level can be much more potent in furthering his interests than isolated efforts.

It would be impossible and inappropriate to attempt to list here all the national organizations directly or indirectly concerned with promoting the various phases of health, physical education, and recreation. A few of the more prominent agencies whose particular interest lies in developing professional leadership will be cited.

American Association for Health, Physical Education, and Recreation

The original organization, called the American Association for the Advancement of Physical Education, was founded in November, 1885, by a group of 35 men. They were called together by Dr. William G. Anderson, then of Adelphi Academy, Brooklyn, who later (1892) became medical examiner and director of physical education at Yale University, where he remained until his retirement. Today the Association is the largest professional association for health, physical education, and recreation in the world, and occupies a top-ranking position among professional education groups in size, influence, prestige, and service.

The Association now serves nearly 50,000 members and is one of the largest affiliates of the National Education Association. Its headquarters are located in the NEA Building in Washington, D.C. To improve regional services, six district associations have been formed on a geographical basis. The Association has official organizational structures in every one of the fifty states, as well as in Guam, Puerto Rico, and the District of Columbia; each has representation in the Representative Assembly of the national organization. The proposed 1974 reorganization of the Association as an Alliance of related groups is structured to administer professional programs and projects through seven associations: National Association for Sport and Physical Education, National Dance Association, Association of Councils and Societies, American School and Community Safety Association, Association for the Advancement of Health Education, National Association for Girls and Women in Sport, and National Association for Recreation and Leisure.

There are 23 national organizations affiliated with the Association, many of which sponsor programs at the national convention. These are:

American Academy of Physical Education
American Association of College Baseball Coaches
American College of Sports Medicine
American Corrective Therapy Association, Incorporated
American School Health Association
American Youth Hostels, Incorporated
Canadian Association for Health, Physical Education, and Recreation
Delta Psi Kappa
Health and Physical Education Directors Associations of YM-YWHA's and Jewish Community Centers
National Association for Intercollegiate Athletics
National Association for Physical Education of College Women
National Athletic Trainers Association
National Collegiate Athletic Association
National College Physical Education Association for Men
National Intramural Association
National Soccer Coaches Association of America
Phi Delta Pi
Phi Epsilon Kappa
Physical Education Society of the YMCA's of North America
Sigma Delta Psi

Society of State Directors of Health, Physical Education, and
Recreation
United States Volleyball Association
Young Women's Christian Association of the U.S.A.

The first official publication of the Association appeared in
1896; it continues under the title of *Journal of Health, Physical Education, and Recreation* (JOHPER). The *Research Quarterly* began
publication in 1930. During the past decade, the publication activities
of the Association have been considerably expanded, to include the
School Health Review, published six times per year, and *Update,*
a newspaper published monthly from October through June. The
current list of over two hundred publications ranges from leaflets
to rule guides, filmstrips, loop films, and research abstracts to the
522-page *Research Methods* book, now in its third edition.

The Association sponsors many professional meetings, in addition to its annual conventions. Recent events of national significance
include student seminars, national institutes on coaching and athletics, symposia on federal support programs, regional and national
conferences on elementary school, secondary school, and college
physical education, dance, aquatics, and school health, and national
and international seminars and meetings on undergraduate professional preparation, graduate education, perceptual-motor development, international relations, sports safety, intramurals, biomechanics,
sports medicine, aging, school-community recreation, research and
programs for the handicapped.

The broad scope of Association services includes participation
in international professional efforts, as the following examples will
indicate:

1. Formation of the International Council on Health, Physical
Education and Recreation in August, 1959, marked a significant
development in the international orientation of the profession. The
ICHPER is an integral part of the structure of the World Conference
of Organizations of the Teaching Profession.

2. The International Relations Council of the Association has
sponsored a project for the collection of books for foreign libraries.
During the years since its inception, books have been sent to Yugo-
slavia, Iraq, India, Pakistan, Taiwan, the Philippines, Burma, Li-
beria, Thailand, and Colombia. The Council planned the 1967
National Conference on International Relations Through Health,
Physical Education, and Recreation, which approved a series of

recommendations directed toward increasing the depth and breadth of international interest and work throughout the whole structure of AAHPER.

3. The Youth Fitness Test has been translated and officially adopted for use in Japan, Burma, Pakistan, Saudi Arabia, Portugal, Mexico, Cuba, Ecuador, Colombia, and Peru.

4. The Association is represented by officers and staff in international planning sessions for the Department of State's American Specialist Program, the Agency of International Development (AID), International Union for Health Education of the Public, and many other organizations. As a result of this cooperation, highly qualified personnel are being sent all over the world. Many have written their experiences in the pages of the *Journal*.

5. The Association was co-host to the Fourth International Congress of Physical Education and Sports for Girls and Women held in Washington, D. C., August, 1961.

Students are referred to the April, 1960, anniversary issue of JOHPER for historical information on the Association and biographies of early leaders, and to current issues of *Update* for information on reorganization of Association structures. The Association also publishes an Annual Directory of Supplies and Equipment and current publications reviews and listings in JOHPER.

American Academy of Physical Education

The American Academy of Physical Education, as stated in its constitution, "shall be concerned with the art and science of human movement. . . . The Academy shall promote its purposes by: Extending knowledge in this field; transmitting knowledge about human movement; fostering philosophic considerations regarding issues, values, and purposes; electing to membership Fellows of outstanding achievement; bestowing honors for outstanding contributions to this field; conducting and sponsoring scholarly and social meetings."

The Academy was originally conceived in 1926 by five leaders in physical education, but was not officially founded until 1930, when a constitution was adopted by twenty-nine charter members. Each year, since 1950, the Academy has sponsored a special speaker at the AAHPER Convention in honor of its founder, R. Tait McKenzie.

He was one of the great pioneers of our profession, serving as president of the AAHPER during several of its formative years and as first president of the Academy. From its inception, the Academy has directed its efforts toward the expansion of scholarship in the fields of health, physical education, and recreation. Membership is limited and by invitation only, on the basis of contributions through research, writing, and exceptional service. The R. Tait McKenzie Lecture[34] is one of the Academy's many contributions to the profession. Publications which have resulted from national meetings, originally titled *Professional Contributions,* and more recently, *Academy Papers,* are an invaluable addition to any professional library.

National Association for Physical Education of College Women

Although meetings of women college directors were held as early as 1910, no definite society was formed until 1915.[1] This organization was known as the Association of Directors of Physical Education for College Women, and its membership was designed to include "Directors or Heads of Departments of Physical Education for College Women in colleges and institutions of similar standing in the eastern section of the United States." Two years later, and no doubt inspired by the professional spirit engendered in the eastern association meetings, the midwestern society was organized and, for a similar reason, was followed by the formation of the western society in 1921. At a joint meeting in 1924, these three societies were merged into one, to be known as the National Association of Directors of Physical Education for College Women. The purposes of this new association were broadened somewhat, and included not only discussion of points of administration and organization, but also study of the problems and promotion of the interests of departments of physical education for women, presentation of research papers, and cooperative effort "in advancing the standards of education and the ideals of the profession." During the period of World War II, the word "directors" was removed from the association's name, thus broadening the scope of the organization.

Over the years, many successful summer workshops have been held. In 1958, in combination with the Division of Girls' and

Women's Sports of the AAHPER, the Association held a national conference on social changes and their implications for physical education, and on sports aspects of recreation for girls and women. The Association sponsors biennial conferences on topics, problems, and issues of current interest. Annual district conferences offer further professional stimulation to members.

In 1967, NAPECW sponsored the First Annual Amy Morris Homans Lecture, "for purpose of paying homage to one of the early pioneers in the profession." Miss Homans established the Boston Normal School of Gymnastics in 1909 and later moved it into Wellesley College. She originated NAPECW and had a tremendous impact on an entire generation of professional leaders. Each year, an outstanding speaker is selected to deliver this address at the annual luncheon during the AAHPER Convention.

A joint semiannual publication with the National College Physical Education Association for Men, titled *Quest,* first appeared in December, 1963. *Quest* was initiated in order to provide a creative, literary contribution to the profession and, in the words of the first editor, is "committed to publishing scholarly papers of philosophical and scientific interest." It is important reading for students of physical education.

National College Physical Education Association For Men

This organization, originally called the Society of College Gymnasium Directors, was organized in 1897 for the purpose of advancing the work of physical education in institutions of higher learning. Membership in the early years of its existence "was restricted to directors of gymnasiums, and they were concerned primarily with growth, development, physical examinations, anthropometric tests, and systems of gymnastics." In 1908, the name of the organization was changed to the Society of Directors of Physical Education in College, and teachers in college departments for men were admitted to membership.

Later, in 1933, the name of the organization was changed to the College Physical Education Association, and in 1962 the organization became known as the National College Physical Education Association for Men. The Association's membership is now in excess of twelve hundred, and the *Proceedings* of the Association, which are published each year, form a very valuable part of our professional literature. One outstanding contribution was the study of the "Committee on Curriculum Research," the results of which have been published in monograph form.[20]

A reading of the stated objectives of the Association indicates the breadth and scope of interests represented in the membership and reflected in the professional leadership which it offers:

1. To improve the contributions of physical education and, where appropriate, the related fields of health, education, and recreation to higher education.

2. To identify and define the major issues and problems confronting the profession, particularly those of higher education, and resolve them in the best possible ways.

3. To gather, analyze, interpret, and organize the research needed to resolve the major issues or problems facing the profession of physical education, especially those which are concerned with higher education.

4. To develop interdisciplinary relationships with kindred fields of knowledge for the light they may shed on the nature and values of physical education (e.g., anthropology, psychology, sociology, sports medicine, and so forth).

5. To improve public relations through increasing public understanding of the nature and purposes of physical education in American and world life.[35]

Society of State Directors of Health, Physical Education, and Recreation

Though necessarily quite small in membership, this organization occupies an important place in professional leadership throughout the country. "Because of the strategical position of the state officers, the society from its beginning took cognizance of national problems and endorsed and sponsored worthy procedures by unanimously passing resolutions on vital tactics and policies."[38] The society has maintained, since its founding in 1926, close contacts with the National Education Association, the American Association for

Health, Physical Education, and Recreation, the National College Physical Education Association for Men, the National Congress of Parents and Teachers, and the National Recreation Association, and has been particularly helpful in influencing national thinking in the fields of health, physical education, and recreation. Informal programs on a committee basis are maintained, and cover a wide range of topics, including state certification, school curricular requirements, safety education, and athletic policies and programs.

The purposes of the society are: "(1) to promote sound programs of health, safety, physical education, and recreation throughout the United States; (2) to study problems in these areas and seek solutions to them; (3) to provide a basis for exchange of ideas and programs among members of this organization; and (4) to cooperate with other professional organizations in furthering the development of programs in health, safety, physical education, and recreation." A recent statement of "Basic Beliefs" is an important contribution which offers guidelines for school health, physical education, and recreation programs.[37]

American College of Sports Medicine

A group of representative physicians, physical educators, and physiologists founded the American College of Sports Medicine in 1954 for the following purposes: (1) to promote and advance scientific studies dealing with the effect of sports and other motor activities on the health of human beings at various stages of life; (2) to cooperate with other organizations concerned with various aspects of human fitness; (3) to sponsor meetings of physicians, educators, and other scientists whose work is relevant to sports medicine; (4) to make available postgraduate education in fields related to the objectives of the College; (5) to initiate, encourage, and correlate research; and (6) to publish a journal dealing with scientific aspects of activity and their relationship to human fitness.

The College is affiliated with AAHPER and the Fédération Internationale de Médecine Sportive. It holds an annual national convention, and the College's regional chapters conduct scientific meetings on a regional basis. It publishes a regular newsletter; a quarterly journal, *Science and Medicine in Sports,* began publication in 1969.

The Encyclopedia of Sport Sciences and Medicine, a volume of approximately 1500 pages, including 1200 articles by 550 authors, was published in 1972 and is a major contribution to the profession. Subjects reported cover many facets of sport sciences, ranging from growth and development, physiology, psychology, and sociology, to safety of participation, rehabilitation, orthopedics, pharmacology, and measurement and evaluation. The work has an international flavor, since the authors are citizens of 35 different countries and the 6000 bibliographical references include many international publications.

International Organizations

Membership in certain international organizations is on an association as well as an individual basis. The individual physical educator may gain a great deal through participation in programs sponsored by international groups, and through reading publications of these organizations and reports of their conferences. Even if his own participation in international activities must necessarily be limited, the significance of physical education in international relations and the impact of international factors on the future development of his profession make the work of these associations important to him.

The International Council on Health, Physical Education and Recreation held its Fifteenth Anniversary Congress in London, England, in August, 1972. AAHPER is a national member of ICHPER, and its immediate past-president serves as the official delegate to the ICHPER Assembly. The Council publishes annually: four issues of the *ICHPER Bulletin,* a newsletter reporting significant professional developments and activities; four issues of *Gymnasion,* a journal treating professional issues of international concern; proceedings of the annual international congress; and other research reports as developed and made available. In its first fifteen years of existence, ICHPER has strengthened the profession at the international level immeasurably, providing channels for communication among physical educators of different nations, and a framework for operation with other education bodies through its relationships with the World Confederation of Organizations of the Teaching Professions. The history and activities of the organization are summarized in *A Decade of Progress: ICHPER 1958–67,*[6] prepared for the 10th Anniversary Congress.

The International Association of Physical Education and Sports for Girls and Women is an organization of more than 50 countries. "Its purpose is to bring into active cooperation and participation women of many countries working in the fields of Physical Education and Sports; to cooperate with other organizations in encouraging the particular services which women contribute to society; to strengthen international contacts; to afford opportunities for the discussion of mutual problems; to promote the exchange of persons and ideas among member countries, and research into problems affecting Physical Education and Sports for women." The IAPESGW was founded in 1949 and held its first Congress in Copenhagen. Congresses have been held at four-year intervals since that date in Paris, London, Washington, Cologne, Tokyo, and Teheran.

The International Olympic Academy is located in a permanent setting near Olympia, and houses the Museum of the History of the Modern Olympic Games as well as living facilities, library, and sports facilities for the participants. Although it was founded in 1949, the first session convened in 1961; annual sessions have been held each succeeding summer. The general activities of the IOA embrace lectures, seminars, question and answer sessions, general discussions, tours, films, and recreation. Subject matter is selected and programs are conducted in accordance with the general purpose of continuation of the high ideals and true spirit of the Olympic movement. English and French are the two official languages of the Academy.[4]

Other international organizations of particular interest to the physical educator include the International Council of Sport and Physical Education, The Fédération Internationale d'Education Physique, and the Fédération Internationale de Médecine Sportive. The First International Seminar on the History of Physical Education and Sports, held at the Wingate Institute for Physical Education, Tel Aviv, Israel, in April, 1968, was sponsored by ICSPE, ICHPER, and FIEP.

U.S. Department of Health, Education, and Welfare

In the fields of school health and physical education, the work of the Office of Education is largely consultative, advisory, and promotional. The staff engages in compiling and disseminating information concerning all phases of health education, physical education, and recreation, and in sponsoring and conducting conferences on numerous problems relating to these three areas of human welfare. A bibliography of the publications of this office is available; many of the pamphlets are provided without charge, and for the others a nominal charge is made. The official publication of the office is *American Education.*

Federal support to education has expanded tremendously during the past decade, particularly through public funds appropriated under the Elementary and Secondary Education Act of 1965 and the Higher Education Act of 1965. Funds allotted to these programs were administered initially through the U.S. Office of Education.

The National Institute of Education (NIE) came into being in August, 1972, as a separate agency within the Department of Health, Education, and Welfare. Title III of the Education Amendments of 1972 established NIE to provide leadership in the conduct and support of scientific inquiry into the educational process.[46]

Professional Fraternities

Delta Psi Kappa, Phi Delta Pi, and Phi Epsilon Kappa are national professional fraternities, the first two for women and the third for men. Each is interested primarily in developing among its members and the profession in general high ideals and a desire for service, and each sponsors a professional magazine. The official publication of Delta Psi Kappa is *The Foil* (semiannual); of Phi Delta Pi, *The Progressive Physical Educator* (semiannual); and of Phi Epsilon Kappa, *The Physical Educator* (quarterly). These organizations have done much to stimulate professional leadership.

Athletic Institute

In 1934, a group of America's leading producers of athletic equipment formed a nonprofit organization, with its major objective to be "the expansion of opportunities for participation in physical education and recreation." Since its inception, the Athletic Institute has proved to be a highly significant force in the area of professional leadership. The promoting and financing of national conferences—notably a series on planning facilities,[5,31] one on undergraduate professional preparation,[33] one on graduate study,[15] and one on effects of altitude on physical performance[9]—have stimulated important professional developments. The published results form a contribution to the professional literature which is widely used and highly respected.

In line with the aim and purpose of the Institute, as stated in its 25th Anniversary Announcement in 1960—to aid, guide, and strengthen the development of sports and recreation as an essential means of enriching life—its scope of activities has been greatly expanded. A brief mention of but a few of its projects includes: the production of 35mm sound slide-films and accompanying instructors' guides and students' manuals in over thirty sports; development of a series of more than a hundred 8mm loop films on track and field, tennis, gymnastics, wrestling, swimming, and golf; the conduct of professional field services which make the experiences of several of the nation's leading recreation authorities available to schools, city recreation departments, and park commissions to solve local problems of program and organization; the sponsorship of an excellent series of 16mm movies on a variety of pertinent subjects; the distribution of sports information to schools, colleges, newspapers, magazines, and individuals; and the conduct of national surveys of various types.

Lifetime Sports Foundation

The Lifetime Sports Foundation was established as a private foundation to gain public and private support for programs which offer opportunities to learn sports skills, concentrating on those sports that last a lifetime. The Lifetime Sports Education Project, initiated in the summer of 1965, was the first to be funded by the Foundation. Until 1973, the Project was a special project of AAHPER, with its director serving as a member of the National Headquarters Staff. Project staff conducted clinics for teachers throughout the United States in archery, bowling, golf, tennis, and badminton. They demonstrated techniques of large group instruction and the utilization of gymnasia and playing fields, improvised materials, and innovative teaching aids. A 17-minute 16mm sound film, "Lifetime Sports in Education," designed to interpret the need for broader physical education programs to lay groups, was made available through state directors of health, physical education, and recreation. The Project sponsored, in addition, clinics in elementary school physical education.

Selected References

1. Ainsworth, Dorothy S. "The National Association of Physical Education for College Women." *J. Health & Phys. Educ.*, 17: 525–526, 575–576 (November, 1946).
2. American Association for Health, Physical Education and Recreation. *Certification of High School Coaches.* Washington, D.C.: AAHPER, 1970.
3. "The Big Package for Education for the Handicapped." *American Education,* 8: 39 (May, 1972).
4. Brown, James K. "Sunrise on Greece." *J. Health, Phys. Educ.-Rec.,* 39:89–90 (March 1968).
5. *College and University Facilities Guide.* Chicago: The Athletic Institute, 1968.
6. *A Decade of Progress: ICHPER 1958–67.* Washington, D.C.: National Education Association, 1967.
7. Downey, Robert J., Davis, Elwood C., McCann, June V., and Stitt, Elizabeth Ann. *Exploring Physical Education.* Belmont: Calif.: Wadsworth Publishing Co., Inc., 1962.
8. "Educational Expenditures as a Percentage of the Gross National Product." *American Education,* 9:33 (February, 1973).
9. *The Effects of Altitude on Physical Performance.* Chicago: The Athletic Institute, 1967.
10. "Estimates of School Statistics, 1967–68." *NEA Research Bulletin,* 46:14 (March, 1968).
11. "Facts on American Education." *NEA Research Bulletin,* 44:35–41 (May, 1966).
12. Gilbert, Bil, and Williamson, Nancy. "Are You Being Two-Faced?" *Sports Illustrated,* 44–54 (June 4, 1973).
13. Gilbert, Bil, and Williamson, Nancy. "Programmed to be Losers." *Sports Illustrated,* 60–73 (June 11, 1973).
14. Gilbert, Bil, and Williamson, Nancy. "Sport is Unfair to Women." *Sports Illustrated,* 88–98 (May 28, 1973).
15. *Graduate Education in Health Education, Physical Education, Recreation, Safety, and Dance* (report of a national conference). Washington, D.C.: American Association for Health, Physical Education, and Recreation, 1967.
16. Hebb, D. O. *Organization of Human Behavior.* New York: John Wiley and Sons, Inc., 1964.
17. Hutton, Linda I., and Silkin, JoAnne. "Needed: Women Athletic Trainers." *J. Health, Phys. Educ.-Rec.,* 43:77–78 (January, 1972).
18. Joint Committee on Physical Education and Athletics, AAHPER, NCAA, and NCPEAM, Robert Weber, Chairman. "Professional Preparation of the Administrator of Athletics." *J. Health, Phys. Educ.-Rec.,* 41:20–23 (September, 1970).
19. *Journal of Health, Physical Education-Recreation,* 31:4 (April, 1960). Special issue prepared for the 75th Anniversary of the founding of the American Association for Health, Physical Education and Recreation.
20. LaPorte, William R., and Cooper, John H. (eds.). *The Physical Education Curriculum.* Los Angeles: Parker and Company, 7th ed., 1968.
21. Leslie, David K., and McLure, John W. "The Preparation of Physical Educators

for Expanded Leadership and Service Roles," *J. Health, Phys. Educ.-Rec.*, 43: 71–75 (November-December, 1972).

22. Maetozo, Matthew G. (Ed.). *JOHPER* Series on Certification of High School Coaches, September 1970 through June 1971.

23. Maier, Henry W. *Three Theories of Child Development.* New York: Harper & Row, Publishers, rev. ed., 1969.

24. Meyer, Harold D., Brightbill, Charles K., and Sessons, H. Douglas. *Community Recreation.* Englewood Cliffs, N.J.: Prentice-Hall, Inc., 4th ed., 1969.

24a. Miller, Donna Mae. *Teaching and Coaching Women in Sport.* Philadelphia: Lea and Febiger, 1973.

25. Nash, Jay B. *Opportunities in Recreation and Outdoor Education.* New York, Vocational Guidance Manuals, 1963.

26. "The Nature of a Discipline." *Quest,* IX (December, 1967).

27. Noonan, William E. "Lifetime Sports Education Project." *J. Health, Phys. Educ.-Rec.,* 40:10–12 (September, 1969).

28. Pape, Laurence A., and Means, Louis E. *A Professional Career in Physical Education.* Englewood Cliffs, N.J.: Prentice-Hall, Inc., 1963.

29. "The Physical Educator as Professor." *Quest,* VII (December, 1966).

30. Piaget, Jean. *The Origins of Intelligence in Children.* New York: International Universities Press, 1965.

31. *Planning Areas and Facilities for Health, Physical Education, and Recreation.* Chicago: The Athletic Institute, rev. ed., 1965.

31a. Poindexter, Hally B. W., and Mushier, Carole L. *Coaching Competitive Team Sports for Girls and Women.* Philadelphia: W. B. Saunders, 1973.

32. "Professional Growth of Teachers in Service." *NEA Research Bulletin,* 45:25–27 (March, 1967).

33. *Professional Preparation in Health Education, Physical Education, Recreation Education* (report of a national conference). Washington, D.C.: American Association for Health, Physical Education, and Recreation, 1962.

34. "R. Tait McKenzie Lecture." *J. Health, Phys. Educ.-Rec.,* 32:73 (October, 1961).

35. "Report of the Committee on Function and Structure." *Proc. Coll. Phys. Educ. Assoc.,* 1957:31–32.

36. "School Enrollment Continues Upward." *American Education,* 8:4⁚ (May, 1972).

37. *The School Programs in Health, Physical Education, and Recreation: A Statement of Basic Beliefs.* Kensington, Md.: Society of State Directors of Health, Physical Education, and Recreation, 1972.

38. Schrader, Carl L. "The History of the State Directors' Society." *J. Health & Phys. Educ.,* IV:3 (December, 1933).

39. Schurr, Evelyn L., and Philipp, Joan A. "Women Sports Officials." *J. Health, Phys. Educ.-Rec.,* 42:71-72 (November-December, 1971).

40. Schwank, Walter C., and Miller, Sayers J. "New Dimensions for the Athletic Training Profession." *J. Health, Phys. Educ.-Rec.,* 42:41–43 (September, 1971).

41. *Status of the American Public-School Teacher, 1970–71. NEA Research Bulletin,* Washington, D.C.: National Education Association (March, 1972).

42. "Support for Nonpublic School Children." *American Education,* 8:36 (June, 1972).

43. Sweeney, Don. "Bridging the Public-Nonpublic School Gap." *American Education,* 8:4–10 (June, 1972).

44. "Trends in the Number and Size of Local Public School Systems." *American Education,* 8:37 (June, 1972).

44a. "Trends in Public School Systems: 1967–68 to 1972–73." *American Education,* 9:33 (August–September, 1973).

45. Ulrich, Celeste. "The Physical Educator as Teacher." *Quest,* VII:58–61 (December, 1966).

46. U.S. Department of Health, Education, and Welfare. *The National Institute of Education: A Brief Outline of Its History, Status, and Tentative Plans.* Washington, D.C.: Department of Health, Education, and Welfare (NIE 73-25000), February 23, 1973.

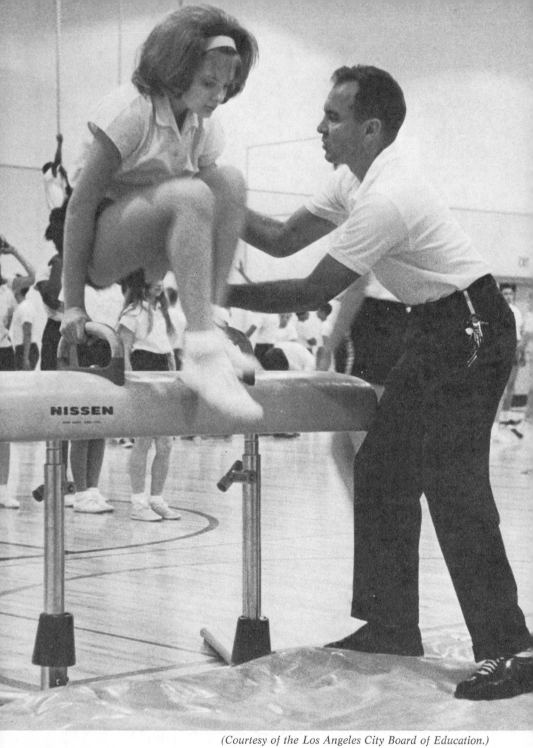

(Courtesy of the Los Angeles City Board of Education.)

Chapter Two

PROFESSIONAL PREPARATION

Physical educators in the last quarter of the twentieth century will play a changed and changing role in American society. Statesmen, acknowledged leaders in all professions, and influential individuals within each of the myriad sub-cultures recognize the crucial role of public education. In the world of today no man is an island, nor is any nation or profession. United States citizens accept a continuing and strengthened commitment to revitalize educational programs in terms of national priorities, to support flexibility in institutional organization and procedure, and to restructure American school and college curricula within the mainstream of modern living.

Civic leaders, administrators, and teachers in other fields of specialization recognize the potential contributions of physical education in the educational enterprise, and are demanding more in professional services from physical educators. Furthermore, greater understanding of the significance of human movement phenomena in contemporary living is opening up new career fields for physical educators. As the need for expertise in dealing with problems involving movement knowledge and skill is increasingly recognized in a wide variety of non-teaching private enterprises and public programs, the demand for qualified specialists grows. We are now looking to professional preparation institutions for competent human movement specialists for non-teaching as well as teaching roles.

The challenge to physical education has become one of quality contribution. The student who chooses to qualify as a professional

39

physical educator today elects to prepare himself for uniquely diversi-
fied, stimulating, demanding, and rewarding careers.

THE CHALLENGE

Pressures from within the teaching profession, the consciousness
of needed improvements, and self-evaluation have combined with
pressures from outside the profession from parents, statesmen, taxpayers, and other groups to bring about many changes in the whole
structure of the school system. Teachers are faced with new challenges. The specific problems crucial in today's society and the particular needs of the current student generation call for substantial
reorientation in the professional preparation of the physical educator.

Accountability

The 1970's are characterized by re-examination of all public
institutions with the spotlight on cost effectiveness and responsibility
to a public trust. Industry is being required to demonstrate integrity
in the provision of consumer services and profits limited to serve
the broader public interest. Professional preparation must respond
to such demands.

Teacher certification is placing more emphasis on the demonstration of competence in particular aspects of teaching performance.
Teacher education programs are being revamped to focus attention
on the development of identified competencies. In many institutions,
new approaches to building curricula, guiding students, and evaluating student achievement have resulted.

Programs designed to provide professional preparation for
physical education specializations other than public school teaching
are facing similar demands. Particular competencies needed for research careers, for administration of public fitness programs, for
planning movement experiences of preschool children, for providing
movement therapy experiences, for working in urban public assistance programs, are being analyzed as the basis for offering appro-

priate professional preparation experiences. Certification requirements are being formalized and upgraded for a variety of specializations such as athletic training, secondary school coaching, aquatics program management, corrective therapy, and sports administration. Prospective physical educators must now demonstrate their qualifications in competency-based preparation programs as well as prepare themselves for continuing accountability in a selected professional career.

Humanistic Education

The demand for accountability increases the challenge of maintaining a humanistic orientation in professional preparation. While American society is demanding accountability, it is also calling for more concern for individual freedom and autonomy. The two goals are not necessarily incompatible; in fact, accountability is valued primarily as a protection for the individual rights of the average citizen. Humanistic education places the integrity of persons above the maintenance of a technological or status system.

Humanistic educators accept the following assumptions:

1. The goal of every learner is to become all that he is capable of becoming, to actualize himself on his own terms, emotionally, intellectually, and socially.[20]

2. Sound contemporary education is designed to assist a person to live in tune with his environment, through developing his abilities to enjoy life in a changing environment. It provides him with the skills for adapting selectively to changing life demands. It fosters positive attitudes toward change.

3. Education is concerned with both scientific knowledge and aesthetic knowledge. Scientific or empirical knowledge and aesthetic or self-knowledge complement each other. Science and art "give a dignity to our culture which is larger than either"; the ethics of science and self are linked to give "a place and a hope to the universal identity of man."[2]

4. Modern education views communication as a central focus. It seeks to create environments "which help people reach each other and live with an expanding common consciousness—one which not

only embraces the traditional liberal values of mutual respect and protection of the rights of others, but also reaches out to explore the development of expanded human experiences through new dimensions of relationships with others."[20]

5. Today's education seeks to meet individual needs by creating alternatives. In the past decade, American education has moved from innovations, through radical reforms, to alternatives.[14] Individuals learn to interact successfully with the environment, achieve self-actualization, integrate empirical and aesthetic knowledge into a single ethic, and develop effective communication through selection of options from among positive, constructive, and imaginative alternatives. The modern school has become a learning center, offering to its patrons a smorgasbord of alternatives.[20]

The challenge to the physical educator, whether he chooses to make his contribution as a teacher or through an alternative professional specialization, is to prepare himself to interpret selected phenomena of human movement in terms of the interests and ideals of persons. He seeks to extend knowledge about movement phenomena and to assist others in using this knowledge to find personal meanings and achieve individual fulfillment. He can play a key role on the current scene. Our discipline is not a special subject on the periphery of the educational enterprise; it is an essential medium for learning and self-actualization. Voluntary movement is a significant function of man from infancy across the total life span. It is essential to successful environmental coping wherever human beings live. We are only at the threshold of our potential contributions to expressive and communicative abilities. Movement activities offer an exciting range of alternatives for self-actualization through both scientific knowledge and self-knowledge.

Interpersonal Understanding

Idealists of earlier generations envisioned the United States of America as a "melting pot" in which peoples of differing cultural origins and varying experiences could seek common goals, a nation in which assimilation led to the enrichment of life for every individual and the attainment of liberty and happiness for all. Today we are beset by difficulties attesting to the lack of common values and inter-group understanding. Racial conflict has made the public school both a target and a tool for civil rights advances. The struggles of ethnic minorities for equal status, affirmative action efforts demanding equal opportunities for women, the prejudices directed against individuals identified with particular religious faiths, and the demands of low-income groups for higher living standards are all reflected in American schools. The generation gap is of increasing concern. Parents worry about the availability of narcotics, increasing sexual license, teenage rebellion, and student riots. Increasing juvenile delinquency, crime rates, drug abuse, mental and emotional illness, and violence disturb us all.

Continuing the dialogue between opposing segments of the population is more and more difficult. The challenge to educate for inter-group understanding is not limited to the continental boundaries. Physical educators of the new generation are learning to understand sports and physical education as a vehicle for broadening understanding and friendship between American citizens and people of other nations. International competitions have highlighted the part sport plays in the struggle of competing ideologies. Perhaps even more significant is the extensive cultural interchange through conferences and educational exchange programs.

In many communities, teachers themselves are faced with a choice between reliance on professional organizations or labor unions to accelerate progress toward better working conditions and salaries commensurate with education and quality of services rendered. Schools must face squarely the responsibility to educate for inter-group understanding. Teachers must learn to facilitate growth toward social responsibility, discover methods for increasing social understanding and find better ways to guide the development of skills for dealing with social problems and for participating in their constructive solution. The school has a vital role in working toward greater integration of our fragmented society, and the prospective teacher faces a crucial challenge in preparing himself to pursue this goal effectively. The professional physical educator preparing to work in a governmental, industrial, small business, private agency, or research setting has an equally important responsibility to equip himself to use his talents and skills as a human movement specialist, to increase interpersonal understanding in our society.

Creative Teaching

Demonstrating accountability while supporting the development of individual autonomy and strengthening interpersonal understanding requires creative professionals. For those physical educators who choose teaching, creativity may indeed be the key, for the quality of teaching is acknowledged to be the basic educational problem. Good teachers for tomorrow's children will need new knowledge and skills we have not yet learned. They will need to be creative individuals, prepared to utilize their own creativity in identifying and expanding the creative potentials of their students.

The creative physical educator is an innovator. He looks for new content to enrich the traditional offerings of the physical education curriculum. He finds new ways of organizing familiar content to facilitate meaningful learning. In his quest for new knowledge and greater effectiveness as a teacher, he searches for answers to new questions, as well as for new answers to continuing questions.

Today's physical educator is responsible for creating learning environments which provide varied stimuli, encourage exploration, and enhance the motivations of students to achieve desired outcomes. He designs learning opportunities to facilitate personal variations in movement performance, to stress individual solutions of movement problems, and to encourage inventiveness and extend creative abilities in movement expression. Clearly, it is a more difficult task for the prospective physical educator to prepare himself for creative teaching than for the more completely structured role which was appropriate in the schools of an earlier era.

Physical Education as a Profession of Specializations

This is an age of specialization. Although greater emphasis is being given to a broad and comprehensive general education for all teachers, regardless of their special field of study, tomorrow's physical educator will also be expected to qualify as a specialist within his profession. In addition to his understanding of human growth and development within the total life span, and of the learning process as it applies to the whole range of learning behavior from the preschool child to the adult, he will be expected to develop particular understandings and skills for working effectively with the age group on whom he chooses to focus his efforts. Perhaps he will elect to qualify for work with the physically handicapped, emotionally disturbed, mentally retarded, culturally disadvantaged, or other specialized population.

He will need a depth of knowledge and understanding concerning the nature of human movement and considerable insight into basic principles and key concepts of movement. He will also need specific abilities for applying these general principles and utilizing his movement skill and understanding in teaching and coaching others in selected activities in which he is especially qualified.

As an author, speaker, or researcher helping to advance his chosen profession, he should be prepared to make a special contribution in one of the sub-fields which constitute the subject of physical education. Those who wish to plan for a career which focuses on human movement, but in which teaching is not the primary responsibility, will find that such specializations are increasing in number and job opportunity. Already there are many individuals with undergraduate preparation in physical education who are building careers in newly emerging sciences and interdisciplinary fields.

BACKGROUND FOR ENTRANCE TO THE PROFESSIONAL CURRICULUM IN PHYSICAL EDUCATION

Colleges and universities are becoming more and more selective in the admission of students to physical education curricula. The process of selection may assume many forms, beginning with qualifying tests and ending with the elimination of the less competent by the high standards of scholarship and accomplishment demanded by accredited educational institutions. The physical educator has a unique opportunity to contribute in the broadest sense to the wholesome growth and development of others. Thus sound procedures for selection, admission, and retention of candidates are essential.

One of the first steps in advising the student with regard to his career is to determine the extent of his high school background and experience. It is desirable that the student come to his preparation from the secondary school with some exposure to the sciences, such as physics and chemistry. It should be remembered that he is entering a profession for which a scientific background is basic. The lack of such background may not preclude his entrance into professional preparation, but it does constitute a deficiency that in many cases may have to be made up at the college level.

Competence in verbal expression is also a prerequisite for success. The potential physical educator will need skill in reading and writing English sufficient for intensive study in many academic areas selected to further his liberal education as an undergraduate. If he achieved only minimum standards of English composition and reading comprehension in his high school preparation, remedial opportunities may be available to him in the college setting, but he will be handicapped in completing his curriculum creditably until he overcomes this deficiency.

The student who aims to become a human movement specialist needs a background as a participant in physical activity. It will be particularly helpful if his activity background has been a broad one in every sense of the word. While a high level of skill in selected sports in which the individual has particular interest is a definite asset, the prospective student should have had a wide variety of movement experiences and extensive participation in all the common forms of athletic, gymnastic, and rhythmic activities. Competitive sports experience is an asset. Leadership experiences in school clubs and activities, in youth agencies, as camp counselors, playground directors, or lifeguards, are all considered desirable.

Physical education is a professional field encompassing opportunities for individuals of varying temperaments, personalities, and abilities. Those who select teaching specializations should recognize that teaching is a vocation with a social service orientation. To find satisfaction in teaching, the individual must enjoy working with others, recognizing that he will seldom be free to select the individuals with whom he works. Because he works with human beings, the results of his efforts are neither fully subject to his control nor highly predictable.

PROFESSIONAL PREPARATION

Patterns for professional preparation in physical education are many and varied. All provide for professional specialization in a college or university setting. Such curricula have three major emphases: (1) liberal studies or general education, designed to extend the individual's familiarity with the major fields of organized knowledge, to permit him to seek deeper personal meanings in areas of individual interest, and to equip him to function effectively as a citizen of his society; (2) disciplinary studies designed to develop knowledge and competence in the subject-field concerned with human movement phenomena; and (3) specialized professional education designed to prepare him for his responsibilities as a specialist utilizing human movement as his focus and his medium. The prospective physical educator will be concerned with all three emphases in his preparation at the college level.

The Undergraduate Curriculum

The student who majors in physical education strengthens his general education background, while establishing the foundations for his professional career, through studies in the biological and physical sciences, the behavioral sciences, and the humanities. To acquire competence in his subject-matter discipline, he works toward mastery of a wide variety of concepts relating to human movement phenomena. These areas of knowledge include human growth and development, physiology of muscular activity, neural bases of movement, human anatomy, kinesiology, perceptual-motor learning, sport psychology, sociology of sport, rhythmic structure of movement, philosophy of sport, dance philosophy, and history of dance, sport, and related movement activities. He becomes knowledgeable in his discipline through study of the basic concepts, participation experience in many forms of physical activity, skillful performance of selected dance or sport movement forms, and laboratory analysis of human movement phenomena.

The authors recommend that the general education background of physical educators be kept as flexible as is consistent with essential foundation work in basic arts and sciences; most colleges and universities have all but eliminated college-wide requirements for all students. All undergraduate majors in physical education, irrespective of individual career goals, need similar experiences with the subject-matter discipline of human movement. Beyond these minimums, however, the prospective physical educator should pursue a curriculum tailored to his selected career specialization and his personal interests. The department, school, or college of physical education should provide orienting, advising, and screening experiences in a systematic manner. The student should be assisted in examining the potential of physical education as a professional field, in determining his own suitability for performing particular professional roles, in becoming acquainted with the designs and resources for the various program options, and in developing an appropriate instructional plan.[18]

The trend in undergraduate teacher education and certification is toward competency-based programs and requirements. The AAHPER Professional Preparation Conference held in New Orleans in January, 1973, used this approach to develop possible competencies and possible experiences relating to basic human movement understandings, physical education movement patterns, professional competencies in methodological, administrative, curricular, and co-curricular analysis, and in evaluation.[1]

Physical education teachers need experiences and competencies required by teachers in all fields in such areas as human development, learning, school and society, communications, media and technology. They share with other physical education specialists interests and undergraduate preparation in movement analysis, movement performance, and study of the human movement professions. As physical education teachers they require extensive professional laboratory experiences in working with individuals and groups in both movement and nonactivity settings and specialized competencies in the guidance of movement learning. Further individualization in programs is indicated according to personal choices to become elementary specialists, high school teacher-coaches, college or university teachers, dance teachers, aquatic teaching specialists, teachers of the handicapped, urban teachers, or other types of teaching specialists.

While there is lack of agreement as to specifics, there is general agreement that students must be prepared to cope with new and constantly changing social conditions. Opportunities are increasing for students to be challenged and stimulated through experiences with new organizational patterns and instructional media and devices: team teaching, modular scheduling, honors programs, educational television, and a variety of new technical aids including electronic devices, video and audio tapes. The growing list of institutions offering degrees in physical education which are accredited by the National Council for Accreditation of Teacher Education (NCATE) offers evidence of the desire of the profession to support and maintain the search for excellence in American education.

The recommendations of knowledgeable and concerned student professionals for strengthening undergraduate teacher education curricula are of particular interest and importance. At the 1973 AAHPER Professional Preparation Conference, the Student Action Council presented seven resolutions.[30] These included recommendations for more practical exposure to teaching situations, inclusion of coaching and officiating preparation for prospective women teachers, more sport psychology and sociology, more encouragement for students to become involved in professional organizations, increased emphasis in health education, motor learning, adaptive methods and skills, and mathematics for research potentials, and immediate and thorough reviewing and restructuring of current undergraduate programs. Teacher educators should give prompt and careful attention to these recommendations.

Students planning careers in human movement professions other than teaching also need studies in movement analysis, movement performance, and orientation to related professions, including physical education teaching. In making their personal instructional plans, they will select professional experiences in coaching, athletic training, administration, development of aquatic facilities, choreography, child psychology, urban sociology, behavioral disabilities, juvenile rehabilitation, continuing education, research techniques, and other content areas, as appropriate for the particular specialization. Some specializations will require qualification for state certification. Most will require some type of intensive professional, clinical, field, or laboratory experience. Many departments permit major students to assist with large activity classes and to work with officiating and other aspects of the intramural sports program. The professionally interested student will voluntarily take advantage of every opportunity to become better acquainted with every phase of his department's program.

Opportunities are often available for participation in professional meetings where students and faculty take part, where outside speakers are invited to meet with groups on the campus, and where problems are discussed which have local and national significance. Sometimes physical education clubs are joined with national professional fraternities whose objective is the advancement of the profession. As a supplement to the more formal professional education program, the advantages to be gained by such group meetings may be very important.

Another type of education which has many advantages is that provided by campus recreational events in which major students act as hosts and leaders for the campus public. More and more college administrators express the viewpoint that recreation is an important phase of the services to be offered all students. One aspect of a college recreation program involves participation in physical activities, usually coeducational, including swimming, volleyball, badminton, shuffleboard, table tennis, and deck tennis, as well as social, folk, and square dancing.

Early in his preparation the student should start to assemble a professional library, so as to become acquainted with the literature of the field and the reliable sources of information to which he may turn for future guidance. Textbooks may well be the basis for such a library. The quality and quantity of books in the field are growing every year. The American Association for Health, Physical Education, and Recreation has a list of publications, many of which should be in every student's library. A professional library is an indispensable asset and can be gradually acquired and augmented from a modest beginning. The student, with the advice of members of the teaching staff, should be alert to new contributions and should add continually to his library even at some personal sacrifice.

The Graduate Curriculum

For the student who is ambitious to prepare himself for a position of greater responsibility, or who may be especially interested in pursuing research, the graduate curricula now available in physical education offer ample opportunity, challenge, and reward. The complexity of American culture and the pressing need for solutions to many professional problems require that colleges and universities offer graduate study which will provide well qualified teachers, leaders, administrators, and creative scholars. Graduate education and advanced degrees are increasingly included in criteria for professional progress and promotion.

The curriculum designed for each individual should depend to a large extent upon his needs; that is, a specified pattern for all graduate students should not be attempted. Included in the graduate program will be education in methods and techniques of research, as well as seminars offering advanced work in such phases of the field as curriculum, supervision, administration, history, philosophy, sociology of sport, motor development, perceptual-motor learning, kinesiology, physiology of exercise, measurement and evaluation.

Because the foundations of physical education are laid in the fields of the natural and social sciences, it is particularly desirable for the graduate student to receive additional specialized preparation in these areas according to his particular interests. These may include one or more of the following: anthropology, anatomy, child development, education, history, neurology, philosophy, physiology, psychology, and sociology.

RESPONSIBILITIES TO RELATED PROFESSIONS

There is agreement throughout the profession that the ultimate goal for all teachers assigned to health education is a major in this area. The trend toward employing fully qualified health educators in secondary schools is gaining momentum. In the meantime, physical education teachers are still carrying the major responsibility for the teaching of health education in the junior and senior high schools. Evidence shows that more often than not the physical education teacher will be given responsibility for health education, even though this assignment may not have been anticipated in college and may be a responsibility the teacher is reluctant to assume.

The result of this misalliance is often a poor quality of teaching and an adverse reaction on the part of students. The assumption by administrators that a teacher can adequately discharge his responsibilities in physical education and at the same time plan and direct curricular experiences in health for the school population demonstrates that inadequate importance is attached to both areas.

There are a number of responsibilities in matters pertaining to health which the physical education teacher has as an integral part of his teaching assignment. These include:

1. Complete cooperation with school medical personnel in findings of health examinations and their application.

2. The cleanliness of the physical education plant and the individuals in the program.

3. Safety in the use of facilities and in the operation of the program.

4. Provisions for first aid and emergency care in cases of illness or injury.

5. Attention to emotional health.

6. Incidental instruction regarding such matters as fatigue, rest, conditioning, warm-up, training, diet, sleep, injuries, and so forth.

7. The promotion of a vigorous program which, among other purposes, will assist in the development of organic power and vigor,

and of efficient body movements in work as well as play, and realization of the fun and recreation which can come from skillful use of the physical mechanism.

8. The wise use of information regarding health matters which should receive the attention of medical personnel, and referral of serious health problems to proper community health agencies.

While safety is a problem for all education, school physical education is particularly concerned because of the large percentage of accidents which occur in the gymnasium, on the playground, and in organized sports. The special phases of safety coming under the immediate supervision of the department of physical education, therefore, relate to safety in the gymnasium, in the swimming pool, and on the athletic field. So far as we teach safety in our own field, we should not only provide protective measures but also try to develop a safety consciousness which will make students considerate of their own personal safety as well as the safety of those with whom they are associated in activities. By attempting to develop a safety consciousness in our activities, we hope that an attitude of consideration may be aroused which will carry into activities and relationships in out-of-school hours.

In discussing the functions of physical education in the school program, educational administrators have emphasized the excellent opportunity offered to physical education teachers for guidance. It is quite apparent in educational thinking today that the guidance of boys and girls should not be entirely confined to one or two specialists in the school organization, but that it is the function of every teacher —an opportunity to be grasped whenever the need for adjustment and choice arises.

Unusual opportunities are offered the physical education teacher by the very nature of the activity. Here the child participates naturally and normally, showing his true emotional behavior. Situations are constantly presented in which the boy or girl can be observed under stress, where no inhibitions are present. There are great possibilities for the establishment of personal relationships which are potentially useful in guidance with reference to a number of areas: recreation, health, personal problems, civic and social behavior, and vocational choice.[5] As an opportunity for service, guidance offers to the physical education teacher the possibility for an outstanding contribution to the total education program and for the integration of his field with the other phases of the school curriculum.

Selected References

1. American Association for Health, Physical Education and Recreation. *Professional Preparation in Dance, Physical Education, Recreation Education, Safety Education, and School Health Education.* Report of New Orleans Conference (January, 1973).

1a. American Association for Health, Physical Education, and Recreation. *Preparing the Elementary Specialist.* Proceedings of the April, 1972 National Conference at Lake Ozark, Mo. Washington, D.C.: AAHPER, 1973.

2. Bronowski, J. *The Identity of Man.* Garden City, N.Y.: Natural History Press, 1971.

3. Browder, Lesley H., Jr. *Emerging Patterns of Administrative Accountability.* Berkeley: McCutchan Publishing Corporation, 1971.

3a. Browder, Lesley H., Atkins, William A., Jr., and Kaya, Esin. *Developing an Educationally Accountable Program.* Berkeley, Calif.: McCutchan Publishing Corporation, 1973.

4. *Career Education.* U.S. Department of Health, Education, and Welfare Publication No. (OE) 72–39.

5. Cassidy, Rosalind F. *Counseling in the Physical Education Program.* New York: Appleton-Century-Crofts, Inc., 1959.

6. "Creativity and Learning." *Daedalus,* 94:No. 3 (1965).

7. Delforge, Gary, and Klein, Richard. "High School Athletic Trainers Internship." *J. Health, Phys. Educ.-Rec.,* 44:42–43 (March, 1973).

8. Dougherty, Neil J. "An Experience Based Teacher Training Program." *J. Health, Phys. Educ.-Rec.,* 44:57–58 (February, 1973).

9. Ersing, Walter F. "Current Directions of Professional Preparation in Adapted Physical Education." *J. Health, Phys. Educ.-Rec.,* 43:78–79 (October, 1972).

10. Field, David A. "Accountability for the Physical Educator." *J. Health, Phys. Educ.-Rec.,* 44:37–38 (February, 1973).

11. *Forward Plan for Career Education Research and Development.* Career Education Development Task Force, National Institute of Education, Education Division, Department of Health, Education, and Welfare (April, 1973).

11a. Gage, N. L. *Teacher Effectiveness and Teacher Education: The Search for a Scientific Basis.* Palo Alto: Pacific Books, 1972.

12. Goodlad, John. "The Reconstruction of Teacher Education." *Teachers College Record,* 72:61–72 (September, 1970).

13. *Graduate Education in Health Education, Physical Education, Recreation, Safety, and Dance* (report of a national conference). Washington, D.C.: American Association for Health, Physical Education, and Recreation, 1967.

14. Gross, Ronald. "From Innovations to Alternatives: A Decade of Change in Education." *Phi Delta Kappan,* LIII:22–24 (September, 1971).

15. "The Growing Dimensions of International Education in the United States." *Phi Delta Kappan,* XLIX:169–240 (December, 1967).

16. Hoffman, Hubert A. "National Survey of Professional Preparation for the Elementary School Physical Education Specialist." *J. Health, Phys. Educ.-Rec.,* 43: 25–28 (February, 1972).

17. Huelster, Laura J. "A Time to Re-conceive 'Physical Education'." The Sixth Amy Morris Homans Lecture. St. Louis: National Association of Physical Education for College Women, 1972.

18. Jewett, Ann E., and Mullan, Marie R. "A Conceptual Model for Teacher Education." *Quest,* XVIII:76–87 (June, 1972).

19. Johnson, Lois. "Optimistic Prospects in Elementary School Physical Education Professional Preparation." *J. Health, Phys. Educ.-Rec.,* 43:29–31 (February, 1972).

20. Joyce, Bruce. "Curriculum and Humanistic Education: Monolism vs. Pluralism." *Curriculum Improvement in Secondary School Physical Education.* Washington, D.C.: American Association for Health, Physical Education and Recreation, 1971, pp. 1–31.

21. Kaufman, Wayne, and Pace, Judy. "Teaching Internship." *J. Health, Phys. Educ.-Rec.,* 43:28–72 (December, 1972).

22. Love, Alice, and Barry, Patricia. "The Teacher Education Center in Physical Education." *J. Health, Phys. Educ.-Rec.*, 42:33–34 (April, 1971).
23. Nelson, Barbara. "Bridging the Gap between Theory and Practice—A Model Teacher Preparation Program." *J. Health, Phys. Educ.-Rec.*, 44:55–57 (February, 1973).
23a. Nixon, John E., and Locke, Lawrence F. "Research on Teaching Physical Education," *Second Handbook of Research on Teaching*, Travers, Robert M. W. (ed.), 1210–1242. Chicago: Rand McNally Company, 1973.
24. Orphan, Milton. "Aquatic Programs for Professional Development." *J. Health, Phys. Educ.-Rec.*, 44:67–68 (March, 1973).
25. *Perceiving, Behaving, Becoming.* Washington, D.C.: Association for Supervision and Curriculum Development, National Education Association, 1962.
26. Pommerenke, Robert L. "Basic Books in Physical Education." *J. Health, Phys. Educ.-Rec.*, 42:35–71 (April, 1971).
27. Richardson, Deane E. "Preparation for a Career in Public School Athletic Administration." *J. Health, Phys. Educ.-Rec.*, 42:17–19 (February, 1971).
27a. Rosenshine, Barak. *Teaching Behavior and Student Achievement.* New York: Humanities Press, 1972.
28. Schwank, Walter C., and Miller, Sayers J. "New Dimensions for the Athletic Training Profession." *J. Health, Phys. Educ.-Rec.*, 42:41–43 (September, 1971).
29. Smith, B. Othanel. *Research in Teacher Education: A Symposium.* Englewood Cliffs, N.J.: Prentice-Hall, Inc., 1971.
30. "Student Action Council Resolutions." *J. Health, Phys. Educ.-Rec.*, 44:55 (April, 1973).
31. *Teachers for the Real World.* Washington, D.C.: American Association of Colleges for Teacher Education, 1969.
32. "Teaching Teachers." *Quest*, XVIII (June, 1972).
33. Teeple, Janet. "Graduate Study in Physical Education—What Should It Be?" *Quest*, XII:66–70 (May, 1969).
34. Travers, Robert M. W. (ed.). *Second Handbook of Research on Teaching.* Chicago: Rand McNally & Co., 1973.
34a. "Trends in Public School Systems: 1967–68 to 1972–73." *American Education*, 9:33 (August-September, 1973).
35. "Washington State Mini-Conference on Preparing Teachers in a Changing Society." *J. Health, Phys. Educ.-Rec.*, 42:8–10. (November-December, 1971).
36. "What Should Higher Education Be Like for the Physical Educator?" *J. Health, Phys. Educ.-Rec.*, 43:66–72 (May, 1972).
36a. Woods, John B., Mauries, Thomas J., and Dick, Bruce V. *Student Teaching: The Entrance to Professional Physical Education.* New York: Academic Press, 1973.
37. Ziegler, Earle F. "A Recommended Irreducible Minimum for Graduate Study in Physical Education and Sport." *J. Health, Phys. Educ.-Rec.*, 42:85–86 (February, 1971).

(Courtesy of the Department of Physical Education and Athletics for Men, Stanford, University.)

Chapter Three

THE NATURE AND SCOPE OF PHYSICAL EDUCATION

Anthropological and historical research has established that physical recreation and sport have been fundamental aspects of all cultures throughout the history of the world. Physical education and recreation are among the oldest arts in the humanities.[2,11] Physical education is a fundamental mode of human expression, and it is an essential form of non-verbal communication, as are music, art, literature, and drama.

In its broadest interpretation, physical education focuses on selected aspects of human experience that are described as the art and science of voluntary, purposeful human movement.[25] Although physical education encompasses all of man's movements, its studies and programs are concentrated in areas of movement designated by such terms as dance, sports, aquatics, gymnastics, and designed exercises. We agree with the view expressed in *Tones of Theory** that physical education should be conceived of as one component in a broad category of human activities called "human movement phenomena." Teachers and scholars in other fields, such as human engineering, recreation, physical therapy, physical medicine, and human ecology, also have a primary interest in selected human movement phenomena.

---

* Celeste Ulrich and John E. Nixon, *Tones of Theory*, 1972. Washington, D.C.: American Association for Health, Physical Education, and Recreation, 26 pp.

A PROFESSION AND AN ACADEMIC DISCIPLINE

The term "physical education" evolved in America in the early 1900's from the more restrictive label, "physical training." "Physical education" became a generally accepted term in schools and colleges in this country in the first half of the twentieth century. Since World War II, professional educators have increased their efforts to correct the limited and inaccurate concept implied by the assumed mind-body dichotomy, and have sought to interpret physical education as a program concerned with the development and learning of the complete human being.

Another shift of emphasis has occurred in recent years that broadens the basis of physical education programs from a school-centered activity to a modern physical education program which provides valuable services for all people of all ages and all degrees of health, individually, in school, and in other social institutions.

A recent elaboration in the conception of the nature and scope of physical education developed in the early 1960's. Concerned individuals, university physical education faculties, and professional organizations worked to establish physical education as an academic discipline with its own unique body of knowledge. In a landmark article, Franklin Henry* asserted that physical education is indeed an academic discipline, and he presents a persuasive argument for this viewpoint. Physical education is, in fact, now regarded as an academic discipline in the community of scholarly disciplines in many colleges and universities throughout this country.

"Movement as a dynamic function of man" is often identified as the area of central concern which gives physical education its unique identity. Metheny[28] indicates that study and research in physical education is directed toward understanding man, with particular reference to his ability to move, the ways in which he utilizes this ability, and the ways in which his use of this ability are related to other aspects of his functional organization as a whole person, and is in some way related to every aspect of man's being and behavior.

There have been many proposals concerning the major areas of concern within the over-all body of knowledge of physical education. Five categories of knowledge frequently appear in these lists: (1) the history and philosophy of physical education; (2) the sociology

---

* Franklin M. Henry, "Physical Education, an Academic Discipline." *Journal of Health, Physical Education, and Recreation,* Sept., 1964, 32, 33, 35, 69.

and anthropology of sports, dance, and physical activity as an essential element in all cultures from primitive times to the present day; (3) the biomechanics, or kinesiology, of human movement; (4) exercise physiology involving the adaptation of the organism to exercise stress under a variety of environmental conditions; and (5) motor development, motor learning and related phenomena, and the neurological bases underlying motor learning and kinesthesis. Additions and variations related to the above list are prevalent in recent physical education literature.

The subject matter of physical education is centered in certain types of movement experiences and behavioral patterns suggested by such terms as exercise, sports, dance, gymnastics, athletics, and movements commonly required for the activities of daily living. These movement experiences exemplify man's personal efforts to act in significant and meaningful ways as he seeks to understand his own human existence and its purpose in his own life and within his cultural surroundings.[25]

Thus, in considering the nature and scope of physical education we may now describe it as (1) an educationally based "profession," and (2) a discrete "academic discipline" with its own unique body of knowledge.

Confusions, contradictions, and misunderstandings have always existed concerning this term, and these difficulties persist today. We believe that more effective interpretation of the purposes and substance of physical education is being carried on today than in the past, but continuous efforts are required to make this interpretation even more clear and persuasive to laymen, as well as to members of the profession itself.

Some examples of the confusion which currently exists concerning basic understanding of the nature and purposes of physical education follow.

The individual whose concept of physical education is limited to the development of the purely physical aspects of the human organism, "body building" and "physical fitness," will scarcely understand the language of another who thinks of physical education as a process concerned primarily with the development of creative movements and patterned movement skills. And neither of them will be in full accord, in word or deed, with other persons who speak of physical education as an agency for the promotion of "good citizenship" or of "health." The advocates of "movement education" create additional uncertainty and misconception in the minds of persons who have long held to the traditional view of physical education as "sports, games and rhythms." Also, many school administrators and curriculum coordinators are unable to distinguish between the unique purposes of physical education and health education, preferring to regard these two areas as components of one broad field of educational experience.

Pleas of increasing intensity have been heard from around the country to change the designation "physical education" to one which more accurately symbolizes the central nature of this subject. In its annual Conference in 1973 members of the American Academy of Physical Education arranged a formal program on this topic, and heated debate concentrated on the desirability of the term "physical education." Other names were suggested to supersede it, such as biomechanics, movement education, kinesiology, and human kinetics. The Academy voted to seek a name change acceptable to a majority of its members. Despite widespread dissatisfaction with the term "physical education," perhaps the greatest difficulty will be to achieve a strong consensus among physical educators about a new title to use in its place.

One approach to clarification of the meaning of the term "physical education" is to propose a rationale for the fundamental nature of all of "education" as a framework within which the school program of physical education is an essential component. Before presenting this rationale, we desire to assert that, in our view, physical education as a broad concept encompasses more than just the formal subject called "physical education" in a school or college curriculum. We will elaborate on the broad perspective we hold for physical education after the following exposition of the fundamental nature of education.

EDUCATION AND PHYSICAL EDUCATION

Schools and Schooling

Traditionally, "education" has been thought of by the layman, and even by some educators, as a process of acquiring knowledge through the medium of the school. A strong emphasis on "concept" learning has been developed in recent years in such subjects as mathematics, biology, physics, chemistry, and more recently, in the social studies and in health education. The important notion under-lying all of these curricular projects is that the body of knowledge in each discipline should be organized around a unique conceptual structure. Thus, we hear the phrase "structure of knowledge" as the central element in teaching the new math, the new science, and so forth. Children are given the objective of learning selected "key concepts" and the most important lower level concepts in the hierarchically structured knowledge framework of a given subject. Today's schools place great stress on acquiring knowledge of "con-cepts" as the most efficient means for the human central nervous system to receive, collect, classify, store, retrieve, and utilize essential elements from the vast reservoir of rapidly increasing and ever changing human knowledge. Also, pupils are given practice in using some of the basic modes of inquiry germane to a field of knowledge at a rudimentary level. The idea is that students will learn to think like researchers or scholars in the discipline.

A few forward looking curriculum experts believe this trend tends to fragment the educational experience, and to place too much emphasis upon discrete subject matter areas per se, at the expense of equal concern for the nature of the individual child and for the cultural milieu in which he learns and lives. These leaders predict that the school curriculum next will evolve in the direction of a more "humanistic" approach, which will seek a balance between the sub-ject matter, the pupil, and his environment, and that the focus will be on the optimum development of the total potentialities of the student, mentally, physically, socially, emotionally, and spiritually, in the humanistic tradition. It is pertinent to note that this book, since its initial publication in 1934, has maintained steadfastly a commitment to this philosophy of the purpose of education and to the unusual opportunities physical education has to contribute to this over-all aim of education in the lives of young people everywhere. This view permeates this edition, for we believe most sincerely that the phy-sical educator can touch the lives of many students in highly significant ways through his subject matter and through his personal example, thus adding to the meaning and significance of human life.

Perceptive educators and laymen no longer regard education merely as "schooling," and not altogether as "learning." Neither is education only those experiences which are formulated and directed by an institution of society known as a school during a few selected hours and days in the year.

This is an era of widespread dissatisfaction with the curricula of many schools and colleges around the country. A wide variety of "alternative" schools and curricula have sprung up in every state. Many critics of public education have leveled heavy broadside barrages against current curriculum models and instructional methods. "Free" schools, "open" schools, schools without walls, parkway schools, and other intriguing labels are being used to symbolize the contrasting educational philosophies of the innovators and creators of these alternative forms of education.

One of the major thrusts of most of these new schools is to offer children more personal freedom, choice, and responsibility in such areas as attendance at school, course election, goal setting within a course, self-evaluation, emphasis on direct experience, multi-sensory learning opportunities, and using relevant environmental conditions in or outside of the school location to provide an optimum learning environment. All students of professional education should become acquainted with pertinent examples of this vast literature and the proposals being offered to replace the traditional public school.

Likewise, most public schools are undergoing intensive scrutiny by concerned citizens and are engaged in both internal and external examination of their programs and instructional modes. Widespread changes are evident in schools and colleges across the country. Educational change is occurring at a faster pace than ever before. Physical education is changing too. In a later chapter we will discuss selected changes which seem to hold promise to improve the quality of physical education curricula and instruction.

Much of this national discontent is prompted by a desire to make the child rather than the subject matter the central concern in the educational process, to provide a learning environment which will emphasize the uniqueness of each student, and to give more weight to personal and human values in the primary goals being sought through formal education.

Learning Theories

A brief review of four major learning theories which are prominent today is necessary as a background for clarifying our views on the fundamental nature of physical education. Space does not permit a detailed explanation of each theory. The physical education major will be exposed to more extensive study of learning theories later in his professional preparation program. Learning can occur without directly imposed formal instruction. In school classrooms and laboratories teachers arrange "learning conditions" in an effort to help children engage in purposeful learning.

Klausmeier and Ripple* describe six steps which are essential to purposeful learning:

1. The learner becomes motivated; sets goal.

2. Appraises situation; means-goal relationship.

3. Tries to attain goal; productive thinking and physical activity.

4. Confirms responses or rejects responses.

5. Reaches goal or does not reach goal.

6. Experiences satisfaction: remembers and applies learning. Or, modifies goal, modifies responses, or withdraws.

Four major theories of learning today are (1) conditioning, (2) modeling and imitation, (3) cognitive restructuring, and (4) information processing.

Conditioning. Conditioning theory usually is divided into two parts, classical and operant conditioning. In classical conditioning a new stimulus is inserted closely preceding the original stimulus. The new stimulus is called the "conditioned" stimulus. After repeated episodes of the new and original stimuli in close association, causing consistent response, the original response continues to occur when the original stimulus is removed: the same response is provoked by the conditioned stimulus. This response is called the conditioned response.

B. F. Skinner has made operant conditioning a household word. It differs from classical conditioning in that a reinforcing stimulus (reinforcer) is deliberately introduced soon *after* a subject has made a response in the form of what the teacher regards as a "desirable" behavior, a behavior which indicates student progress toward the attainment of a learning goal. Operant conditioning theorists contend that prompt positive reinforcement of desirable behaviors influences the learner to attempt to display the desired behavior again.

It is believed that conditioning is most applicable to affective learning which deals with emotional feelings, values, interests, attitudes and similar concepts in human learning and motivation. Con-

---

* Herbert J. Klausmeier and Richard E. Ripple, *Learning and Human Abilities,* 3rd ed. New York: Harper and Row, Publishers, pp. 35–42, 1971.

ditioning also has its place in cognitive learning and in motor learning. In fact, it is well known in connection with programmed learning.

Modeling and Imitation.[1]   The main emphasis in this learning theory is on observation by the learner of accurate models displaying the behavior to be learned. The learner attempts to make new, modified responses after observing the model of the performance he seeks to emulate. Models can be actual persons such as the teacher, a pupil who is an expert performer, parents, siblings, and others. Or, models can be symbolically presented through pictures, drawings, books, TV tapes, motion pictures, loop films, and oral and written instructions.

It is important that the real life model be prestigious, or highly regarded by the learners. It is also desirable that the model have the authority to bestow rewards upon learners who improve through this imitation process. Positive reinforcement can be a powerful reward. Rewards can take other forms both intrinsically and extrinsically. Self-reward is one of the most effective rewards. It is obvious that the teacher must provide a model of behavior in such a way that the student can understand the goal of the performance so that he can produce a series of behaviors which move him in the direction of the learning goal over time. Finally, students from differing cultural and educational backgrounds must be provided with appropriate models in consonance with their previous experiences. One model may not suffice for all members of a large class.

Modeling and imitation theory supports desirable teaching practices in the motor learning domain. Also, it is effective in affective learning. Because the act of modeling does not necessarily possess a consistent internal logic within the learning task it is not as applicable to learning tasks in the cognitive realm.

Cognitive Restructuring.   This theory of learning relies on the concept of "subsumption" as defined by Klausmeier and Ripple*:

> Subsumption of the trace of the correct learning task by an already established ideational system, or *cognitive structure* (italics added), provides anchorage for the new material. . . .

Rather than learning knowledge in isolated bits the teacher assists the pupil to associate new knowledge with existing knowledge stored in his neural system. Each new segment of information or

---

* Herbert J. Klausmeier and Richard E. Ripple, *Learning and Human Abilities*, 3rd ed. New York: Harper and Row, Publishers, p. 37, 1971.

knowledge is seen in the light of previously learned concepts. This melding of new concepts with the existing conceptual system thus is described as "cognitive restructuring." Concepts, principles, generalizations, theories, facts, laws, and other forms of cognitive input are arranged in meaningful relationships which promote desirable learning results. The teacher exerts cognitive and perceptual influence to assist the learner to recognize the relationship or cues of a concept or of a principle to the potential solution of a problem. In presenting a new lesson involving cognitive materials the teacher should emphasize clear advance organizers which are short expository statements which provide a description of the "anchor" Klausmeier and Ripple mentioned in the quote above as the chief vehicle for facilitating cognitive restructuring. Learning materials are presented to the students in final form such as books, motion pictures, TV film, teacher prepared notes and memoranda, and similar forms. This theory of learning applies only to learning materials which can be presented to the learner in final form. It does not replace or substitute for conditioning theory or modeling and imitation theory.

Of particular interest to the physical educator is that little, if any, research has been undertaken to determine the extent to which concepts which are best learned through movement experiences, as contrasted to learning them from books or pictures, can be "restructured" into the existing cognitive system of the learner.

Information Processing. Gagné* describes a newer theory of learning which encompasses the three theories we have just discussed, as well as others. It is called the "information processing" model. Recent research demonstrates that incoming stimuli are processed in the central nervous system (CNS) in a variety of complex ways. The old school of connectionist learning is now considered to be too simplistic to be a viable explanation of how learning and remembering occur in the CNS.

Stimuli received through the various sensory organs are now labeled as "information." It is now believed that when the sensory systems initially register incoming information it is stored for approximately thirty seconds in its original form. This information is not immediately altered as was formerly believed. It is held in "short term store." Because our sensory systems constantly bombard the CNS

---

* Gagné, Robert M. "Some New Views of Learning and Instruction," *Phi Delta Kappan,* 43, May, 1970, 468–472.

with new incoming information the older information is forced out of the storage area. While in the short term store a "rehearsal buffer" acts upon the new information to organize and rehearse it. From the short time store the rehearsed information is transferred into "long term store" by a process called "coding" which prepares it for economical storing and later retrieval. Of course the information processing model is much more complicated than indicated above but brief mention of these major components serves to introduce this recent theory which is gaining wide acceptance.

Gagné believes that the key element in learning is the "prior learning of prerequisite capabilities." Spaced reviews are vital to long term retention. The individual must learn coding and retrieval strategies. These ideas tend to weaken long held beliefs that practice and repetition result in improved retention. Rather, "advance organizers" and "anchoring ideas" seem to be extremely important.

Gagné relates the above theory to instruction by teachers as follows:

> . . . instruction becomes not primarily a matter of communicating something that is to be stored. Instead, it is a matter of stimulating the use of capabilities the learner already has at his disposal, and of making sure he has the requisite capabilities for the present learning task, as well as for many more to come.

Summary. The physical education teacher, the athletic coach, and the dance instructor should be knowledgeable about the major elements of these learning theories which seem to be most acceptable as a basis for selecting desirable learning opportunities for pupils and for deriving appropriate theories and principles of teaching in order to most effectively facilitate learning by pupils in relation to educational goals. For example, Hilgard and Bower* present a series of suggested teaching practices based on their interpretation of learning theories at the time of the publication of their book.

Fundamental Generalizations

The brief explanations about schools, schooling, and learning theories provide a background for our beliefs about the meaning of

---

* Ernest R. Hilgard and Gordon H. Bower, *Theories of Learning,* 3rd ed., 1966. New York: Appleton-Century-Crofts, Inc., pp. 562–565.

the term "education." In our view, education is regarded as a continuous, lifelong process of change, modification, or adjustment of the individual—in school or out of it—resulting from his own responses to the stimuli or situations of his external or internal* environment.[7,20] These rather stable or permanent changes in behavior, resulting from the learner's own activity, affect the mental, physical, emotional, and moral or ethical aspects of his life. Societal values and cultural and sub-cultural norms determine the extent to which such behavioral changes are desirable or "valued."

Substantial evidence from psychology, physiology, and neurology provides commonly acceptable generalizations which explain this concept of education.

1. All Educational Changes or Modifications Come About Through the Individual's Own Activities.[17] Some changes occur through the influence of normal growth and development based on

---

* The internal environment consists of the conditions, influences, or forces within the organism itself, particularly within the blood and lymph. For example, the hormones are powerful influences.

hereditary predispositions and maturational processes. Such changes are not regarded as educational modifications. Many educational changes are deliberately selected and sought by the teacher and are stated as educational objectives. The pupil is engaged in a planned series of educational experiences which have as their purpose "learning" or rather stable changes in behavior which approximate the behaviors described in the objectives.

The pupil must be engaged, directly and actively, in this learning process. The learner must define clear, realistic, attainable goals. Motivational conditions suitable to the learning tasks and to the state of the learner are an essential ingredient in this process of behavior change. The learner must participate in frequent repetition of learning opportunities. He should engage in learning activities which will provide for multisensory stimulation and for the neural integration of a variety of stimuli.

Not all specific changes in pupil behaviors are overtly planned and taught by instructors. Artistic teachers in any field will provide learning opportunities which encourage divergent, creative behaviors. Problem solving situations are formulated which encourage the child to find acceptable responses or answers by virtue of his own intellectual efforts. Self-discovery and heuristic learning experiences are fundamental aspects of curriculum and instruction at all levels of formal education. In this type of learning there is no one "predictable" solution but, rather, a range of possible responses of equal "correctness." Boys and girls should be encouraged to engage in expressive behaviors which reflect their feelings and emotions. Nonverbal behaviors which communicate ideas, moods, preferences, and idiosyncratic personality traits are to be encouraged. None of the above behavioral changes are preplanned to the extent of specifying performance objectives in advance but all are valuable educational outcomes developed under the guidance of a sensitive, "open" teacher.

2. *Educational Experiences Are Responses to Stimuli Presented to the Individual by the Internal or External Environment.* "Stimuli," in the sense employed in the above generalization, refers to total learning situations, not to isolated, unplanned stimulus-response reflexes or reactions. When the quarterback changes the offensive play with an "audible" call at the line of scrimmage, all teammates respond by revising their planned actions to conform to the specifications of their assignment for that new play, and they place themselves

in the highest possible degree of physical and mental readiness to carry out their duty effectively. Basketball players spend hours of practice time learning to recognize instantaneously various defensive maneuvers, such as "switches," "presses," "over-playing," and other stratagems, so that in turn they may almost reflexively respond with a counter move which takes full advantage of a new weakness inherent in the opponent's move. The golfer sizes up the width of the fairway, the distance of the fairway trap in front of the tee, the direction of the prevailing wind, the best approach to the green and the pin for the second shot, and other relevant factors before he makes his drive. He analyzes the total situation before responding with a drive and develops a mental plan which, hopefully, is executed to serve a calculated purpose. Distance runners are coached by mentors knowledgeable about the effects of fatigue upon performance. The runners respond to planned practices in order to react favorably to influences from both external and internal environmental conditions during the race.

Individual responses to total learning situations are based on prior opportunities for practice in varied contexts, which enhance the likelihood of generalizable responses which are discriminating in later environments. Thus, the fundamental response can be adapted and utilized under varying conditions.

In general, learning is most efficient when it starts with experiences organized first as simplified wholes, which then in turn are expanded to complex wholes as the learner progresses.

There is a risk that reference to "stimulus" and "response" will imply a type of rote, automatic learning. This notion is not intended in this discussion of change or modification through educational experiences. Learning opportunities should be devised with comprehension and understanding as integral facets. Likewise, the student should be encouraged and rewarded (reinforced) for attempts to think and act divergently or creatively, as well as convergently or logically. The full human potential for learning will not be realized if it is restricted to logical, expected, predicted responses.

3. *All Responses to Learning Situations Change, Modify, or "Educate" the Individual in Some Way.* The football players, the basketball players, the golfers, and the long distance runners have reacted in various total learning situations to different types of stimuli, and thereby are changed or modified in some manner and to some degree. As these athletes are changed or modified, it may be assumed

that they become increasingly more effective in attaining the specific objectives set forth for them; that is, they more nearly approximate the ideal behavior set for them in the objectives formulated by their coaches. Likewise, students engaging in creative, problem solving, expressive, and non-verbal communicative behaviors are changing during these educational episodes and their behaviors are changed as a result of these experiences. Obviously, competent instruction in the full and complete sense of the term is a necessary prerequisite to these educational achievements.

Actually, each time the golfer practices his drive, he hits the ball a little differently from any other time. On each hit he receives "feedback," or knowledge of results, both externally and internally, concerning how successful the drive was in distance and accuracy. His kinesthetic feedback system operates with unbelievable speed to inform him that he "hit from the top" too soon, or that he did not keep his left arm firm. He can tell from the "feel" of the hit whether or not it was "good." He can observe the flight of the ball, its height, and its degree of deviation in flight as a hook or slice, as well as where it lands and rolls, and thus he can assess the quality of that particular stroke as a basis for determining what adjustment to make in the next try. Externally, his coach may be observing him, and can explain to him verbally the error he made and can offer a suggestion for improvement next time. The instant playback portable television camera also is an external feedback source being used as an instructional aid in the teaching of physical skills.

In general, modifications or changes in behavior in specified directions occur most efficiently when learned in small, progressive steps based on the feedback mentioned above. Successful change should be "reinforced" by appropriate "rewards" from the instructor, such as verbal encouragement or a compliment.

4. All Responses Involve the Integrated Human Organism.[12] The manifold behaviors which an individual exhibits at any given time are organized into a complex, unique system which is called "personality." Each person attempts to organize and structure his patterns of behavior to enable him to adapt successfully to the society in which he lives.[23]

All of the responses of the individual are subject to a continual process of integration. Education is concerned with the whole individual, not just with parts of him. We may observe that the experimental subject's pulse rate rises to 200 beats per minute on the bicycle ergometer, and we may thoughtlessly believe that this performance represents an isolated physiological response. The quarterback may be heard issuing an audible change in signal at the line of scrimmage, which superficially seems only to be a rapid mental adjustment and response. The boy who wins the one hundred yard dash in the conference track meet erupts with unbridled joy by prancing around the track, smiling broadly, and waving to the audience, seemingly an emotional response. Yet, in every case, modern knowledge about the totally integrated functioning of all the systems of the human organism assures us that the effects of each of the above experiences modify the boy in some way. It is the cumulative state of these integrated responses which determines the individual's personality at any given time.

Stable changes which occur as a result of learning probably evolve through a variety of types or kinds of learning conditions. It is hypothesized that increasingly higher levels of learning depend upon the mastery of the ones below it. An integrated theory of learning levels has been proposed by Gagné,[14] which is illustrated in his hierarchical learning model. He postulates eight levels of learning: (1) signal learning (the classical conditioned response); (2) stimulus-response (a connection is learned which can produce a precise response); (3) chaining (two or more stimulus-response connections); (4) verbal association (learning of chains which are verbal); (5) multiple discrimination (making a number of different identifying responses to as many different stimuli); (6) concept learning (ability to make a common response that classifies an entire class of objects or events); (7) principle learning (learning a chain of two or more concepts); and (8) problem solving (developing a higher order principle from an appropriate new combination of two or more principles).

Although physical educators have not achieved a large measure of success in implementing this position, some physical education theorists have advocated this integrated view of learning and teaching for a considerable period of time. We suggest that the implementation of an integrated view of learning may be facilitated by the construct of a "motor" domain for identifying educational objectives and analyzing motor performance behaviors. The term "motor" in preference to "psychomotor" is based on the need to view physical education's developmental potential in a more integrative context. This position will be explained more fully in a later section.

Application

The four generalizations discussed can be summarized by the statement that fundamentally all education is concerned with (1) the individual, his purposes, needs, abilities, aptitudes, interests, attitudes, and personality; (2) the situation (or stimulus) as perceived by the individual—the setting (learning environment) in which education occurs; (3) the response (reaction) of the individual, and the interaction between the individual and the situation (or stimulus); (4) the changes or modifications or stable adaptations in behaviors, which are brought about as a result of responses to the situation (or stimulus); and (5) the total integration of these responses and subsequent altered behaviors to mold the ever evolving human personality.

These generalizations and conclusions apply to physical education just as to any other form or phase of education. Fundamentally, physical education is concerned with individuals, situations, responses, and modifications. In the final analysis, the only distinction between physical education and other forms of education lies in the fact that physical education is concerned largely with situations and responses characterized by overt movement activities such as sports, dance, aquatics, and designed exercises. Keeping in mind the fact that all responses of the individual involve the integrated human organism, we still recognize that certain responses are characterized mainly by intellectual activity, others by emotional activity, and still others by vigorous muscular movements. It is the last-mentioned type of activity with which physical education is primarily concerned, although it is also fundamentally concerned with intellectual, social, and emotional changes in behavior and personality.

This statement is not to be taken to mean that physical education is concerned exclusively with muscular reactions and resultant physiological and anatomical changes in the individual. It is true that rational muscular exercise, among other effects,[20] promotes growth and development,[23] strengthens and enlarges muscles, improves muscle tone, and increases the power and vigor of the organic systems of the body.[19] But it would be a rare system of physical education indeed which could be conducted without involving the individual in situations calling for mental and emotional responses, with resultant modifications in habits, attitudes, appreciations, or skills. The nearest approach to such a barren and limited program is to be found in those "systems" in which the individual gains his physical education through the medium of drills, dumbbells, wands, gripping devices, mechanical horses, or vibrating belts driven by electric motors.

Studies in neurophysiology and kinesiology are producing strands of evidence which now lead us to believe that the contribution of the sense of kinesthesis to intellectual development is more crucial than previously realized.[29] Steinhaus* says: "Every movement, every body position, every tension in muscle, tendon, and joint structure contributes to the formation of concepts or ideas that form the building stones with which we construct our thought life."[37] In a more recent review of current research in neurology and physiological psychology, Steinhaus also develops the startling notion that "your muscles see more than your eyes."[38]

DEFINITION OF PHYSICAL EDUCATION

When we consider education in such fundamental terms as have been presented above, we are drawn logically to the conclusion that physical education should be defined as *that phase of the total process of education which is concerned with the development and utilization of the individual's movement potential and related responses, and with the stable behavior modifications in the individual which result from these responses.*

In the light of this definition, we see that the school program of physical education consists fundamentally of a specialized environment, characterized by many situations and stimuli intended to induce or provide opportunity for physical, social, emotional, intellectual, and other responses on the part of the student, through which he may become changed, modified, or educated. The swimming pool, the running track, the tennis courts and other facilities, and the equipment and supplies are a part of the specialized environment, as are the teacher or leader, the schedule of contests, and the athletic tradition of the school.

Just what physical education will mean for any school, for any group within the school, or for any individual will depend upon the

---

* Arthur H. Steinhaus, *Toward an Understanding of Health and Physical Education.* Dubuque, Iowa: William C. Brown Company, Publishers, 1963, p. 10.

types of responses induced in the students, hence the vital importance of selecting physical education teachers of high moral standards and outstanding character. If the total situation results in no more meaningful reactions than "exercises" done on command, then physical education in this particular school will mean little aside from strictly "physical training." But if, on the other hand, the total situation results in frequent and desirable reactions of an intellectual, social, and moral nature as well as physical, the program becomes one of vital educational significance. Physical education now is generally regarded as an essential educational experience, in which all pupils should regularly engage throughout elementary, secondary, and higher education as an integral phase of the total school curriculum.[6,35]

Steinhaus,[37] along with others, is a vigorous spokesman for the expanded view of physical education which is concerned with all degrees of human physical activity, from a state of complete relaxation with relatively little human energy being expended, to the condition of the highly trained, competitive athlete producing maximum effort at high energy cost in championship events. As in the case of restricted thinking about the involvement of agencies promoting physical education, the profession likewise has tended to emphasize training and interest in the more "vigorous" physical activities, exemplified by exercises, formal calisthenics, school games and sports, and dance and body mechanics activities.

The physical educator today should be trained to select and conduct programs of varying degrees of physical activity and stress, adapted to the specific needs of each individual. One of the most significant problems facing the physical education teacher in the public schools today is that of individualizing instruction.[31] He should have the scientific background knowledge which classifies him as a professional person who is fully qualified to select, organize, and conduct appropriate programs.

There is a trend now to devote more attention to the place and function of relaxation, rest, and recovery from fatigue as one phase of physical education.[34] At the other end of the activity scale, research in exercise physiology at submaximal and maximal output of energy seems more and more to be undertaken by specialists in physical education, as less interest is shown in this phase of physiological research by the physiologists. Many colleges and universities in recent years have established well endowed exercise physiology laboratories. In several of these laboratories, well known physiology researchers have been employed because of their continuing interest in research concerning exercise stress. An increasing number of young physical education research specialists are obtaining advanced graduate training in physiology and neurology in order to qualify themselves to conduct sophisticated research in these laboratories, which have been accorded various descriptive titles such as "Human Physical Performance Laboratory," "Physiology of Exercise Laboratory," "Physical Fitness Laboratory," and similar appellations. Coaches and athletic trainers are becoming more knowledgeable about the effects of various conditioning regimens upon the performance of their athletes in sports requiring "all-out" physical exertion. Much of this new evidence is empirically based, although basic research also is producing more and more experimental data.

Much is being learned about degrees and types of physical activity appropriate to persons of all ages and varying health conditions. There is an entire specialty called Physical Medicine, which deals with the recovery of medical patients by use of therapy involving selected physical activities appropriate to the medical problem.

The role of physical activity in proper growth and development of young children is abundantly documented in the child psychology literature.[4] The role of exercise in relation to the aging process is becoming better illuminated as additional research evidence and empirical information become available.[19] The effects of physical activity upon the condition of so-called sedentary males of middle age are being dramatically indicated by recent laboratory and clinical studies.[13]

The fundamental relationship of physical activity to weight control and nutritional principles, described by new research findings in recent years, has significantly changed our beliefs about this basic aspect of health and well-being, and adds importance to the role of the physical educator and his program.[3,24]

The use of physical activities as a medium of therapy in the treatment of the mentally and emotionally ill[22] likewise is more heavily indicated by research and clinical evidence than ever before.

In summary, the physical educator of today needs to be fully informed and deeply concerned about the proper roles of physical education, in relation to the full range of human activity, for persons of all ages, and for varying degrees of health. The physical educator must broaden his horizons concerning the contributions he can make to human welfare through a greater understanding, interpretation, and application of knowledge about the significance and meaning of movement in the lives of children, youth, and adults.

Selected References

1. Bandura, Albert: *Social Learning and Personality Development.* New York: Holt, Rinehart and Winston, 1963.
2. Berelson, Bernard, and Steiner, Gary A.: *Human Behavior: An Inventory of Scientific Findings.* New York: Harcourt Brace Jovanovich, Inc., 1967.
3. Bogert, L. Jean, Briggs, George M., and Calloway, Doris H.: *Nutrition and Physical Fitness.* Philadelphia: W. B. Saunders Company, 9th ed., 1973.
4. Breckenridge, Marian E., and Vincent, E. Lee: *Child Development: Physical and Psychologic Development Through Adolescence.* Philadelphia: W. B. Saunders Company, 5th ed., 1965.
5. Bucher, Charles A.: *Foundations of Physical Education.* St. Louis: The C. V. Mosby Company, 6th ed., 1972.
6. Bush, Robert N., and Allen, Dwight W.: *A New Design for High School Education: Assuming a Flexible Schedule.* New York: McGraw-Hill Book Company, Inc., 1964.
7. Cannon, Walter B.: *The Wisdom of the Body.* New York: W. W. Norton & Company, Inc., rev. ed., 1963.
8. Cassidy, Rosalind F.: *Counseling in the Physical Education Program.* New York: Appleton-Century-Crofts, Inc., 1959.
9. Cassidy, Rosalind F.: "The Cultural Definition of Physical Education." *Quest,* IV:11–15 (April, 1965).
10. Cassidy, Rosalind: "Should We Drop the Designation Physical Education in Favor of a Different Name?" *Academy Papers,* No. 6. Louisville, Kentucky: American Academy of Physical Education, 1972.
11. Cozens, Frederick W., and Stumpf, Florence S.: *Sports in American Life.* Chicago: University of Chicago Press, 1953.
12. Cronbach, Lee J.: *Educational Psychology.* New York: Harcourt Brace Jovanovich, Inc., 2nd ed., 1963.
13. Cureton, Thomas K.: *Physical Fitness and Dynamic Health.* New York: The Dial Press, 1965.
14. Gagné, Robert M.: *The Conditions of Learning.* New York: Holt, Rinehart and Winston, Inc., 2nd ed., 1965.
15. Henry, Nelson B. (ed.): *Learning and Instruction.* Forty-ninth Yearbook, Part I, National Society for the Study of Education. Chicago: University of Chicago Press, 1950.
16. Hetherington, Clark W.: *School Program in Physical Education.* Yonkers, N.Y.: World Book Company, 1922.
17. Hilgard, Ernest R., and Atkinson, Richard C.: *Introduction to Psychology.* New York: Harcourt Brace Jovanovich, Inc., 5th ed., 1971.
18. Hilgard, Ernest R., and Bower, Gordon H.: *Theories of Learning.* New York: Appleton-Century-Crofts, Inc., 3rd ed., 1966.
19. Jokl, Ernst: *Physiology of Exercise.* Springfield, Ill.: Charles C Thomas, Publisher, 1964.
20. Karpovich, Peter V., and Sinning, Wayne E.: *Physiology of Muscular Activity.* Philadelphia: W. B. Saunders Company, 7th ed., 1971.
21. Klausmeier, H. J., and Ripple, Richard E.: *Learning and Human Abilities: Educational Psychology.* New York: Harper & Row, Publishers, 3rd ed., 1971.
22. Layman, Emma M.: "Contributions of Exercise and Sports to Mental Health

and Social Adjustment." Chapter 29 in Johnson, Warren R.: *Science and Medicine of Exercise and Sports.* New York: Harper & Row, Publishers, Inc., 1960.

23. McDonald, Frederick J.: *Educational Psychology.* Belmont, Calif.: Wadsworth Publishing Company, Inc., 2nd ed., 1965.
24. Mayer, Jean: "Exercise and Weight Control" in *Exercise and Fitness.* Chicago: The Athletic Institute, 1960
25. Metheny, Eleanor: *Connotations of Movement in Sport and Dance.* Dubuque, Iowa: William C. Brown and Co., 1965.
26. Metheny, Eleanor: "The 'Design' Conference," *J. Health, Phys. Educ. and Rec.,* 37:6 (May, 1966).
27. Metheny, Eleanor: *Movement and Meaning.* New York: McGraw-Hill Book Company, Inc., 1968.
28. Metheny, Eleanor: "Physical Education as an Area of Study and Research," *Quest,* IX:73–78 (December, 1967).
29. Metheny, Eleanor: "The Unique Meaning Inherent in Human Movement." *The Physical Educator,* 18:3–7 (March, 1961).
30. Nash, Jay B.: *Physical Education: Interpretations and Objectives.* Dubuque, Iowa: William C. Brown and Co., rev. ed., 1963.
31. Nixon, John E., and Jewett, Ann E.: *Physical Education Curriculum.* New York: The Ronald Press, 1964.
32. Oberteuffer, Delbert, and Ulrich, Celeste: *Physical Education.* New York: Harper & Row, Publishers, 4th ed., 1970.
33. Rathbone, Josephine L., and Hunt, Valerie V.: *Corrective Physical Education.* Philadelphia: W. B. Saunders Company, 7th ed., 1965.
34. Rathbone, Josephine L.: *Relaxation.* Philadelphia: Lea & Febiger, 1969.
35. "Resolutions on School and College Health and Physical Education" passed by the House of Delegates of the American Medical Association, Miami Beach, June, 1960. *J. Health, Phys. Educ.-Rec.,* 31:18 (October, 1960).
36. Siedentop, Daryl: "What Did Plato Really Think?" *The Physical Educator,* 25: 25–26 (March, 1968).
37. Steinhaus, Arthur T.: *Toward an Understanding of Health and Physical Education.* Dubuque, Iowa: William C. Brown and Co., 1963.
38. Steinhaus, Arthur H.: "Your Muscles See More Than Your Eyes." *J. Health, Phys. Educ.-Rec.,* 37:38–40 (September, 1966).
39. *This Is Physical Education.* Washington, D.C.: American Association for Health, Physical Education, and Recreation, 1965.
40. Williams, Jesse F.: *The Principles of Physical Education.* Philadelphia: W. B. Saunders Company, 8th ed., 1964.

(Courtesy of the Department of Physical Education and Athletics for Men, Stanford University.)

Chapter Four

THE PURPOSES OF
PHYSICAL EDUCATION

In recent years, diverse, powerful forces and events have evoked a continuous and intense reappraisal of public education in the United States at all levels. In the 1950's, the launching of the first Russian Sputnik resulted in national consternation about the quality of education in this country, particularly in scientific fields. Other important influences have been the financial, social, and educational problems of minority groups in urban areas; rapidly increasing costs of education at all levels, which are now straining tax sources and which seem to have reached a barrier of taxpayer resistance; the concentration on curriculum reform, based on the concept approach, in subject fields such as mathematics, physical science, chemistry, physics, biology, foreign languages, social studies, English, and health education, buttressed by substantial grants from governmental and foundation sources; student and teacher unrest and militancy; the development of public and private alternative and "open" schools; and the insistence of the public that teachers and schools be held explicitly "accountable" for the instructional competence of teachers based on measurable learning gains by pupils.

In this broad context, physical education likewise has been reappraised, and has been subjected to weighty pressures, both from within and from outside its own professional boundaries. All of the Presidents of the United States since 1956 have demonstrated a personal interest in, and concern for, the physical fitness of the citizens of this country, and they have given support to the work of the President's Council on Physical Fitness and Sports, an agency of the Department of Health, Education, and Welfare. The Lifetime Sports Foundation has significantly influenced school programs across the country. It employs advertising, workshops, instructional clinics, audio-visual instructional materials, and modified equipment to present its aim of introducing a greater number of lifetime sports into the curriculum.

Movement education has come into widespread acceptance, particularly in elementary school programs. Since about 1960, there has been a development of interest in self-discovery, problem solving, and inquiry development through movement experiences at the elementary school level. American physical educators finally recognized the potential contributions of this type of physical education, which has been common in countries such as West Germany,[13] England, Austria, and others for many years. Perceptual–motor learning experiences recently have been emphasized in physical education classes in lower elementary grades, as physical educators, reading consultants, and general curriculum coordinators have become acquainted with the studies and clinical experiences of cognitive and developmental psychologists, and with the work of medical specialists in the neurological bases of human movement and kinesthesis.

Rapid advances in the adaptation and utilization of instructional technology for the improvement of teaching and learning have caused many physical educators and administrators to rethink the physical education program and the way it is organized and conducted. Modular scheduling, made possible by the capabilities of the computer, has provided a method for planning a more highly individualized program of study for each pupil, based on his interests and abilities. It has opened up new opportunities for independent study and practice in physical education in an "open laboratory" setting and in physical education resource centers. New findings concerning differentiated staff duties and utilization provide for viable alternatives for planning and conducting physical education programs of higher quality and greater breadth of content and experience.

A national project, directed by Ann Jewett, under the auspices of the American Association for Health, Physical Education and Recreation to develop a "concept" curriculum for physical education from kindergarten through college, and a study to identify and describe the theoretical structure of physical education as an area of scholarly study and research, have helped to cause reevaluations of the purposes of physical education in the school program and of the status of this field as a substantive discipline in higher education.

All of these influences, and others as well, have caused a continuous concern for and review of the purposes of physical education in schools and in other societal agencies. It is little wonder that physical educators, administrators, school board members, faculty colleagues, parents, and taxpayers at times are confused about the major purposes of physical education.

Since its inception as a school program in this country, physical educators, both individually and through their professional organizations, have worked to promote a greater understanding of the purposes of this field.[10,20,31,34,36] Many statements and publications have been developed to provide clear interpretations of these purposes for the edification and understanding of the lay public as well as for members of the physical education profession and other educators.

In recent years, intensified efforts have been made on many fronts. Three noteworthy examples were the National Conference on the Interpretation of Physical Education[39] in 1961; the publication *This Is Physical Education*,[43] a statement prepared by the Physical Education Division of the American Association for Health, Physical Education and Recreation in 1965 by an editorial committee under the chairmanship of Eleanor Metheny; and the Conference of Twenty in 1969 which was the highlight of the AAHPER long term Project on the Theoretical Structure of Physical Education.

The Report of the National Conference on Interpretation of Physical Education was a milestone in the history of physical education. It contains a series of "basic beliefs" hammered out and agreed to in principle by 53 leaders of the profession, representing its many specializations and educational levels.

This Is Physical Education provides a succinct, dynamic, and clear exposition of the present day interpretation of physical education through its description of "broader and deeper understandings." It explains the major objectives of physical education which are relevant to any phase of the school or college program. It indicates the necessity to base the selection of educational opportunities for the students on a needs assessment. The major curriculum elements which should be included at each educational level are described. The role of continuous evaluation and feedback in curriculum and instructional processes is stressed. The entire statement, although relatively brief, is couched in a framework of practical educational philosophy which stimulates and challenges the physical educator to broaden his aspirations and to improve the quality of his service to youth through the recommendations presented.

Since the early 1960's the AAHPER has sponsored a project to explore and develop a theoretical structure of physical education. National and regional conferences have been held over the years to promote this project. A recent AAHPER publication, *Tones of Theory—A Theoretical Structure for Physical Education, a Tentative Perspective,* 1972, by Celeste Ulrich and John E. Nixon,[44] Project Primary Co-Investigators, summarizes the work of many individuals over a ten-year period and presents a tentative theoretical framework of physical education.

Many other projects have been completed in recent years, and still others are underway currently to explain the purposes of physical education to various "publics." Undoubtedly, these efforts will continue unabated in the years ahead.

This chapter presents an approach to the understanding and conceptual organization of the purposes of physical education as conceived by the authors. The term "purposes" is used in the inclusive sense and will be elucidated in detail through a definition and description of such terms as aim, objectives (general, instructional, performance, specific and behavioral), and goals. Obviously, there is not just one acceptable framework for viewing physical education purposes. Therefore, frequent reference is made to the works of other individuals and a variety of professional organizations which propose alternative structures. The professional student should be exposed to as many of these views as possible as a basis for developing his own conceptual framework within which he can organize his views and understandings about the purposes of this field. Virtually every act the physical educator performs is based on the purposes he values whether implicitly held or explicitly enunciated.

A perusal of professional literature readily reveals that there is no consistent use among authors of such terms as "aims," "purposes," "objectives," "goals," and "outcomes." Often two or more of these words are used interchangeably or synonymously. There is no standard acceptance or agreement concerning a differentiated definition for each of these terms. Thus, it is indeed difficult to attempt to order one's thinking about the purposes of physical education, and to compare and contrast the many varying shades of philosophical exposition found in the vast quantity of physical education literature which has accumulated in recent years.

The authors believe that a consistent understanding and use of these terms is desirable and possible. The "aim," as explained later in this chapter, is the ultimate, ideal conceptualization of the end result to be attained. It is so idealistic, so distant, and so broadly constructed that it probably never will be fully realized by any one pupil in a school program. Nevertheless, it serves the crucial function of providing the ultimate "aiming point" (hence the use of the term "aim"), which gives over-all guiding direction to the educational effort. It sets the course for the educational voyage, for without it, the program, and the students in it, would drift aimlessly like the ship lost at sea.

General objectives are the major subdivisions of the aim. They, too, are broad, extensive, and idealistic. Like the aim, they usually are couched as expectations that are beyond complete fulfillment by any mortal being. However, they serve the function of separating and clarifying the essential elements of the total aim. There are unique characteristics which differentiate each general objective from the others. Together they comprise the aim. They are discrete, but when considered inclusively they account for the commitment of the aim. As with the aim they, too, have the essential function of providing navigational guidance for the educational journey. They point the way. They are closer to the practical "nitty gritty" of everyday educational practice. Still another imperative function for general objectives is to reflect the values of the society which the schools are directed to promulgate. In doing so, these objectives point the way.

Instructional objectives constitute the next level of analysis. Each general objective is scrutinized to discover its essential elements. What must the student accomplish, master, perform, know, understand, value, and appreciate, in order to progress in the direction of the general objective, and hence toward the aim? This analysis, if conducted rigorously and thoroughly, will yield a large number of instructional objectives for each general objective. Objectives are stated at a level of preciseness which permits actual accomplishment by the student.

Instructional objectives encompass "behavioral" and "performance" objectives as well as "expressive" objectives. Behavioral or performance objectives are stated as specific descriptions of actual stable behavioral changes which are thought to be desirable by the end of the learning experience. The two terms have become interchangeable.

"Expressive objectives" is a term used for describing pupil behaviors which are not amenable to precise quantitative measurement. The quality of a poem or a painting constructed by a pupil cannot be evaluated by normal objective methods. However, the teacher may want to insure that each pupil in the art appreciation class has attempted to create an original work of art in water color, in pencil, and in clay. The expressive objective would be for each student to have the personal experience of creating an art product of his own design in each of these media.

"Goals," like behavioral objectives, represent terminal performances, or descriptions of stable behaviors through which the teacher attempts to develop a planned set of educational experiences. Goals can be considered synonymous with specific or behavioral objectives. Elementary and high school teachers and administrators are more likely to use the term "goals" than are college and university physical educators. Also, the word "goals" seems to hold more appropriate usage in discussions with pupils, and in challenges and assignments issued to students in the current trend toward the encouragement of "pupil goal setting" in physical education programs.

"Outcomes" refers to a description of the actual overt, describable behaviors exhibited by a student on the last day of instruction. If evidence can be accumulated to show that a pupil has attained a rather stable behavioral change or adaptation due to the effects of practice, he has "learned" and has evolved a new set of behaviors called outcomes. Outcomes may, then, be compared to the specific objectives or goals set before the instructional unit begins and the extent of achievement of these goals can be assessed.

THE BASIC AIM

The conceptual framework of physical education purposes logically evolves from the *ultimate purpose* toward which physical education is directed. This broad, unified, all-inclusive proposition concerning what physical education is and what it aspires to do is, by definition, the *aim* of physical education.

American public education at various school levels still faces the dilemma of the existence of ambiguous, vague, and widely divergent aims as proposed by state legislatures, school boards, educational writers, curriculum commissions, and other sources. One can readily locate a diversity of statements of aims described in the following ways: "to train the mind"; "to develop the intellect"; "to master prescribed bodies of knowledge"; "to learn the basic concepts of selected disciplines"; "to develop the character"; "to develop the human potentialities of the individual so he will become an effective, participating member of a democratic society"; "to develop the rational powers"; "to develop the ability to think"; "to develop the capacity to make wise decisions, in order to become an effective citizen in the democratic processes upon which this free country depends;" and "to learn to learn for a lifetime."

Perhaps the task of deriving the over-all aim of physical education can best be accomplished by analyzing two fundamental concepts about education in general, which seem to be well substantiated by carefully validated scientific evidence. These two basic generalizations, which were described in more detail in the previous chapter, are (1) that education is a process of stable change or modification of the behavior of the individual resultant from his own activities and reactions and his interaction with his environment; and (2) that formal, organized education is concerned with the promotion of modifications of the individual which will enable him more nearly to reach his maximum possible development in all phases of life and his finest possible adjustment to the world in which he lives.

Definition

Statements of purposes of physical education found in recent literature quite generally agree on the importance of providing favorable opportunities in school programs for individuals to engage in selected kinds of human movements (such as sports, dance, designed exercises, gymnastics, and aquatics) and related activities, which are voluntary, purposeful, and overtly observable. These statements also stress the need for adequate facilities and for exemplary leadership in order to provide favorable opportunities for educational activities best suited to produce desirable changes in behavior, growth, and development. Following this line of reasoning, we may define the aim of physical education as follows:

Organized physical education aims to make the maximal contribution to the optimal development of the individual's potentialities in all phases of life, by placing him in an environment which will promote the movement and related responses or activities that will best contribute to this purpose.

Misconceptions

Despite a widespread flow of current literature which provides interpretations concerning the purposes of physical education and its nature, scope, and contributions, vital misunderstandings still exist in the minds of many people, including physical educators themselves. The major confused or inadequate concepts of the aim and purposes of physical education which have developed in the past and which still remain current in certain quarters are described briefly.

Physical Education and Health Education. A certain amount of confusion in regard to physical education arises out of a general failure to distinguish between physical education and health education.[9] It is common to think of these two phases of education as identical, or of one of them as being part of the other. In some states and local school districts, health education and physical education are regarded, philosophically, as comprising one discipline, and are organized and scheduled as one program in the school curriculum. In other states and districts, health education and physical education have been regarded as separate disciplines in recent years, and have been organized and scheduled separately. In some of these areas there are pressures being exerted to combine these two fields again into one discipline, although this movement does not have the support of professional leaders in health education and physical education.

We have pointed out before that physical education must be thought of as that phase of education which comes about through, or in connection with, vigorous movement activities. Health education comprises all training which contributes in any way to the sum total of the individual's health knowledge, health habits, and health attitudes. Health education and physical education may go on together.[33] This happens in the case of the individual whose ambition to excel in sports stimulates him to the practice of desirable health habits and to the acquisition of information about healthful living. A formal course in health education should not be regarded as physical education. Learning to wash the hands before eating may be a valuable item of health education, but it has little connection with physical education.

Physical Education and Physical Fitness. The present-day emphasis on physical fitness in the school program tends to confuse the essential differences between physical fitness, physical performance, and physical education. Some literature by both professional organizations and individual physical educators employs these terms synonymously. Newspaper articles in particular frequently seem to present an uninformed viewpoint concerning the crucial differentiation of these terms. Physical fitness is discussed in more detail in another chapter. It will suffice to state here that physical fitness activities in themselves do not constitute a total physical education program. Many exercise programs advocated in the name of physical fitness are physical training, not physical education. Oberteuffer[35] and Brackenbury[2] clearly describe the difference between the two concepts. Physical fitness is a worthy objective of physical education, but it is only one of several objectives, and cannot be regarded as the ultimate aim of physical education, although some physical educators today are tending to give this impression to the public because of their strong allegiance to the physical fitness objective.

Another aspect of confusion in this area of physical exercise is the often heard statement, particularly in the elementary school, that children need a physical education period in order to "blow off steam" or to "release the tensions" they have built up in the classroom. In this view physical education is not recognized as having educational potentialities. It is merely regarded as a catharsis or a relief from the more serious and emotionally demanding formal learning activities in the school. There are people who genuinely believe that young children will play long enough and hard enough daily to meet the natural demands of their bodily systems and that, therefore, no physical education class time is required. Such natural activity can be performed during recess and during non-school hours, while school time should be reserved for more important intellectual experiences.

This situation indicates the failure of the physical education profession to interpret the nature, scope, and values of this medium of education, a failure which leads to faulty and misguided understandings of the aim of physical education, particularly in this realm of exercise and natural play.[18]

That "physical education aims to make people healthy," or, put another way, that "physical education aims to promote healthful living," is a claim which in the past has been used frequently to win support for the physical education program. But the more we attempt to define "health," and the more clearly we understand the causes of disease, the more dangerous this claim seems to be to the cause of physical education, when put forth in the usual loose manner. Health is now thought of, not merely as freedom from disease, but as a condition of all-round efficiency of the human organism mentally, socially, and physically, which enables one to live fully and completely.

If we accept this modern concept of health, we can defend with some assurance the statement that physical education aims to keep people "healthy." For, in this sense of the word, all aspects of organized education aim at health. However, proponents of health as the chief aim of physical education should not argue that the individual maintains freedom from disease by means of muscular exercise, because there is no scientific basis for any such general claim.[42] Immunity to diseases and infections is highly specific, and has little or nothing to do with muscular activity. Undoubtedly rational exercise, through its influence upon muscle tone, metabolism, excretion, and vasomotor regulation, may be regarded as a valuable aid in the battle against certain degenerative diseases which are highly destructive to civilized man.[25] However, modern health education teaches us that the battle against disease, especially infectious disease, depends much more upon the proper utilization of sanitary measures, immunization, and isolation of the infected person, than upon building up physical power through muscular activity.

The Correction of Physical Defects.   In the past the claim was made frequently that the main purpose of physical education is to correct physical defects. Although this notion is seldom heard today, there does exist considerable controversy concerning the place of corrective physical education in the total education program, and the role of physical education teachers in the corrective program.[38]

Physical examinations of millions of young men in recent wars resulted in the rejection of a significant percentage of them from military service. To place upon physical education any great measure of blame or responsibility for these conditions is to engage in muddled thinking.[28] The most prevalent physical defect in school children is dental decay. Defective sight and hearing are also very common. To say that these and many other defects are the responsibility of physical education to prevent or correct, is erroneous. Here is a situation which challenges the whole social order, and is not one to be lightly passed over to a particular group of educators.

So far as existing defects are concerned it is true that certain types are amenable to correction through the medium of appropriate muscular activities. But for the great majority of defects there is need for the services of the physician, orthopedist, surgeon, dietitian, dentist, oculist, physical therapist, or school nurse, rather than for the help of the educator. The physical educator frequently weakens his position and interferes with the ultimate solution of the problem by attempting to perform the functions of these specialists. Even in cases calling for instruction in healthful living, such instruction may better be given by the specialist in health education, unless the physical educator is also qualified in this field.[12]

Physical education should be regarded as a type of education rather than as a therapeutic agency. It should be interested in any desirable changes in the individual which can be promoted through educational procedures; it should not, however, attempt to invade the fields of medicine, surgery, and nursing. So far as it becomes incumbent upon us to accept responsibility for formal corrective procedure, we should recognize the service as a special undertaking. We should find it necessary to qualify ourselves especially for the work, and we should employ all available help of specialists in this important undertaking.[16]

It is feasible to work out a plan whereby the regular physical education teacher can conduct physical activity regimens for these pupils under the supervision of the physician in charge, who makes the diagnosis of the medical problem and prescribes the activities to be administered by the physical education teacher. These careful distinctions of roles are the key to full understanding of the purposes of physical education, both for normal children and for those with medical problems.

Physical Education and Body Building. Many persons in past years believed that the aim of physical education was "body building." This notion was stimulated by the Charles Atlas physical culture advertisements in popular magazines, and by Bob Hoffman and other professional weight-lifters who commercialized this activity. This aim was never fully accepted by the physical education profession, because it did not have the necessary properties of a desirable "educational" experience, and there was no sound scientific basis to support the claims of its advocates.

However, owing to new scientific evidence and to successful experiences with weights used by many athletes, in which improved athletic performance is linked with stepped-up weight training, coaches, athletes, physical educators, team physicians, and trainers, by and large, have now accepted weight training as a legitimate phase of the physical education and athletic program.[21] Weight training is to be distinguished carefully from weight-lifting.[47] In recent years, considerable evidence and experience have accumulated which indicate that weight training can develop strength and promote general conditioning, which in turn facilitate improved athletic performance in a wide variety of sports. Also, boys and girls in physical education classes, and many adults as well, have come to realize the values of general conditioning regimens properly suited to each person's individual health status, and many of these conditioning programs include elements of weight training in them, or may even consist of weight training exclusively.

In addition to training dynamically with weights, which involves exercises in which the muscles contract against resistance (called isotonic exercise), another type of weight training has developed called isometric exercise. This is a static exercise in which the muscle exerts force against a fixed object for a few seconds during which time there is no shortening of muscle fibers. The relative merits of isotonic and isometric exercises for specific purposes is still a matter of debate, although very recent thinking by research leaders seems to be leading to more and more agreement that isometric exercise has been overrated. Additional research evidence is needed in order to answer with more assurance the many questions being raised on the subject.

The program of body building ranks strength, muscular development, and personal bodily appearance as being of supreme importance. Its particular appeal lies in the ease with which this type of development can be observed and measured, and in the fallacious concept that strength and muscular development are somehow certain indices of health and efficiency. This latter conclusion is not sustained by scientific evidence. Muscle tone and the ability to use muscles effectively are important qualities, but have little to do with the size of muscles. This erroneous concept of physical education has been promoted in the public mind largely by the exponents of "systems" and "physical culture," whose income depends upon their ability to sell their services to the public, and whose appeal often involves misleading claims for the virtue of enormous muscular development. We should not hold that our profession exists primarily to build large muscles. However, we must remember that muscular strength and power result from physical education activities,[6] and that increased strength attained through proper programs of weight training can be an asset to improved performance in sports activities where strength is a significant factor. It has been demonstrated that weight training can be carried on satisfactorily not only in the "off season" of a sport but also, in moderate amounts, during the season of a sport.

Weight training is beneficial for girls and women, as well as for boys and men, when properly adapted to each individual and when conducted under the instruction of highly qualified physical educators. The cultural bias against this activity for females gradually is being overcome as its potential benefits become more fully recognized.

So, with the above considerations in mind, we conclude that while body building per se is not a legitimate objective of physical education, weight training, when properly prescribed and administered, is an acceptable phase of the program, but should not be regarded as the broad aim of physical education.

Physical Education and Neuromuscular Coordination. The cultivation of a general quality of neuromuscular coordination, sometimes designated as "gracefulness" or "physical efficiency," has often been advocated as the main purpose of physical education. Unquestionably, physical education experience should result in the improvement of skills. As the individual learns a variety of skills, he should become more graceful or physically efficient.

Recent evidence from the investigations of Henry,[19] Cratty,[11]

Fleishman,[17] and others has significantly altered the old view of a unitary trait or general quality of coordination, a concept which previously was thought to be the basis for the success of the highly skilled decathlon performer who could score well in ten diverse types of track and field events.

New theories are being developed which place more emphasis on task specificity. The individual who appears to have what was popularly called "general motor ability" is now believed to possess many specific abilities in the upper ranges of skilled performance. This view represents a significant change of theoretical insight into the problem of physical coordination or coordinations.

In addition to the current belief that coordinations are quite specific, recent evidence also indicates that there may be several abilities which underlie motor performance, such as (1) ability to utilize space efficiently during accurate movements; (2) ability to mobilize and to produce full speed and maximum force at the precise crucial moment during a skilled movement; (3) ability to relax while performing; and (4) ability to think about and logically analyze a complex motor task to be performed. It seems probable that these general abilities can be explained as relatively stable constitutional factors which are determined by hereditary predispositions, basic organic structure, and physiological functioning.[11]

Cratty proposes a four-part theory of perceptual-motor behavior which includes the two parts just discussed. The third part of the theory postulates the presence of "ability traits," which seem to operate when optimum effort is exerted relative to a motor performance. These abilities involve agility, body equilibrium, flexibility, speed of limb movement, static and dynamic strength, explosive strength, trunk strength, and ability to manipulate weights with both feet and arms. McCloy, Guilford, Fleishman, and other investigators have identified abilities which could be appended to this list.

The fourth part of the theory also indicates that personal preferences, or "personal equations," are variables which influence performance. Examples are the individual's ability to persist with a task even though it is painful or uncomfortable, an individualized sense of rhythm and tempo at which the movement is performed, the preference of the individual for the use of space to accomplish the purposes of the performance, and the unique way the person employs force efficiently.

Fleishman[17] adds to the controversy by reporting careful research which identified nine components of what he calls "physical proficiency." These nine components are: (1) extant flexibility; (2) dynamic flexibility; (3) explosive strength; (4) static strength; (5) dynamic strength; (6) trunk strength; (7) gross body coordination; (8) gross body equilibrium; and (9) stamina. Fleishman concludes from his studies that physical proficiency is not a single general ability; rather, it consists of several relatively independent factors. He relates these factors to physical fitness by saying that, as an individual scores higher on a greater number of these factors, he becomes more physically fit.

The physical educator should keep abreast of the evolving evidence and changes in theoretical positions which subsequently occur to explain the conditions and factors which underlie skilled motor performance. The final answer is not yet in, so the student is encouraged to study the evidence and formulate his own conclusions.

One of physical education's primary objectives is to teach skill development in a wide variety of interesting physical activities. The individual who improves his skill in a certain activity is more likely to have the motivation and interest to continue active participation in that activity over an extended period of time. Thus, while it is appropriate to regard the development of a variety of skills as a highly desirable objective of physical education this development should not be considered its ultimate aim.

Physical Education and Good Citizenship. There is one other claim about the purpose of physical education which, while meritorious in its sentiment, is yet too hazy and too indefinite to inspire complete confidence or to serve as a reliable guide in our procedure. This is the claim that the chief purpose of physical education is the promotion of "good citizenship." In a general sense, this aim may be regarded as the aim of all education, if we think of a "good" citizen as one who attains and maintains a full measure of development and efficiency, physically, mentally, and socially. But as a statement of the aim of physical education, the expression "good citizenship" is too vague and needs too much explanation. Furthermore, the physical educator cannot cite scientific evidence that such an aim is in fact promoted by physical education experiences. He can only assert his subjective judgment to support his contention. Many critics are dubious about such a claim, and point to lack of convincing evidence as well as to examples of personal incidents where "good citizenship" was not displayed in a physical education context.

In a similar vein, one author has challenged the "sportsmanship myth."[3] He points out that, even if the teacher or coach can educate his pupils to act in sportsmanlike ways during an athletic contest, there is no assurance or evidence that the same individuals will behave honestly or ethically in a business transaction in later years. In other words, he casts serious doubt on the assumption of "transfer of learning" from physical education experiences to other areas of life experiences in the future with respect to desirable qualities of "citizenship."

OBJECTIVES

Innumerable books, pamphlets, curriculum guides, and magazine articles contain descriptions of broad physical education objectives. It is startling and instructive to construct a long list of physical education objectives from these sources and to categorize each under various headings. First, one is impressed with the diverse terminology used to express each author's precise meaning. If the reader can attach clear meanings to these many descriptions then the analysis naturally leads to an attempt to classify them for inherent similarity and for distinctiveness. It soon becomes apparent that physical education objectives from various sources cover an exceedingly wide range of expectations for changing human behavior through this medium of education.

This diversity of "claims" has worked to the detriment of the field. One of the most frequent charges levied against physical education is that it claims too much, that it purports to be "all things to all people," and that it puts itself on a pedestal. Indeed, certain objectives appear to be self-serving. An exaggerated list of objectives weakens the position of physical education and undermines the strength of the interpretation and understanding it seeks.

Objectives should be tentatively held, even though some of them are strongly advocated at the moment and seem to be well supported by valid evidence. New evidence and varied experience, combined with increasing ability to examine them carefully and to reflect on them periodically, undoubtedly will cause each physical educator to revise his objectives, and even, at times, to alter his selection of them. The continual revision of objectives is a fact of professional life for the perceptive physical educator. Every educational decision he makes, in curriculum planning, in selecting and carrying out instructional strategies, in choosing and employing teaching techniques, and in his evaluation procedures and conclusions about pupil learning, emanates from the clarity of his objectives and his commitment to them.

Selectivity and Priority

Another trend in the study of objectives, both in education and in physical education, is to determine the *priority* of their relative importance. In the past, the typical procedure was to list a set of objectives and to imply, if not to state explicitly, that each was of equal value, and then to teach on the basis of that assumption. Modern thought holds that the school should be more selective in the purposes it expects to fulfill, performing those functions for which it is uniquely qualified. The home, the church, and other institutions must share in the tremendously large total task of educating youth to meet the expectations of society. Therefore, the school must select its objectives on a priority basis and devote its energies to their fulfillment, and must not dissipate its specialized resources and its limited time by attempting to achieve too many diverse objectives.

Classification

One other aspect of a discussion of objectives in physical education has to do with recent attempts to classify them as being "unique," or "primary," or "shared." For example, some physical educators have asserted that physical fitness and the development of movement skills are the "unique" functions of physical education. By such a contention, they imply that, because no other subject in the curriculum lists these particular objectives, no other field can make a substantial educational contribution. Sober reflection will reveal that physical fitness really cannot be completely isolated as a unique objective of physical education if we accept the complete definition of the term. Any broad definition must consider nutrition, dental hygiene, hereditary predispositions to specific health deficiencies, and other influences, in addition to the role of exercise. Several of these essential factors obviously are not the sole responsibility of the physical education program.

If we do want to insist that muscular strength, muscular endurance, cardiovascular efficiency, flexibility, balance, and agility are among the most essential elements in a total concept of physical fitness, we should modify our claim and replace the qualifying term "unique" with the word "primary."

Other objectives to which physical education makes solid claim may be regarded as "shared" objectives, meaning that one or more of the other subjects in the curriculum also makes significant contributions to the achievement of these purposes. For example, most physical educators believe that their field makes important contributions to social behaviors, such as sportsmanship and cooperation, and that it exerts a favorable influence on character development. Surely teachers of other subjects feel that they, too, help develop sportsmanship, cooperation, and character. Thus, the physical educator should regard such objectives as "shared."

In the category of "shared" objectives, we should decide on a small number of purposes to which physical education contributes most effectively, and assign them highest priority in our professional work and public interpretation.

Categories of Objectives

Another problem facing anyone who attempts to state his personal objectives for physical education is the varying degrees of abstractions that are possible in expressing them. The aim we propose in this chapter is the most abstract type of purpose, obviously beyond the point of full realization by any individual. However, it is a useful way of describing the role of the school and its program as an agency of society. As the term indicates, the aim provides an "aiming point"; it acts as the guiding star which gives direction to the educational journey being undertaken by the student.

If educational objectives are stated only in general abstract terms, at least two major difficulties ensue. First, there are many problems in the planning of "proper" or "best" or "most efficient" learning experiences to achieve these broad purposes. Second, we encounter difficulty in evaluating the extent to which desired behaviors have in fact occurred, because the concepts and descriptions of these behaviors are so vague.

In order to overcome these difficulties, it becomes necessary to subdivide the general, abstract objectives into more concrete statements of objectives.

General Objectives. The authors subscribe to the following *general objectives* of physical education:

1. To develop a basic understanding and appreciation of human movement. This broad objective involves (a) the development of an understanding and appreciation of the deeper, more significant human meanings and values acquired through idea-directed movement experiences; (b) an appreciation of human movement as an essential non-verbal mode of human expression; (c) the development of a positive self-concept and body image through appropriate movement experiences; and (d) the mastery of key concepts through volitional movements and closely related non-verbal learning activities.

2. To develop and maintain optimal individual muscular strength, muscular endurance, and cardiovascular endurance. It is customary to refer to this purpose as the "physical fitness" objective. Many authors expand it to include such factors as flexibility, balance, agility, power, and speed. It is essential to develop not only skills, but also knowledge and understanding relevant to physical fitness.

3. To develop individual movement potentialities to the optimal level for each person. Physical education instruction concentrates on the development of selected neuromuscular skills, and on refinement of fundamental movement patterns basic to specific skills.

4. To develop skills, knowledges, and attitudes essential to satisfying, enjoyable physical recreation experiences engaged in voluntarily throughout one's lifetime. Normal mental and emotional health is enhanced by participation in voluntary physical recreation.

5. To develop socially acceptable and personally rewarding behaviors through participation in movement activities. Physical education instruction seeks to develop desirable social habits, attitudes, and personal characteristics.

The authors take the view that physical educators should select only those objectives for which persuasive evidence exists, and which are relative to rather stable changes in human behavior (called learning) which can result from appropriate educational experiences. A more detailed discussion of the evidence, professional judgments, and basic beliefs which underlie these objectives is to be found in several chapters of the book.*

Instructional Objectives.   Each general objective should suggest a number of instructional objectives depending upon the individuals concerned. The term instructional objectives has come into prominence with the refocus of emphasis on the *consequences* of instruction or the results teachers achieve in changing pupil behaviors. Formerly, emphasis was on what the *intentions* of the teacher were before the lesson started.

Popham,** whose work on the formulation of statements of objectives is well known, says:

> An instructional objective stated in performance, behavioral, or measurable terms is simply an assertion of what you want to happen to learners as a consequence of instruction.

This statement implies that a teacher must describe a learner's probable behavior at the end of the unit in measurable terms. Popham says:

> I think there are almost no goals, however general, which are not amenable to some form of operationalization in order to provide the educator with better clues as to whether the goal has been achieved.

Behavioral and Performance Objectives.   The two terms, behavioral objective and performance objective, have become interchangeable. Although critics of the term "behavioral" read into it a set toward the dehumanization of the pupil, a forced shaping of behavior, and a mechanized form of learning, perhaps "behavioral" still has the most widespread usage in this country. Whatever label

---

* Organic power and vigor (physical fitness) are dealt with in this chapter and in Chapter 8, Biological Foundations. Motor skills development is considered in Chapter 7 also. Social habits, attitudes, and personality development are referred to in more detail in Chapter 6 on Socio-cultural Foundations. The recreational objective is enlarged upon in Chapter 11 on Leisure and Physical Education. The Selected References at the end of each chapter provide a rich source for the detailed study of the evidence, professional judgments, and basic beliefs which underlie these and other frequently stated objectives of physical education.

** "Instructional Objectives, An ER Dialogue With Researcher, Supervisor, and Teacher," *Educational Researcher*, Vol. No. 9, Sept., 1972, 8–12.

is applied, these objectives are stated as specific descriptions of actual stable *behavioral changes* which are thought to be desirable by the end of the learning experience. These learned behaviors are described with an emphasis on action verbs which permit direct observations and objectified evaluations in terms of the specific expectations inherent in each objective. From this process come the common expressions "stating objectives in behavioral terms," describing them "operationally," and formulating "performance objectives."

In order to state a behavioral objective clearly while planning a teaching unit, the instructor must have considered carefully what the overt behavior of the pupil will be when he has mastered that particular objective. Mager [29] calls this the "terminal" behavior. The description includes not only what the pupil can do or *perform* in observable ways, but also states the *conditions* under which the behavior is to be elicited, and an acceptable *level of performance* of the behavior. Such statements must utilize overt action verbs. Infinitives such as "to know," "to understand," or "to appreciate" are not precise enough. Such abstract verbs are appropriate in general objectives, but not in behavioral ones.

In preparing behavioral objectives, the teacher actually plans a unit of instruction backwards. He begins with a clear description and understanding of the final, over-all, larger terminal objectives he expects pupils to demonstrate overtly by the time the unit is completed. Then, working back through the lesson sequence, he subdivides these terminal performance objectives into *subordinate* behavioral objectives to be accomplished step-by-step along the way. The decisions the teacher makes about the complexity, variety, and type of these smaller behavioral objectives throughout the unit will depend upon the initial experience, ability, understanding, and motivation of each pupil on the first day of the unit. The more the teacher knows about the capabilities of each student, the more effective he will be in providing an instructional climate which will produce the desired behavioral changes.

Obviously, objectives of this kind can be stated at varying levels of specificity. One hierarchical model is the following:
    (1) ultimate behavioral objective
    (2) terminal behavioral objective
    (3) terminal intermediate behavioral objective
    (4) intermediate behavioral objective
    (5) sub-behavioral objective

(Courtesy of the Los Angeles City Board of Education.)

Of course there are several other models for sub-dividing instructional objectives.

It is quite well agreed that all worthwhile objectives are not amenable to formulation in the form of behavioral objectives. Even Popham*, a leading advocate of the performance objectives approach, admits that "The really worthwhile goals of education are invariably the most difficult to measure." However, he goes on to say ". . . an outcome-oriented approach to education is the only defensible stance open to the responsible educator." Rather than abandon this approach because of the difficulty in stating some highly desirable objectives of education in performance terms it is preferable to plan as much instruction as possible around measurable objectives. Popham, Mager, and others explain and demonstrate in their writings how to approach the problems of stating and assessing behavioral changes related to the "more difficult to measure" objectives.

---

* W. James Popham, "Focus on Outcomes—A Guiding Theme of ES '70 Schools," *Phi Delta Kappan,* Vol. 51, Dec., 1969, p. 208.

In summarizing the arguments in favor of using performance objectives we can assert that teachers should (1) describe objectively the changes in pupil behaviors they believe to be desirable, (2) carefully plan instructional strategies and procedures which will most effectively develop these behaviors, and (3) develop and utilize the most valid assessment techniques available at the end of the lesson or unit to ascertain accurately the *terminal* performances of the students.

Eisner[15] and others caution that it is not always appropriate to state objectives behaviorally, for several reasons. First, it is not always possible to predict in advance exactly the nature of behavioral changes which will in fact occur. In the very complex and dynamic teaching experience, innumerable teacher interactions with pupils occur, many of them entirely unforeseen. The possible consequences of these interactions are beyond control and forecast. Also, unforeseen "teachable moments" will develop almost instantaneously, and the alert teacher will take advantage of them. By and large these "moments" are not planned in advance. The creative teacher will not be tightly bound to one prescribed set of objectives. In essence, in a favorable instructional atmosphere there are far too many potential educational outcomes possible to be specified in advance.

Second, performance behavior statements are more appropriate to the purposes of some subjects than others. They are quite relevant to physical education, language, science, typewriting, industrial arts, and other subjects characterized by overt motor learning. In certain other subjects, such as the fine arts, an important objective is to encourage novel, creative responses, and to ferret out unique relationships. Thus, unpredictable pupil behavior is encouraged; it cannot be described in advance.

Third, not all educational outcomes are capable of objective measurement. There is no objective way to assess the quality of a poem, or the meaning of a picture, or the impact of a musical score. So-called creative outcomes can only be judged subjectively. Outcomes in terms of curiosity, insight, and creativity are important, but are not measurable.

Fourth, many teachers regard objectives stated in the planning stage as "initiating consequences" which give direction to instruction early in the unit. These objectives are subject to alteration and revision as the instructional experiences progress. Thus, objectives are tentative, ever changing, and in fact are not thought to be capable of being definitely described before a unit is taught. This view rejects the notion that educational objectives need to be stated precisely as a basis for the selection and organization of the content of the subject.

Raths* makes some additional thoughtful objections to proposals that all learning activities should be based on performance objectives. He suggests that it is important for pupils to have the opportunity to decide on some of the educational activities they are interested in and want to pursue. Also, these pupils should have opportunities to learn to evaluate their own progress. The curriculum should provide for problem solving experiences both in personal and in social realms. Students should have experience in debating controversial ideas, they should practice formulating and testing hypotheses, they should search for basic assumptions, and they should develop skill in raising and formulating pertinent questions. Learning should not be so mechanistic that it diminishes the wholesome, free expression of human emotions and deep rooted feelings. Pupils should be encouraged to apply one kind of learning to a new or novel situation in order to learn how to "generalize" their understanding and application of human knowledge and experience. This advice includes use of multi-sensory modes of learning, or, in effect, direct learning in a variety of situations. Boys and girls should be urged to continue to learn beyond the boundaries of the terminal objective, they should be reinforced and motivated to improve their performances over the longer term, and not to be satisfied with momentary or single success. Relate learning opportunities to the unique interests and preferences of each student. Encourage students to engage in divergent and heuristic learning activities without being fearful of disappointment, or even of failure in a particular instance. Take calculated risks against criticism, unanticipated obstacles, and a heavy time and energy commitment when the potential learning and experiential outcomes are so unusual that they are worth the gamble. A final caveat: relate learning opportunities to individual student preferences, interests, and abilities.

The preceding discussion has summarized the strengths and weaknesses of the currently popular behavioral objective approach to curriculum and instruction, and has attempted to show its relevance to physical education. There is one more extension of this notion, namely, the competence approach to selection of activities

---

* James D. Raths, "Teaching Without Specific Objectives," *Educational Leadership*, April, 1971, 714–720.

within a physical education program, or the possibility of exemption from a requirement.

Behaviorally stated objectives, when sufficiently developed and validated, should provide us with a detailed description of the "physically educated" person, at least at certain crucial stages of progress, such as at high school and college graduation. Some institutions are working on this concept as the primary criterion for the fulfillment of the institutional physical education requirement. The student who can demonstrate, by relevant skill peformance, attitude, knowledge, and consistent behavior patterns, that he fully meets the criteria of the physically educated person is deemed to have fulfilled the requirement in physical education.

Expressive Objectives. Eisner* clarifies the nature of expressive objectives as follows. This type of objective describes an educational experience such as a problem to solve, a project to be planned and carried out, or a poem or painting to be created. It does not describe the terminal behaviors the student will possess at the end of the encounter. It encourages the pupil and the teacher to seek, decide, try out, and vary learning opportunities which seem to possess potential elements of value in terms of the interests and abilities of the student. They are not prescriptive as are behavioral objectives. Rather, they are evocative. The students engage in diverse learning activities so that the development of personalized meanings becomes an essential characteristic of educational experiences which are derived from expressive objectives. The educational products pupils develop are diverse and often unique. They cannot be evaluated by a common standard stated in advance and applied broadly for all members of the class.

Examples of expressive objectives are:
1. Write a personalized interpretation of the meaning of *Captains Courageous.*
2. Construct a clay model of a human head and face.
3. Attend an orchestral performance and describe your emotional responses to it.

Note that these objectives do not state in precise terms the behaviors students should exhibit as a result of engaging in the edu-

---

* Elliot W. Eisner, "Instructional Expressive Educational Objectives: Their Formulation and Use in Curriculum." Unpublished report, School of Education, Stanford University, Stanford, California, 1968, 28 pp. mimeo.

cational activity. They do specify the nature of the educational opportunity to be encountered. As in aesthetic criticism the student
evaluates the product and gives his own reactions to its qualities and
meanings. Criteria for evaluation are not stated in advance.

In summary it may be noted that performance objectives pertain
to knowledge and skills already well accepted as "known." Expressive objectives interpret, extend, and modify the "known" and sometimes create something which is completely new.

Many teachers have taught mainly in this way in past years. Few
have taught by the performance objective method until recently.
Physical education involves a wide variety of educational purposes.
Some are amenable to the performance objective approach, others
to the use of expressive objectives. The thoughtful physical educator
probably is best advised to make judicious use of both types of
objectives to promote optimum learning.

Physical Education Taxonomies

In recent years considerable work has been accomplished to
classify various educational objectives. Probably the two best known
taxonomies are by (1) Bloom and colleagues,[1] concerning the cognitive domain, and (2) by Krathwohl and co-authors,[24] on the affective
domain. Similar studies in physical education have not appeared in
national publications until recently. The label "psycho-motor domain"
has gained common acceptance for this realm of objectives. The three
categories listed above, when combined, presumably account for all
of the objectives for which American schools generally are held
responsible.

Three tentative taxonomies which may have relevance for physical educators in the development of motor objectives can be identified. One of the first classification systems for the psychomotor
domain was developed by Simpson,[41a] a home economist. The Simpson
classification has five major categories, identified as perception, set,
guided response, mechanism, and complex overt response. Each category is subdivided into several subcategories. Clein and Stone[8] have
built upon the Simpson classification, stating physical education
objectives in terms of how a student would learn a motor skill. Jewett
and her colleagues[22] have proposed a taxonomy which postulates

three major movement process categories for the "motor domain." These categories are described as generic, ordinative, and creative movement processes. An additional taxonomical model intended "to help behavioral objective writers and curriculum developers classify student learning experiences and define objectives as meaningful descriptions of student behaviors" has been developed by Harrow.[17a]

Student Goals

It seems plausible to believe that practically all students have certain goals in mind as they participate in the school physical education program. These goals may differ considerably among individual pupils. If the teacher does not provide favorable opportunities for the expression of these goals, verbally, in writing, or both, he will never be certain as to the goals which have the most significance for each member of his class. It seems self-evident that the teacher must be fully informed of the goals held by the members of his class if he is to provide optimal learning opportunities on an individual basis.

Unfortunately, many physical education teachers will only superficially, if at all, discuss their objectives for the class and provide communication channels through which pupils may state their goals and their reactions to teacher-imposed objectives. The students cannot know precisely what the teacher has in mind in such cases. Thus, they lack the assurance and confidence they need to attempt to achieve their own goals. In such situations, it is little wonder that pupils regard the physical education class as a "free play" period, or even as the equivalent of "recess" as they knew it in elementary school.

There is some difference of opinion among teachers as to the extent of agreement which should exist between explicit statements of objectives formulated by teachers, and those which might be expressed by students when they are asked to respond to an attitude inventory, or to answer such a question in a class discussion. Some educators hold that, while it is the primary responsibility of the teacher to develop and state the instructional objectives of his class, there should be opportunity for pupil discussion and suggestions in the process of formulating these objectives. Also, once the class objectives have been selected, the good teacher should explain these objectives carefully to the students, and, by sound motivational and teaching techniques, strive to achieve maximum understanding and acceptance of those objectives by all class members.

Other educators believe that it is not necessary for students to hold in mind the identical objectives stated by the teacher. This view is illustrated by the following example. If the teacher of a basketball class has as an objective the "development of an attitude of fair play in basketball," the skillful teacher need not be concerned about whether or not the students also state explicitly that "fair play" is an important objective to them. The teacher need only ask that the pupils have a strong liking for the game, a keen desire to play it with others, and an ambition to "make the team" if it is at the interscholastic level. Given these conditions, the teacher can undertake to see that the student learns fairness without any conscious effort on the part of the pupil.

A third view now coming into practice is for teachers to provide encouragement and guidance to each pupil to set his own goals for an announced instructional unit. The pupil selects his own goals, in terms of performance expectations, which he hopes to achieve by the end of the unit. He discusses the goals with his teacher, with his classmates, and with his parents, if he so desires, before making his final choices. He then writes down these personal goals on his physical education class cumulative record file, which is continually available to him throughout the instructional unit. Periodically, he assesses his progress toward these goals, and he writes his performances on the record form. This type of pupil goal setting, based on interaction with teacher and classmates, stimulates individual responsibility for educational planning, and provides opportunity for steadily increasing self-reliance and self-monitoring toward the accomplishment of personal goals which are important and meaningful to the student. Of course the pupil is provided the opportunity periodically to revise and reformulate his goals in relation to the progress he has made up to that time. He should not become too discouraged because of failure to accomplish goals set at some previous time. Likewise, he should be encouraged to proceed at a faster learning pace than his original goals predicted if he shows this capability. Such goals are tentative and flexible. In a sense they are an expression of the student's *level of aspiration*. Research has shown that most students learn more effectively when they aspire to learning goals which are within their capabilities but which are neither too easy to attain nor so difficult that they may be beyond reach.

In general, it seems difficult to argue against the view that there should be genuine compatibility between teacher objectives and student goals. Perhaps the difference in the various views just discussed is more related to differences in methodology than to a difference in basic beliefs about the relation of teacher and student objectives. It seems obvious that any teacher could write a long list of objectives which he might assist a pupil in achieving, at one time or another, in any subject. "Concomitant learning" is involved also. The opportunity to capitalize on the "teachable moment" in physical education, as explained by Nash,[34] likewise can contribute to the realization of important objectives, including those which might not necessarily appear in writing on a teacher's course outline.

Perhaps this whole question of relation and congruence between teacher and pupil objectives is made more confusing by the difference in language used to describe these objectives. Usually, the teacher and the administrator writing curriculum guides and lesson plans will use educational jargon to state objectives, while students, when given the opportunity, write or speak in their natural manner of expression. Thus, there appears to be a greater difference between objectives held by teachers and those expressed by pupils than actually is the case. In any event, it is fundamentally important to take student objectives into consideration in the total process of developing and stating course objectives.

Probably the normal and natural physical education goals of boys and girls include the following:

To have fun.

To be with the group.

To learn more about the game and become more skillful.

To develop strength and endurance.

To make the team.

To develop a better physique—to be better looking.

To get away for a time from the confinement associated with study.

A physical educator should be very happy if he finds the boys and girls under his direction holding such goals. He should then plan carefully to merge the students' goals with his own objectives in order to provide for the sincere, thoughtful selection of further goals by pupils, with his guidance, on the basis of individual abilities and interests.

Not only are more teachers encouraging students to set their own goals in physical education classes but they also are encouraging and aiding pupils to evaluate their progress in relation to individualized goals. Again, teachers provide helpful guidance as the need is perceived but pupils are urged to take increasing responsibility for this function. This procedure helps boys and girls to develop a realistic self-concept and to grow and develop more fully in the direction of a self-actualizing, mature adult, a concept which is discussed in more detail in another portion of this book.* Another promising trend is to facilitate peer evaluation among students. Again, providing guidance and training in this skill is an important role for the perceptive teacher to play.

NEEDS AND OBJECTIVES

The objectives of any school physical education program should be developed cooperatively by the staff and the administration. Many educators advocate the use of pupil representatives, parents, and representative citizens on committees which develop educational philosophy and curriculum. Some school districts appoint citizens' advisory committees for each subject in the school curriculum.

Physical education objectives grow out of the needs of the individuals served by the program and of the society of which they are a part. Therefore, these needs must be determined as accurately as possible. Having determined the needs and having set the objectives, activities are then selected which are most likely to help bring about the objectives sought. Finally, a program is organized and conducted which will best satisfy the needs and attain the objectives.

We may restate the curriculum development procedures as a series of questions to be answered:

1. What are the needs, in terms of growth, development, and adjustment, of the individuals to be "educated"?

2. What educational activities will best contribute to the satisfaction of these specific needs?

---

* See Chapter 7.

3. What should be the characteristics of the school environment in which we can best conduct these desirable activities?

DETERMINING THE NEEDS OF THE INDIVIDUAL

One of the major problems facing the school physical education program is how to provide an individualized program which best meets the *needs* of each student. Far too often in the past we have lumped all students together into a class, and then into squads, and have directed them in rather authoritarian ways through a standard curriculum, with little regard for their individual differences and individual needs. By such a practice, we seem to assume that one prescribed program of activities is equally valuable (educative) for all pupils.

The teacher who genuinely believes that individualized learning experiences should be based on individual needs has an obligation to understand the nature of needs, and their relationship to motives, and to the goals which we have previously discussed. McDonald aptly weaves these three concepts together.*

> Curriculum organization has profited from the conception of basing the curriculum on the needs of children. . . . Modern educators have built a curriculum derived from conceptions of what the majority of children will need in order to be useful members of society, with provisions for the needs of particular groups of children. This reorganization of the curriculum has not simplified or resolved the problem that has always confronted teachers—the problem of motivating students to work for specific goals. The teacher faces children with varying needs and learned goal expectations. The teacher's task is to broaden children's conceptions of their goals, foster the acquisition of new needs, and through this process enhance the total development of the child.

Needs are defined as rather stable and relatively permanent dispositions or tendencies in persons, to be motivated in specific ways. Unsatisfied needs developed from either external stimuli from the surrounding environment or internal bodily changes may arouse or

---

* Frederick J. McDonald, *Educational Psychology.* Belmont, Cal.: Wadsworth Publishing Company, 2nd ed., 1965, p. 152.

direct activity toward goals which will presumably satisfy those needs.

The current status of research and theory on the concept of needs is too complex and extensive to summarize here. Hilgard and Atkinson* provide a detailed basic discussion about needs and related concepts such as drives, motives, incentives, appetites, aversions, and other highly interrelated concepts. The physical educator should study these topics as a basis for understanding current knowledge and theory and their relationship to teaching and coaching principles and practices.

Controversy still exists between competing theories of needs. We believe in the theory of self-actualization as pioneered by Maslow** and we use it to provide theoretical and philosophical direction for the major emphases and beliefs which form the basic structure of this book. Therefore, we will present briefly Maslow's hierarchy of needs as one example of a dynamic theory which concentrates on the energizing and directing of human behavior, tasks in which all teachers are continually engaged.

The basic need in man, according to Maslow, is that of self-actualization. This concept refers to the need to constantly strive to become a person who adequately functions in society according to the potential he possesses for developing adaptive behaviors. Persons who succeed in meeting this self-actualization need in a relatively satisfactory manner are assessed as being the healthiest and best adjusted in our society. The basic structure of Maslow's hierarchy of needs is as follows:

Needs to know and understand

↑

Self-actualization needs

↑

Esteem needs

↑

Love and belonging needs

↑

Safety needs

↑

Physiological needs

---

* Ernest R. Hilgard and Richard G. Atkinson, *Introduction to Psychology*, 4th ed. Harcourt, Brace, and World, Inc., New York, 1967, 118–162.

** A. H. Maslow, "A Theory of Human Motivation." *Psychological Review*, 50, 370–396.

In general, the individual must find adequate need satisfaction at all lower levels before a higher need can be met. Satisfaction of higher needs is based on fulfillment of lower needs. Most normal persons are both partially satisfied and partially unsatisfied at each level but in varying degrees. It is not a matter of "all-or-none." However, it is generally observed that the degree and numbers of unmet wants or needs increase in each higher category. Thus, it can be said that man is a continually "wanting" organism.

Other scholars have identified alternative categories and descriptions of needs. We have constructed our own list of needs which are highly relevant to the teacher's understanding of his pupils and the factors which motivate their goal-directed behaviors.

The needs we shall discover in the case of any individual cannot, of course, be foretold. However, the following examples of developmental and adjustment needs have been found common to a great percentage of children and youth in America.

Physiological Needs

Urbanization and automation in America have tended largely to eliminate the survival activities characteristic of former ages, leaving a large percentage of the young without the necessity, or even the opportunity, of engaging in a variety of challenging and exciting vigorous physical activities, which are the only means of developing organic power and vigor.*

Normal growth and development in childhood demand large amounts of activity. As a rule, children play and exercise, even under the most adverse circumstances, but in many cases the amount of activity is too limited and the type not fully beneficial. The limitations of city life are particularly significant in this connection.[27] Specific needs arise from:

---

* The term "organic" refers to the cardiovascular system, digestive system, nervous system, and so forth. These systems can only be exercised, developed, or trained through the medium of muscular activity. While muscular power is no longer directly important for the social and economic success of a majority of the population, it is indirectly so because of the dependence of organic power upon muscular activity, and because of the stress placed upon the vital organs by modern conditions of life.

1. Lack of adequate muscle tone, and accompanying faults of posture, owing to inadequate muscular activity.

2. Abnormalities in bodily growth and development, often attributable in part to lack of sufficient muscular activity.

3. Lack of regular habits of exercise, which are necessary under modern conditions of living. The marked trend toward sedentary living in America is generally regarded as a serious menace to the health status of our people.

Psychological Needs

1. Need for the development of emotional control.

2. Need to overcome "awkwardness" by developing control of a variety of voluntary bodily movements.

3. Need for the development of resourcefulness, initiative, and the capacity for quick and accurate mental reactions when under pressure.

4. Need for the opportunity for wholesome expression of human tendencies to action. (Many abnormalities of personality and many forms of antisocial behavior are found in connection with this need.)

5. Need for the development of interest in wholesome recreational activities, as contributions to the joy of living and as a means of relief from the mental and emotional strain engendered by the pressure and speed of modern life.

6. The need to engage in creative, divergent thinking and novel activities during part of one's daily life. It is stultifying, restricting, and psychologically detrimental to be expected to act and think solely in conforming, logical, and expected ways.

Social Needs

American society, based on democratic ideology and concepts, derives societal needs which a majority of young people acquire as a result of cultural influences which operate on them almost from the date of birth. Several important social needs of youth are:

1. Need for the cultivation of an attitude of fairness, which will habitually take into account the rights and welfare of others.

2. Need for the cultivation of an attitude of cooperation in enterprises intended for the common good.

3. Need for the development of interested participation in stimulating activities with a strong emotional element, to counteract the influence of the television, radio, motion pictures, and other sedentary forms of entertainment which tend to make youth an age of vicarious emotional experience and synthetic participation.

4. Need for favorable opportunity to participate in socializing activities, to counteract tendencies toward injurious or vicious forms of play and various types of juvenile delinquency.

5. An almost universal need in the adolescent group for the acquisition of physical skills in recreational activities which can be enjoyed in later life.

6. Need for the development of capacity for quick adjustment to the motives, needs, and intentions of others, so as to be better equipped to meet the changing conditions of modern society.

Selected procedures for determining individual needs include:

1. A thorough medical examination for each individual at intervals not greater than every three years to determine his organic and anatomical condition, defects, and deficiencies.

2. Frequent tests of the individual's skills in physical activities and his ability to control bodily movements.

3. Periodic evaluation of the individual's social characteristics and needs.

4. Evaluation of the individual's interest in physical education activities in relation to his other interests (on the basis of observation and by use of interest inventories).

5. Evaluation of cultural and occupational situations in which the individual is involved when out of the physical education environment.

6. Determination, so far as possible, of the probable social, cultural, and occupational status of the individual in later years, with a view to determining also his probable future needs in forms of recreation and exercise.

7. Evaluation of changing social, cultural, and economic conditions in America, with implications in terms of human needs now and in the future.

SUMMARY

Thus, as McDonald and others indicate, curriculum development considers pupil needs, pupil goals, and individual motivation. Based on the most accurate available knowledge relative to these factors concerning each student, the curriculum decision makers should select educational opportunities which hold the greatest promise for promoting desirable behavioral changes. These educational opportunities should be analyzed by professional judgment, and should be placed in a scope and sequence framework with respect to learning progression, grade placement, and time allotment. This procedure is recommended for developing an articulated, sequential curriculum in physical education.

CONCLUSION

We believe in physical education as an integral part of the curriculum in any scheme of education, and in its broader aspects, including recreation, health, and rehabilitation, as important instruments in the total picture of life in today's world. In fact, we believe that regular physical education experiences for all children through the twelfth grade are more essential in the school program than ever before, owing to the changing environment in which we live. A majority of the population in the United States now lives in crowded urban and suburban areas, with highly restricted open spaces, usually near polluted lakes and rivers, in smog, and under continuous tension-inducing conditions of work and transportation. The style of life the typical American, adult or child, now lives is biologically and psychologically unsuited to the natural physical endowments of the human organism as it has evolved and adapted during the past several million years. The opportunity for regular, vigorous, stimulating, and enjoyable physical recreation and activity is one of the few remaining fundamental antidotes to these severe, artificial, and stressful conditions which man has now imposed upon himself.

Physical education should imbue every child with a wholesome respect for the particular human organism with which he is endowed at birth. The word "wholesome" is used advisedly, because concentration on physical development as manifested in the "body beautiful" cults is as unbalanced an approach as was medieval asceticism with its denial of the flesh. It is the responsibility and the privilege of teachers of physical education to help each child to a realization that this mechanism is the vehicle through which he must ultimately express his dreams, aspirations, and accomplishments. It makes no difference what his eventual destiny will be, for so long as he lives, his highest achievements, mentally, spiritually, culturally, and artistically, must be expressed through the medium of his physical being. This wholesome respect implies, in addition to acquiring knowledge of its proper care, a maximum ease, competence, and wholehearted pleasure in the use of his body. [32,40]

No "system" of physical education, American, British, Swedish, German, or any other, could possibly meet the demands of such a broad concept of physical education. The greatest possible contribution is to be made by well-trained teachers with a background of knowledge covering the biological, psychological, and socio-cultural aspects of their profession, and with vision to accommodate their teaching to the particular situation at hand by an intelligent and judicious application of the tools of the profession. Better than a static curriculum is the freedom to choose, from multitudinous tools, just the right one for the particular challenge. To make a dynamic and effective response to the undeniably dynamic human material at hand is our challenge and opportunity.

Selected References

1. Bloom, Benjamin S., Engelhart, Max D., Hill, Walker H., Furst, Edward J., and Krathwohl, David R.: *Taxonomy of Educational Objectives, The Classification of Educational Goals.* New York: David McKay Company, Inc., 1956.
2. Brackenbury, Robert L.: "Physical Education, An Intellectual Emphasis?" *Quest,* I:3-6 (December, 1963).
3. Calisch, Richard: "The Sportsmanship Myth." *The Physical Educator,* X:9-11 (March, 1953).
4. Cassidy, Rosalind: "The Cultural Definition of Physical Education." *Quest,* IV: 11-15 (April, 1965).
5. *Central Purpose of American Education.* Educational Policies Commission. Washington, D.C.: National Education Association and the American Association of School Administrators, 1961.
6. Clarke, H. Harrison: *Muscular Strength and Endurance in Man.* Englewood Cliffs, N.J.: Prentice-Hall, Inc., 1966.
7. Clarke, H. Harrison, and Clarke, David H.: *Developmental and Adapted Physical Education.* Englewood Cliffs, N.J.: Prentice-Hall, Inc., 1963.

8. Clein, Marvin I., and Stone, William J.: "Physical Education and the Classification of Educational Objectives: Psychomotor Domain." *The Physical Educator*, 27:34 (March, 1970).

9. Cornacchia, Harold J.: "A Critical Issue: Are Health Education and Physical Education Separate Disciplines?" *CAHPER Journal*, XXIII:4-5, 9 (March-April, 1961).

10 Cowell, Charles C., and France, Wellman L.: *Philosophy and Principles of Physical Education*. Englewood Cliffs, N.J.: Prentice-Hall, Inc., 1963.

11. Cratty, Bryant J.: *Movement Behavior and Motor Learning*. Philadelphia: Lea & Febiger, 2nd ed., 1967.

12. Daniels, Arthur S.: *Adapted Physical Education*. New York: Harper & Row, Publishers, 2nd ed., 1965.

13. Diem, Liselott: *Who Can*. Frankfurt, Germany: Wilhelm Limpert Publishers, 1962.

14. Eisner, Elliot W.: "Educational Objectives: Help or Hindrance?" *The School Review*, 75:250-260 (Autumn, 1967).

15. Eisner, Elliot W.: "Instructional and Expressive Educational Objectives: Their Formulation and Use in Curriculum." *Instructional Objectives*, AERA Monograph Series on Curriculum Evaluation, No. 3. Chicago: Rand McNally, 1969.

16. Fait, Hollis F.: *Special Physical Education—Adaptive, Corrective, Developmental*. Philadelphia: W. B. Saunders Company, 3rd ed., 1972.

17. Fleishman, Edwin A.: *The Structure and Measurement of Physical Fitness*. Englewood Cliffs, N.J.: Prentice-Hall, Inc., 1964.

17a. Harrow, Anita J. *A Taxonomy of the Psychomotor Domain*. New York: David McKay Company, 1972.

18. Hein, Fred V.: "Not Just Exercise." *Hygeia*, 25:350-351, 376-380 (May, 1947).

19. Henry, Franklin M.: "Specificity vs. Generality in Learning Motor Skills." *Proc. Coll. Phys. Educ. Assoc.*, 1958:126-128.

20. Hetherington, Clark W.: *School Program in Physical Education*. Yonkers, N.Y.: World Book Company, 1922.

21. Hooks, Gene: *Application of Weight Training to Athletics*. Englewood Cliffs, N.J.: Prentice-Hall, Inc., 1962.

21a. Jewett, Ann E. "Physical Education," *Curriculum Handbook for School Executives*. Arlington, Va.: American Association of School Administrators, 253–271 (1973).

22. Jewett, Ann E., Jones, L. Sue, Luneke, Sheryl M., and Robinson, Sarah M.: "Educational Change Through a Taxonomy for Writing Physical Education Objectives." *Quest*, XV:32-38 (Jan., 1971).

23. Jones, Harold E.: "Physical Ability as a Factor in Social Adjustment in Adolescence." *Journal of Educational Research*, 40:287-301 (December, 1946).

24. Krathwohl, David R., Bloom, Benjamin S., and Masia, Bertram B.: *Taxonomy of Educational Objectives, Handbook II: The Affective Domain*. New York: David McKay Company, Inc., 1956.

25. Kraus, Hans, and Raab, Wilhelm: *Hypokinetic Disease*. Springfield, Ill.: Charles C Thomas, Publisher, 1961.

26. Kroll, Walter P.: *Perspectives in Physical Education*. New York: Academic Press, 1971.

27. McCloy, Charles H.: "Home Recreation for Fitness" *J. Health, Phys. Educ., Rec.*, 29:12, 22, 64 (April, 1958).

28. McCloy, Charles H.: "The Significance of the Draft Statistics." *The Physical Educator*, XV:47-49 (May, 1958).

29. Mager, Robert F.: *Preparing Objectives for Programmed Instruction*. San Francisco: Fearon Publishers, 1961.

29a. Mathews, Donald K., and Fox, Edward L.: *Physiological Basis of Physical Education and Athletics*. Philadelphia: W. B. Saunders Company, 1971.

30. Metheny, Eleanor: *Body Dynamics*. New York: McGraw-Hill Book Company, Inc., 1952.

31. Metheny, Eleanor: *Connotations of Movement in Sport and Dance.* Dubuque, Iowa: William C. Brown and Co., 1965.
32. Metheny, Eleanor: "The Third Dimension in Physical Education." *J. Health, Phys. Educ., Rec.,* 25:27-28 (March, 1954).
33. Moss, Bernice: "Health Teaching—A Physical Educator's Responsibility." *J. Health, Phys. Educ., Rec.,* 25:15, 24 (November, 1954).
34. Nash, Jay B.: *Physical Education: Interpretations and Objectives.* Dubuque, Iowa: William C. Brown and Co., rev. ed., 1963.
35. Oberteuffer, Delbert: "The Role of Physical Education in Health and Fitness." *Am. J. Pub. Health,* 52:1155-1160 (July, 1962).
36. Oberteuffer, Delbert, and Ulrich, Celeste: *Physical Education.* New York: Harper and Row, Publishers, 4th ed., 1970.
37. Popham, W. James: "Objectives, '72." *Phi Delta Kappan,* LIV:32–35 (March, 1972).
38. Rathbone, Josephine L., and Hunt, Valerie V.: *Corrective Physical Education.* Philadelphia: W. B. Saunders Company, 7th ed., 1965.
39. *Report of the National Conference on Interpretation of Physical Education.* Chicago: The Athletic Institute, 1961.
39a. The School Programs in Health, Physical Education, and Recreation: A Statement of Basic Beliefs. Kensington, Md.: Society of State Directors of Health, Physical Education, and Recreation, 1972.
40. Schurr, Evelyn L.: *Movement Experiences for Children: Curriculum and Methods for Elementary School Physical Education.* New York: Appleton-Century-Crofts, Inc., 1967.
41. Sheehan, Thomas J.: "Sport: The Focal Point of Physical Education." *Quest,* X:59-67 (May, 1968).
41a. Simpson, Elizabeth J. "The Classification of Educational Objectives: Psychomotor Domain," Vocational and Technical Education Grant Contract No. OE 5-85-104 (Washington, D.C.: U.S. Department of Health, Education, and Welfare, 1966).
42. Steinhaus, Arthur H.: *Toward an Understanding of Health and Physical Education.* Dubuque, Iowa: William C. Brown and Company, 1963.
43. *This Is Physical Education.* Washington, D.C.: American Association for Health, Physical Education, and Recreation, 1965.
44. Ulrich, Celeste, and Nixon, John E.: *Tones of Theory—A Tentative Perspective.* Washington, D.C.: Physical Education Division, American Association for Health, Physical Education, and Recreation, 1972.
45. Updyke, Wynn F., and Johnson, Perry B.: *Principles of Modern Physical Education, Health and Recreation.* New York: Holt, Rinehart and Winston, Inc., 1970.
46. Vendien, C. Lynn, and Nixon, John E.: *The World Today in Health, Physical Education, and Recreation.* Englewood Cliffs, N.J.: Prentice-Hall, Inc., 1968.
47. *Weight Training in Sports and Physical Education.* Washington, D.C.: American Association for Health, Physical Education, and Recreation, 1962.
48. Williams, Jesse F.: *The Principles of Physical Education.* Philadelphia: W. B. Saunders Company, 8th ed., 1964.

(From Daughtrey, G. Effective Teaching in Physical Education for Secondary Schools. *Philadelphia: W. B. Saunders Co., 1973.*)

Chapter Five

THE NORMATIVE FOUNDATIONS OF PHYSICAL EDUCATION
Historical, Philosophical, Comparative

History, philosophy, and comparative education are known as *normative* fields because they continuously seek to define and describe more clearly the goals and behaviors a given society values so that individuals are bound together into a cohesive cultural entity. In this sense "normative" refers to a desired and desirable state of affairs to be achieved by all members of the collective social enterprise.

At any given time some persons have already attained the stated or implicit norms. Others are still striving to reach them. Norms are an expected set of behaviors which the reference group values and seeks to inculcate in its members.

The study of the history and philosophy of physical education, and of comparative physical education, focuses on these cultural expectations and the basic value systems of the social groups whose members are the patrons of and participants in physical education programs.

This chapter summarizes briefly (1) the major influences in the history of mankind which have been forerunners to the development of organized programs of physical education in American formal educational institutions (2) the roles and functions of the discipline of philosophy and the contributions of educational philosophy, and the philosophy of physical education, to the analysis and improvement of the conduct of physical education programs; and (3) a cross-cultural perspective and analysis of similarities and differences between systems of physical education in various countries around the world.

In all of these ways the American physical educator can better understand his own value systems, and that of the school and the societal agencies which control the institution he teaches in; he can more effectively evaluate the strengths and weaknesses of the policies, principles, and practices which determine what and how he will teach; and finally, the perceptive, thoughtful teacher can develop skills and insights which will enable him to evolve more effective teaching and learning conditions and activities so as to facilitate changes in pupil behaviors in the direction of the approved norms of the culture.

HISTORY OF PHYSICAL EDUCATION

Evidence from archaeology, anthropology, and history indicates that sports and games, dances and festivals, and the endless play of children have formed cultural patterns inseparably woven into the history of man wherever and whenever he has lived. The most primitive of men undoubtedly undertook to instruct their young in various physical activities involved in securing food, in self-defense, and in other phases of self-preservation. Archery is still a popular activity in the physical education program, but how many tens of thousands of years ago the first instruction in archery was given, no one knows. Such play activities as wrestling, tag games, and others are as old as the human race. Ball games belong to the earliest eras of history of which we have any knowledge.

Thus we see that certain features of modern physical education come down to us from time immemorial. Our principal concern here, however, is to trace the influences which have affected our school programs of physical education, and to do this it is necessary to go back only as far as the Greeks of the fifth century B.C. For while it is true that the history of the older civilizations—China, Egypt, Persia, and others—indicates the presence of more or less systematic schemes of physical training long before the golden age of Greek civilization, these systems can hardly be thought to have influenced our present-day theory and procedures in this field.[40]

Ancient Greece

The philosophy and ideals of Greek education, together with the significance which the Greeks attached to physical education in relation to their whole conception of the adequate training of the young in mind, body, and spirit, still exert an influence on the thinking of those who concern themselves with speculation about education in relation to human welfare and human destiny.

The impact of Greek theory and practice upon later thought and procedures in the realm of education may be attributed largely to the brilliance of the civilization with which these theories and practices were connected. The Golden Era of Greece was fully developed in the sixth century B.C. Each city, and the surrounding area, was regarded as a separate state with its own government and military force, and having the complete loyalty of all the people. Greece was not a unified nation at this time but rather was a collection of city-states. Corinth was a noted business center; Sparta was famed as a strong military power; and Athens was becoming recognized as an intellectual and cultural center. Thus, the role of physical education differed in each area of Greece according to the dominant values of each city-state. Sparta and Athens, when viewed in historical perspective, seem to have provided the strongest influences on physical education theory and practice, which were passed down through the centuries by historians and philosophers of educational practice.

Sparta. Because of its emphasis on military strength, Spartan boys were raised to become healthy, strong warriors, and girls were trained to become physically fit mothers. Sickly children were weeded out shortly after birth by the elders and often left to die on Mount Taygetus. The boys were raised in the home until age seven when the state assigned them to "packs" in which they remained until they were fourteen. During this time they engaged in rigorous physical training and conditioning as a base for the military training to follow. The "packs" were scheduled into a variety of physical education activities including archery, ball games, wrestling, boxing, javelin throwing and hunting.

Music and songs were also an important part of the education of the Spartan youth. They exercised to music and marched to the beat of martial music. The accompanying songs extolled the virtues of dead war heroes. The laws of the state were set to music and memorized in this fashion.

From age fourteen to twenty the boys were trained for military service. From then on they were available for military campaigns on call.

Spartan girls were raised at home, although they too were organized into "packs." Thus, state-supervised physical education played a prominent role in the education of all of the girls of Sparta. The program stressed weight control and physical fitness to prepare for motherhood. The girls participated in running, jumping, discus and javelin throwing, ball games, mountain climbing, and dancing. This training continued until age twenty. Most young girls developed strong, attractive physiques. Overweight was not allowed to occur. These young women were admired for their physical beauty, clear complexion, and general vigor.

Dancing was very popular with both the boys and the girls. The men believed that warfare resembled dance, so the dance forms symbolically emphasized the warriors in battle, the raiments of battle, and the accompanying music of the flute. Dance was regarded as instrumental in communicating the glory of the state through victory in war and paid honor to the valiant deeds of the warriors. Dance was not necessarily valued for its intrinsic aesthetic contributions to human development and emotional expression.

In summary, Sparta succeeded in developing strong, healthy young men and women who were the envy of the other nation-states in Greece. Spartan athletes were dominant in the Olympic Games and in lesser athletic contests throughout the land for centuries. However, this educational system gradually failed because it did not produce well rounded citizens who knew how to lead a civilized life of peace. The defeat of the Spartan armies at Leuctra in 371 B.C. sealed the doom of this physical and military system.

Athens. It has been suggested that, if one were to indicate by lights upon a map of the world those regions in which civilization has in the past reached its highest development, the smallest but brightest of these lights would mark the little city-state of Athens in

Greece. In the fifth century B.C., this small community of a few thousand free citizens produced more men of the highest rank in human history than the whole world has ever produced in an equal period of time. It is doubtful whether the brilliance of Greek art, literature, and philosophy of this period has ever been approached in any age by any nation or people.

Naturally, a people which produced Socrates, Plato, Aristotle, Phidias, Ictinus, Pericles, Aeschylus, Sophocles, Myron, and other immortals deserves to have consideration given to its theories of education, because it is fair to assume that the system of education in vogue must have contributed in some measure to the phenomenal development of genius which marked the age.

Modern students of Greek education have been impressed particularly by the emphasis the Greeks placed upon the idea of the unity of life. The Greeks seem to have been the only people of ancient times to attain this conception. They recognized the physical, mental, and spiritual aspects of life, but at the same time, they fully appreciated the interdependence of these elements. Their philosophy of education insisted upon harmonious development of all the powers and capacities of the individual.

The education of the Athenian boy consisted of "literature," "music," and "gymnastics." Literature was studied under the direction of a grammarian. The term "music" included artistic, literary, and musical training. "Gymnastics" involved the whole range of physical education activities which included, among others, throwing the javelin and discus, running, jumping, wrestling, and free play. An equal amount of time was devoted to "music" and "gymnastics." This latter fact ought to carry more weight than it does with some modern educators who tend to balance several hours of intellectual study with a daily allowance of ten to thirty minutes of physical education.

The Greeks did not regard physical education as a palliative agency to counteract too long-continued and intensive mental effort, or as an aid to discipline, as do many modern educators. On the contrary, they saw clearly that only through muscular activity is it possible to develop the beauty and perfection of the human body, which appealed so strongly to their sense of the artistic, and to lay sound foundations for health and physical vigor. But above and beyond these results, the Greeks recognized the value of the physical education program in the development of such personality and character traits as poise, confidence, self-control, and courage. This conception was indicated by Plato when he said that music and gymnastics were both designed for the improvement of the soul.

The present-day physical educator must be cautious about citing isolated quotes from Plato and other Greek philosophers as support for the place of physical education in the school program today. A careful reading of Plato shows clearly that, as an exponent of classical idealism, he held a dualistic position concerning man, which regarded the soul as immortal and the body as mortal. He did regard the body and soul as separate entities and he held the body to be very inferior to the soul. In a penetrating analysis of Plato's writings, Siedentop[37] establishes that the two purposes of physical training were for military preparation to protect the city-state and to develop a healthy body as the receptacle for the soul. There is some merit in presenting Plato's views as a historical and philosophical base for the interpretation of present-day physical education. However, his philosophy was a dichotomous one which we hear paraphrased frequently today as "the sound mind in the sound body." This interpretation no longer is consistent with the well-established scientific knowledge of the integrated nature of man. The physical educator does this field a disservice to use the historical dualistic cliché as justification for today's program.

While our present civilization owes much to Greek ideals in relation to education in general, and physical education in particular, it must be remembered that in Athens, which is regarded as the ideal Greek state, only about 20,000 of the total population of approximately 200,000, or 10 percent, were free male adult citizens. To these people alone, and to their sons, the Greek ideal of education applied.

The Roman Empire

Throughout the period of Roman ascendancy, narrower conceptions of life and of the destiny of man took such complete control of human thought and custom as to obliterate almost entirely the Greek ideals of complete harmonious development and fullness of living. It is true that the Roman scheme of education included much physical training, but only to contribute to military efficiency. The Campus Martius at Rome was dedicated to the training of the young men of the city, but the training had a militaristic emphasis.

Modern physical education owes little to the Romans. The

Romans attributed only slight worth to the individual and valued the human being only in relation to the state. This is a political philosophy with which we became quite familiar before and during World War II, in connection with the Nazi and Fascist regimes. The Romans developed no philosophy of education which would make paramount the complete development of the human being. Their interest in sports was largely spectator interest. Professional sports and gladiatorial combats held their attention, to the exclusion of any general participation in play. Many observers of modern American life profess to see in our enthusiasm for professional baseball, football, and other sports a development of spectator interest which bodes ill for the America of the future. The same critics see a similar threat in the commercializing of college sports.

The Middle Ages

The disintegration of the Roman Empire marked the beginning of a period of about a thousand years designated as the "Dark Ages," "Middle Ages," or "Medieval Period." In this era, marked by the supremacy of the invading barbarian tribes, the learning of the Greeks and Romans was largely lost sight of, and formal education was not only neglected but commonly despised. It is true that the lamp of learning was kept lighted in the medieval monasteries and universities, but organized education in the modern sense was practically nonexistent.

And yet, out of the Dark Ages emerged a number of influences which are still of significance to modern physical education. Of these influences, those favorable to physical education were, first, the character of the barbarian tribes which invaded the Roman Empire; and, second, the development of sports, particularly among the English people.

The Teutonic invaders, as a people, were physically vigorous and hardy, and they possessed traits of character which made them superior in many ways to the more degenerate Romans whose supremacy they overthrew. Inured to a vigorous, hardy, outdoor life, these "barbarians" brought to the civilized world new vitality, new customs, and new manners of life.

The development of sports in England during the Middle Ages is one of the most specific of all historical influences on American physical education. Our heritage of sports, a significant feature of American life, comes almost entirely from the English people. The Middle Ages in England saw the development of such sports as archery, football, tennis, and many others. Carried down into modern times, this English love of sports, brought to America by the colonists, has been instrumental in the development of our modern programs of physical education.

The Middle Ages also spawned two influences which even today often form a barrier to a general understanding and appreciation of the true significance of physical education. These influences are scholasticism and asceticism.

Scholasticism. Scholasticism may be thought of as an attitude which would glorify the mental or intellectual aspects of life to the neglect or even degradation of the physical. This attitude, developed among the university scholars of the Middle Ages, was probably a reaction against the general ignorance and brutishness of the times.

It is particularly important for the physical educator to note that the spirit of scholasticism is still influential in the modern world, particularly among university faculties. Some present-day "scholars" still are inclined to set the mental life in opposition to the physical, as though the two were incompatible—in spite of one of the most significant discoveries of modern science, that life is a unity and there can be no successful separation of mind, body, and spirit. If the scholastic mind accepts physical education at all in the school curriculum, it is only as a palliative or disciplinary agency, or as a necessary evil. This attitude is being broken down gradually, but it still constitutes a challenge which physical education must meet by a program of interpretation and education.

Asceticism. Asceticism is an attitude of austere self-denial which commonly sets the soul and body in opposition, and finds it necessary to degrade the latter in order to glorify the former. This attitude also still troubles the physical educator. The Protestant Reformation during and after the sixteenth century strengthened the influence of asceticism and its later descendant, "puritanism."

Originating early in the Christian era as a revolt against the sensuality of the decadent Romans, asceticism displayed itself successively in the extreme self-degradation of the early hermits, in the life of the monasteries, and in the harsh and joyless existence of many of the later Puritans. Out of asceticism have come such expressions as "the flesh and the Devil," to indicate the prevailing attitude toward all things physical; the idea that play is childish, foolish, or vicious; and the belief that happiness is prima facie evidence of sinfulness. In its extreme form, asceticism has never been able to see good in joyousness, to tolerate freedom in self-expression, or to find value in physical perfection. This spirit even today opposes the expenditure of time and money involved in the modern program of sports education for the young. It is incapable of understanding the truth about human nature, and is still obstinately set upon warping human beings into a mold for which they were never intended, and into which they can never be fitted successfully.

The Renaissance

The "revival of learning" which characterized the Renaissance in the fourteenth and fifteenth centuries marked the beginning of modern theories, practices, and philosophies in education. Of special interest to the educator is the fact that the revival of learning called attention again to the Greek ideals and practices in education described by Plato and other classical writers. For the student of education, it is possible to trace the development of our modern philosophy of physical education from the age of Vittorino da Feltre of Mantua, early in the fifteenth century, to the present. The Renaissance educators, breaking away from the authoritarianism and scholasticism of medieval times, proposed and put into effect new programs of education which gave a place of prominence to physical training and to training in manners and morals. To these pioneer educators of the modern world, and to an unbroken line of successors reaching down to the present day, physical education owes thanks for the measure of acceptance and appreciation it has attained in our generation.

AMERICAN PHYSICAL EDUCATION

The historical influences described so far must be thought of as significant for physical education generally. It remains now to give a brief account of the more immediate influences upon the development of organized physical education in America, and to fit it into the world picture.[44]

British. The colonists who established this country, being largely of British ancestry, brought with them traditions of education which were in many ways admirable but were also largely tinctured with scholasticism and puritanism. In the main, their conception of education gave no place of worth to physical education. It is interesting to note that games were forbidden to the students of certain institutions of higher learning in early America. Such activities were regarded as undignified and detrimental to an atmosphere of scholarly endeavor. Incidentally, this is the identical position of the college professor of today who deplores interest in sports as incompatible with "the things we come to college for." However, the founders of our nation also brought with them the age-old British tradition of sports which no scholastic or puritanical regulations were ever able to obliterate. It is out of this British heritage of sports, more than from any other source, that our present-day program of physical education has developed.

German. American school children have always played—generally without adult supervision. The first organized effort to direct the physical activities of school children in America came to us from the Germans. Early in the nineteenth century there developed, out of the leadership of Guts Muths and Jahn, a system of gymnastics which later became a powerful influence in German education. The introduction of the Turner gymnastics into America, and later into the American public school system and institutions of higher learning, may be attributed to the great immigration of German people into America beginning about 1848. In such centers of German influence as Kansas City, Cincinnati, St. Louis, Davenport, and many others, Turnverein societies were established, and gymnastics were promoted with great enthusiasm. After the introduction of gymnastics into the school curriculum in Germany, pressure began in German communities in the United States, which resulted in the establishment of gymnastics as a part of the curriculum in many public school systems before the beginning of the present century.

Swedish. During the early development of American physical education, the German system of gymnastics came into conflict with the Swedish system developed by Ling at the Royal Central Institute of Gymnastics in Stockholm. The Swedish system was supposed to have a scientific basis in studies of human anatomy, whereas the German gymnastics had been a more spontaneous development. With scientific backing, the proponents of the Swedish system challenged the German gymnastics, and throughout Europe and America a controversy over the relative merits of the two systems raged for several decades. In American schools, a compromise was reached in many cases. The American school and college gymnasium of the early 1900's commonly displayed apparatus of two types—the German horses, bucks, and parallel and horizontal bars, and the Swedish stall bars, booms, climbing ladders, poles, balance boards, and inclined ropes. Light apparatus, such as wands, Indian clubs, and dumbbells, was popular.

The schoolmen of America, during the quarter century from 1890 to about 1915, looked with marked favor upon the German and Swedish systems of physical education. Both were regarded as having great disciplinary value; they required a minimum of special training, and only a few minutes of time daily. The Swedish calisthenics were particularly economical of time and money. Therefore, while both these systems have been discredited in their original forms, in many school systems their influence lingered, and prolonged the development of more modern procedures in physical education.

Rise of New Concepts

The German and Swedish systems of physical education were developed among foreign peoples and under social and political conditions which were very different from those in America. They were a product of autocratic and militaristic cultures. In the light of our present knowledge, these systems violated the best practices involved in the learning process. Gymnastics still form a part of the curriculum in some secondary schools and colleges, but they tend to be taught in a more and more Americanized form, with certain adaptations from German, Swedish, and Danish systems. This turbulent historical development of physical education has aptly been referred to as "the battle of the systems."

Since physical education in any country is an outgrowth of the culture of that country, the diminishing influence of systems of gymnastics as a vital part of programs of physical education in the United

States was inevitable. The United States presents an intensely demo-cratic, highly individualistic, and competitive society, where a higher premium is placed on the independent initiative of the individual than upon his blind obedience. The abundance of open spaces and the availability of easy transportation have made active out-of-door participation possible to so many people that the appeal of formal systems of gymnastics has dwindled. However, credit must be given to the proponents of German and Swedish gymnastics for the first establishment of organized physical education in American schools.

This historical account of the rise of the modern American physical education curriculum in no way indicates that gymnastics no longer constitute an important phase of the educational program. On the contrary, a wide range of tumbling, fundamental gymnastics, rhythmic gymnastics, and other gymnastic activities are considered to be basic elements in the physical education curriculum at all school levels. A criticism of many school and college programs is that they do not include as many gymnastic units and activities as they should. Curriculum leaders are urging more modern gymnastics in the phys-ical education program, as well as an expansion of gymnastic teams in interscholastic and intercollegiate sports programs.

The tendency in American physical education today is toward a program emphasizing the teaching of sports skills and providing for participation in a wide variety of sports activities. The transition from formal systems of gymnastics to sports programs came about gradu-ally. Knowledge drawn from the fields of sociology, biology, and psychology contributed to our understanding of the learning process and of growth and development. The twentieth century brought with it the recognition by educators and psychologists alike that play was an important part of the educational process. It also brought condi-tions of living (for example, urbanization and industrialization) which tended to deprive children of both opportunity and space for play.

Efforts were made to find solutions to the problems involved. One attempt was the widespread establishment of playgrounds. More often than not, the opportunities provided by the playgrounds were not integrated with the schools, and a situation developed where gymnastics were conducted in the schools, and sports and games were played during out-of-school hours. Physical education has been work-ing toward a gradual integration of the school program with the students' out-of-school physical recreation activities, inculcating skill and enthusiasm for these activities in the youngsters while not neglecting the potential contribution of this recreation to their lives as adults. The "community-school" concept, so successfully exemplified by the "Mott program" in Flint, Michigan, has made significant contributions to this philosophy and is being adopted by many schools throughout the United States today. Physical educators should exert leadership to develop community school programs in their areas.

The Opening of the Twentieth Century

The passage of more than 70 years of the twentieth century provides sufficient perspective to assess the role of some of the more important influences that have affected programs of physical education in schools and colleges during this period. For purposes of comparison, a brief browsing through early issues of the *American Education Review* provides an excellent background picture of conditions as they were at the turn of the century.

In the year 1900, announcement was made of a written examination of applicants for licenses as teachers of physical training in any or all of the boroughs of the City of New York. The applicant was required to be at least 18 years old and of good moral character, a graduate of high school, its equivalent, or a higher rank school, and a graduate from a professional course of at least one year in the teaching of physical training, with at least one year of successful teaching experience in physical training. Salary scales for elementary teachers were $900 to $1200 for women (married women not eligible) and $1100 to $1400 for men. For high school teachers the range was $1100 to $1900 for women and $1300 to $2400 for men. By 1903, there were some 52 normal schools offering courses to prepare students for teaching gymnastics in the public schools, even though the teaching of physical education was required in only a few of the states.

In 1905, the results of a questionnaire to which 555 cities responded revealed that only 128 cities employed teachers of physical training, of whom 102 were men and 189 women. Of the 555 cities, 125, or 23 percent, had one or more high school gymnasiums. Swedish gymnastics were the most frequently used method of instruction in the program. Competitive athletics in high school were approved by 115 of the 128 cities with special teachers, and by 323 of the 427 cities without special teachers. Incidentally, 243 of the 427 cities without special teachers of physical education *did* have high school athletic organizations.

The Annual Report for 1899 of the Commissioner of Education, a publication of the United States Bureau of Education, contained a section on physical training. In the portion of the report devoted to "athletics," the statement was made that the best interests of rational and effectual physical training have suffered from the undue prominence accorded to college athletic contests and contestants by "an uncritical public and an injudicious press."

Two years later, in 1901, the *Review* reported that physical training was established in some form or other in 270 colleges and universities, 98 were doing organized work, 72 required physical exercises, and 24 gave credit for physical training in courses which counted toward a diploma.

The American Association for the Advancement of Physical Education was fifteen years old in 1900, and had been publishing a magazine for four years. The National Council consisted of nine individuals, six of whom were medical doctors. The Association's membership had increased from 49 members in 1885 to 703 in 1900, and the reported expenditures for the year 1900 were $1000.

Vacation schools and playgrounds in New York City opened in the summer of 1900 with 5000 children enrolled. Facilities included five outdoor gymnasiums, 31 school playgrounds, seven roof gardens, ten swimming baths, six recreation piers, and five kindergarten tents. In Philadelphia, 28 playgrounds and five vacation schools were operating. For the first time in the history of vacation schools in Buffalo, the city bore the expense. Teachers volunteered their services. In Chicago, four vacation schools had operated during the previous summer of 1899. Three outdoor gymnasiums were open for summer use in Boston and also "one municipal bath house with 30 sprays and three tubs for men, 11 sprays and six tubs for women. More than 2000 have taken these baths in a single day."

In 1903, the City of Chicago passed a $5,500,000 bond issue for the establishment of additional parks and the erection of field houses in the South Park System. The following year, 1904, the City of Los Angeles set up a board of playground commissioners. Admiration and esteem is due the pioneer efforts of individuals and communities throughout America who had the bravery and vision to undertake these early programs. This is particularly true in view of the widespread conviction of a large percentage of taxpayers—and of city, state, and federal officials—that the provision of facilities for play was a proper function of charitable organizations, but not a fitting use of public funds.

Research of a sort had begun in the early years of the century. It was predominantly medical, or was confined to areas which today might seem peripheral to the central problems of physical education. An awareness of the deficiency of much that was being done was demonstrated when the editor of the *Review* wrote in 1900 that physiologists and psychologists were interested in "all considerations of physical exercise as applied to bodily development." He then commented that the profession must find out what is fact and what is fancy, and do away with all haphazard methods of investigation!

A reading of the various titles of research papers reported in the early years of the century will supply ample evidence of the orientation of efforts at that time. Attention to postural defects and the deleterious effect of seating arrangements in schools were endlessly discussed. Anthropometic measurements of every conceivable type were taken. Hygienic and dietary problems of all sorts absorbed the time and energy of many investigators. Much of the work is useful, today, only as a historical reflection of what occupied the time and attention of the Association members of that day.

In 1901, an address given by the president of the Boston Physical Education Society contained a statement that would not be out of place in tomorrow's newspaper: "The tremendous pressure of American life, the rush, the tension, the steadily increasing demands of life, are pauperizing the community in a physical way."

Important Developments Since World War I

Wartime Influence. In common with other systems of physical education throughout recorded history, American physical education has been profoundly affected by war and the threat of war. American involvement in World War I accelerated the spread of physical education in the public schools with a speed that the efforts of patient and hard-working professional people alone might have taken many years to accomplish.

Preparation for America's entry into the war, the public reaction to the high percentage of rejections among drafted men, and the pressures exerted by professional people brought about the enactment of legislation in many states for required public school physical education. To a large extent this legislation was sold on a "health" basis. The erroneous idea that physical education could make people "healthy" gave the program an impetus which it could not have gained in any other way.

Raising of Standards.   State certification of teachers in physical education came as a result of the institution of required programs. Broader and better professional training courses were set up by colleges and universities, and professional leadership steadily improved, both in quality and quantity.

The negative side of this picture was evident in the "emergency" certification of teachers to provide the immediately needed personnel to implement the required programs. Many of these individuals were poorly trained and unsuited for the teaching profession. They remained in service in the period between World Wars I and II, and were sometimes more of a liability than an asset to a profession earnestly struggling to attain genuine status and acceptance.

Increased Number of Playgrounds.   The playground movement continued to grow following World War I. The "games" program readily found its way into school physical education and influenced both objectives and curricular content. Undoubtedly the widespread interest in the play movement did much to strengthen programs of physical education in the school.

The part played by municipalities in providing leadership and facilities for vigorous recreation received tremendous impetus through the expenditure of federal funds during the depression years of the 1930's. A considerable share of WPA and PWA funds was used for the building of school sports facilities—gymnasiums, swimming pools, tennis courts, and athletic fields. By 1937 it was estimated that $75,000,000 had been spent for such projects.

The availability of community facilities for golf, tennis, badminton, and swimming helped bring about the inclusion of many individual sports in the school instructional program.

Improved Use of Leisure Time.   Following the enunciation of the Seven Cardinal Principles of Education in 1918, one of which was "the worthy use of leisure," physical educators became increasingly alert to their possible contributions to the accomplishment of this objective. It must have been a great source of satisfaction to many physical education teachers to have the mantle of respectability and acceptance draped around an objective many had long cherished. Now some of the pressure of the program for fitness, health, and strength could be legitimately and openly directed to education for the use of leisure time. Perhaps there was, even in 1918, a dawning realization that leisure and its use would become a major national problem in the decades to follow.

Since the worthy use of leisure was prominent in the objectives of numerous youth organizations, both semipublic and private, not all of the progress during these years is attributable directly to school personnel in physical education. The leadership provided by many agencies outside the school has given impetus to the over-all program. Boy and Girl Scouts, YMCA's and YWCA's, Boys' Clubs, fraternal organizations, and church groups of all denominations have provided both leadership and facilities for programs of vigorous recreation. Other agencies have emphasized the sports program and its use in the prevention and control of delinquency. The American Red Cross, through its intensive campaigns in swimming and water safety, has done much to bring to the favorable attention of the public the necessity for teaching these activities in the school program. In the forty-year period from 1922 to 1962, over 75,000 persons received Red Cross instructor training to enable them to teach the essentials of water safety at camps, pools, lakes, and beaches.

Increased Freedom for Women.   The transformation in attitude with regard to the role of girls and women in the twentieth century has influenced school and college programs of physical education and the whole gamut of ideas as to the amount and kinds of activities in which they should participate. The schools could not be said to have taken the lead, but they did follow along as a greater freedom for women became acceptable in the culture as a whole. The girls today who swim in a brief bathing suit, play tennis in comfortable shorts, and swing over the golf course in a short skirt and sweater are hardly conscious of the long battle that preceded their privilege to do such things without fear of ridicule or censorship.

In many localities in the United States there are still more money spent, more time devoted, and more facilities provided for physical education for boys and men than there are for girls and women. The disparity is gradually diminishing, and most educators today fully

appreciate that it is just as important to provide many opportunities for participation, good programs of instruction, and adequate facilities for girls as it is for boys. It is neither necessary nor desirable that the programs should be *identical*, but certainly one should be as rich and rewarding as the other.

The first woman president of the American Physical Education Association, Mabel Lee, was elected in 1930, and within the following two years the National Section on Women's Athletics became a recognized section. The establishment of a Women's Athletic Rules and Editorial Committee allowed the women to carry on their publication of rules handbooks and to promote desirable standards for girls' and women's sports as an accepted and integral part of the Association.

Scientific Discoveries. Research has made significant contributions to the development of programs of physical education in the twentieth century, and has resulted in changes in philosophy, in curricula, and in methods. A considerable number of physiological and psychological studies have been made which offer an increased understanding of the efficiency of the human mechanism and its adaptations to stress. Many of the problems involved in motor learning have been investigated, and studies are available which contribute to a more rational approach to problems of teaching methods, administrative practices, and curriculum content. The growth of graduate work in colleges and universities indicates an attitude on the part of professional people which strengthens all phases of physical education.

The most salutary effect of research has been to make responsible representatives of the profession less naive in their claims with regard to what physical education can or cannot be expected to accomplish. There is less uncritical acceptance of biased information obtained in the name of research and greater demand for the objectivity of competent scholarly work. Every individual should have faith in the profession to which he gives his allegiance, and a profound belief in the importance of its role in education. But faith should not be mistaken for indisputable evidence. The continuing struggle to attain and maintain firm status in the academic world must be based on incontrovertible evidence of the intellectual integrity and sound educational background of the personnel representing the profession.

Growth of Competitive Sports in the Schools.   The growth of competitive sports in schools has had a considerable influence upon program content. In large measure, the current programs include both team and individual sports. The design and construction of gymnasiums and swimming pools have been directly influenced by the incorporation into the program of these activities, and these facilities are now used for class instruction and intramural participation as well as for interscholastic competition.

Improved safety measures involving medical examination and supervision, vastly improved equipment and facilities, and constant attention to the elimination of hazards, as well as appropriate rule changes, have all made a contribution to the success of the program.

Sports for Children Outside of School.   The tremendous interest in programs conducted by organizations other than the schools is one of the outstanding developments in the history of American sports. It is estimated that more than one million youngsters now participate in Little League baseball in this country, and thousands of others are playing in an ever expanding number of countries around the world. Countless thousands of boys and girls are competing in programs of Pop Warner football, Iddy Biddy basketball, Babe Ruth baseball, swimming clubs, tennis clubs, and many other types of sports activities. In fact, the effect of highly competitive athletic participation upon young children is one of the controversial issues facing the physical education profession today.

Highly competitive athletics for elementary school children sponsored by agencies and organizations which are not school or community recreation sponsored are the subject of controversy and debate. It has been charged that the widespread popularity of Little League, Pop Warner Baseball, and similar youth programs is due to the failure of the schools and community recreation agencies to provide suitable sports programs for these youngsters. The tremendous participation figures, which total in the millions in this country and others, are direct evidence of the popularity of these varied sports programs, many of which are administered and conducted by volunteer adults who lack professional preparation in education and sports.

Major issues involved in the controversy about the values and potential dangers in these programs include (1) the qualifications of the sponsoring and coaching adult leaders; (2) the safety and sanitary conditions under which many of these games are conducted; (3) the intense emotional pressure which can be exerted upon very young children by enthusiastic parents and other adults who strive to win the league championship, the city playoff, the regional, state, and national championships; (4) the possibilities of physical injury; (5) the possibilities of developing unbalanced feelings of importance and overemphasis at such an early age range; and (6) the supplying of large amounts of money, equipment, facilities, and leadership for the benefit of a relatively small percent of highly skilled youngsters.

Educational organizations and committees of the American Medical Association have published official statements of standards which should be observed in the promotion and conduct of these sports programs. Many individuals who are professionally prepared in education, sports, and medicine are volunteering their services to the local sponsoring agencies of these sports in order to interpret these professional standards and to provide inservice education and guidance to the adult leaders so that these recommended standards will be adopted and observed.

Fitness Groups.   In 1956, as a result of research indicating that European children were more "physically fit" than American children, President Eisenhower established a President's Council on

Youth Fitness, composed of the Vice-President of the United States and five members of the Cabinet. Established at the same time was a Citizens' Advisory Committee on the Fitness of American Youth, composed of a large number of nationally prominent leaders from a cross-section of areas representative of American life. The function of this group was to "consider and evaluate existing and prospective governmental and private measures conducive to the achievement of a happier, healthier, and more completely fit American youth." Great impetus to physical education has resulted from the work of these groups and from consequent developments at state and local levels throughout the country. The subjects of "fitness" and "physical fitness" are discussed in detail in Chapter 8.

PHILOSOPHY OF PHYSICAL EDUCATION

Originally the term "philosophy" connoted love of wisdom or knowledge. As a formal discipline the word now has elaborate definitions and connotations which are beyond the scope of this book. Basically, it refers to the organized study of human thought and conduct. It is concerned with identifying and clearly formulating laws and principles which underlie all knowledge and reality and which explain the universe and man's thoughts and beliefs in relation to control of his existence.

Roger Burke* says that:

> The content of philosophy is a rational consistent, systematic set of pervasive general principles which explain existence, perceived facts, and causations. . . . It provides a framework, a rational theory, a logical method, a penetrating explanation and a universal guide for the problems of human existence.

Zeigler** defines philosophy as ". . . that branch of learning (or that science) which investigates, evaluates, and integrates knowledge of reality as best as possible into one or more systems embodying all available wisdom about the universe."

---

* Elwood C. Davis. *The Philosophic Process in Physical Education.* Philadelphia: Lea and Febiger, 1961, p. 26.
** Earle F. Zeigler. *Philosophical Foundations for Physical, Health, and Recreation Education.* Englewood Cliffs, New Jersey: Prentice-Hall, Inc., 1964, p. 12.

Philosophy is arbitrarily subdivided into branches or domains in a variety of ways by different authors. It is standard to list four main branches of philosophy, namely:

Metaphysics (the nature of reality)
Epistemology (the nature of knowledge)
Logic (the nature of relationships between ideas)
Axiology (the nature and sources of values)

There are numerous subdivisions of these main branches. Brubacher[7] describes twelve categories of philosophy:

Pragmatic Naturalism
Reconstructionism
Romantic Naturalism
Existentialism
Organicism
Idealism
Realism
Rational Humanism
Fascism
Communism
Democracy

There are three major categories of philosophical method:

Speculative, which involves synthesis of facts or ideas in order to present an overview or an integrated picture;

Normative, which refers to the formulation of goals, norms, and standards of behavior for individuals or groups under study; and

Critical, which involves the careful, precise study of terms and propositions about thought and practice in any area of human endeavor for the purpose of generating the greatest possible clarity of meaning and understanding.

Educational philosophy is a branch of philosophy applied to the study of educational aims and practices. Traditionally, the major approaches of educational philosophers have been (1) to describe various schools of philosophical thought and relate each to the problems, responsibilities, and challenges of educational institutions in an attempt to provide useful guidance; and (2) to attempt to clarify educational problems in terms of the basic tenets of the various fundamental branches of philosophy such as metaphysics, epistemology, logic, and axiology. In these two approaches philosophical schools and guiding principles were described first and then educational problems were analyzed in an effort to seek clarification and

solution. Thus, the starting point was with philosophy and educational philosophy with subsequent application to educational problems and issues.

In recent years this process has been reversed. Educational problems become the central focus of concern and the point of origin of study and analysis. Philosophy becomes secondary or ancillary. The tools of philosophical analysis are applied to educational problems and practices to aid in the search for more significant and effective strategies and practices for governing and administering educational enterprises and for developing an atmosphere which will be more conducive to improved learning by the pupils. There are several category systems for classifying schools of educational philosophy as derivations of the parent field.

Physical educators have "philosophized" about their field both orally and in writing for a long, long time. However, it has only been in recent years that a few interested physical educators undertook advanced graduate study in philosophy in order to qualify themselves properly in the subject matter and the methodology of research and analysis of philosophy as applied to the study of physical education. Several leading books on the philosophy of physical education are cited in the reference list for this chapter.

For example, Zeigler[46] and colleagues have made a detailed philosophical analysis of fourteen persistent problems in the history of physical education. This analysis is conducted in terms of three leading philosophical positions, namely, experimentalism (or pragmatic naturalism), realism, and idealism. Each of these major categories has variations and differing shades of interpretation within it which can be labeled with other philosophic terms which Zeigler provides. He also discusses existentialism and describes how it can be the basis for analysis of physical education problems and practices. Elwood C. Davis and Donna Mae Miller,[9] Howard Slusher and Aileene Lockhart,[38] Seymore Kleinman,[28] and others[15,41] have made significant contributions to literature concerning the philosophy of physical education.

Every physical educator should have a basic understanding of philosophy, philosophy of education, and philosophy of physical education. This knowledge will enable the teacher, coach and administrator to better analyze his basic assumptions, clarify his goals, bring more consistency to his reasons for teaching as he does, and to formulate more appropriate evaluation and assessment techniques to deter-

mine how suitably he is performing in his assigned educator roles, as well as assisting pupils to judge their own progress toward educational objectives.

Perhaps the basic step is for the teacher to learn to comprehend more clearly and state more explicitly the value systems, both personal and educational, which are the foundation of his work with students. This process will enable the teacher to think and act more consistently and will sharpen his perception of, and his dedication to, the pursuit of priorities in the educational development of his students. Values are discussed in more detail in Chapter 6.

PHYSICAL EDUCATION AROUND THE WORLD

Although not all countries of the world today may agree on a name by which physical activities are known—physical education, physical recreation, physical culture, athletics, sports, or games—such activities form a necessary ingredient of the cultural life of each nation. With the formation of new nations throughout the world during the past two decades, a multiplicity of economic, political, social, and educational problems have arisen. In the social and cultural development of new nations, sports and physical education, because of their dynamic quality, accompany the general development of human community life, in that they are sensitive to social and cultural impulses and reflect individual as well as national aspirations, pride, and pursuits.

Sports and physical education are a part of the struggle of ideologies in the current world. In the Soviet philosophy, sports are apparently conceived primarily as a tool of propaganda, an instrument of national policy, a means of strengthening the party line of Soviet superiority and further indoctrinating Communists. Under the American philosophy of sports, conversely, athletes act as ambassadors of good will, spreading ideas, ideals, and democratic concepts in the foreign countries they visit. The American public, through Congress, gave the State Department a mandate to conduct an educational exchange program with the free countries of the world, in order to know each other better. Within this program, teachers, students, scholars, and national leaders are exchanged. In sending various representatives of American life abroad, the sports area was not

excluded, for to do so would have resulted in a distorted picture of American life. When William Faulkner, Chief Justice Warren, and Robert Frost went abroad, others from various walks of American life—great sportsmen like Bob Mathias, Jesse Owens, and Sammy Lee—went also, to present a balanced picture of the American scene.

International Athletic Competitions

This exchange of cultural concepts not only emphasizes the value of some current athletic events, but has also contributed to a further extension of sports competitions which assume a variety of forms on an international scale. Vendien and Nixon[43] describe a variety of international competitions.

The Olympic Games. From their beginning, the Olympic Games have promoted interest in sports around the world. Participation has become a matter of national prestige. The Olympics, as well as other forms of competitions, have developed from individual competitions into competitions between countries. Despite the sporting ideologies, restrictive rules, and control of international federations, the Olympic Games have become the platform where countries, as well as individuals, compete among themselves for a superiority in sports. The number of countries in the Olympics has increased from 59 in 1948 to 124 in 1972, when the Games of the XXth Olympiad were held in Munich, West Germany, in August. The Games were spectacularly staged and were seen by millions of people —the largest viewing audience ever to see a TV program—all over the world via satellite transmission. The facilities were beautifully designed and soundly constructed. The men and women athletes from around the world continued their assault on Olympic and world records in many events.

Tragically, the Games were marred by international violence— the "Israeli incident." It is important to observe that in recent years the Olympic Games have become a vehicle for political propaganda. The use of the Games as a public forum for the promotion of intense nationalism is now widespread. There is great concern over this trend which completely negates the original, laudable reason why the modern Olympic Games were revived in 1896. Many proposals have been made in various quarters for changes in the policies and rules which govern the conduct of the Games so as to solve the major problems which are now associated with them. Other critical problems, in additional to excessive nationalism, are the extremely high cost of conducting the Games by the host country, and the complex issue of the eligibility of so-called "professional" sportsmen and women to participate in the Games.

Competitions Between Two or More Countries. International matches among a small number of countries have, year after year, met with popularity and publicity. A basic reason for this trend is that countries have freedom to choose as their adversaries those who, because of similar cultural and sporting resources, are most suitable for the reciprocal arrangement. This makes it possible for a small country to compete with other small countries with equal possibility for success. The Asian Championships and the Pan-American Games exemplify this form of competition.

World Championships. World championships are held in a variety of sports. There is no consistent pattern among sports as to frequency of meeting, host countries, or eligibility for participation. Of course the Olympic Games is the most renowned of this level of championships. Other examples include world championships in archery, association football, basketball, gymnastics, ice hockey, skiing, and swimming.

Other Competitions. Annual challenges between countries in specific sports have proved to be mutually satisfying. The Ryder Cup challenge in men's amateur golf between Great Britain and the United States and the Wightman Cup Tennis competitions involving British and American women are of international significance. The Davis Cup and Wimbledon, as well as other tennis tournaments with international flavor, bring together outstanding players to compete for supremacy in that sport.

The United States and the U.S.S.R., in a joint communiqué in January, 1958, provided for exchanges in cultural, technical, and educational fields. These exchanges continue on an even larger scale today. More American sports teams are visiting a greater number of countries than ever before. Of particular interest is the initial visit of the United States table tennis team to mainland China in 1972. This visit was a planned, symbolic gesture by China and the United States as the first step to the development of diplomatic relations between these countries. President Nixon's historic visit to China followed soon thereafter. This unique episode has since been referred to as "ping pong diplomacy." More exchanges of sports teams between the U.S.S.R. and the United States, particularly in basketball and gymnastics, are indicative of intensified diplomatic activity between these countries in recent years. This widely publicized use of sport as an instrument of international politics merits close scrutiny by interested sports fans and scholars of political science alike. Using sport as one major vehicle to symbolize a mutual policy of improving international political relationships is indeed a striking phenomenon! Writing in the Department of State Bulletin in 1962, the words of Lucius D. Battle, formerly an Assistant Secretary for Educational and Cultural Affairs, are cogent:

> When we come to communication between people, however, we want more than a formal dialog. It is for this reason that our Government's programs in education and the arts have come to play a more and more significant role in contributing to the attainment of United States foreign policy objectives, often producing results that cannot be achieved in any other way. For they provide direct access to people —people who are glad to purvey as an illumination of the quality of our lives and an enrichment of their own. . . . In the long run they can create a world-wide common market of ideas, cultural attainments, and human discourse. . . . By arising above ideological differences, education and the arts make possible intuitive contacts that can ripen into mutual trust and understanding and enduring friendship.[3]

Recent Conferences

The extension of international competitions has exerted a definite positive influence on the exchange of ideas in health, physical education, and recreation. These subjects have served as discussion topics for many national and international groups. Some of the more important recent conferences are the following.

Health and Fitness in the Modern World. A collection of papers presented in Rome, Italy, in 1960, by outstanding international authorities and published by the Athletic Institute in cooperation with the American College of Sports Medicine emphasized problems which confront the individual and society, and described how the scientific disciplines of medicine, science, and physical education are directed toward the solution of such problems. "Medicine contributes toward the elimination of disease and its draining effects; science toward an understanding of the normal and maladjusted individual as a physical, mental, emotional, social being; and physical education toward knowledge of the individual and the care and development of the human body."[14]

Seventh International Congress on Physical Education and Sports for Girls and Women. This Congress, attended by approximately 500 delegates from 30 countries around the world, was held in Teheran, Iran, in August, 1973. The theme of this Congress was "Physical Education and Sport for All." The Congress continues to gain in popularity and in attendance. It provides an excellent forum for the exchange of information and views on important topics of mutual concern to women physical educators from all countries. It is held every four years.

Fifteenth Annual Congress of the International Council on Health, Physical Education and Recreation. The World Confederation of Organizations of the Teaching Professions is the parent agency of ICHPER. The Congress met in London in August, 1972. Approximately 300 delegates from 34 countries attended. This anniversary conference featured general sessions on educational developments in Canada, on what research tells physical education teachers about selected topics, on modern interpretations of physical education, and on recommendations endorsed by the General Assembly. ICHPER Congresses continue to attract world leaders of Health, Physical Education, and Recreation, and maintain their reputation for high quality programs.

Scientific Congress, "Sport in the Modern World—Chances and Problems." The Organizing Committee for the Games of the XXth Olympiad sponsored this one-time international conference from August 21 to August 25, 1972 as a prelude to the Olympic Games in Munich. The federal government of West Germany subsidized the expense of the Congress. The announced aim of the Congress was to promote the development of sport science by treating questions and problems arising from the vast field of sport and jointly discussing them with experts representing the various scientific and humanistic disciplines from many countries of the world. Although it was never officially announced it seems likely to those who attended that another major purpose of the Congress was to provide a cultural, artistic, and academic atmosphere within which to frame the spectacle of the XXth Olympic Games. This was indeed a unique conception in the modern history of the Olympic Games as well as in the annals of international conferences concerning physical education and sport.

More than 2,000 delegates from approximately 100 countries attended the Congress. Most of them were official representatives sponsored by the national governments of their respective countries. The elaborate program involved speakers and panel members from a broad spectrum of academic disciplines having legitimate relevance to the problems, issues, and analyses of the phenomenon of "sport" as studied from a variety of perspectives. Approximately 120 scholars, each a national or international expert in his specialization, were on the program.

Many valuable materials were prepared in advance for distribution to the conferees, most notable of which is a book entitled *The Scientific View of Sport*.[2] Also, another valuable publication was a selected bibliography, "Sport in Our Time—Chances and Problems," containing citations to pertinent literature from around the world. A post-Congress report of the major addresses was another highly worthwhile document.

The Congress probably was unique in the history of international meetings on sport because of its emphasis upon interdisciplinary analysis and critique, engaged in by so many famous experts from around the world, before a vast international audience of men and women who are engaged daily in carrying out their professional roles in the field of sports.

People to People Sports Committee

This committee, which grew out of a White House Conference in 1956, is composed of individual memberships as well as patron and club memberships. Its purpose is to enable private citizens to supplement the efforts of government in broadening understanding and friendship between American citizens and people of other nations. Typical projects promoted or conducted by the committee included sending a junior baseball team on a three weeks' tour of Japan and Korea, hosting a test cricket team from Pakistan for fifteen days, and providing equipment and training materials to sports clubs, including groups in Thailand, Rhodesia, Spain, Italy, and Brazil.

The Peace Corps

The establishment of the Peace Corps by Congress in September, 1961, "to promote world peace and friendship" has been significantly successful. Developing nations around the world have requested the Peace Corps to send physical education teachers and sports specialists because these programs develop pride, national prestige, and interest in international competition. Sargent Shriver, former director of the Peace Corps, has stated that these representatives "are revealing, on an unprecedented scale, the value of sports as a tool in building that world of independent, friendly nations that is the major goal of America's foreign policy."

The International Olympic Academy

A proposal for the establishment of The International Olympic Academy was first made in 1949 to the International Olympic Committee at its Rome meeting. The Academy was formally organized in 1961 under the sponsorship of the Hellenic Olympic Committee and the auspices of the International Olympic Committee. The Academy has acquired 100 acres in Olympia, Greece, in close proximity to the ancient Olympic stadium.

The objective of the Academy is to maintain and promote the Olympic spirit. It studies and applies the educational and social principles of competitive sport and interprets the Olympic ideal. For approximately two weeks each summer, the Academy sponsors sessions concerning the history of the ancient Olympic Games, the ideals of the Games, the development of moral and spiritual values through sports, the evolution of the theory and techniques of coaching the various sports, and scientific foundations of training and coaching. The National Olympic Committee of each country nominates participants. A Report of each of these summer sessions is published by the Hellenic Olympic Committee.

Comparative, International, and Development Studies

Traditional comparative education research has been conducted for many years both in this country and in other countries around the world. Physical educators in America have to date contributed few really significant comparative studies. They have written many articles for professional journals describing systems of physical education and sports in other countries as viewed through American eyes. But this endeavor cannot be classified as comparative research.

Bereday[4] says:

> Comparative education seeks to make sense out of the similarities and differences among educational systems. It catalogues educational methods across national frontiers; and in this catalogue each country appears as one variant of the total store of mankind's educational experience. If well set off, the like and the contrasting colors of the world perspective will make each country a potential beneficiary of the lessons thus received.

The research methodology involves the analysis of various national educational systems by placing in historical and contemporary juxtaposition relevant educational data, and then evolving cross-national comparisons.

This traditional approach has been changing in recent years. International education may involve some of the steps of comparative education but it goes further and concentrates on cross-national cooperation and relationships and the mutual exchange of educational experts. International relations and cooperation are stressed, as are the exchange of educational materials, technology, students, teachers, and financial aid. International and cross-national mutual understanding and goodwill constitute a third objective. We are seeing these purposes being carried out to some degree by American physical educators through the Fulbright program, the U.S. State Department educational and sports consultant programs, exchanges through educational institutions, and similar programs. Of course the many international conferences in health, physical education, recreation, sports, and sports medicine discussed elsewhere in this chapter are prime examples.

Development education has superseded the famous "fundamental education" and Point Four programs of the 1950's through which the United States government filtered vast quantities of aid to many other countries. Community and personal health programs were stressed along with literacy education. Except for the medical aspects of sports and fitness, physical education programs rarely were central to these development education projects. Educational programs are basic to nation building in underdeveloped countries. Russia, East Germany, England, and other countries are deeply involved in assisting new nations and poor countries with economic support around the world. Sport has become an important political vehicle for assisting these countries. The United States does not seem to be as aware as other countries are of the impact that aid through sport can make on the people and the governments of the lesser developed countries. We make some minimal, token efforts, but nothing of significance. One wonders why.

Selected References

1. Alley, Louis E.: "A Report to the Membership on the ICHPER Meeting (15th)." *J. Health, Phys. Educ.-Rec.*, 44:11, 12 (Jan., 1973).
2. Baitsch, Helmut, Bock, Hans-Erhard, Bolte, Martin, Bokler, Willy, Grupe, Ommo, Heidland, Hans-Wolfgang, and Lotz, Franz: *The Scientific View of Sport.* Berlin: Springer-Verlag, 1972.
3. Battle, Lucius D.: "Cultural and Educational Affairs in International Relations." *Dept. of State Bulletin*, XLVII (July 9, 1962).
4. Bereday, George Z. F.: *Comparative Method in Education.* New York: Holt, Rinehart and Winston, Inc., 1964.
5. Brackenbury, Robert L.: "Physical Education, an Intellectual Emphasis?" *Quest*, I:3-6 (December, 1963).
6. Brown, Roscoe C., Jr., and Kenyon, Gerald S. (eds.): *Classical Studies on Physical Activity.* Englewood Cliffs, N.J.: Prentice-Hall, Inc., 1968.
7. Brubacher, John S.: *Modern Philosophies of Education.* New York: McGraw-Hill Book Company, Inc., 4th ed., 1969.
8. Cooper, John M.: "ICHPER 13th International Congress." *J. Health, Phys. Educ.-Rec.*, 42:25-27 (Jan., 1971).
9. Davis, Elwood C., and Miller, Donna Mae: *The Philosophic Process in Physical Education.* Philadelphia: Lea & Febiger, 2nd ed., 1967.
10. Dixon, John G., McIntosh, Peter C., Munrow, A. D., and Willetts, Ronald F.: *Landmarks in the History of Physical Education.* London: Routledge & Kegan, Paul, Ltd., 1957.
11. "First Annual Peace Corps Report." Washington, D.C.: U.S. Government Printing Office, 1963.
12. Gardiner, E. Norman: *Greek Athletic Sports and Festivals.* New York: The Macmillan Company, 1910.
12a. Gerber, Ellen W.: *Sport and Body: A Philosophical Symposium.* Philadelphia: Lea and Febiger, 1972.
13. Hackensmith, Charles William: *History of Physical Education.* New York: Harper & Row, Publishers, Inc., 1966.
14. *Health and Fitness in the Modern World.* Chicago: The Athletic Institute, 1961.
15. Hellison, Donald R.: *Humanistic Physical Education.* Englewood Cliffs, N.J.: Prentice-Hall, Inc., 1973.
16. Howell, Maxwell L.: "Toward a History of Sport." *J. Health, Phys. Educ.-Rec.*, 40:77-79 (March, 1969).
17. *ICHPER 12, The Twelfth International Congress of the International Council on Health, Physical Education, and Recreation.* Washington, D.C.: NEA Publication, 1969.
18. *International Council on Health, Physical Education, and Recreation, 1970— 13th Congress Report.* Washington, D.C.: American Association for Health, Physical Education, and Recreation, 1971.
19. *International Council on Health, Physical Education, and Recreation, 1971— 14th Congress Report.* Washington, D.C.: American Association for Health, Physical Education, and Recreation, 1971.

20. Jernigan, Sara S., and Frost, Reuben: "International Olympic Academy." *J. Health, Phys. Educ.-Rec.*, 36:53-55 (November-December, 1965).

21. Jernigan, Sara Staff and Vendien, C. Lynn: *Playtime, A World Recreation Handbook.* Hightstown, N.J.: McGraw-Hill Book Company, Inc., 1972.

22. Johnson, William (ed.) *Physical Education Around the World*, Monograph #1. Indianapolis: Phi Epsilon Kappa Fraternity, 1966.

23. Johnson, William (ed.) *Physical Education Around the World*, Monograph #2. Indianapolis: Phi Epsilon Kappa Fraternity, 1967.

24. Johnson, William (ed.) *Physical Education Around the World*, Monograph #3. Indianapolis: Phi Epsilon Kappa Fraternity, 1969.

25. Johnson, William (ed.) *Physical Education Around the World*, Monograph #4. Indianapolis: Phi Epsilon Kappa Fraternity, 1970.

26. Johnson, William (ed.) *Physical Education Around the World*, Monograph #5. Washington, D.C.: AAHPER Publications, 1971.

27. Kistler, Joy W.: "Eleventh International Congress of the International Council on Health, Physical Education, and Recreation." *J. Health, Phys. Educ.-Rec.*, 40: 42,43 (Jan., 1969).

28. Kleinman, Seymour: "Will the Real Plato Please Stand Up?" *Quest*, XIV:73-75, Spring Issue, 1970.

29. Kolatch, Jonathan: *Sports, Politics, and Ideology in China*. New York: Jonathan David, Publishers, 1972.

30. Metheny, Eleanor: "A Directive from History." *J. Health, Phys. Educ.-Rec.*, 20:514, 548-550 (October, 1949).

31. Nixon, John E.: "Comparative, International, and Development Studies in Physical Education." *Proc. Nat. Coll. Phys. Educ. Assoc. for Men.* 1968:114-123.

32. "Peace Corps Asks for Physical Educators." *J. Health, Phys. Educ.-Rec.*, 33:4 (April, 1962).

33. "People to People Sports Committee." New York: People to People Sports Committee, Inc.

34. Rice, Emmet A., Hutchinson, John L., and Lee, Mabel: *A Brief History of Physical Education.* New York: The Ronald Press Company, 5th ed., 1969.

35. Russell, Bertrand: *An Outline of Philosophy.* Cleveland: World Publishing Company, 1967.

36. Semotiuk, Darwin M.: "References for Comparative Physical Education and Sport." *Gymnasion*, 22, 23 Summer, 1970.

37. Siedentop, Daryl: "What Did Plato Really Think?" *The Physical Educator*, 25: 25-26 (March, 1968).

38. Slusher, Howard S., and Lockhart, Aileene S.: *Anthology of Contemporary Readings: An Introduction to Physical Education.* Dubuque, Iowa: William C. Brown and Co., 2nd ed., 1970.

39. "Tenth Anniversary, International Council, Health, Physical Education, and Recreation." *J. Health, Phys. Educ.-Rec.*, 38:21-24 (November-December, 1967).

40. Van Dalen, Deobold B., Mitchell, Elmer D., and Bennett, Bruce L.: *World History of Physical Education.* Englewood Cliffs, N.J.: Prentice-Hall, Inc., 1953.

41. Vander Zwaag, Harold J.: *Toward a Philosophy of Sport.* Reading, Mass.: Addison-Wesley Publishing Company, Inc., 1972.

42. Vendien, C. Lynn, Johnson, William, and Kidess, A. A.: "References for Comparative Physical Education and Sport." *Gymnasion*, 21, 22 Spring, 1970.

43. Vendien, C. Lynn, and Nixon, John E.: *The World Today in Health, Physical Education, and Recreation.* Englewood Cliffs, N.J.: Prentice-Hall, Inc., 1968.

44. Weston, Arthur: *The Making of American Physical Education.* New York: Appleton-Century-Crofts, Inc., 1962.

45. Zeigler, Earle F.: "A Comparative Analysis of Educational Values in Selected Countries: Their Implications for Physical Education and Sport." *Proc. Nat. Coll. Phys. Educ. Assoc. for Men*, 1971:169-174.

46. Zeigler, Earle F.: *Philosophical Foundations for Physical, Health, and Recreation Education.* Englewood Cliffs, N.J.: Prentice-Hall, Inc., 1968.

47. Zeigler, Earle F.: *Problems in the History and Philosophy of Physical Education and Sport.* Englewood Cliffs, N.J.: Prentice-Hall, Inc., 1968.

(From Daughtrey, G. Effective Teaching in Physical Education for Secondary Schools. Philadelphia: W. B. Saunders Co., 1973.)

Chapter Six

SOCIO-CULTURAL FOUNDATIONS

Physical education and physical recreation have been essential elements of every culture known to man, according to evidence from anthropology and history. The place and extent of physical education and physical recreation in American culture today is widespread, and undeniably significant in many respects, although the accurate assessment of this assertion is not yet possible with existing tools of social and anthropological analysis. One can scarcely imagine what American life would be like if legitimate and socially acceptable forms of sports and dance were somehow suddenly removed from existence. Sports and dance in one form or another impinge directly or indirectly on most persons. Compelling evidence of the tremendous involvement of sports and dance in many facets of culture is suggested by Boyle,[2] Maheu,[27] and McIntosh.[25]

ANTHROPOLOGY

Anthropology is generally viewed as the study of the races, physical and mental characteristics, distribution, customs, and social relationships of mankind. Its major fields of study are archaeology, physical anthropology, and cultural anthropology. All have foundational content important to physical education.

Archaeology

The archaeologist's focus is on the scientific study of the life and culture of ancient peoples. His approach to the search for new knowledge is primarily through excavation of ancient cities, relics, and artifacts. Understandings gained through such studies provide important insights into the history of sport and physical education and the role of physical activities in earlier civilizations.

Physical Anthropology

Physical anthropology is concerned with human morphology and adaptability, cultural and ecological factors influencing the composition and structure of human population, expression and distribution of genetic character within and between populations, racial differences, constitutional studies, and measurement and description of human variation. Constitutional studies which relate motor capability and behavior to particular body types depend upon the findings and methods of physical anthropology. Studies concerned with the physiological responses of different groups to heat, cold, altitude, nutrition, exercise, and disease stresses are of particular concern to physical educators. Variations among different human populations in motor performance abilities is another area of important research activity.

Cultural Anthropology

The cultural anthropologist is particularly interested in the customs, institutions, and social relationships of human groups. He investigates variations of human cultures throughout the world, makes comparative studies of human institutions, and analyzes processes of acculturation and cultural change.

The concept "culture" has approximately 175 definitions reported in the scholarly literature on the subject. Obviously, these definitions represent a wide panorama of divergent perspectives. In the analysis and summary of 164 definitions of "culture" in 1952, noted anthropologists A. L. Kroeber and Clyde Kluckhohn[20] indicated that commonly accepted definitions included the following notions: culture is a product; it has historical bases; it involves values, ideas, and patterns; it involves selectivity; it is learned; it is predicated on symbols and it is an abstraction from behaviors and the products of behaviors. Culture concerns the abstracted "nonbiological conditions" of human life. It fundamentally influences man's physiological, psychological, and sociological dimensions. It is shared with one's fellow man. It affects reciprocal interacting human behavior. It is acquired early in the formative years, it is strongly ingrained, and it is typified by an atmosphere of compelling emotional force. Various facets of man's cultural development seek interrelationships, hence leading to development of cultural patterns. Finally, a sense of unity operates to blend diverse aspects into a "cultural integration."

Murdock, a noted anthropolgist, suggests that although there are vast differences readily observable among the many cultures extant throughout the world, there are also "cultural universals" present in every culture. The long list includes athletic sports, dancing, education, games, hygiene, and other elements fundamentally associated with physical education and physical recreation.

We know that today in the educational world there are many informal, implicit assumptions underlying statements made by teachers and administrators concerning sports in relation to culture. Often the expression is heard that "our college offers a wide variety of cultural events and also has an extensive sports program." This statement infers that sports are not "cultural." Sometimes teachers of art or music lament that boys in particular spend too much time in baseball, basketball, or other sports, and not enough time in cultural activities such as playing a musical instrument or learning to paint a picture. Again, the same inference is present.

Undoubtedly this present-day confusion concerning the modern definition of the term "culture" stems from its etymology. It is derived from the verb "to cultivate," which also means to "create." Historically, the term "culture" has thus been used to mean artistic or intellectual endeavors as composing the "cultured" life. Modern anthropological studies have modified and broadened this concept to include the total way of life of a people, with the patterns and content of their learned behaviors and beliefs. The physical educator should be familiar with modern interpretations of the concept of "culture" so that he may authentically interpret, to those who still hold a narrow, historical view, the fundamental contributions which sports undisputably make to American cultural life.

All of us live in a world consisting of our cultural traditions. Schools must recognize that all of us, to some degree, have a responsibility for the transmission of, and hopefully for the improvement of, these traditions. Children today are living in a world of rapid change and confusing social life. Social institutions and practices are not as stable as they were in years past. Schools must educate pupils to seek appropriate means for developing some degree of stability and orderliness in their lives. Teachers can improve their abilities to make such contributions to their pupils by studying relevant generalizations which have been evolved by the research of psychiatrists, clinical psychologists, social psychologists, sociologists, and anthropologists. Topics of particular pertinence for teachers are cultural dynamics, interpersonal and intergroup relationships, and personality in culture. Administrators and teachers can construct their own "guides to action," in making wise educational decisions and in formulating effective teaching strategies, through acquaintance with this literature.

Cassidy[6,7] articulates a "cultural definition" of physical education. Physical education is culturally determined. Man's view of his body, his self-concept, and his notions about how his body should be developed and educated are central to the nature of the culturally evolved definition. The role of movement in human life also contributes fundamentally to this definition based on the development of "self-values" and "becoming." Societal determinants of human movement range from time-place values to economic determinants, political determinants, and cultural beliefs and values.

An analysis of sports as a variety of culture is developed in a fascinating manner by Maheu.[27] He regards sport not as incompatible with culture or inferior to it, but as a variety of it. Important ethical values are thought to be promulgated more effectively through sport than by any other means. Sport may not yet have achieved full cultural expression, but it will when the humanism of the body is fully established. A subtle difference between art and sport is described. The presence of "signs" in works of art endows them with immortality, whereas sport is wholly involved with action of the moment. He pleads for efforts to close the gap between sport and culture. This kind of analysis is thought-provoking, and subject to debate, depending upon the definition of "culture" from which the argument emanates.

Sports, dance, and other forms of human movement as esthetic expressions of beauty are receiving increasing attention in the physical education literature. Cowell and France,[8] Jokl,[16] Metheny,[30] Gray,[13] Kaelin,[17] and others contend that physical educators are artists, and that sports and dance performances can be viewed as artistic expressions of beauty, emotions, feelings, and internalized values. These and other human movements possess qualities which evoke in observers emotional reactions such as esthetic quality, sensitivity, taste, and beauty. Through "kinesthetic imagery" a person can feel an appreciation, or empathy, for the movements of another as an art form. Sport can be regarded as a performing art. It is different from most art forms in that the actual performance is of the moment; it is fleeting, and when it is concluded it no longer exists. The only way it can be preserved for posterity in its active form is through the medium of the motion picture, videotape or television film. Sports can be referred to as "kinesthetic arts." Metheny* states it succinctly when she says, "My thesis is that the sensory experience of movement is as inherently meaningful as the sensory perception of color, design, and musical sounds."

In order to more fully understand and appreciate the vast potentialities his field has for the esthetic development of students, the physical educator should devote systematic study to basic literature in esthetics, the fine arts, and philosophy. The recent interpretations by physical education and dance specialists likewise should be noted. Cozens and Stumpf[9] reported in the early 1950's that physical education is one of the oldest of the arts of the humanities. It is an anomaly that this realization has been so little attended to in the modern preparation and thought of most physical educators, with the exception of the dance specialists and the human movement theorists.

SOCIOLOGY

Men and women are, biologically, animals with certain basic physiological functions and reactions. Each individual possesses a physiological make-up which can be, and is, studied intensively in relation to individual differences, ability to learn and rate of learning

---

* Eleanor Metheny, *Connotations of Movement in Sport and Dance*, 1965. Dubuque, Iowa: William C. Brown and Co., p. 117.

time, reaction time, and personality differences which are intimately related to motivation and level of aspiration. However, all that man is or does or thinks takes place in a sociological setting. This sociological background, the culture in which he lives, has a very close interrelationship with what sort of animal he is, both physiologically and psychologically. Sociology is the discipline directed toward the study of the history, development, organization, and problems of people living together as social groups. Huelster[14] has identified the specific content in sociology foundational to professional competence in physical education as including "the cultural patterns and systems of action in play and work, competition and cooperation, and the study of populations in geographic areas." The nature of physical education is largely determined by the values, institutions, and social relationships of the particular culture which it serves and which, to some degree, it shapes.

As we consider the sociological foundations of physical education, we are concerned with the insights which the social scientists have contributed to our understanding of the human individual functioning in our particular society. We need to utilize such understandings in planning physical education curricula; in working with individual learners in our classes and in such social groups as competitive teams, activity clubs, community recreation organizations, and adult education groups; and in contributing to the improvement of our society as responsible citizens.

The social scientists focus their investigations on understanding man as a member of a group. They are concerned with studying (1) the structure of his society; (2) the institutions which exist to promote its functioning, such as schools, churches, business organizations, labor organizations, and governments; (3) social class, symbols of social status, and avenues of social mobility; (4) the agencies and techniques for social change; and (5) patterns of living, both within the family group and within the rural, suburban, and large urban communities. They explore and describe the characteristics of American culture as a whole. They also study the infinite variations which characterize particular regional cultures and particular subcultures; e.g., the school within the larger community, selected ethnic groups within a total city population, the factory workers within the overall labor force, or the bowlers as a segment of the sportsmen. They are vitally interested in studying the place of the individual, in the different social groups in which he participates and in his society as a whole. They identify the values exemplified by human behavior in particular cultures and analyze the nature and probable causes and effects of such changing values.

Physical education in all its forms, from the solving of simple movement tasks to highly organized sports and complex dance choreographies, is primarily a cultural product, and must be understood as such, even though its incidence and formal development rest on considerations of a biological and psychological nature. Sociological research is concerned with the problem of seeing physical education and sport in the larger framework of human society. Social scientists have contributed much knowledge that is foundational to improving the conduct of physical education. Physical education research can contribute to increased understandings of certain cultural concepts. A few illustrations of sociological concerns especially relevant to physical educators are mentioned in the following paragraphs.

Our Technological Society

Automation and labor-saving devices have developed at a rapid rate. Automation affects employment by taking a few individuals and giving them responsibilities which require high intelligence and advanced levels of education. These individuals are subjected to increasing stress and anxiety because of the nature of their responsibilities. At the same time, many other persons are working at jobs which demand only a fraction of their human abilities, and for which their schooling is frequently irrelevant. These individuals are subjected to the stresses of boredom, a sense of meaninglessness, and anxiety about their personal roles in the scheme of current society. Still others are unemployed because, for any of several reasons, their job skills and personal characteristics do not match the demands of today's workaday world. Their stresses and anxieties are expressed in apathy, revolt, sickness, and civil disobedience. The children and youth of all of these citizens are in our physical education classes.

Cybernetics has changed the nature and structure of our schools and colleges. It has even changed our techniques of instruction. We have moved from machine-scored examinations and machine-controlled registration and recording procedures to unbelievably diverse teaching machines. We have brought modular scheduling into school administration, programmed learning into the classroom, data retrieval systems into individual study carrels, video tape recorders into the gymnasium, and computers into research design.

The effects of electronic communications upon modern man have been dramatic. Mass media are acknowledged to have brought about profound changes in American society. Marshall McLuhan has popularized a view of mass media as "extensions of man":

> The medium, or process, of our time—electric technology—is reshaping and restructuring patterns of social interdependence and every aspect of our personal life. It is forcing us to reconsider and reevaluate practically every thought, every action, and every institution formerly taken for granted. Everything is changing—you, your family, your neighborhood, your education, your job, your government, your relation to "the others." And they're changing dramatically.[26]

Unbelievably rapid technological advances in our society have changed our schools, our work, our recreation, and even the limits of our world as our scientists continue to penetrate the mysteries of outer space with astonishing speed. The sedentary nature of our work calls for a different kind of physical education in our schools. The great success which sport has achieved in the sphere of mass communication media has led to noticeable changes in leisure-time pursuits. The new horizons of our future world will require significant adaptations in patterns of human movement. The machine systems resources available in our schools should lead to major changes in physical education programs.

Changing Roles of Work and Leisure

Technology has made it possible for fewer workers to produce much more, both in goods and services, to supply the needs and the desires of our population. The fact that less human labor is required to meet the demands of human existence has led to very significant changes in contemporary culture. The average work week in 1900 was 67 hours for farm workers and 56 for those in industry; a work week of less than 40 hours has now become standard. Some predictions suggest a work week reduced to 20 hours within the next decade, a two-hour workday by the end of the century, and the probability that before long our work force will have 200 free days in the year.[29] Clearly we will have more leisure; but it is not so clear that we will learn to use it leisurely.

The United States is traditionally a work-oriented culture. Our society has regarded highly the hard-working individual and has encouraged us to value work as a good in itself. Work has typically been viewed as central in the individual's life. Work is a status symbol in our work-oriented society. Such a value is not consistent with current social conditions. In a society in which unprecedented productivity and abundance do not require a maximum of energy for most of the citizens—in which we have achieved a long-sought goal of considerable free time from the necessity of work—it is far more important that leisure be well used for the improvement of society. It is vital that the best in each person be discovered, and that human capacity for leisure be restored. Only when we recognize that the capacity for leisure and the capacity for work have equal importance and must complement each other will we be able to free the creative energies of our nation for genuine cultural advancement.

Sociologists have identified marked differences in patterns of leisure participation according to socio-economic class, occupational status, or ethnic affiliation. Kraus[19] points out that the poor are automatically prevented from enjoying most of the forms of private or commercial recreation available to the rest of society, that their leisure needs must necessarily be met through organized recreation services provided by government and voluntary agencies, and that these services tend to be inadequate in accessibility and in the variety and quality of the program. In addition to class differences in patterns of leisure participation, leisure activities, notably athletics, sometimes serve as a medium of social mobility.

The culture of the United States today is an anxiety culture which threatens individual significance and individual security. Cassidy stresses the need "for greater self-awareness, for a deeper self-knowledge through a movement literacy and a movement vocabulary, for knowing how to spend energy according to one's tempo and biochemical make-up and ways to find relief from tension and strain."[6] It is quite possible that many individuals will not work at all, in our present sense of work, by the turn of the century. If their lives are to have meaning, and if the nation is to benefit from the best use of time free from work, then leisure must be better understood, and individual and national resources for leisure more thoughtfully developed. Physical education has an important role to play in this process.

Changing Concepts of Social Responsibility

Americans have historically championed free enterprise and their own particular brand of capitalism. The United States has been slower than many other western nations to adopt social welfare programs. The first U.S. Security Law was enacted in 1935; many steps have been taken since that time to adopt measures leading us in the direction of a "welfare state." The GI Bill, which provided educational training for World War II veterans, was a major step toward accepting greater national responsibility for higher education. Sweeping revisions in the 1965 Social Security Law included establishment of a medical care and health insurance program. The Elementary and Secondary Education Act and the Higher Education Act, both enacted in 1965, and the many diverse programs federally financed since, including the Emergency School Aid Act of 1972, are indicative of the changing attitudes of Americans. More and more the American taxpayer is accepting the necessity of a total social responsibility for ensuring the minimum essentials for human dignity and an adequate standard of living to every individual citizen. Proposals for the future, such as a guaranteed annual income not dependent upon employment, suggest that this trend will continue.

It is quite clear that more and more of this responsibility will be assumed by the taxpayers on a national basis, as the federal government's role becomes increasingly greater and the state, local, and private agencies accept distinctive but secondary roles. The problems of the inner city cannot be solved on a local basis. Equal educational opportunity is possible only with a broader base than the local and state governments can provide. Federal funds are essential for any realistic attack on the central problems of poverty in this country.

Current concepts of social responsibility include assigning an increasingly significant role to public education. The civil rights movement and the problems of the disadvantaged continue to play a major role in reshaping the nation's thinking about the nature and function of education in contemporary society. There is a growing consensus that higher education should be made available to all who can benefit from it. Emphasis is being placed on productivity and accountability in the attempt to increase the capacity of the schools, colleges, and universities to meet the increasingly extensive and diverse demands our citizens are placing upon the "educational establishment." More and more is asked of the schools and colleges. Elementary and secondary schools are viewed as key institutions in building a truly integrated society. It is expected that appropriate educational programs will be offered in the future for citizens with all kinds of special needs, from those who are physically handicapped to those who require remedial reading, from the culturally disadvantaged to the overprivileged, from the emotionally disturbed to the intellectually gifted. Colleges and universities are expected to prepare professional leaders for a constantly expanding variety of specializations, and, at the same time, to serve as the common training ground for American adult life. They are expected to provide refresher programs and advanced seminars for alumni and diverse extension services for all segments of the population. They are expected to produce scholarly writings and to conduct research in support of numerous national goals. All of these demands upon public education confront the physical educator, as they do teachers in all fields, with a tremendous challenge to increase the effectiveness of his contribution toward national goals.

Social Disorganization

Certain critics suggest that American society is disintegrating. Few of us view our present status with quite so much pessimism. But there is no question that our present culture embraces some great social problems, and that there are elements of disorganization in our society. Many citizens are expressing profound concern for the U. S. racial situation, for U. S. foreign policy, for corruption in government, for the problems of increasing urbanism, and for new religious elements.

Edward Stainbrook, in discussing the behavioral sciences and the nature of man, asks: "Can societies successfully maintain the risk of organizing for individual creativity and freedom?"[36] Stainbrook raises the question in reference to possible social control of biological action. But it is pertinent to ask whether we also risk social disintegration as we emphasize the value of individual freedom and self-fulfillment.

There is some evidence that one or more characteristics of our

present social organization has led to the alienation of too many individuals from the human essence that is man. We speak of dehumanization, of isolation, of meaninglessness. We note increasing personal withdrawal into delinquency, drug addiction, crime, violence, and suicide.

Social organizations and institutions should be systems for effective human adaptations, changing rather than standing as inflexible realities to which the individual is forced to adjust. Failure to adapt our social arrangements to changing human needs leads to such phenomena as student rebellion and riots of militant civil rights groups. "The task of achieving and maintaining human dignity in the contemporary world is demonstrably much more the problem of managing what goes on between people rather than what goes on inside bodies."[36]

The sociology of the college or university is itself one of the more pressing problems in contemporary education.[36] Youth in secondary schools as well as in higher education appear to be more

164

outspoken, more irresponsible, more independent.[38] Today's students are uncommitted to traditional values, but they are deeply concerned over society's problems and are fighting to feel useful in a world they often find hostile. They have become more international-minded and more socially conscious. Possibly one in ten college students works off-campus in community service projects.[38] In some instances, students have succeeded in becoming a force for social change through the Peace Corps abroad, in picket lines all over the nation, and in political campaigns.

Threats of social disorganization pose a serious challenge to our entire society. Educational institutions are clearly on the firing line. James Billington, Professor of History at Princeton University, made the following statement in discussing student unrest in the tumultuous 1967–68 academic year:

> The American version of the international student upheaval demands not just a new structure, as in Paris, and new politics, as in Prague, but new substance in higher education itself. Our collegiate discontent arises largely among well-fed students in the humanities and the social sciences and is the consequence of a spiritual poverty in academia that, in some ways, is as explosive as the material poverty in the ghetto. . . . The university, as the center of rational criticism in our civilization, has an obligation to become its own most searching critic. . . .[1]

The school represents a social system of its own. Students, teachers, administrators, and non-academic staff members interact with one another as they perform their particular roles within the system. Schools, from the nursery school to the university level, must find ways in which all participants can relate, which will result in greater social integration as well as a higher level of individual need satisfaction. Much social interaction centers on physical skill. Physical education and athletics may serve as common denominators to bring together youth from various social, economic, and ethnic groups.

One recurring sociological phenomenon of particular interest to educators is the cultural lag that always exists between what is actually transpiring in the culture and the means and methods of operation of the social institutions within the culture. This lag exists in the schools as it does in all other institutions. An understanding of the role of the school, and specifically of physical education in our present-day society, will require a fundamental examination of social requirements, social patterns, and social responsibilities. This is urgently needed if educators are to exert leadership in minimizing the cultural lag in modern American society.

Sociology of Sport

Sociology of sport is a relatively recent subdiscipline of sociology.[23] Loy provides a convincing case for sociology of sport as a field of inquiry.[22,23] A major point in his argument is as follows:

> . . . sport is such a pervasive social phenomenon, intruding upon nearly all aspects of daily life, that it deserves sociological attention in its own right. Sport . . . is a social institution having its own distinctive value orientations, important social concerns, modes of interaction, and strategic structural relationships with other significant social institutions.[23]

The relatively uncomplicated social system of sport facilitates examination of "basic social structures and fundamental social processes such as social stratification, socialization, and social change."[23] Loy also makes a strong case for analyzing sport situations to generate significant sociological propositions and for constructing useful models and middle-range theories as well as using sport as a suitable proving ground for trying out sociological instruments and methodologies and testing sociological theories. Sociology of sport may appropriately include the study of sport as a game occurrence, sport as an institutionalized game, sport as a social institution, and sport as a social situation.[22]

Sport sociologists have provided some insights concerning varying aspects of socialization in sport and physical education.[18,34,40] It appears that instructional programs in physical education are not particularly effective in socializing participants in diffuse social roles, but that interscholastic and intercollegiate athletics may achieve more socialization. In analyzing the situational context within which sport activity occurs, it is hypothesized that the most important variables are: (1) the degree of involvement in the activity by the participants; (2) voluntary or involuntary selection and/or participation; (3)

instrumental or expressive socialization relationships; and (4) the prestige and power of the socializer, and the personal and social characteristics of the participants.[34]

ROLE OF PHYSICAL EDUCATION IN SOCIALIZATION

The school is a social institution. It is an agency of the society which supports it, established to maintain, transmit, and improve a particular social order. The children and youth—and in lesser but growing numbers, the adults—who become the students in our schools learn as whole individuals. A holistic view of human development and learning does not allow us to distinguish "social education" from the total educational process, any more than it permits the separation of physical education from "academic education." It is possible, however, to focus on particular educational objectives which are directed toward the development of socially acceptable and personally rewarding behaviors essential to citizens in our democratic society.

The substantive concern of socialization via play, games, and sport is an important one.[22] It is an almost frightening challenge for the school to guide this socialization process in ways which will not limit, but extend, the horizons of self-actualization. The physical educator is a member of a professional team composed of many educators who must coordinate their efforts to provide an environment in which the socialization needed can be achieved and our society changed in the directions desired.

Sociological research supports the general assumption that members of the immediate family are key agents in the socialization process. In the United States, it has been a traditional expectation that the public school should serve to strengthen values developed by the home, church, and other social agencies in the preschool years. All educators in a democracy are responsible for fostering and reinforcing individual value systems which encourage behavior consistent with democratic values. Each individual educator responds to this challenge differently, according to the particular potentialities of his specialization and the uniqueness of his personal style of teaching. The following paragraphs attempt to describe channels for social development which seem to have special import for physical educators.

Valuing Difference

The attitude toward individual differences often distinguishes democracy from autocracy. In a democratic learning environment, students are encouraged to cooperate as unique individuals and yet relate as equal human beings. Erich Fromm[12] points out that most of our efforts toward equality in the twentieth century have resulted ultimately in more conformity and sameness. The educator's task is to help children and youth recognize essential humanness and to relate as equal human beings while guiding them to appreciate and value the uniqueness of each individual.

The physical education class situation, supplemented by intramural and interscholastic athletic programs, provides for a high degree of interpersonal interaction. The movement activities which typify physical education experiences add another dimension to communication among peers. Success in the physical education situation often emphasizes different abilities than does success in the usual classroom setting, thus facilitating the valuing of those individuals whose strongest talents are most clearly evident in motor activities. In every game worthy of the name, situations constantly arise which call for appraisal of the contestant, the teammate, or oneself. Participants can learn to appreciate and give proper credit to the skill and ability of the opponent and the cooperation of a teammate. All of these characteristics of learning opportunities in physical education can be utilized to guide the student in understanding and valuing differences among his classmates.

Sports are a fundamental form of human expression and a basic part of all cultures. Physical education can contribute to understanding other cultures and valuing difference by providing opportunities to experience physical recreation activities of different cultures. Such learning opportunities can be directed toward understanding other subcultures represented within the local school population and other regions of the United States, as well as other national cultures. The teacher's primary concern in planning is to organize the learning activities so that the student, in developing an appreciation of "the other fellow's game," increases his understanding and appreciation of his fellow classmate and of his counterpart in another region or nation.

The growing realization that nations all over the globe are now our close neighbors makes it imperative for all of us to try to understand thoroughly the conditions of life and the attitudes and problems of other nations. Throughout the world, the play life of any people reflects their ideals and their social and economic conditions. Physical education can make a considerable contribution by teaching the history and significance of games, sports, dances, and other physical recreation activities, including the part they have played in the development of nations.

Teachers who would help students learn to relate as equals, yet as unique and different individuals, must learn to create an atmosphere for learning which is cooperative, trusting, friendly, accepting, challenging, and experimental. A democratic climate is basic. In such a physical education climate, learning to value difference can be stimulated by variety in program activities, such as coeducational experiences and games more typical of other cultures; by flexible student groupings, which permit involvement in well-integrated social groups, like effective teams, as well as friendly individual competition and informal group participation with many differing individuals; and by increasing reliance on student leadership and control, which provides better opportunities for personal interaction among students and for unique individual abilities to develop.

Social Responsibility

The individual's responsibility in a democracy goes beyond respect for others and valuing individual differences. Superficial interpretations of such popular and significant educational goals as the pursuit of excellence and individual self-actualization have sometimes led to a deemphasis on social responsibility. But thinking Americans are agreed that an awareness of responsibility toward others and toward society as a whole is increasingly necessary to the maintenance of our free society.

Every society establishes some limitations upon individual behavior in the interests of the public welfare. A basic social responsibility is a willingness to accept properly constituted authority and to respect reasonable limitations set up for the common good. Regulations for governing the behavior of school "citizens" can be seen as parallel to laws for regulating certain interactions of adult citizens. The rules of a game introduced in the physical education class or an athletic contest with students of another school can be viewed similarly. Physical education settings can be useful in guiding students toward a recognition of the role of authority in a democracy, provided learning climate is genuinely democratic, attention is focused on the need for rules and the proper role of officials, and there is satisfying participation for all.

Social responsibility goes beyond respecting properly constituted authority, to desiring to obey the spirit as well as the letter of the law. The concept of sportsmanship has often been extolled as exemplary for interpersonal behavior in broader social contexts. In an analysis of the relationship between play and culture, Johan Huizinga[15] reports:

> Real civilization cannot exist in the absence of a certain play-element, for civilization presupposes limitation and mastery of the self, the ability not to confuse its own tendencies with the ultimate and highest goal, but to understand that it is enclosed with certain bounds freely accepted. Civilization will, in a sense, always be played according to certain rules, and true civilization will always demand fair play. Fair play is nothing less than good faith expressed in play terms.

Accepting his responsibility as a member of the social group requires the individual to be a thinking person who identifies and analyzes problems in rational ways. Aggressive behavior is redirected into constructive, positive means of overcoming obstacles. It is conceivable that problem-solving approaches in meeting movement challenges, and the emphasis on using skillful movement and effective strategy to achieve specific goals of highly organized games, rather than using overwhelming power and strength, can contribute to the development of thinking adults. The leader must not be too quick to solve the problems which confront the learner. Life now demands that the individual display willingness to attack personal problems and a measure of ability to solve them. A play situation in which all the problems and difficulties confronting the student are cleared away by the teacher or leader, without effort on the part of the learner, is not a lifelike situation. The help which the leader offers the student should relate to the technique of problem-solving rather than to the solution itself.

A responsible citizen recognizes his obligation to assist in making his community a better neighborhood, city, or nation. His school physical education experiences should prepare him to accept a share of responsibility for improving facilities for developing fitness in his community, for strengthening local public recreation programs, for increasing opportunities for sound movement education experiences for preschool children, and for giving leadership in social welfare programs utilizing movement skills. A good list of possible course experiences for learning the needed leadership skills is provided by Brown and Cassidy.[4] The future progress of the community, on the local, national, or international level, will inevitably necessitate social change. Education, including those aspects for which the physical educator is responsible, must value change. The teacher and coach should put less emphasis on the "right" way in skill performance, and should open up more opportunities for the individual to solve movement problems, to develop experimental strategies for achieving game objectives, to develop new games and dances, and to express himself through creative movement.

The development of social responsibility through the physical education curriculum requires that a concerted effort be made to arouse and enlist interested cooperation in the projects promoted on the playground. Life in general, under modern conditions, involves interdependence and cooperative effort in large measure. The activities must seem to the learner to belong to the student and to his group rather than to the leader. The learner must not be allowed to feel that all responsibility for the successful conduct of the activities belongs to the leader. The learner must especially feel that to him belongs a large share of the responsibility for the social and moral tone which permeates the play situation. American life calls for such individual assumption of responsibility, and it is highly important that we develop this lifelike quality in the play situation. Brown and Cassidy[4] have offered some excellent suggestions for working toward the development of democratic social skill, including the following:

> In working with this objective, a unit of work or a course, perhaps entitled "Game Theory and Democratic Philosophy" or "Democratic Sportsmanship," would be included in the program. Teacher and students together may well study democratic values as built-in to sports and games. They could well evaluate procedures used in many sports today to help young people identify and realize how games and game values are changed. The students may then try to operate democratically in game situations after taking this class as a specific and clear cut knowledge–laboratory experience. Within such a course students may try to develop new games with built-in contemporary democratic values.*

---

* From *Theory in Physical Education*, Lea and Febiger, p. 160.

The competitive athletic program is often cited for its potential in developing democratic behavior. In a discussion of competition, conflict, and cooperation as social values, Leslie Malpass[28] points out that intergroup competition usually encourages within-group cooperation. He states that competition is a desirable social value when its chief aim is excellence in performance; that conflict typically occurs when rules for competition are disregarded and opponent degradation supersedes striving for excellence; and that intra-group cooperation encourages more effective effort in intergroup competition. The place of competitive sports and athletics in physical education is discussed in more detail in Chapter 10.

Learning Social Roles

Role, in sociological-anthropological tradition, consists of the activity the individual would engage in were he to act solely in terms of the normative demands upon someone in his position.* Role is the basic unit of socialization. It is through roles that tasks in society are allocated, and that arrangements are made for their performance. Individuals learn to play roles expected of them or desired by them. Individuals play different roles in differing social groups; individuals play different roles within a given group at different times; given roles within a particular group are played by different individuals at different times. Socialization encompasses the learning of adequate techniques for playing certain key roles. Games have been analyzed from the standpoint of the various roles to be performed. It is suggested that learning to meet certain selected role expectations in the physical education setting may be of particular value to the individual and to society at large.

The role of *competitor* has probably received the most attention in analyzing the contributions of sports to education in a free society. The competitor is expected to exhibit a strong will to succeed, to persevere in spite of discouragement, to maintain poise and emotional control, and to give his best for the success of the cause, but also to have respect for and to be fair to the opponent.

The *cooperator* is a particularly important role to learn, since variations occur in all areas of group living. The *teammate* is a

---

* Erving Goffman, *Encounters.* Indianapolis: Bobbs-Merrill, 1961, p. 85.

particular role definition of cooperator, but opportunities for developing cooperative behavior need not be limited to formal team experiences. The cooperator is expected to identify his own strengths and make such contributions as he is able to the common effort, giving his best to the cause without considering personal gain or glory.

The *leader* is an essential role in any group activity. Whether the leader is appointed or elected, whether he is actually designated as a leader or simply recognized as such by the group, the group holds certain expectations. The leader is expected to help the group clarify its goals, to maintain sufficient integration for the group to achieve its goals, and to provide means for achieving identity to individual group members. Particular forms of leadership experience common in physical education contexts include team captain, squad leader, and game official.

In guiding students in learning any of these role concepts, the physical educator must give particular attention to providing environments which will reinforce the particular role behaviors which the society values. Unfortunately, the play situation offers equal opportunity for the development of undemocratic role performance, if leadership is inexpert.

One other aspect of role performance should be mentioned in this discussion. Young people growing up in America need to clarify their roles as male or female members of the social group. Many adolescents, both boys and girls, experience considerable difficulty in meeting cultural expectations of masculinity or femininity. Contemporary social philosophy suggests that the idea of masculinity and femininity may not be compatible with democratic values, that we stress humanness rather than masculinity or femininity. In any case, physical educators need to examine their responsibility toward such role expectations as a masculine preference for combative sports, a feminine satisfaction with skill at the novice level, and stereotypes concerning participation of either sex in particular physical recreation activities.

Key Problems

Social development through physical education has long been recognized as a major concern of the curriculum. Yet there is precious little evidence of successful teaching in this respect. Some of the crucial problems which have limited the effectiveness of physical education in this important area should be identified.

To begin with, there is insufficient agreement concerning the specific behaviors to be learned. Considerable confusion and inconsistency exists among the physical education teachers and coaches themselves, reflecting similar confusions in the larger society. Should the game really belong to those who play it? To what degree ought it to be controlled from the sidelines or the stands? What do we really mean by "amateurism"? Must college athletes be amateurs? What constitutes fair play in defensive strategy? Can eligibility rules be enforced so as to provide equal opportunity to all participants? Examples of inconsistency in our ideals and our practices are legion. We cannot expect to influence our students toward desired social standards if we are not clear concerning our own interpretations of these standards in physical education.

Secondly, the available techniques for measuring and evaluating social development are quite unsatisfactory. How do we measure the social qualities of an individual or the progress he is making in socialization? How do we know whether he is learning a love for the activity or a distaste for it as a form of drudgery; whether he is learning respect for authority as represented by a respected teacher or hatred for all authority as represented by an overbearing drillmaster or a brutal football coach; whether he is learning an attitude of fairness toward the opponent in the game or whether his outward conformity to the code only covers an inner determination to take advantage of every favorable opportunity to play "dirty"? Social scientists are developing techniques for evaluating behavioral change, but they are limited in application and are often very difficult to administer. The collection of longitudinal data is crucial in measuring such change, but it is tedious, time-consuming, and expensive.

Perhaps the greatest obstacle to utilizing the school as an agency for social learning is the problem of carry-over or transfer of learning. Even if we can insure that desirable social learnings occur in the physical education class or on the athletic field, how can we be assured that these learnings will be applied outside the school environment, functioning effectively in the everyday life of the student? The transfer of concept learning—and the truly important social learnings must be classified as concepts—involves transfer of learning on the basis of symbolic mediating responses. This usually means verbal mediation and is affected to a large extent by transfer of learning from the subject's past experience.* Transfer is facilitated by making physical education learning situations as lifelike as possible and by teaching for transfer.

Unless teaching is consciously directed toward transfer of learning, no amount of effort to promote right conduct on the playfield can be expected to result in behavioral change of importance beyond the physical education class.

Selected References

1. Billington, James H. "The Humanistic Heartbeat Has Failed." *Life*, 64:32-35 (May 24, 1968).
2. Boyle, Robert H. *Sport—Mirror of American Life.* Boston: Little Brown and Company, 1963.
3. Brim, O. G., Jr. "Socialization through the Life Cycle." In Brim, O.G. Jr., and Wheeler, S. *Socialization after Childhood.* New York: John Wiley and Sons, 1968.
4. Brown, Camille, and Cassidy, Rosalind. *Theory in Physical Education: A Guide to Program Change.* Philadelphia: Lea & Febiger, 1963.
5. Callois, Roger. *Man, Play, and Games*, tr. Meyer Barash. New York: Free Press. 1964.
6. Cassidy, Rosalind F. "The Cultural Definition of Physical Education." *Quest*, IV: 11-15 (April, 1965).
7. Cassidy, Rosalind. "Societal Determinants of Human Movement—The Next Thirty Years." *Quest*, XVI:48-54 (June, 1971).
8. Cowell, Charles C., and France, Wellman L. *Philosophy and Principles of Physical Education.* Englewood Cliffs, N.J.: Prentice-Hall, Inc., 1963.
9. Cozens, Frederick W., and Stumpf, Florence S. *Sports in American Life.* Chicago: University of Chicago Press, 1953.
10. Cratty, Bryant J. *Social Dimensions of Physical Activity.* Englewood Cliffs, N.J.: Prentice-Hall, Inc., 1967.
11. "The Cultural Context of Physical Education." *Quest*, XVI (June, 1971).
12. Fromm, Erich. "The Moral Responsibility of Modern Man." *Merrill-Palmer Quarterly*, 5:3-14 (Fall, 1958).
13. Gray, Miriam. "The Physical Educator as Artist." *Quest*, VII:18-24 (December, 1966).

---

* Arthur R. Jensen, "Individual Differences in Concept Learning." Chap. 9 in *Analyses of Concept Learning* (Klausmeier and Harris, editors). New York: Academic Press, 1966, p. 144.

14. Huelster, Laura J. "The Physical Educator in Perspective." *Quest,* VII:62-66 (December, 1966).
15. Huizinga, Johan. *Homo Ludens: A Study of the Play Element in Culture.* London: Routledge & Kegan Paul, Ltd., 1949.
15a. Husman, Burris. "Sport and Personality Dynamics." *Seventy-Second Proceedings of the National College Physical Education Association for Men.* Washington, D.C.: American Association for Health, Physical Education, and Recreation, 56-69 (1968).
15b. Johnson, Warren, and Hutton, Daniel. "Effects of a Combative Sport Upon Personality as Measured by a Projective Technique." *Research Quarterly, American Association for Health, Physical Education, and Recreation,* 26:49-53 (Dec., 1955).
16. Jokl, Ernst. *Medical Sociology and Cultural Anthropology of Sport and Physical Education.* Springfield, Ill.: Charles C Thomas, Publisher, 1964.
17. Kaelin, E.F. "The Well-Played Game: Notes toward an Aesthetics of Sport." *Quest,* X:16-28 (May, 1968).
18. Kenyon, Gerald S. "Sociological Considerations." *J. Health, Phys. Edu.-Rec.,* 39:31-33 (December, 1968).
19. Kraus, Richard G. "Recreation for the Rich and Poor: A Contrast." *Quest,* V:48-58 (December, 1965).
20. Kroeber, Alfred L., and Kluckhohn, Clyde. "Culture." *Papers of the Peabody Museum,* 1952:47.
21. "Leisure Today: Research and Thought about Children's Play." *J. Health, Phys. Educ.-Rec.,* 43:25-26 (June, 1972).
22. Loy, John W., "The Nature of Sport: A Definitional Effort." *Quest,* X:1-15 (May, 1968).
23. Loy, John W. "A Case for the Sociology of Sport." *J. Health, Phys. Educ.-Rec.,* 43:50-53 (June, 1972).
24. Loy, John W., and Kenyon, Gerald S. *Sport, Culture and Society: A Reader on the Sociology of Sport.* New York: Macmillan, 1969.
25. McIntosh, Peter E. *Sport in Society.* London: C.A. Watts, 1963.
26. McLuhan, Marshall, and Fiore, Quentin. *The Medium Is the Message.* New York: Bantam Books, Inc., 1967.
27. Maheu, Rene. "Sport and Culture." *J. Health, Phys. Educ.-Rec.,* 34:30-32, 49-50, 52-54 (October, 1963).
28. Malpass, Leslie F. "Competition, Conflict, and Cooperation as Social Values." *Values in Sports.* Washington, D.C.: American Association for Health, Physical Education, and Recreation, 1963.
29. Martin, Alexander Reid. "Man's Leisure and His Health." *Quest,* V:26-36 (December, 1965).
30. Metheny, Eleanor. *Movement and Meaning.* New York: McGraw-Hill Book Company, Inc., 1968.
31. Rath, Louis, Merrill, Harmin, and Simon, Sidney B. *Values and Teaching.* Columbus, Ohio: Charles E. Merrill Books, Inc., 1966.
32. Sarbin, T. R., and Allen, V.L. "Role Theory." In Lindzey, G. and Aronson. E., *The Handbook of Social Psychology,* Vol. I. Reading, Mass.: Addison-Wesley Publishing Company, 1969, 491.
33. Singer, R.N., Lamb, D.R., Loy, J.W., Malina, R.M., and Kleinman, S. *Physical Education: An Interdisciplinary Approach.* New York: Macmillan, 1972.
34. Snyder, Eldon E. "Aspects of Socialization in Sports and Physical Education." *Quest,* XIV:1-7 (June, 1970).
35. *Social Changes and Sports.* Washington, D.C.: American Association for Health, Physical Education, and Recreation, 1959.
36. Stainbrook, Edward. "The Behavioral Science and the Nature of Man." *Quest,* III:57-66 (December, 1964).

36a. Sipes, Richard G. "War, Sports, and Aggression." *American Anthropologist,* 75(1):64-86 (Feb., 1973).

36b. Stevenson, Christopher L., and Nixon, John E. "A Conceptual Scheme of the Social Functions of Sport." *Sportwissenschaft,* 2:119-132 (1972).

37. *Students and Society.* Report on a conference. New York: Center for the Study of Democratic Institutions, 1967.

38. "To Keep Pace with America." Editorial, Projects for Education, Inc., 1966.

39. "Toward a Theory of Sport." *Quest,* X (May, 1968).

40. Ulrich, Celeste. *The Social Matrix of Physical Education.* Englewood Cliffs, N.J.: Prentice-Hall, Inc., 1968.

(From Daughtrey, G. Effective Teaching in Physical Education for Secondary Schools. *Philadelphia: W. B. Saunders Co., 1973.)*

Chapter Seven

PSYCHOLOGICAL FOUNDATIONS

Psychology is one of the sciences that study human behavior in order to arrive at a better understanding of man and how and why he functions as he does. Psychologists also study the behaviors of lower forms of animal life because these findings give clues to the study and understanding of human behavior. Furthermore, it is easier to control the conditions of laboratory study under which animals are studied. Basically, psychology is a biological science because its central concern is with the bodily processes which activate and control human activity. The central nervous system is of primary interest although the skeleton, muscles, and endocrine glands are also fundamentally associated with human behavior.

Hilgard and Atkinson[20] outline the major areas of study undertaken by psychologists. Man as a behaving organism is the focus. Stimuli which are received from the external and internal environments, responses which result from brain and central nervous system controls, the movements of the skeleton utilizing power provided by the muscles, and the functioning of the glands all are the province of the researcher in psychology.

Perception, or how an individual discovers and understands his world through his sensory systems as controlled by the nervous system, is another major concern. Growth and development studies focus on the ongoing processes of progressing from a new-born baby to a fully grown adult with emphasis on child development. Physiological maturation is a focal topic of study.

Learning and thinking are areas of research of special interest to psychologists. This topic is discussed in more detail in later pages. Emotion and motivation play central roles in the development of man. Needs of humans are the bases of motivation which in turn give crucial direction to the kinds of behaviors humans adopt as they grow and mature.

Virtually everyone lives in a social environment with other people. Each person is in some way a unique individual unlike any other in the world. He is shaped in this uniqueness by influences of heredity and environment. His personality is distinctive. Each person is a "self." The psychologist is interested in all of these topics.

Because most people live with and among other persons the psychologist is interested in how man relates to other humans, how he reacts in groups under varying conditions, and how his responses differ in social situations as the composition of the group changes. A brief section on social psychology elaborates on these topics later in this chapter.

Finally, the broad concept of the mental health of individuals is important not only to each person but also to the society in which he lives. Conflict, frustration, and "adjustment" are notions of relevance here. Thus, it is apparent that psychology covers a wide span of territory concerning behavioral realms of man in action as an individual and as a member of various social groups.

The physical educator must make continual use of the theories, concepts, and research findings of psychology concerning teaching and learning and the related topics listed above as he attempts to influence individual behavior in consonance with the educational objectives discussed in another chapter. The study of psychology does not provide the teacher with a "bag of tricks" for use concerning a particular instructional problem. Psychology contributes to the educational background of the teacher by: (1) providing information about the conditions which cause human behavior, in order that he can plan learning opportunities to influence student behavior as indicated by the objectives; (2) helping him to classify and assess student abilities and knowledges as a basis for planning and evaluating instruction; and (3) offering insights into methods of research for further investigation of human behavior.

GROWTH AND DEVELOPMENT

Growth and development constitute an area of psychological study of vast importance to physical educators and coaches. Four basic principles form a foundation for detailed analyses of how babies grow and develop into young children, then adolescent youth, and finally into adulthood. (1) In general, the developmental processes are gradual and continuous. There seldom are spurts or plateaus except for speeded up height increases occasionally. (2) Gesell and others have demonstrated that specific forms of human behavior occur in the same order for all children. There is a lawful order to human development. Therefore, a particular child's development at any point in time can be compared with general expectations of all children. (3) Skills, knowledges, and other basic responses develop from the general to the specific. (4) Children tend to have personal qualities or abilities which, in general, are of similar levels. Scientific evidence shows a positive (but low) correlation between qualities and abilities. A major conclusion from recent research is that human beings are the end products of all the experiences they have undergone from date of birth, and also of prenatal influences, for that matter.

Hilgard and Atkinson[20] report twelve conclusions from growth and development research. Of particular interest to physical educators are these concepts. Maturation and learning are the influences which strongly shape the development of human beings. Maturation studies show that human development occurs at an individual rate for each person somewhat independently of environmental influences. However, a necessary level of environmental quality must be present for normal development to take place. There is a constant interplay between environmental quality and maturational readiness to take the next developmental step. Apparently, there are certain time periods when the individual is most receptive (ready) to take on a new behavior form which will facilitate optimal development later on.

Recent studies of human growth and development have brought out facts which call for a complete revision of the older systems of physical education for children. Some of these facts are primarily physiological, while others are psychological or sociological in their significance. The following points may be cited to show the importance of this study.

While it is now generally believed that a normal heart cannot be damaged permanently by exercise, the fact remains that great numbers of children have had their hearts damaged by infectious diseases to the point that strenuous activity is dangerous. This fact calls for cardiac examinations for all children, at regular intervals such as 1st, 7th and 10th grades. There should be careful supervision of programs of activities for those whose physical exertion should be restricted.

Systematic muscular exercise is a factor in the growth, height, weight, and vital capacity of children and youth.[33] Regular physical activity will eventually increase bone density and elasticity of connective tissues, increasing their resistance to stress and strain. Experimental research has demonstrated that muscles which have lost their motor nerve supply atrophy within a period of a few weeks.[26]

It is known that normal children require, for their best growth and development, amounts of physical activity ranging from four to six hours of activity every day. Rarick reports the following:

> Experience has shown that children who lead an active and vigorous childhood have firmer, stronger, and more supple muscles, with sturdier physiques and less adipose tissue than children who follow a more sedentary existence. From the evidence now available it appears that exercise promotes the nitrogen retention and protein-building powers of the body, thus contributing to the effective use of the nutrient supplied to the cells.[32]

Chronological age is known to be a highly unreliable indication of the child's development, needs, or characteristics. Rather, we must take into account the child's mental and physiological ages if we are to deal intelligently with him. Many children are far in advance of others of the same chronological age in such respects as intelligence and physical development, and it is certain that no program of activities will be equally interesting and beneficial to all groups.

Another important fact is the increasing rate of maturity among children in elementary schools today. It is not uncommon for girls of 8.5 years and boys of 9.5 years to have entered the preadolescent period of accelerated growth. American children tend to be taller, heavier, and in better health today than ever before in our history. At the same time, there have not been accompanying increases in muscular strength and physical abilities.

The general morphological characteristics of the individual tend to persist throughout the growing years despite environmental influences, suggesting that inherent factors play a significant role in growth. But observable changes in physical dimensions are not the most important, in any case. The most dramatic effects are those related to skill development, improvements in efficiency and economy of muscular movement, and gains in muscular power and endurance.

Skills appropriate to developing behavioral patterns are most easily acquired. The rate of development is steady even under varying conditions of stimulation. Attempts to speed up the acquisition of a new behavior will fail, or at best be a temporary improvement, if maturational readiness is not present. Imposing premature training can be harmful if it is too intense. A child who is the victim of environmental deprivation or of strong stimulation at an early stage (first two years) of maturation may become somewhat deprived of normal response behavior in later years.

It is not yet verified whether development is primarily continuous or whether major advances occur at somewhat discrete stages. The personality development of the child begins almost immediately after birth as he is taught to conform to the requirements of the culture in which he is raised. Appropriate body contact with parents and other close adults is important in very early emotional and personality development. By the ages of 6 to 10 years children may have developed personality characteristics which can be quite predictive of adolescent, and even adult, behaviors, especially as related to sex-role standards.

H. Harrison Clarke,[7] Espenschade and Eckert,[16] Halverson,[18a] Rarick,[32] and Seefeldt,[35a] among others, are physical education researchers who have specialized in child growth and development with emphasis on physical growth and motor development. Some ideas of importance to physical education teachers and coaches follow.

By the age of three, normal children are able to walk automatically (without conscious thought). From this time on most of the child's physical activities throughout the day involve play. Many specialists consider the child's play to be his most serious business in these formative years. Therefore, proper selection of "appropriate" toys, play materials, and the play environment, both indoors and out, is of great significance.

In later childhood (ages 6 to 10 or 12) growth is relatively slow and constant in trend so energies can be applied to the improvement of basic motor skills which were learned in early childhood and which now need to be adapted and generalized so they can be applied to a wide variety of situations.

Girls mature skeletally faster than boys from birth and achieve physical maturity about two years earlier. Also, the rate of maturity has increased in recent years.

Studies of boys in Little League baseball programs, and also of superior athletes in upper elementary school and junior high school found these subjects to have significantly advanced skeletal ages compared to "non-athletes."

In elementary school boys there is a significant superiority in strength and also in body size. Boys are slightly superior in running and jumping abilities. In general, boys are superior in activities based on strength and gross motor movements. Girls excel in activities requiring finer coordinations. Of course there is great variability in performances of both sexes at all ages and thus there is a considerable area of overlap concerning skill performances of girls and boys at the same age levels.

In adolescence, the physical skills performances of girls tend to level off just before reaching biological maturity, which is three years earlier than skeletal maturity. Boys show continued improvement in skills with increased skeletal maturity. The earlier maturing boy is more likely to excel in physical performances during adolescence than later maturing boys.

Cultural influences are instrumental during the adolescent period in determining the extent to which girls are discouraged from physical activities, or at best treated with indifference, while boys are strongly encouraged and find many types of stimulating rewards for their successful participation.

Finally, in adulthood the greatest variation in human physical performance occurs because of cultural patterns and influences, hereditary factors, socio-economic environment, and years of developing interests, preferences, and antipathies to various forms of physical performance.

As one grows older chronologically there is a decrement in all human physical functioning to some degree. However, evidence indicates that people who have maintained a regimen of an active, physical life tend to decline in physical performance at a slower rate. It is clear that individuals who have learned physical skills in younger years and thus found pleasure in participation develop habits and attitudes which persist into adulthood and result in frequent engagement in pleasurable physical activities in adult years.

NEUROLOGY AND KINESTHESIS

Voluntary and reflexive human movements are controlled and directed by the central and peripheral nervous systems. The physical education teacher and athletic coach should study the basic control mechanisms and how they function as a basis for enlightened instruction of pupils under his direction. Physiology, anatomy, physiological psychology, and kinesiology, among other courses, basically contribute to one's understandings of these highly intricate neural systems.

The central nervous system (CNS) is composed of the spinal cord and the brain which are housed in the skull and vertebrae. Further protection is provided by the cerebrospinal fluid and the ligamentous connections in the spine. Nerve cells are called neurons. The largest portion of the brain (upper portion) is called the cerebrum, which consists of millions of cell bodies (grey matter) rather than neurons. Human thought and conscience reside in the activity of these cells.

The cerebral cortex exerts the highest level of motor control. Responsibility for the control of certain types of motor activity has been identified in regions of the cortex called the motor area and the pre-motor area. These areas control precise voluntary muscular movements. There is also a sensorimotor (or somesthetic) area which controls the basic sensations of touch, pressure, heat, and cold. This area also detects changing spatial relationships of the body and its limbs relative to joint movements and touch sensations.

The mid-brain also is crucial in the control of muscular contractions and appears to regulate movements through its effect on the tonic contraction of muscles.

The hindbrain has three important structures. One of these structures, the cerebellum, coordinates movements which originate in other sectors of the central nervous system. However it cannot initiate movement. It also is involved in the reflex control of bodily balance, or equilibrium, as detected by the inner ear. It apparently coordinates postural movements and locomotor activity. As the body and its segments move in space the cerebellum monitors these constantly changing positions and provides a continuous flow of rapid feedback information concerning the direction and amplitude of these movements. Whenever the body starts to deviate from an intended movement the cerebellum sends out a corrective signal and the body attempts to adjust its movements to its intentions. The cerebellum also anticipates the positions body and limbs will be in within a few seconds and thus alerts the body to sudden danger within a time span sufficient for an attempt to make corrective action to avoid injury or other disaster. Finally, the cerebellum is highly instrumental in the control of bodily equilibrium and coordinates information from the vestibular system, the proprioceptive system, and the visual system.

The brain stem connects the cerebellum and the cerebral cortex which send out motor fibers, and the spinal cord which ascends into the brain stem. It is an integrative area for consolidating all sensory information with motor information. It mediates much of our automatic motor responses, especially postural and locomotor. The brain stem performs other motor functions reflexively with respect to posture and equilibrium.

The spinal cord also contributes to the control of muscular movements. It is a center for reflexes which have been innately developed and which are continuously active as modifiers of human movement. The stretch reflex produces the well known "knee jerk." There are many other types of reflex movements which are controlled at the spinal cord level.

The peripheral nervous system consists of the spinal and cranial nerves and the peripheral part of the automatic nervous system which controls bodily functions not directly concerned with skeletal movement, such as the heart, blood vessels, glandular secretions, and smooth muscles. There are 31 pairs of spinal nerves which enter the spinal column at various levels. They all receive sensory messages from various bodily parts, transmit these messages to the spinal cord, and return a message to the muscles in the area of the original stimulus.

Sage[35] defines kinesthesis as "the discrimination of the positions and movements of body parts based on information other than visual, auditory, or verbal. It is the bodily sense which informs us of the position of bodily segments at any given time, total body position, direction and amplitude of limbs and trunk movements, and configurations of total bodily movement." Sage[35] indicates that "kinesthesia" is the sense of position and movement of the joints. Receptors, called Golgi tendons, are located in the tendons near their muscular origin and also are in the connective tissue of muscles. Whenever the connective tissue or tendons are stretched the resultant pressure acts on nerve endings and causes messages to be relayed to the central nervous system. Pacinian corpuscles are spread throughout the fascia of the muscles and are especially concentrated beneath the tendon insertions to the joints. They are embedded deeply in skin layers. When muscles stretch or contract the nerve endings are stimulated and messages are relayed to the central nervous system. Under the skin lie touch and pressure receptors which also are important to skilled movements. They help to identify the location of limbs, and the position of the body while moving. Some of these neural impulses set off by touch or pressure will result in reflexive movements, others will be transmitted to the cerebellum for integration into complex voluntary movements.

Vision and balance are also important sensory sources of information relevant to reflexive and voluntary movements. It is evident that eyesight is another sensory mode which supplies rapid, fundamental information to the central nervous system as a basis for initiating and controlling physical movements. Likewise, the utricle and the semicircular canals are important sources of information regarding movements. The utricle is sensitive to varying head positions in relation to the force of gravity and helps one to maintain an upright, balanced position. The three semicircular canals, located in the inner ear, monitor rotary movement. Thus, movement in all planes is sensed and this information is relayed to the central nervous system.

Kinesthetic information seldom is acted on by the CNS in isolation; rather, it is combined with information being provided at the same time from other sensory systems. In experiments where kinesthesis and other sensory modalities have been manipulated for combined and partial efficiency of human movement, it was found that reduction in proprioception alone resulted in greater decrement of performance than when any one other sensory system was reduced. It is debatable as to whether or not kinesthesis can be improved with practice. Research results to date are inconclusive. Kinesthesis can be affected by heavy fatigue and muscular tension. Various forms of motivational stimuli do not seem to improve kinesthetic perception.

Probably the outstanding modern discovery about the human mechanism is the new realization of the extremely close integration of the various parts and functions of the body. The highly intricate and effective systems of intercommunication, control, and coordination throughout the human mechanism, having their basis in the nervous system and in the glands of internal secretion, form one of the most amazing, as well as the most significant, phenomena of human life. The new knowledge of the close relationship of every part and function of the body to every other part and function has made it necessary to revise or abandon a great deal of the older theory of education, particularly the theory that it is possible to train or educate acceptably one phase of life entirely apart from any other. We know now that when the individual reacts—when he thinks, feels, or moves —he reacts with his whole mechanism, and not only with some specific part of it, such as the brain, heart, or a muscle group.

This fact makes it necessary for us, in all areas of education, to scrutinize our methods and activities, to determine whether the learning experience is good for an individual as a whole, rather than whether it is good for his mind, muscles, or morals. For we may be sure that any form of education is going to have some effect—good or bad—upon the whole individual, regardless of how specifically it is aimed at a particular part of that individual. In view of these facts, physical education can no longer be looked upon as purely muscular training or "physical training." Every muscular movement sets up reactions which ultimately influence, in some measure, the whole living mechanism. It is easy to see that fatigue may lessen mental keenness, cause "round shoulders," or cause the individual to fall asleep in church; a headache may come from fallen arches, the ballplayer may fumble or strike out because he is angry, or he may be angry because he strikes out; a missed golf shot in a bunker may spoil the day for the whole family; an attack of indigestion may have its beginning in a too-difficult assignment in mathematics.

LEARNING THEORIES

Many specific subjects studied by psychologists have direct relevance to teaching and learning in physical education, and this section briefly discusses some of them. Because scientists do not know in absolute terms the answers to such questions as how the brain works, how muscles contract, or how nerve fibers conduct impulses, psychological theories should be regarded as hypotheses.

"Bond" Psychology. In the past, theories of teaching and learn-

ing skills in complex muscular activities were mainly based upon the "bond" psychology and the "Laws of Learning." Exponents of these theories believed that a skill has been learned when we have, by repetition, established certain paths and connections in the nervous system so that the nerve impulses unfailingly pass over these particular pathways and stimulate the appropriate muscles, and when we have so trained the nervous system by practice it becomes perfect in the control of the timing and intensity of the nerve impulses.

It is argued that the acquisition of skills is a process of trial and error in the beginning. Out of the large number of more or less uncoordinated muscular movements involved in our early attempts, we tend to retain and practice further those which seem to make for success and satisfaction, at the same time discarding those elements of the performance which seem not to lead to success. Then we try still other movements, and the above process is repeated. Out of this building-up process, we eventually hit upon a fortuitous combination of proper timing, regulation of intensity, and direction of nerve impulses which results in the most effective accomplishment of the motor act. The satisfaction of this way of doing tends to cause us to repeat it. The remainder of the process of acquiring a skill or a coordination is a matter of trying to repeat (practice) this exact way of reacting without variation until the whole process is so thoroughly ingrained in the nervous system (overlearned) that it becomes automatic. Assumptions about ingraining messages in exact paths in the nervous system have been discredited in recent years.

Behaviorism. Behaviorist or "conditioning" psychology, which developed somewhat later than the "bond" psychology, abandons all theorizing about how the "mind" works or about what goes on in the nervous system during the process of learning. Its chief qualification as a truly scientific system lies in the fact that it draws conclusions from experimentation, and observations of behaviors, and that these conclusions can be examined by other scientists. Its most significant conclusion is that learning is a process of conditioning, meaning that people learn to behave in specific ways as a result of associating these ways of behaving with particular kinds of stimuli and with rewards or reinforcements. The conditioning theory is one of the basic assumptions underlying the use of teaching machines and programmed instruction. It is discussed in more detail in Chapter 3.

Gestalt Theory.   The Gestalt or organismic psychologists believe that learning is not a trial-and-error process. Practice in the usual sense of the word does not enter into the procedure, for connections and pathways fixed in the nervous system by practice do not exist, and skill is never automatic. On the other hand, even the most uncoordinated responses to any situation are not random or experimental movements. The movements may be "undifferentiated," but taken together they represent the effort of the total human organism attempting to reach a goal (for instance, a perfect shot to the eighteenth green) by the "shortest route"—the "Law of Least Action." We never actually practice, because we never perform the act exactly the same way twice. If we actually practiced the act, we could never improve, because we should always be doing it in the same imperfect way. The improvement attributed to practice—repetition of the act— is really due to increasing insight or understanding of the total situation or "stimulus pattern." Increased skill is attained through the "structuralization" of the whole to the different parts—the learning process consists of "differentiation" of the whole from the parts, rather than the addition of the parts to produce the whole. The degree of skill is dependent not upon amounts of exercise or practice, but upon the degree of "insight." Coordination in an athletic skill represents not an automatic functioning of the nervous system, but an improved "conceptual configuration" or understanding of the total situation. The coordinated response is "configurational," because the individual, functioning as an integrated unit, has arrived at the goal (possibly a home run into the right-field stands) by the shortest possible route.

Comparison of Theories.   Thus all schools of psychologists meet again at the starting point, which was, "How is skill in complex movement activities improved, and how do we help the learner to improve?"

In respect to the method by which we develop skills (coordinations) in complex muscular activities, the theories of psychology seem at first sight to be irreconcilable. One school would build up coordinations by the gradual addition of new elements of learning to what has been acquired, so that ultimately one perfects the whole skill; this is in accord with the Law of Exercise and the Law of Effect and is an accumulation process. Another (organismic) would arrive at the same skill by taking the whole or total reaction of the

beginner, awkward and uncoordinated as it is, eventually refining the response through a process of helping the learner to gain "insight" or understanding of the total situation, so that ultimately the coordination becomes perfected.

The first method calls for practice in the activity. The second denies that we learn by practice, since in learning we improve by doing the act differently each time. But to the physical educator, it is apparent that "practice" in some sense of the word is necessary in either procedure—in the one case to strengthen the connection between the situation and the correct responses, and in the other to help the learner to gain the necessary insight or understanding which we have always thought of as "getting the hang of the thing" or "getting the feel of it."[11]

A comparison of these theories of the learning process implies mainly that the physical educator should scrutinize his methods, to determine whether his students have been "practicing" in a purposeful manner and whether he has been helping them sufficiently to attain a thorough understanding of all phases of the situation, including the activity itself; for it is apparent that mere repetition does not guarantee progress. What is going on in the neurons and synapses is none too certain, but this knowledge is not so essential to the teacher as the assurance that he is lending efficient assistance to the student engaged in learning.

Chapter 3 reconciles the elements of current theories of learning which seem to be most adequately supported by research evidence. That chapter states four broad generalizations which describe how an individual is "educated," or how he "learns." A review of those four generalizations would be useful in summarizing and integrating current views about the psychology of learning.

PERCEPTUAL-MOTOR LEARNING

Current psychological theory seeks to understand man in dynamic terms. We now look at human beings, not through the eyes of an outsider only, but also in terms of how things look from the behaver's own point of view.[40] The perceptual view holds that the behavior of an individual is a function of his ways of perceiving. In the words of Arthur W. Combs:

> Modern perceptual psychology is helping us to see the problem of learning in a somewhat different way. Learning, we are coming to understand, is not simply a matter of motivation, repetition, presentation, stimulation, conditioning, and the like, although, of course, all of these things are part of the problem. Learning, we are coming to understand, is a problem of total personality. It is a problem of an individual's total discovery of meaning.[40]

Perception is "man's awareness of sensory stimuli, his attention to them, and the meaning he attaches to them."[5] It is frequently noted that, although two individuals may observe the same measurable reality, they perceive it differently. The individual's perception is discriminatory, depending upon his past experience, present state of attention, emotion, and other sensory stimuli. Movement is one medium through which his perception can be extended. The teacher can help him to broaden his perception through making available experiences which are appropriately challenging.

From the moment of birth the infant begins to learn about his external world through his sensory systems. His experiences are transmitted to the central nervous system in the form of sensations (sight, sound, smell, pressure, balance, etc.). These sensations are received at various levels in the central nervous system and are stored for further reference by a process of classification which converts them into perceptions. Perceptions give meaning to individual instances of incoming sensate data. A process of mediation occurs which converts specific sensory inputs into meaningful perceptions. Perceptions, in turn, are organized into concepts. Concepts range from highly concrete to broadly abstract. The individual continually uses his store of perceptions and concepts as data for generating responses to stimuli he receives both from his internal and external environments.

All of the sensory systems monitor the child's environment and relay messages to the central nervous system to keep him informed of all that is transpiring around him. The sensory systems involved are:

> auditory—hearing
> visual—seeing
> kinesthetic—spatial awareness
> bodily position
> muscle stretch
> olfactory—smelling
> gustatory—tasting
> tactile—touch
> vestibular (inner ear)—balance.

Perceptual abilities are developed with experience. Movement is very important in enabling the individual to develop a wide repertoire of perceptual abilities. On the other hand, voluntary human movements necessarily involve some degree of perceptual awareness and information provided by the sensory system. The more accurate the perceptions, the more likely the individual is to evoke successful, coordinated motor acts. Thus, there is a continuous reciprocal relationship at work between the incoming perceptual information and outgoing messages guiding voluntary motor acts. A rapid feedback system operates to keep the stimulus sources cognizant of the degree of congruence at any given time between the perceptions and the motor responses thereto. The central nervous system utilizes this feedback information to correct errors in movement in order to assist the person to more accurately perform a motor task at hand.

All voluntary motor performances are basically *perceptual-motor acts.*

In recent years, specialists in early childhood education, psychologists, optometrists and other specialized physicians, and physical educators have become interested in the study of perceptual-motor development, both for normal children and for those with learning disabilities which appear to be related to perceptual deficiencies. A major theoretical construct which underlies this work is that a fundamental motoric development in the first six years of life is basic to eventual, normal, perceptual and conceptual development.[30] If the child's gross motor learning experiences are inadequate or incomplete or delayed in developing, he may not be able to perform adequately perceptual tasks in his daily school work in English, reading, arithmetic, and other basic subjects.

There are various perceptual-motor screening tests[1] available to assess a child's status administered usually in the kindergarten or first grade, although such tests can be given whenever the teacher sees behavioral indications which suggest the need for an evaluation. Likewise, there are perceptual-motor training programs which can be administered individually, or to groups of children, for the avowed purpose of helping them to "make up" perceptual deficiencies incurred in earlier years. Examples of perceptual-motor skills emphasized in these tests and programs include directionality, laterality, depth-perception, spatial discrimination, balance, time-awareness, manipulative skills, and locomotor activities. Many physical educators maintain that physical education programs in the elementary school are in reality perceptual-motor programs.

Numerous elementary classroom teachers, physical education teachers and consultants, and reading specialists have become acquainted with the various perceptual-motor training programs now available, and have hopefully employed them in an attempt to improve the reading skills of children who score well below the age norm on reading tests. Other adults hope that such programs will improve spelling, handwriting, and arithmetic skills. Unfortunately, research to date has not demonstrated conclusively that such programs will necessarily result in improvement in these academic skills by all or most of the children involved.

Many elementary school physical educators *believe* that a broad based program of movement education, adapted to the individual capabilities of each child, can contribute significantly to the more rapid development of perceptual-motor abilities, as well as help to make up motor deficiencies incurred in earlier years.

LEARNING MOTOR SKILLS

The concept of behavioral loops is now being used to emphasize that a measurable unit of motor performance depends upon both external and internal events. The human being acts as a self-correcting mechanism, constantly adjusting to changes in his external and internal environment. Perception and motion are inseparable units of behavior. In learning a motor skill, the learner typically depends upon the sensory feedback of an external visual-motor loop. As he becomes more highly skilled, more dependence is placed upon the internal loops involving kinesthetic feedback. Research is providing more information concerning the effects of feedback in motivating, regulating, and reinforcing human behavior. Such research contributes to the physical educator's understanding of how to utilize knowledge of performance and of results as factors in increasing the rate and accuracy of learning.

Physical practice is essential to skill learning. In order to retain that which is practiced, there must be overlearning, to the point of automatic action. Repeated practice under differing conditions leads to consistency of performance in varying situations.

The teacher's role is to short-cut the learning process. An essential part of this role is to provide external cues, to stimulate the internal cues, and to help the student develop a clearer concept of the movement problem to be solved. These cues may be verbal, visual, or manual. They can help to elicit an automatic movement pattern, but the pupil must also perceive, think, and plan during instruction if he is to learn successfully. Stereotyped movement response is particularly to be avoided when the objective is movement exploration, kinesthetic awareness, or self-expression through movement.[26]

Motivation is necessary for learning. The learner must focus his efforts on a well-defined goal if learning is to result. Personal involvement is essential. There must be a need which drives the learner into action. The behavior which results from that need may then be directed by some type of incentive. The teacher or coach can influence learning through the use of such incentives.

Transfer among learning episodes has always been of concern to students of the learning process. Planned instruction has little justification unless we can expect that what the student learns in school will have some effect upon his behavior in situations beyond the formal curriculum. Klausmeier and Ripple,[22] Clayton,* and other psychologists suggest ways in which learning can be structured to facilitate transfer as follows:

1. Through identical elements. These may be identical in terms of facts or information, skills, methods, or principles of organization.

2. Through principles or generalizations from one learning situation or organized system that apply to other situations.

3. Through conscious efforts to perceive relationships and to make applications of any learning.

4. Through developing an active intention to transfer or an attention to transferable phases.

5. Through greater stress on divergent thinking, open systems, or creative thinking that enhances transferability or decreases the rigidity of boundaries.

There is a rapid accretion of research reports, magazine articles, and books by motor learning specialists appearing on the professional scene around the world. Likewise, there is a recognized core of literature on the general topic of skill learning. Selected references on both of these topics are included at the end of this chapter.

A considerable variety of phenomena are investigated in motor learning research. Teachers and coaches constantly are seeking instructional hints from the findings of these studies. Examples of areas of research are: ability grouping, class size, motivation, goal perception, whole versus part learning, modeling and demonstration, degree of difficulty, non-directed practice, programmed learning, verbal assistance, motor plans, speed and accuracy variables, physical assistance, open and closed skills, knowledge of performance and of results, types of feedback, learning plans, mental practice, massed and spaced practice, and use of drills.

---

* Thomas E. Clayton: *Teaching and Learning: A Psychological Perspective.* Englewood Cliffs, New Jersey: Prentice-Hall, Inc., 1965, p. 87.

A review of recent motor learning studies reveals some clues for teachers and coaches to consider as they plan and conduct their instruction. Motor learning research is not yet conclusive enough to tell the teacher "how to teach" in any prescriptive sense. Tentatively, the following findings seem to be worthy of the teacher's consideration.

A given amount of school time can be divided in different ways throughout a week (i.e., three days per week, or five days per week) without affecting the results of the instruction. Teachers who are more knowledgeable about the skill they are teaching and who themselves are more highly skilled in it seem to be more effective instructors and this correlation increases as the complexity of the skill increases. Provide the students with equipment and mechanical aids which permit a larger number of "tries" and improved learning may accrue. There are some indications that larger class size ultimately results in lower skill achievement. Research to date does not support the notion of skill ability grouping.

It seems to make little difference whether classes are segregated by sex or not. One of the strongest indications from a substantial number of research studies is that some form of whole learning is superior to part or progressive-part methods. It appears that there are a variety of progressions which can be employed with equal success in teaching the development of a complex motor skill. A few studies suggest that a student can learn effectively through self-study. Knowledge of abstract principles of motor skill performance does not correlate significantly with increased skill learning. The teacher should emphasize accuracy in the instruction if accuracy is the most important element. Likewise, concentrate on speed if speed is the crucial variable in the skill. When accuracy and speed are of relatively equal importance have the pupil practice under actual performance conditions.

Perhaps the strongest evidence exists to support the belief that feedback to the learner, both from internal and external sources, is the single most effective variable which aids motor learning. Imaginary performance has been found to be positively correlated with gains in learning.

The above listing is indicative of the diversity of variables which researchers have investigated in recent years in an effort to throw light on how people learn complex motor skills. Refer to current motor learning texts for full coverage of this subject.

SOCIAL PSYCHOLOGY

Social psychology is the study of the behavior of groups of people. Interactions between groups, between an individual and the group, and between individuals in the group are of interest to the social psychologist. As the name implies, he uses the research methodologies of both psychology and sociology.

The physical education class, the sport team, and the dance group are social organizations within which teachers and coaches spend most of their instructional energies and time. They also are members of, and work with, other groups in school and out, such as the school faculty, the PTA, the departmental staff, professional organizations, booster clubs, service clubs, and similar groups. Thus, it behooves the physical educator to learn all he can about the principles of group behavior so that he is better able to provide optimal learning and social environments for his pupils. He also needs to understand that each student is a member of various social groups such as the family, his peer group friends, the neighborhood, an ethnic group, a recreational club and so on. Each group makes its own special demands on its members, both implicitly and explicitly. Group "pressures" can be very powerful influences on the motivations and behaviors of young people. Understanding teachers should be cognizant of the existence of these influences and appreciate their importance. Finally, the teacher needs to recognize that he, too, is subject to pressures from the groups he belongs to and that there are times when he has difficult personal or professional decisions to make because of the pressures.

The behaviors of social groups exert powerful influences on the types of physical activities young people elect to engage in as well as the degree of skills they are able or desirous of attaining. Friends, parents, coaches, spectators, and others are examples of sources of influence. Numerous studies have indicated that high skill levels in physical performances are related to general social approval of peers, especially with respect to boys from 10 to 14 years of age. The relationship does not seem to be so strong in the case of girls, or of boys at other age levels.

There is some evidence that boys and girls with marked deviations from the norm in height, weight, and general body structure (thin, or obese) tend to be associated with low self-concept and poor body image. On the other hand, students who are "well built" frequently are looked upon as capable and dependable.

Cooperation and competition describe important behaviors taught by physical education teachers and coaches. Group influences can be powerful socializers with respect to these behaviors which are discussed in more detail in the chapter on competitive athletics.

Cratty* has chronicled the role of the family in shaping attitudes toward, and providing opportunities for, participation in physical activities:

> The efforts of the child are continually evaluated by the parents, and as a result his relative need for subsequent achievement is molded. Socioeconomic status and race also influence the child's opportunity for proficiency in physical activity.
> The child's parents influence both his inclination for physical activity and his proficiency in various physical skills.

One of the most renowned studies of the influence of sports on high school boys was conducted by Coleman in mid-west high schools several years ago. Although we cannot be certain that he would find similar results if he were to replicate his study today, an abstract of it is noteworthy in highlighting the extreme importance which young high school students have attached to interscholastic sports in the schools studied. Similar situations are frequently attested to even today by teachers and coaches across the country. Coleman** summarizes:

> Research—based on the visibility of athletic stars, on most desired achievement, on the composition of the leading crowd, on status criteria in leading-crowd membership, on popularity—demonstrates conclusively that athletics is far and away more important as a value among high school students than intellectual achievement. And the school itself seems to encourage rather than discourage this relative evaluation. There must be basic reasons for these phenomena, and these may be discerned in the functions performed by athletics not only in the school but also in the community. Among boys, for example, it has been found that athletics has a democratizing effect, break-

---

* Bryant J. Cratty. *Social Dimensions of Physical Activity.* Englewood Cliffs, New Jersey: Prentice-Hall, Inc., 1967, p. 100.

** James S. Coleman, "Athletics in High Schools," *Annals of the American Academy of Political and Social Science,* November, 1961, 33-43. Reprinted in *Sport and American Society,* George H. Sage, Editor, Reading, Mass.: Addison-Wesley Publishing Company 1970, p. 84.

ing up organization based on background and reconstituting it on the basis of common activity or achievement. Athletics serve an important function in motivating students. It generates strong, positive identification with the school; without athletics the school would be lifeless for the student, deficient in collective goals. With athletics, it is possible for all students to identify with their teams. Not only schools but whole communities depend upon the collective enthusiasm generated by their local high school athletic teams.

Social psychologists conduct research using a variety of methodologies such as laboratory and field, correlational and experimental, individual and survey, and archival and observational. Many findings of the studies of social psychologists are relevant to the work of the physical education teacher and athletic coach. Young researchers in physical education are electing to receive doctoral training in social psychology in order that they may investigate phenomena of interest to them in the settings of dance, sport, designed exercise, aquatics, and other activity areas in physical education programs.

Some of the important behaviors of man and his social groups, and related phenomena, of interest to the physical educator and coach are:

1. affiliation, or the extent to which man is gregarious either by genetically determined characteristics, or by dependency necessity;

2. how people form impressions of others;

3. the extent to which people like each other as basic to personal interaction;

4. aggression, or concern for behavior that is aggressive and also for aggressive feelings and the relationship of frustration and annoyance to aggression;

5. how individuals function in social groups, including communication methods, the emergence of informal and formal leaders, the power of the leader, and the leader's influence on the group;

6. conformity and adaptive behaviors, trust, deviancy, security, anonymity, self-esteem;

7. group dynamics, including social facilitation, cooperation and competition, incentives, threats, motivation, group problem solving, group cohesion, deindividuation;

8. social forces which influence an individual's behavior, such as external pressure, situational pressure, and social justice;

9. cognitive dissonance;

10. attitude formation and change.

This partial listing of important behaviors of individuals and groups will readily reveal self-evident applications to teaching and coaching objectives, to instructional methodologies employed, and to individual and group evaluation responsibilities teachers must shoulder. There is a growing physical education literature which is including more and more of these topics and their relevance to individuals and groups involved in the physical education setting. Selected references at the end of this chapter are provided to guide the interested reader.

Selected References

1. *Annotated Bibliography on Perceptual-Motor Development*. Washington, D.C.: American Association for Health, Physical Education, and Recreation, 1972.
2. Berlin, Pearl and Gentile, A. M. (eds.): "Skill Learning and Performance." *Res. Quart., Am. Assoc. Health, Phys. Educ., and Rec.*, 43, Washington, D.C. (Oct., 1972).
3. Bilodeau, Edward A. (ed.): *Acquisition of Skill*. New York: Academic Press, 1966.
4. Bloom, B. S. "Mastery Learning." In J. H. Block (ed.): *Mastery Learning, Theory and Practice*. New York: Holt, Rinehart and Winston, Inc., 1971.
5. Breckenridge, Marian E., and Vincent, E. Lee: *Child Development: Physical and Psychologic Development Through Adolescence*. Philadelphia: W. B. Saunders Company, 5th ed., 1965.
6. Brown, Camille, and Cassidy, Rosalind: *Theory in Physical Education: A Guide to Program Change*. Philadelphia: Lea & Febiger, 1963.
7. Clarke, H. Harrison: *Nature and Extent of Individual Differences and Their Significance for Physical Education and Athletics*. Eugene, Ore.: Oregon School Study Council, School of Education, University of Oregon, 1967.
8. Cratty, Bryant J.: *Intelligence in Action: Physical Activities for Enhancing Intellectual Abilities*. Englewood Cliffs, N.J.: Prentice-Hall, Inc., 1973.
9. Cratty, Bryant J.: *Movement Behavior and Motor Learning*. Philadelphia: Lea & Febiger, 2nd. Ed., 1967.
10. Cratty, Bryant J.: *Psychology in Contemporary Sport: Guidelines for Coaches and Athletes*. Englewood Cliffs, N.J.: Prentice-Hall, Inc., 1973.
11. Cratty, Bryant J.: *Teaching Motor Skills*. Englewood Cliffs, N.J.: Prentice-Hall, Inc., 1973.
12. Cronbach, L. J.: "Comments on Mastery Learning and Its Implications." In. E. W. Eisner (ed.): *Confronting Curriculum Reform*. Boston: Little, Brown and Company, 1971.
13. Cronbach, Lee J.: *Educational Psychology*. New York: Harcourt Brace Jovanovich, Inc., 2nd ed., 1963.
14. Dunham, Paul, Jr.: "Learning and Performance." *Res. Quart., Am. Assoc. Health, Phys. Educ., and Rec.*, 42:334-337 (Oct., 1971).
15. *Early Childhood Education*, Part II, Seventy-first Yearbook National Society for the Study of Education. Chicago: The University of Chicago Press, 1972.

16. Espenschade, Anna S., and Eckert, Helen M.: *Motor Development*. Columbus: Merill Books, 1967.
17. Fitts, Paul M., and Posner, Michael I.: *Human Performance*. Belmont, Calif.: Brooks/Cole Publishing Company, 1967.
18. Frost, Reuben B.: *Psychological Concepts Applied to Physical Education and Coaching*. Reading, Mass.: Addison-Wesley Publishing Company, Inc., 1971.
18a. Halverson, Lolas E. "The Young Child . . . The Significance of Motor Development," *The Significance of the Young Child's Development*. Proceedings of a conference sponsored by the AAHPER and the National Association for the Education of Young Children. Washington, D.C.: NAEYC, 1971.
19. Higgins, Joseph R.: "Movements to Match Environmental Demands." *Res. Quart., Am. Assoc. Health, Phys. Educ., and Rec.* 43:312-336. (Oct., 1972).
20. Hilgard, Ernest R., and Atkinson, Richard C.: *Introduction to Psychology*. New York: Harcourt, Brace, Jovanovich, Inc., 5th ed., 1971.
21. Kane, John Edward (ed.): *Psychological Aspects of Physical Education and Sport*. Boston: Routledge and Kegan Paul, 1972.
22. Klausmeier, H. J., and Ripple, Richard E.: *Learning and Human Abilities: Educational Psychology*. New York: Harper & Row, Publishers, Inc., 3rd ed., 1971.
23. Lawther, John D.: *The Learning of Physical Skills*. Englewood Cliffs, N.J.: Prentice-Hall, Inc., 1968.
24. Lawther, John D.: *Sport Psychology*. Englewood Cliffs, N.J.: Prentice-Hall, Inc. 1972.
25. "Learning Models and the Acquisition of Motor Skills." *Quest*, XVII, Winter, 1972.
26. LeWinn, Edward B.: *Human Neurological Organization*. Springfield: Charles C. Thomas, Publisher, 1969.
27. Lockhart, Aileene: "Conditions of Effective Motor Learning." *J. Health, Phys. Educ.-Rec.*, 38:36-39 (February, 1967).
28. Martens, Rainer: "A Social Psychology of Physical Activity." *Quest*, XIV, 8-17 (June, 1970).
29. Morgan, William P.: *Contemporary Readings in Sport Psychology*. Springfield, Ill.: Charles C Thomas, Publisher, 1970.
30. Piaget, Jean: *The Origins of Intelligence in Children*. New York: W. W. Norton & Company, Inc., 1969.
30a. Posner, Michael, and Keele, Steven W.: "Skill Learning," *Second Handbook of Research on Teaching*. Travers, R. M. W. (ed.). 805-831. Chicago: Rand McNally Company, 1973.
31. "The Psychology of Sport and Physical Activity." *Quest*, XIII:1-83 (Jan., 1970).
32. Rarick, G. Lawrence: "Exercise and Growth." From Johnson, Warren R. (ed.): *Science and Medicine of Exercise and Sport*. New York: Harper & Row, Publishers, Inc., 1960.
33. Rarick, Lawrence (ed.): *Physical Activity: Human Growth and Development*. New York: Academic Press, 1973.
34. *Recreation and Physical Activity for the Mentally Retarded*. Washington, D.C.: American Association for Health, Physical Education, and Recreation, 1966.
34a. Rushall, Brent S., and Siedentop, Daryl: *The Development and Control of Behavior in Sport and Physical Education*. Philadelphia: Lea and Febiger, 1972.
35. Sage, George H.: *Introduction to Motor Behavior: A Neuropsychological Approach*. Reading, Mass.: Addison-Wesley Publishing Company, Inc., 1971.
35a. Seefeldt, Vernal: "Concerns of the Physical Educator for Motor Development," *Foundations and Practices in Perceptual Motor Learning—a Quest for Understanding*, Robb, Margaret D. (ed.). Washington, D.C.: AAHPER, 1971.
36. Singer, Robert N.: *Coaching, Athletics and Psychology*. New York: McGraw-Hill Book Company, Inc., 1971.
37. Singer, Robert N.: *Motor Learning and Human Performance*. New York: The Macmillan Company, 1968.

38. Smith, Hope M.: "Implications for Movement Education Experiences Drawn from Perceptual-Motor Research." *J. Health, Phys. Educ., Rec.*, 41:30-33 (April, 1970).
39. Steinhaus, Arthur H.: "Your Muscles See More Than Your Eyes." *J. Health, Phys. Educ.-Rec.*, 37:38-40 (September, 1966).
40. "A Symposium on Motor Learning." *Quest*, VII:1-89 (May, 1966).
41. Torpey, James E.: "Motor-Perceptual Development and Physical Education." *The Physical Educator*, 28:11-12, March, 1971.
42. Wasserman, Burt: "New Directions in Physical Education Skill Acquisition." *The Physical Educator*, 29:135-137 (Oct., 1972).
43. Whiting, H. T. A.: "Overview of the Skill Learning Process." *Res. Quart., Am. Assoc. Health, Phys. Educ., and Rec.*, 43:266-294. (Oct., 1972).

(From Daughtrey, G. Effective Teaching in Physical Education for Secondary Schools. *Philadelphia: W. B. Saunders Co., 1973.)*

Chapter Eight

BIOLOGICAL FOUNDATIONS

Biological research verifies that life in any form must consist of at least the functions of *irritability* (response to stimuli), *motility* (movement), *self-regulation* (control), and *reproductivity* (multiplication). A living organism is distinguished from inorganic matter because of its ability for purposive development and the continuance of structure-function organization. In other words, the living organism is characterized by creativeness and an ability to direct its development or evolution. Homeostasis, or continuous self-direction and maintenance, is the basic drive of the organism. It seeks to progress from its innate potentialities to a degree of self-fulfillment, or "self-actualization," to use Maslow's term.

Moreover, biological research supports the crucial concept of "cooperation" between like organisms. The common notion of "survival of the fittest" and the elimination of the weak members of a species, drawn from a simplification of Darwinian evolutionary theory, has been contraindicated. Aggression does exist in various forms in nature. So do some acceptable styles of competition. But, in addition, it is now supported by substantial evidence that *cooperation* is the strongest drive of all in a biological sense. It is postulated that human development relies more heavily on this principle than on any other one as an explanation of evolution. The principle of cooperation likewise is fundamental in all non-human forms of life which survive and evolve.

The evolutionary principle of "natural selection" is explained by the cooperation principle which states that organisms are most likely to survive and develop in relation to their ability to work together among themselves, and with their physical environment, to facilitate their chances for survival. Competition also is a major factor in the struggle for survival and interestingly enough it seems likely that one competitive group may be more successful than another in its fight for existence to the extent that it engages in higher levels of cooperative activity.

Finally, biological evidence suggests that all forms of life, even the lowest forms, are possessed of some innate tendency toward social relationship. In all probability there is no such thing as a completely asocial organism.

With this brief introduction to complex biological phenomena the following observations on the evolving human species are of significance to the physical educator.

Human biology teaches that man is by nature a creature who must have sunshine, fresh air, interesting physical and mental activity, and a fair opportunity for expression of his inherent tendencies and emotions. Failing to attain these age-old necessities, man fails to grow, develop, or flourish to the maximum of his potential.

The study of evolution also establishes the principle that man is the dominant creature on earth because he is a "generalized" rather than a "specialized" animal. The primary physical asset of man is his erect posture. With this great advantage, including the freedom of use of his hands, man evolved with a steady enlargement of the brain tissue and a corresponding improvement of intellectual power. Then he developed language, and the ability through speaking and writing to transmit knowledge and ideas to his fellow man and to later generations. The discovery and control of fire further differentiated man from all other animals. Then, man developed his tool-making ability. He is the only organism with spiritual beliefs which guide his conduct, and he alone holds a philosophy of immortality.

Physical educators in particular should realize that all too frequently modern man has been thought of as weak, slow, unprotected, unable to fly, and physically inferior to many other animals. His progress has been achieved almost entirely because of the development of his higher rational powers. Actually, evidence indicates that man is a giant among animals. Only a small number of animals are faster, larger, or stronger. Man has the natural ability to kill a large majority of more than one million species of animals on earth, without resorting to the weapons he has invented for the destruction not only of such animals, but also of his fellow man. Man has greater ability to modify and control his environment than any other animal, for, as Plato said more than two thousand years ago, "Mind is ever the ruler of the universe."

GENETICS

The study of hereditary processes, as developed by Mendel and his successors, has brought out many facts highly interesting and significant to physical education. It is now understood that heredity sets the ultimate limits to which the individual may develop in various phases of life, whereas environment determines how nearly the individual will approach these possible limits. The function of education is not to mold each individual child into the same form by one set process, but rather to help each individual make the utmost of such possibilties as are his by inheritance. Recent research suggests that educators have tended to accept unnecesary restrictions in terms of their misconceptions of the inherited potentials of individual children. Science has demonstrated that many limits which were formerly considered fixed by heredity are, in fact, subject to environmental modification; hence it is possible to extend them through improved educational opportunities.

Tragically, it has been demonstrated that some teachers have been guilty of the self-fulfilling prophecy syndrome with respect to their attitudes toward pupils whom they assumed had limited abilities. In one study a group of teachers was informed of the intelligence test scores of their pupils at the start of the school year. At the end of the year grades achieved by these children were correlated with their intelligence test scores. It was found that in general the teachers had awarded significantly lower letter grades to pupils ranging in the lower end of the intelligence scores distribution. The "kicker" in the study was that the teachers had been provided with incorrect information about the pupils with low intelligence test scores. In fact, those children had intelligence test scores equal to the achievement of the high scoring students. Thus, it was concluded that the teachers formed an early hypothesis in their own minds that the children of low intelligence would be unable to achieve high grades in their classes. The teachers proceeded to make this unsound prophecy come true. How often do physical education teachers and coaches commit a similar injustice based on observations of pupil performances in sports skills or on the scores they achieve on a physical fitness test? Teachers should be made aware of this potential mistreatment of children, so that they will encourage each child to fulfill the potential of the physical and mental abilities he possesses.

BIOMECHANICS OF HUMAN MOVEMENT

The human being, belonging to a particular biological species, has certain structural characteristics which facilitate, limit, and determine the nature of his movements. This area of study is known as "kinesiology." In the early days of our profession, prospective teachers followed a wholly mechanistic attack on the study of movement. They memorized the actions of individual muscles and their mechanical relationships to the body segments and joints involved.

> The movements comprising gymnastic maneuvers, and to a lesser degree sport skills, were described in anatomical terms, and lists were then compiled of the individual muscles which ought to contribute to the production of the joint positions assumed. This was a highly artificial kinesiology, based almost entirely on synthetic reasoning.[17]

Human anatomy is still foundational to physical education. But the study of anatomy, because of the development of modern instrumentation serving biological research, has advanced to what Dr. Frances Hellebrandt terms "Living Anatomy." In Dr. Hellebrandt's words, "The Living Anatomy of today is, in effect, Electromyographic Kinesiology."

> Physical educators have all but forgotten the anatomical basis of the activities comprising their programs. For decades biomechanics has usurped the stage. The end-results of the motor acts willed have been translated into mechanical units and then tested and measured by application of increasingly sophisticated methods. . . . The biomechanical kinesiologist has forgotten to ask *why* the behaviors occur, and *how* they are implemented. . . . It is the neurophysiologic approach to kinesiology which has been more or less bypassed at a time when what we know about the functioning of the nervous system has been leaping forward with one brilliant stride after another.[17]

It seems likely that physical educators will always need to study human anatomy and kinesiology in order to plan for their students rich learning opportunities through movement. It is equally likely that they will continue to be challenged and assisted by new knowledge and new questions.

Modern kinesiology utilizes a variety of sophisticated instruments for research investigations and for instructional purposes. Clarke and Clarke* provide an excellent summary of the current methodologies of kinesiological research and instruction.

Electromyography (EMG) employs a complicated electrical machine which records, analyzes, and integrates recordings of the amplitude and duration of electrical impulses generated by muscles under contraction, or immediately prior to contraction. Electrodes are placed across the belly of the muscle under study. Metal plates can be placed on the skin over the area of study, or thin wire can be inserted into the muscles. Lead wires conduct electrical impulses from the muscle fibers to the recording machine which traces irregular lines on fast moving graph paper. These tracings can be read to determine with considerable accuracy just when a muscle begins to "fire," when it ceases, and the varying amplitude of the electrical impulses released. As many as six muscles can be studied simultaneously on some polygraphs. The impulses can be recorded electronically on electromagnetic tape, and they can be viewed on an oscilloscope from which photographs can be made as permanent records. Whenever an impulse from the central nervous system is conducted to a muscle, or muscle group, the thousands of motor units in the muscle are activated and an electrical potential is immediately released which is recorded on the electromyographical machine. The study of the tracings, on a time scale, reveals patterns of muscle actions and indicates clearly when muscles contract and relax in relation to each other. It also informs the physiologist about properties of muscle excitation.

The use of electromyography has replaced the older, traditional methods of external, manual muscle palpation and inference from knowledge of the origins and insertions of muscles on cadavers and skeletons as a basis for determining more accurately what Clarke and Clarke call the "interplay of the musculature participating in a movement." The exact role each muscle, and muscle group, plays as sets of muscles move limbs through a range of motion can be ascertained.

---

* Clarke, David H., and Clarke, H. Harrison: *Research Processes in Physical Education, Recreation, and Health.* Englewood Cliffs, New Jersey: Prentice-Hall, Inc., 1970, pp. 364-394.

Many misconceptions developed from the older methods have been revealed and corrected. Much research remains to be conducted to fill in present voids of knowledge about muscle response in various parts of the body but this information is gradually being obtained. Physical educators and physical therapists are in the forefront of this type of research. Many practical applications for the teaching of efficient movements to normal individuals and for corrective rehabilitation of persons with pathologic and orthopedic problems are evolving throughout the country and the world.

Cinematography is another basic mode of investigation in kinesiological study. Very high speed motion picture cameras are available now which have the capability of shooting 10,000 frames per second. X-ray cameras and stroboscopic cameras add to the accuracy with which the kinesiologist can follow the precise movements of the body and its parts in complex skills performances. Two or more cameras can be placed in different planes to picture the movement on the same time line which provides two and three dimensional analysis. Various types of wooden and metal frames with lines and squares marked off in specific units of distance can be placed behind the performer and recorded in the picture so that the researcher can measure accurately the distances, angles and arcs any portion of the body may have moved over a given time period. Frequently, physical features, such as bony prominences, of the body of the subject are marked with contrasting tape or other material which can be readily identified in the pictures so that an accurate tracing can be made of the trajectory followed by that body part in the pictures over time. Data from cinematographical analysis helps to describe more accurately such phenomena of movement as force, power, velocity, and acceleration.

It is obvious that cinematographical study can be conducted either indoors or out-of-doors, so it can be adjusted to either analysis of skilled movements in formal competitive or demonstration conditions, or to detailed, controlled laboratory conditions either in isolated part study, or in complete, integrated performances. Film readers and analyzers simplify the task of the investigator, although his job is a rigorous and time consuming one at best. He must work with extreme care in the measurements he makes and in the reconstruction of the flow of the movements under study as well as the time intervals involved, including accuracy to the 100th or even 1000th of a second.

Cinematography is indeed a valuable asset in the research methodology of the kinesiologist and obviously is much more complex and difficult than indicated in this brief sketch. The equipment is expensive and the investigator requires much training and experience to become highly proficient. The standard kinesiology books[7,24,41] now report typical studies carried on by this type of research and describe the basic instrumentations available. Technical references are required to identify the various cameras, film, and supporting equipment and supplies. Advanced training is a prerequisite to entry into this type of research. Gradually, more sophisticated analysis of human movement through cinematography is contributing to greater understanding of man's potential for complex human movements and the exposition of the mechanical principles which undergird these performances.

EMG and cinematographic techniques have been used extensively to analyze the performances of skilled athletes in a variety of sports events as well as in human movements of other types. The standard kinesiology books and the physical education journals give extensive coverage to the reports of these analyses. Teachers and coaches can benefit from a periodic review of these reports, which continually advance our knowledge concerning the principles of the mechanics of skilled human movements.

Brief reference will be made here, by way of example, to one EMG study and one cinematographic analysis which analyzed the complex skill of hitting in baseball.

James L. Breen, now a prominent physical educator, was Research Director for the Chicago Cubs baseball team in the National League for several years. In 1967, he performed extensive cinematographic studies and time and motion analyses of a large number of major league baseball players which concerned the "external mechanics of skills" employed in hitting the baseball. He indicates that such studies can accurately measure directions of movement (angles) of segments of the human body, time relationships, and the indirect values of force and velocity. He asserts that data so collected can be interpreted in terms of recognizable scientific principles instead of professional judgment and guesswork.

Breen analyzed the hitting styles of six great hitters: Ernie Banks, Ted Williams, Stan Musial, Henry Aaron, Willie Mays, and Mickey Mantle.* Despite outward differences in style, his analyses verified that all six hitters possessed five mechanical attributes in common:

---

* Breen, James L. "What Makes a Good Hitter?" *J. Health, Phys. Educ.-Rec.*, 38:36–39, 1967.

1. The center of gravity of the body follows a fairly level plane throughout the swing.
2. The batter can adjust his head for each pitch in order to look carefully at the ball for the longest period of time before having to start his swing.
3. As the bat swing begins, the leading forearm starts to straighten immediately, resulting in greater bat velocity.
4. Each hitter retains a highly consistent length of stride, regardless of the type of pitch.
5. After contacting the ball with the bat, the upper body is aligned with the direction of the flight of the ball and most of the hitter's weight is transferred to the front foot.

Hitters with poor batting averages make errors on one or more of these skills. The report is rich in details about the above conclusions and includes sketches of the correct skills involved in hitting.

Kitzman* combined cinematographic analysis with EMG recordings of action potentials of specific muscle groups involved in hitting a baseball. He compared the performances of two professional players with those of two college students who had not competed in inter-school baseball competition. This investigation was a case study rather than an experimental design from which generalized conclusions could be drawn. Such studies provide clues and leads for coaches on the field and for researchers in the laboratory so that they may advance the knowledge about the effective principles of human movements which are involved in complex sports skills.

Kitzman studied the functions performed by the right and the left pectoralis major muscles, the right and the left triceps brachii muscles, and the right and left latissimus dorsi muscles. Analysis of the data indicated several specific differences of activity in the various muscle groups of the two sets of players at various points in time during the swing of the bat. Also, errors in skill performance associated with swinging the bat were detectable. One major conclusion was that the muscles (those studied) of the skilled performers came into their strongest action earlier in the swing than did the muscles of the unskilled batters. Also, the skilled hitters brought their bats back farther at the start of the swing. It was proposed that right-handed batters could increase the force transferred to the bat by undertaking training to strengthen the left triceps brachii muscles.

---

* Kitzman, Eric W. "Baseball: Electromyographic Study of Batting Swing." *Res. Quart., Am. Assoc. Health, Phys. Educ.-Rec.,* 35:166–178 (May, 1964).

This study is an excellent example of the potential for detailed analysis of complex sports skills which is available in EMG and cinematographic research techniques. The article also includes clear pictures of the apparatus in use, and it contains detailed tables of data collected and extensive discussion of findings, conclusions, and implications.

The physical education major will find many opportunities to experience this type of research and analysis in kinesiology classes and laboratories.

The accurate measurement of movements in the various joint areas of the human body refers to the degree of *flexibility* in each joint, or the range of motion. It is recognized that flexibility is important in movement skills. However, there remains much to learn about it as yet. Recent research indicates that flexibility within an individual is specific to the various joint areas. The degree of flexibility attainable is determined by the anatomical properties of the extensibility of the muscles and ligaments surrounding the joint. Flexibility, or greater range of motion, and stability, or more restricted range of motion, can be accomplished to some degree in each joint area through relevant training regimens. The athlete, and the coach, should study the movements required in the sport of concern to determine the requirements of flexibility and stability in each joint area for optimum performance. Then proper training procedures should be developed and carried out, both in season, and out of season. Exactly how much flexibility an individual should possess as a contributor to his general health status has not yet been verified. It does appear to be related to general physical fitness levels. That is, more physically fit individuals seem to possess higher degrees of flexibility than persons less physically fit.

The methodology for measuring joint flexibility depends primarily on three instruments. The double armed goniometer looks like the well known protractor. Two metal or plastic arms are hinged together so that a dial measuring degrees through a 180-degree radius indicates the degree of flexion in a joint when fully contracted and again when the limb is fully extended. One arm of the goniometer is bound to the limb below the joint and the other arm is fastened to the limb above the joint. When the joint moves the degree of flexibility registers on the dial. This manual method is easy to apply. However, it is not as accurate as is desirable. It is a gross method and at best produces data that are not always of high reliability.

Jack Leighton invented the well known Leighton Flexometer a few years ago. Its operation is described in most kinesiology books. It can be strapped on to most joint areas of the body. It consists of a complete rotary circle. There is a weighted point attached to the center of the dial. Both the dial and the pointer are free and independent of each other, and both are affected by the force of gravity. The segment to which the flexometer is attached is placed at any desired stationary starting position of more than 20 degrees off horizontal. The zero point on the dial and the tip of the pointer float freely until they coincide at rest. Then the dial is locked into its position. The limb involved is moved through the desired range of motion. At the end of that motion the needle is locked. Then the reading of the position of the needle indicates the number of degrees of the arc through which the motion has transpired. This instrument has proved to be highly reliable with coefficients well into the .90's. There are strict instructions about how to place the flexometer on the various joints, how to direct the movements of the subject, and how to make accurate readings. Some training is necessary to use this instrument accurately.

Finally, Karpovich has developed the electrogoniometer,[19] called the "elgon." It provides for the continuous measurement of movements of body segments through a range of motion so that patterns of movement can be analyzed minutely. A small potentiometer is attached at the center of the rotation of the joint. Two arms extend from it as with the goniometer. These arms are strapped to the limbs involved in the movement on either side of the joint. As the joint moves resistance is recorded electrically in terms of ohms which can be analyzed to describe the movement of the joint quite precisely.

Because it is a vital factor in efficiency of human movements flexibility will continue to attract the attention of researchers and teachers alike. They will join forces to produce more sophisticated knowledge about this phenomenon and to translate this information into desirable principles of teaching and coaching.

Biomechanics and kinesiology are concerned with a wide range of important phenomena concerning the efficiency of human movement. In addition to the topics listed in the chapter examples of other basic concepts of interest to the teacher and coach include gravity and buoyancy; air, water and wind resistance; equilibrium; rebounds and spins; projectiles; force and work providing impetus to external objects; receiving impetus; moving and supporting the body; ballistic movements and forces; levers; locomotion; and postures.

PHYSIOLOGY OF EXERCISE

Modern physiology teaches that muscular activity is the major source of development of power and vigor in the organic systems of the body. The essentiality of vigorous muscular activity for increasing endurance, strength, and agility is one of the most potent of all arguments for the inclusion of physical education in the school program at all grade levels. People who exercise regularly are capable of greater efforts and resist fatigue better than sedentary individuals.[4]

The normal heart and circulatory systems become more efficient through use. Exercise leads to improved muscular tone of the heart, increased blood output per minute, and an increase in the number of active capillaries in the lungs. Extended exercise improves lung functioning through increasing the lung expansion, air intake, and oxygen consumption.[1] Strength and endurance are increased by exercise that regularly approaches physiological limits, coupled with adequate rest. Exercise to the point of exhaustion may do harm; but this condition rarely occurs in the untrained person, since he is likely to discontinue his performance on the basis of psychological reactions long before reaching his physiological limit.

Recent physiological research indicates increasing concern for the role of exercise in the aging. Dr. Paul D. White tells us that exercise in the early and middle years of old age can be very beneficial to general health status. A benefit of exercise at any age, but of particular importance to the middle aged and the aging, is its favorable effect in helping to control obesity. Mayer[26] has studied this problem extensively, and concludes that moderate, frequent, and consistent exercise does indeed help in weight reduction.

Recent studies have dealt with such phenomena as energy sources during exercise; aerobic and anaerobic processes; work efficiency; muscle structure, strength, endurance, and flexibility; physical conditioning and training; the physiology of underwater activity and of drowning; temperature regulation during exercise stress; pulmonary ventilation; gaseous exchange and transport; cardiovascular control; respiration and circulation; performance at altitude; body composition and weight gain and loss; fitness and aging processes; physical fitness testing; ergogenic aids in sport and work; and rehabilitation of cardiovascular disorders.

A brief enumeration of some of the equipment and apparatus used by the researcher in exercise physiology follows. Standard treatment of this subject can be found in several well known texts.[1,25,28]

To measure the amount of energy used to accomplish physical work a human subject can be placed in a closed chamber called a calorimeter wherein the total amount of heat produced by the subject at work can be determined. Or, the subject can breathe into a spirometer which makes it possible to measure the amount of oxygen used during exercise. An athlete participating in a strenuous workout in swimming or running can breathe expired air into a Douglas bag at the beginning and end of the workout. Later this air can be analyzed by a spirometer or by passing it through a gas meter. The difference between the pre-race VO_2 value and the end-of-race value represents the oxygen utilized. Expired air can be collected during continuous exercise when the subject is on the stationary bicycle or on the treadmill. It can be analyzed for O_2 and CO_2 content.

The bicycle ergometer and the treadmill are used to aid in the computation of energy expenditure and work output. Various types of work ergometers have been devised to measure work performed by muscle groups surrounding different joint areas of the body.

Blood is subjected to laboratory chemical analyses to determine the effects of exercise on pH levels, lactic acid, red blood corpuscles, erythrocyte sedimentation rate, white blood corpuscles, blood platelets, specific gravity of blood, blood sugar, phosphates, and cholesterol level. Blood pressure readings are taken by use of the sphygmomanometer. Heart rates are elevated by having subjects step up and down to cadence on steps of varying height while monitoring the pulse rate before, after, and even during the exercise.

Measures of body heat are taken by thermometers inserted in the mouth or in the rectum. A special thermometer using a thin needle can be inserted directly into muscle tissue. The Sling Psychrometer, useful for determining environmental conditions on the athletic field, consists of wet and dry bulb thermometers.

Where strength testing is required the investigator uses dynamometers (hand, leg, back), a tensiometer, and a manuometer (grip strength).

The vital capacity of the lungs is tested by use of the spirometer. The subject inhales the largest quantity of air of which he is capable. Then he forcefully expires it gradually, and for as long as he can, into the spirometer. The total amount of air thus expired is the vital capacity.

It is possible to inject a dye, fluorescein, into the blood and to record the amount of time it takes it to reach another area of the body during exercise, thus providing data about the relationship between exercise intensity and blood circulation time.

Body composition can be assessed by various types of calipers which measure skin folds in different regions of the body and also calipers which make accurate anthropometric measurements.

Radio-telemetry has now been miniaturized to the extent that by strapping a small package of instruments on a runner, or other active athletes, electrical signals can be relayed some distance back to the monitoring equipment so that information concerning respiration, heart rate, and blood pressure can be obtained during the ongoing performance of a sport event.

This brief summary indicates the wide domain of inquiry available to the exercise physiologist and the necessity for expensive, sophisticated equipment and facilities to conduct much of the basic and applied research about phenomena of central concern. Needless to say, extensive advanced graduate preparation and laboratory experience are prerequisites to a career in this physical education specialization.

Recent discoveries in the physiology of muscular activity have opened up to us a wealth of information. Such resources help to guide the physical educator in his efforts to provide the types and amounts of physical activity which will benefit the individual to a maximum degree and, at the same time, avoid excessive stresses and strains and types of fatigue which result in temporary or permanent damage. Most important, scientific information serves as a basis for helping students to learn how to plan sound individual exercise programs, and how to adapt them to varying individual needs throughout life. Principles of physical education, which guide our policies and practices, are to a large extent derived from present-day scientific knowledge. The discussion in this chapter has only touched the fringes of this knowledge, but it is hoped that enough has been said to stimulate the professional reader to a further study of this field, in which advances are being made daily, and to development of the ability to make the appropriate applications to his teaching, coaching, and administration in physical education.

PHYSICAL FITNESS

The physical fitness of the American public continues to be a popular subject in schools and colleges. Organizations such as the American Medical Association and the President's Council on Physical Fitness and Sports are conducting stepped-up campaigns to promote better health through physical fitness activities, and the various communications media keep the country informed of recent developments through professional and popular books, magazine articles, research reports, and television and radio programs and advertising. This section recounts the role physical fitness has played in various historical eras and describes selected current developments in this country.

It is possible to identify the civilizations in the history of the world which have stressed physical fitness or physical training as an important objective of the educational program, and to study the curricula and methods of training adopted to achieve this objective. A partial listing[42] of countries, groups, and eras would include the Spartan Greeks, the early Athenian Greeks, the early Romans, the era of chivalry, the individual humanists, the Protestant reformers, the verbal and social realists, the formal disciplinarians, the advocates of naturalism, countries which developed strongly nationalistic systems of education in the nineteenth and twentieth centuries, the German Nazis prior to and during World War II, America during and after World Wars I and II, and up to the present time, many countries of the world.

Historical Background

In American history the physical fitness movement received strong impetus in 1885 when Dr. William Anderson of the Adelphi Academy, an instructor of Swedish medical gymnastics, invited 49 leaders of American youth to attend a conference, for the purpose of considering a scientific approach to the development of physical fitness. As a result of discussions at this conference, and because of the stimulus of outstanding addresses by Dr. Edwin Hitchcock of Amherst and Dr. Dudley Sargent of Harvard, the group decided to form the American Association for the Advancement of Physical Education. This organization was the forerunner of our present-day American Association for Health, Physical Education, and Recreation, a department of the National Education Association.

Next, the American Association for the Advancement of Physical Education appointed an important committee on Statistics and Measurements, composed of Dr. Anderson, Dr. Hitchcock, and Dr. Sargent. The purpose of this committee was to develop a set of anthropometric measurements which would describe the "ideal man," and to set up a program of physical education in which all pupils would work scientifically toward achieving this ideal.

The three committee members returned to their respective institutions and conducted intensive programs of measurement of all students in the three colleges. Approximately 50 measurements were taken of each student, plus a grip strength score measured by a hand dynamometer, an instrument which had just been introduced to America from England. All test scores from the three institutions were averaged together, and these averages were published to represent the "ideal man." In the interest of scientific accuracy, this term was soon changed to "typical man."

The next step was to plan a program which would best develop students to conform as nearly as possible to the measurements of the "typical man." Special apparatus was devised to develop various parts of the body. Cash prizes were offered to boys whose measurements most approximated those of the "typical man." A sculpture of the "typical man" was exhibited at the World Exposition. The YWCA started a similar project for girls, but without much success.

When this project was well under way, Dr. Sargent realized that something was missing: the entire battery of body measurements and strength scores failed to measure the efficiency or the ability of the body in motion. Thus, Sargent recommended a change of approach and emphasis. With his co-workers, he endeavored to identify the basic abilities which were common to the many forms of gymnastics and athletic events of the time.

In 1902, Dr. Sargent published the results of his findings in the form of "A Universal Test for Strength, Speed, and Endurance." The effect of this change of emphasis was a decline in the medical gymnastics approach, and a shift of interest toward an athletic ability basis for physical fitness.

From that time on, American physical education has moved more and more in the direction of the so-called "natural program," emphasizing sports, dance, and other activities which are composed of fundamental skills and movements "natural" to man, such as jumping, running, throwing, balancing, leaping, dodging, hanging, climbing, and catching. Periods of war have brought renewed interest in physical fitness in the United States. Although athletics and sports were retained in school and armed forces programs, there usually was a return to more formal gymnastic and exercise programs for physical conditioning purposes.

Gradually, after World War II, the typical peacetime lack of interest in physical fitness returned to many school programs. Several states and many school districts relaxed or eliminated their physical education requirements, thus resulting in a report in the late 1950's that about one half of the boys and girls in American high schools were not enrolled in any form of physical education. At the same time, many existing school programs moved so far from the direction of play, games, and sports that very little vigorous activity was retained. Studies which ascertained the extent to which pupils engaged in vigorous activities indicated that many pupils in a physical education class were not active, beyond the exercise and exertion required in walking, for more than two or three minutes in an entire physical education period. With few exceptions, physical fitness became a "lost objective" in most school programs of physical education.

Present Status and Concern

In 1955, for the first time in our national history, physical fitness in peacetime became a national concern of top government officials, including the President of the United States.

The President's Council. When the controversial Kraus-Hirschland*[22] research study was brought to the attention of President

---

* Many physical education authorities doubt the validity of the Kraus-Weber test for determining minimum fitness levels of youth. The flexibility item in the test as a determinant factor of fitness levels is particularly subject to challenge. Students are referred to a study published in the *Research Quarterly* of October, 1955, written by Marjorie Phillips and others, titled "Analysis of Results from the Kraus-Weber Test of Minimum Muscular Fitness in Children."

Eisenhower, the President was shocked at the unfavorable "minimum fitness level" test scores made by American children as compared with groups of children from selected European countries. By executive order dated July 16, 1956, he established the President's Council on Youth Fitness and the President's Citizens Advisory Committee on the Fitness of American Youth. The purpose of these two groups was to promote the efficacy of existing fitness programs and the launching of additional programs to enhance the fitness of American youth.

With the election of John F. Kennedy, physical fitness received the strongest support it had ever known in peacetime from a president of the United States. In a move that surely was unique in the field of physical education, John F. Kennedy, while still President-elect, wrote an article published under his own name in the December 26, 1960, issue of *Sports Illustrated*, entitled, "The Soft American," in which he cogently stated his concern for the fitness of the American citizenry and suggested steps for improving the situation. This unprecedented support for physical fitness gave the program a tremendous boost.

After his inauguration, President Kennedy continued to show his

221

strong personal interest in and concern for physical fitness through speeches, television statements, statements to national conferences, and introductions to official publications on the subject. He spoke personally on behalf of the program to periodic conferences of state governors, and urged his cabinet officers and other officials holding high public office to promote and support the program at all times.

Shortly after he took office, President Kennedy appointed the well-known University of Oklahoma football coach, Charles "Bud" Wilkinson, as Special Consultant to the President on Physical Fitness. The President's Council on Youth Fitness was reorganized, and liaison with the White House was strengthened. The staff of the Council was appointed by Mr. Wilkinson. Projects were undertaken immediately to bring about national "action" concerning physical fitness, and to carry out the President's directive to improve the fitness of Americans everywhere. One of the first steps was to publish and disseminate a booklet entitled *Youth Physical Fitness—Suggested Elements of a School Centered Program*,[44] now revised. The recommendations in this publication were adopted by many schools throughout the country.

In 1962, the Council published its second noteworthy booklet, *Physical Fitness Elements in Recreation—Suggestions for Community Programs*.[33] This publication indicates how community recreation agencies can work to promote the physical fitness of all citizens, young and old alike, through recreation.

In order to emphasize its concern for the physical fitness of all Americans, regardless of age, the Council changed its name to the President's Council on Physical Fitness, by executive order on January 8, 1963. In 1967, the name again was changed to the President's Council on Physical Fitness and Sports, which is its title today.

The Council has vigorously promoted and interpreted physical fitness through all media available: motion pictures, public speeches, publications, television programs, advertising on television, radio and in newspapers, press conferences, research publications, popular and scientific magazine articles, and proposed legislation.

In October, 1967, not only was the Council renamed, but its organizational status was changed. It became an agency in the Department of Health, Education, and Welfare. In October, 1970, C. Carson Conrad, former Director of the Bureau of Health, Physical Education, and Recreation, California State Department of Education, was appointed Executive Director of the Council. Captain James A. Lovell (U. S. Navy, Ret.), the famous astronaut, is Director of the

Council and Consultant on Fitness to the President of the United States. In 1971 the President of the United States appointed a one hundred member Advisory Committee on Fitness and Sport and he personally addressed the first meeting of this group to express his concern and interest in the work of the Council. In August, 1971, a Business and Industry Advisory Committee was appointed composed of presidents and other leaders of large, well known corporations and business establishments across the nation. Also in 1971, the Council appointed H. Harrison Clarke, noted physical education scholar and researcher from the University of Oregon, to serve as part-time Consultant for Research and as Editor of a new publication, the *Physical Fitness Research Digest.*

The Council has actively expanded its program activities over the years. Some examples include a Presidential Physical Fitness Award program which, between its origin in 1965, and the end of 1972, had presented citations and awards to 1,143,376 boys and girls throughout the United States. It is interesting to note that more girls than boys have received this honor.

In 1969 the Council began to formally recognize selected junior and senior high schools across the country as "Demonstration Center Schools" because of their exemplary physical fitness programs. Selections are made each year.

In 1970 the Council, in cooperation with the National Collegiate Athletic Association, began an extensive National Summer Youth Sports Program which involved participation of approximately one hundred schools and universities and approximately 35,000 boys and girls ages ten to eighteen. The Department of Health, Education, and Welfare initially funded this summer recreational program with approximately three million dollars. This program has continued each summer on approximately the same scale. In the summer of 1973, 105 colleges in 37 states offered programs to 45,000 boys and girls. Three million dollars from the Educational Opportunity Administration Amendments Act of 1972 provided the financial support.

For the past several years the Council has sponsored regional fitness clinics throughout the nation and provided a majority of the staff participating in these programs. Also, special Symposiums have been held such as the Medical Symposium on Exercise and the Heart.

In 1972 the Council established a national Presidential Sports Award for any man or woman eighteen years old or more. This award may be achieved in any of thirty-one athletic events for participating for fifty hours, in fifty or more different time periods, for at least four months.

In April, 1972, the Council initiated a service which provides the five hundred largest newspapers in the United States with material to use in a weekly physical fitness column.

The Council has been very active in producing its own informative publications and instructional films. The *Newsletter* was begun in November, 1963 and has been produced several times yearly ever since. The *Physical Fitness Research Digest* was started in June, 1971 and is published quarterly. The two best known publications of the Council are (1) *Youth Physical Fitness—Suggested Elements of a School Centered Program,* published in 1961, with a minor revision in 1967; and (2) *Adult Physical Fitness,* in 1963. Both of these pamphlets have been read by literally millions of persons in this country and others and their popularity continues unabated. Plans have been formulated to revise these booklets in 1974. Other valuable pamphlets include *An Introduction to Physical Fitness,* 1970; *What Physicians Say About Physical Education,* 1972; *Interpreting Physical Education,* 1972; and a booklet developed in collaboration with the Campbell Soup Company, *It's Easy to Eat Well . . . For Your Figure, For Your Health.*

Two notable instructional films produced by the Council are (1) "Prescription for Fitness," 1971, and (2) "The School Where Fitness Counts," 1972.

AAHPER Physical Fitness Programs. The American Association for Health, Physical Education and Recreation has given active national leadership to physical fitness throughout its long history. In recent years the Association has expanded its activities in this area even more, and has established close working relationships with the President's Council, the American Medical Association, the American College of Sports Medicine, and other allied organizations having a concern for the health and fitness of the citizens of the United States.

In 1959, Dr. Paul Hunsicker reported the results of his national study for the Association, which established national norms for the AAHPER Youth Fitness Test Manual published in 1961. In subsequent years, the AAHPER test has been administered to millions of pupils in schools throughout the country.

In order to ascertain the progress these school pupils were making in fitness status, Hunsicker and Reiff[18] conducted another national study for the AAHPER, which compared the results of fitness testing done in 1958 with a new national sample of test scores in 1965. This monumental study involved 9627 boys and girls in 110 schools throughout the continental United States, and 1602 pupils in 18 schools in Alaska. In general, the physical fitness levels of this sample of American public school children were significantly improved over the 1958 national scores. There has not been another national survey in recent years.

There is an AAHPER national Physical Fitness Award program for the mentally retarded, in cooperation with the Joseph P. Kennedy, Jr., Foundation.[35] The AAHPER is maintaining its enthusiastic pace to promote increased fitness among the youth and adults of this country. This influential professional organization is serving the cause of fitness with distinction.

Fitness Activities of other National Groups. The American Medical Association has been increasingly active in telling the "fitness story" to the nation. It has disseminated two official statements for public perusal, "Health Problems Revealed During Physical Activity,"[15] a statement by the Committee on Exercise and Fitness; and "Need for Varied Activities in Physical Education Programs,"[30] also by the Committee on Exercise and Fitness.

The AMA also is joint sponsor of two other significant statements, "Exercise and Fitness," Joint Statement of the American Medical Association and the American Association for Health, Physical Education and Recreation;[12] and "Exercise and Weight Control," Joint Statement by the Committee on Exercise and Fitness of the American Medical Association, the President's Council on Physical Fitness and Sports, and the Lifetime Sports Foundation.[13]

In 1966, the National Aeronautics Space Administration established a Physical Stress Laboratory in Washington, D.C. Research is being conducted concerning stress responses to normal occupational exercise and physical training workouts, both in a laboratory situation and in normal work environments. Regional laboratories of NASA also do research on selected physiological phenomena related to the capabilities of pilots and astronauts to endure stress at very high altitudes. Frequently, there is collaboration with physical education researchers and doctoral students in nearby colleges and universities. Research experience and new data produced in these laboratories probably will be valuable in extending the potentialities and horizons of research concerning various types of physiological stress to which school children and adults in everyday life are exposed.

The United States Marine Corps historically has led the other military services in its active interest in the physical fitness of its members, in peacetime as well as in periods of war. In 1967, the Marine Corps founded a Physical Fitness Academy at Quantico, Virginia, for the training of non-commissioned and commissioned officers.

Research in physical fitness has accelerated at such a rapid rate in many countries that the need for greater understanding, communication, and standardization is well recognized. Accordingly, in 1966, Dr. Leonard A. Larson of the United States was chairman of an International Research Program for the Standardization of Physical Fitness Tests.[23] The purpose of this project is to provide scientific instruments to study and to determine the powers and the organic resources of the people living under greatly varying conditions all over the world. Interested individuals and organizations will contribute to the study of the health and physical fitness status of people in all parts of the world. Many international, national, state, and local groups have established fitness councils, held workshops and conferences, developed research projects, implemented new programs, and in a variety of ways stimulated fitness.

Definitions of Physical Fitness

Majority opinion holds that physical fitness should be considered as one aspect of total fitness which has several components, intellectual, emotional, and social, as well as physiological. Improvement in total fitness leads to more effective living. The physical educator has a unique interest in that aspect of total fitness usually called physical fitness, as well as a general interest in the other components of total fitness which can be influenced favorably by a sound physical education program.

Many attempts have been made to define physical fitness and to enumerate and describe its specific factors. The authors accept a widely held viewpoint that physical fitness refers to the organic capacity of the individual to perform the normal tasks of daily living without undue tiredness or fatigue, having a reserve of strength and energy available to meet satisfactorily any emergency demands suddenly placed upon him. One obvious implication of this definition is that physical fitness is an individual matter. The question "Physical fitness for what?" must be answered for each individual in terms of his general health, his occupation, his avocational activities, his interests, needs and capabilities, and many other factors, in order to arrive at a definition of an optimal condition of physical fitness for that person. It is fallacious to hold that there is one "best" level of physical fitness which all persons should strive to achieve. The inherent difficulties involved in identifying and then evaluating the status of the pertinent factors to be considered in setting a physical fitness goal for any individual constitute a formidable challenge to the physical education profession.

Various definitions include a variety of components of physical fitness. Approximately 70 elements have been listed in the definitions cited in the literature to date. An excellent analysis and classification has been made by the New York State Department of Education.[31] Sixty-nine detailed components of physical fitness were found in the definitions proposed in physical education literature. These components fell into three major categories: medical or physiological function, anthropometrical condition, and physical or motor function. Under the medical function, seven major components were listed: function of the nervous system, function of the heart, circulatory system, and blood, function of the respiratory system, function of the digestive system, function of the muscular system, function of the endocrine system, and general health. Seven major components of anthropometric condition were developed: posture, height–weight relationship, flexibility, dead weight, height, body structure, and bone–muscle–fat relationship, and these were reduced to the three major categories of body development, posture, and flexibility. Physical functions had a total of 40 components reduced to six major classifications: accuracy, agility, balance, strength, endurance, and speed.

Clarke and Clarke more succinctly state that the basic elements of physical fitness are organic soundness, freedom from disease, and nutritional adequacy.[6] The professional student should formulate his own definition from a thorough consideration of all factors involved in the problem.

Physical Fitness as an Objective of Physical Education

In our country today, physical fitness rates high in any list of objectives for the modern school program of physical education at all levels. The organic vigor phase of total fitness is primarily a responsibility of the physical education program in the school curriculum.

Physical educators err when they claim "unique" or "full" responsibility for physical fitness as an educational objective rather than a primary concern. Good physical fitness is not only a question of sufficient exercise; it depends upon many other factors as well: proper nutrition, good mental and emotional health, freedom from disease, the correction of remedial defects, and other factors which are the concern of the physician, the school nurse, the dietitian, the other teachers, and the parents. In view of those comprehensive considerations, the physical educator should concentrate on improving three components of fitness, namely, circulatory efficiency, muscular strength, and muscular endurance.

Research evidence shows that the way the organism functions physiologically while at rest has no relation to the way it may function in action. A similar lack of relationship exists between light work and heavy work. This evidence verifies our earlier point that physical fitness is specific; we must ask, "Physical fitness for what?" In addition, we must describe the "what" very carefully and specifically in behavioral terms.

Other studies indicate that all of us are to some degree "unfit," for a large variety of reasons and causes. Therefore, we must be cautious, and should not expect a single performance test to be an accurate diagnostic test of fitness. By the same token, an exercise program alone does not constitute a fitness program.

Clarke cites several studies in Oregon which indicate that "good" physical education programs at various school levels produce a higher physical fitness rating than that achieved by pupils who have had "poor" physical education programs or no physical education at all. Clarke's concluding statement concerning the import of these studies merits serious consideration. He states that there is positive proof that the lack of proper physical education in public schools results in lower physical fitness levels for both boys and girls. Thus as young men and women, they embark on university study in preparation for their life's work and service with a definite and potentially dangerous handicap.[34]

Doornink found that, among University of Oregon students, those with lowest Physical Fitness Index (PFI) ratings compared most unfavorably with students rating high on the PFI, in such areas of student life as chance of successful graduation, earning of varsity athletic awards, winning academic scholarships, being elected to an honor society, probability of being elected to a position of student body leadership, probability of being elected as a leader of a club or society, and the winning of prizes and awards. Not only were the students at the high end of the PFI scale markedly superior in all comparisons, but they were superior to an astonishingly high degree.

Clarke has made an extensive analysis of research findings by various investigators, including his own studies, and he developed a careful analytical conclusion which states ". . . it may be contended that a person's *general learning potential for a given level of intelligence* is increased or decreased in accordance with his degree of physical fitness."*

Other lines of research, which are steadily revealing data and evidence with widespread implications for our concern about fitness, involve the relationship between performance and behavior, differences in human physiques and constitutional factors and their relationships to various elements of fitness, the effects of training of various types and intensities, and the need for a reserve physical capacity for emergencies.

Tests

Teachers can now select from a wide variety of so-called physical fitness test items and test batteries for various grade levels. Many individuals and groups are making physical fitness studies and constructing physical fitness tests on local, state, and national bases. Three quite similar tests have followed in rapid succession in recent years. The similarity is partly owing to the fact that several physical education leaders were involved in the construction of each of these three tests, and partly owing to the general acceptability of certain items in these tests for use nationally as well as regionally. The *California Physical Performance Test* was published in 1958 as an outgrowth of the California Fitness Project. A revision was published in 1962, and another revision in 1966, entitled *The Physical Performance Test for California*. The latest revision is entitled *The Physical*

---

* H. Harrison Clarke: *Application of Measurement to Health and Physical Education*, p. 51. Englewood Cliffs, New Jersey: Prentice-Hall, Inc., 4th ed., 1967.

Performance Test for California (Revised), 1971. The American Association for Health, Physical Education and Recreation published a test which contained several of the items found in the California test, plus certain swimming tests, in 1958. This test was revised in 1965 with only one change. In 1961 the President's Council on Youth Fitness published a physical fitness test in its manual, *Youth Physical Fitness,* which also contained several test items found in the California and AAHPER tests. It was revised slightly in 1967. These three tests in revised editions[5,43,44] are now used throughout the United States and in many foreign countries.

Many teachers, physical education departments, school districts, counties, states, countries, professional organizations, and even commercial interests are producing and using self-constructed physical fitness tests. Many schools and states are developing norms for their own pupils, a procedure which the authors encourage. It is not sufficient to compare an individual pupil's results with national norms only. It may be even more important to know how pupils are progressing in relation to their own performances, their own class, their own school, their own community, and their own state.

An innovation in junior and senior high school programs which is creating extensive student interest in physical fitness is the introduction of Physical Fitness Laboratories. These labs are equipped with standard physiological testing equipment, and technically competent physical education teachers are able to operate them and to conceptualize and carry out sound studies. Students serve as subjects and as laboratory technicians. This program can be integrated closely with the science department in the school, and laboratory credit can be arranged for science classes. Students can learn important physiological concepts in an interesting and challenging laboratory setting. They can learn some of the fundamental principles which underlie physical performance. They can gain experience with some of the modes of inquiry of the biological sciences. The potentialities of these laboratories are limited only by the imaginative, creative talents of the teachers in charge. This innovation seems to hold high promise to make physical education an even more varied and challenging learning experience.

Physical fitness testing and exercise programs are of personal interest to many young people and adults outside of the school. The Armed Forces of the United States have increased their physical fitness requirements for all active duty personnel, and have intensified training programs by including more mandatory physical fitness activity and testing. YMCA's and other organizations are sponsoring adult fitness programs. Community recreation agencies are being urged to make more opportunities for physical fitness activities available to citizens of all ages.

Programs

Four examples of physical fitness programs which have captured the attention of the American public are worthy of note, although many more could be cited. The *Royal Canadian Air Force Exercise Plans for Physical Fitness*[37] have been publicized extensively throughout the United States and now are available in printed form for public purchase. Many physicians recommend these exercise programs to their patients for their general physical well-being. There is a twelve-minute-per-day plan for women, designated XBX, and an eleven-minute-per-day plan for men, called 5BX. One of the chief virtues of these plans is that they permit any individual to begin with exercises appropriate to his own physical condition, and then to gradually increase in difficulty and achievement as he improves his strength and endurance.

A very recent (1972) popularized publication of extensive research, carried on over a period of years and involving thousands of subjects, by Air Force Physiologist Major Kenneth Cooper, entitled *Aerobics*,[8] has commanded the public attention. There is now a companion book entitled *Aerobics for Women*, 1972.[8a] Major Cooper has evolved scientifically a variety of physical fitness regimes which medically sound individuals can follow to build up their condition over a period of time. Cooper's studies indicate that the best exercises are running, swimming, cycling, walking, running in place, handball, basketball, and squash, in that descending order of efficacy.

The system requires that the individual engage in any combination of recommended physical fitness workouts which accumulate a total of 30 points per week, using a scale of points graded to the degree of exertion and the time involved in each activity. Cooper asserts that extensive medical data on many subjects validate the contention that these carefully graded and scheduled workouts do in fact cause a marked training effect.

Two basic principles fundamental to the "aerobic" system are that the exercise must be severe enough to produce a heart rate of 150 beats per minute for at least a five-minute period, and that if the heart rate does not rise to 150 beats per minute, the exercise can be extended for a considerably longer period of time.

The title "aerobic" was selected because this physiological term means that these particular exercises require oxygen consumption, but they don't cause a severe oxygen debt, which would place the cardiovascular system in an anaerobic state. As long as exercise can be performed in an aerobic state, the person can perform over a reasonably long period of time appropriate to his over-all physical condition. Thus, a training effect is "activated."

Another physical fitness activity which is gaining many advocates of all ages and of both sexes is popularly called "jogging."

In various parts of the country, track coaches, physical education teachers, YMCA instructors, athletic trainers, and physicians have given leadership to the establishment of jogging programs as an ideal fitness activity. In 1967 the noted University of Oregon track and field coach William J. Bowerman joined with heart specialist Dr. W. E. Harris in co-authoring a popularized publication entitled *Jogging: A Complete Physical Fitness Program for All Ages*[14]. This paperback book was revised in 1972 and is now authored only by Dr. Harris. Jogging refers to an easy-paced steady run, or slow running alternating with periods of walking, which is within the capability of any individual who has been approved for this activity by his physician.

The advantages of jogging as a fitness activity are obvious. It provides regular, moderate exercise; it is simple, convenient, and inexpensive; it requires only a small amount of time weekly; no special skill is necessary; it applies to any age and both sexes; and it is enjoyable and invigorating. Furthermore, it can be performed alone, or with groups as a social experience. These are the same advantages ascribed to "aerobics."

As with "aerobics," jogging follows prescribed schedules suited to each individual's current fitness status. It involves a slow, steady progression in length and intensity of running, and is based on a time schedule of at least three days per week. Jogging has a longer history than "aerobics," and so has attracted a larger following to date. It seems probable that both types of programs will continue to appeal to more and more individuals throughout the country.

The past three years have seen the rapid rise of warm-up, stretching, and jogging programs for patients with a variety of cardiac disabilities. The individual's personal physician determines when the patient is ready to enter this program. The program is directed by a heart specialist who prescribes the optimum exercise regimen for each participant individually. Frequently, there is regular consultation with the person's private physician as well. These programs are usually conducted in the gymnasia of local YMCAs, YWCAs, schools, or colleges. Sometimes they are held out-of-doors, weather permitting. Some programs include activities other than walking and jogging such as swimming, or riding a stationary bicycle. The results obtained by patients in these programs have been uniformly encouraging in all parts of the country. Research studies are being conducted to test the efficacy of these programs and to determine how to continue to improve their effectiveness. More and more physicians are becoming confident in the results of these programs and are advising their patients to enter them. Recent medical literature reports the findings of these studies.

Conclusion

A final word of caution is that we should keep the physical fitness objective in proper focus and balance with the other valuable objectives of physical education, health education, and recreation programs. The physical education curriculum should not be based primarily on physical fitness testing programs. Overemphasis of this objective might jeopardize gains made in the achievement of other equally valuable objectives. Oberteuffer[32] very clearly points out the danger. The admonition that it would be tragic to reduce the broad contributions of the physical education program to a barren physical training program should be considered seriously by all thoughtful physical educators and school administrators.

Selected References

1. Astrand, Per-Olof, and Rodahl, Kaare: *A Textbook of Work Physiology.* New York: McGraw-Hill Book Company, Inc., text ed., 1970.

2. Basmajian, J. V.: *Muscles Alive: Their Functions Revealed by Electromyography.* Baltimore: Williams and Wilkins Company, 2nd ed., 1967.
3. Broer, Marion R.: *Efficiency of Human Movement.* Philadelphia: W. B. Saunders Company, 3rd ed., 1973.
4. Brouha, Lucien: "Training." From Johnson, Warren R., and Elsworth, Buskird.: *Science and Medicine of Exercise and Sport.* New York: Harper and Row, Publishers, 2nd ed., 1972.
5. *California Physical Performance Test.* Sacramento: California State Department of Education, 1966.
6. Clarke, H. Harrison, and Clarke, David H.: *Developmental and Adapted Physical Education.* Englewood Cliffs, N.J.: Prentice-Hall, Inc., 1963.
7. Cooper, John M., and Glassow, Ruth B.: *Kinesiology.* St. Louis: The C. V. Mosby Company, 3rd ed., 1972.
8. Cooper, Kenneth H.: *Aerobics.* New York: Bantam Books, Inc., 1972.
8a. Cooper, Mildred, and Cooper, Kenneth H.: *Aerobics for Women.* New York: Bantam Books, Inc., 1972.
9. DeVries, Herbert A.: *Physiology of Exercise for Physical Education and Athletics.* Dubuque, Iowa: William C. Brown and Co., 1966.
10. *Drugs and the Coach.* Washington, D.C.: American Association for Health, Physical Education, and Recreation, 1972.
11. Espenschade, Anna S.: "Role of Exercise in the Well-Being of Women 35-80 Years of Age." *Journal of Gerontology,* 44-48, Jan., 1969.
12. "Exercise and Fitness." (Joint Statement of the American Medical Association and the American Association for Health, Physical Education, and Recreation). *J. Health, Phys. Educ., and Rec.,* 35:42-44, 82 (May, 1964).
13. "Exercise and Weight Control." Committee on Exercise and Physical Fitness of the American Medical Association, the President's Council on Physical Fitness and Sports, and the Lifetime Sports Foundation. Washington, D.C.: President's Council on Physical Fitness and Sports, 1968.
14. Harris, W. E.: *Jogging: A Complete Physical Fitness Program for All Ages.* New York: Grosset & Dunlap, 1972.
15. "Health Problems Revealed During Physical Activity." (Statement of the Committee on Exercise and Physical Fitness of the American Medical Association.) *J. Health, Phys. Educ., Rec.,* 36:6-8 (September, 1965).
16. Hein, Fred V.: "Not Just Exercise." *Hygeia,* 25:350-351, 376-380 (May, 1947).
17. Hellebrandt, F. A.: "Living Anatomy." *Quest,* I: 43-58 (December, 1963).
18. Hunsicker, Paul A., and Reiff, Guy G.: *A Survey and Comparison of Youth Fitness 1958–1965.* Ann Arbor, Mich.: University of Michigan, 1965.
19. Karpovich, Peter V., and Sinning, Wayne E.: *Physiology of Muscular Activity.* Philadelphia: W. B. Saunders Company, 7th ed., 1971.
20. Kelley, David L.: *Kinesiology: Fundamentals of Motion Description.* Englewood Cliffs, N.J.: Prentice-Hall, Inc., 1971.
21. *Kinesiology III.* Washington, D.C.: American Association for Health, Physical Education, and Recreation, 1973.
22. Kraus, Hans, and Hirschland, Ruth P.: "Muscular Fitness and Health." *J. Am. Assoc. Health, Phys. Educ., Rec.,* 24:17-19 (December, 1953).
23. Larson, Leonard A. and Michelman, Herbert: International Guide to Fitness and Health. Crown, 1973.
24. Logan, Gene A., and McKinney, Wayne C.: *Kinesiology.* Dubuque, Iowa: William C. Brown and Co., 1970.
25. Mathews, Donald K. and Fox, Edward L.: *Physiological Basis of Physical Education and Athletics.* Philadelphia: W. B. Saunders Company, 1971.
26. Mayer, Jean: "Exercise and Weight Control." From Johnson, Warren R. (ed.): *Science and Medicine of Exercise and Sports.* New York: Harper & Row, Publishers, Inc., 2nd ed., 1972.
27. "A Message from the President of the United States." *J. Am. Assoc. Health, Phys. Educ., Rec.,* 42:12, 13 (February, 1971).

28. Morehouse, Laurence E., and Miller, Augustus T.: *Physiology of Exercise*. St. Louis: The C. V. Mosby Company, 6th ed., 1971.
29. Morgan, William P. (ed.): *Ergogenic Aids and Muscular Performance*. New York: Academic Press, Inc., 1972.
30. "Need for Varied Activities in Physical Education Programs." (A statement by the Committee on Exercise and Physical Fitness of the American Medical Association). *J. Health, Phys. Educ., Rec.,* 36:6-8 (June, 1965).
31. *New York State Physical Fitness Test*. Albany, N.Y.: University of the State of New York, The State Education Department, Division of Health, Physical Education and Recreation, Bureau of Physical Education, 1958.
32. Oberteuffer, Delbert: "The Role of Physical Education in Health and Fitness." *Am. J. Pub. Health,* 52: 1155-1160 (July, 1962).
33. *Physical Fitness Elements in Recreation—Suggestions for Community Programs*. Washington, D.C.: President's Council on Youth Fitness, U.S. Government Printing Office, 1962.
34. *Physical Fitness News Letter*, H. Harrison Clarke (ed.) Eugene, Oregon: VIII (December, 1961).
34a. Rasch, Philip J., and Burke, Roger K.: *Kinesiology and Applied Anatomy—the Science of Human Movement*. Philadelphia: Lea and Febiger, 4th ed., 1971.
35. *Recreation and Physical Activity for the Mentally Retarded*. Washington, D.C.: American Association for Health, Physical Education, and Recreation, 1966.
36. Ricci, Benjamin: *Physical and Physiological Conditioning for Men*. Dubuque, Iowa: William C. Brown and Co., 2nd ed., 1969.
37. *Royal Canadian Air Force Exercise Plans for Physical Fitness*. Ontario, Canada: Simon & Schuster of Canada, 1972.
38. Shephard, Roy J.: *Alive Man: The Physiology of Physical Activity*. Springfield, Ill.: Charles C Thomas, Publisher, 1972.
39. Shephard, Roy J. (ed.): *Frontiers of Fitness*. Springfield, Ill.: Charles C Thomas, Publisher, 1971.
40. Villee, Claude A.: *Biology*. Philadelphia: W. B. Saunders Company, 6th ed., 1972.
41. Wells, Katharine F.: *Kinesiology: The Scientific Basis of Human Motion*. Philadelphia: W. B. Saunders Company, 5th ed., 1971.
42. Wilds, Elmer H.: *The Foundations of Modern Education*. New York: Holt, Rinehart & Winston, 3rd ed., 1961.
43. *Youth Fitness Test Manual*. Washington, D.C.: American Association for Health, Physical Education, and Recreation, rev. ed., 1965.
44. *Youth Physical Fitness*. Washington, D.C.: President's Council on Physical Fitness, U.S. Government Printing Office, rev. ed., 1967.

(Courtesy of the Department of Physical Education and Athletics for Men, Stanford University.)

Chapter Nine

THE PHYSICAL EDUCATION CURRICULUM

Voluntary movement is a significant function of man; it serves many roles in human life. Motor development is of crucial importance in the growth and learning of the preschool child. Physical recreation is important to elementary school children and secondary school youth in their out-of-school hours. Physical activity plays a vital role in the lives of all adults during the productive career years and into retirement living. Professional physical educators are concerned with the importance of their discipline to all of these contexts. School programs of physical education, however, must be thought of as primarily educational.

Organized, formal education helps the individual to develop his capacity to function successfully in the environment in which he lives, to contribute to the improvement of that environment, and to realize his full personal, human potential. Because the time available for schooling is comparatively brief, there exists the problem of the types of contributions upon which the school should concentrate. To what extent is physical education an essential element of a contemporary liberal education?

People need physical education to help them live well in today's world. We need efficient body mechanics, understanding of optimum body alignment for long periods of sitting or standing or specific physical work tasks. We need skills of conscious neuromuscular relaxation to renew enthusiasm and maintain productivity through long periods of stress. We need perceptual-motor training to help us evoke appropriate motor responses to the variety of stimuli by which we are constantly bombarded. We need direct survival skills of water safety and personal self-defense. We need satisfying physical recreation experiences to find personal joy in movement and to share fully in group living in our society.

Not only do we need physical education to live in today's world. We need a physical education to cope with tomorrow's world. Tomorrow's world will certainly require us to adapt movement patterns to conditions of weightlessness, to develop new movement skills for tasks yet undefined, and to condition ourselves for unfamiliar forms of stress. We will need men and women with the knowledges, skills, and physical training, not just to enjoy underwater sport, but to work and maintain themselves for long periods of time far below the ocean surfaces. Human beings will need to learn to adjust to temperature extremes and variability. We will need many experts competent to investigate different factors of human performance.

We need physical education relevant to today's living and tomorrow's coping. But, more important, physical education is needed in this computer space age to emphasize man's humanity. Man retains his humanness only as he is a fully integrated person. Education which emphasizes the wholeness of the individual—as expressed through movement as an avenue of self-expression, movement as a form of participation in wholesome group activity, movement as a means of communication among persons, movement as one aspect of our common humanity—is sorely needed in this contemporary world.

CHANGING CONCEPTS OF SCHOOLING

Originally, the function of the school in America was to teach children to read, write, and figure. The other phases of education were assumed to be taken care of through the media of the home, the church, and community life. But as the social order became increasingly complex, and as the pattern of home and community life underwent many changes, the school assumed wider responsibilities.

During the past 20 to 30 years, the school has come more and more to be regarded as a place where students gain experience in better living and learn to become more effective citizens in a democratic country. These objectives developed as the public school's responsibilities grew to include more than the traditional task of the school to provide knowledge and mastery of the "three R's." Now, since the advent of sputnik and intercontinental ballistic missiles, there has been a continuous and important reevaluation of the purposes and function of public schools in America. Many individuals and groups advocate a return to the "fundamentals," a deemphasis on "social adjustment" and "citizenship" as major aims of the schools, and a primary emphasis on learning the basic concepts and modes of inquiry of the academic disciplines.

There is a real danger that current curricular emphases and the rapid widespread use of instructional technology will lead to the "dehumanization" of the individual. This potential danger has been recognized and discussed publicly and in professional literature by perceptive scholars of curriculum and by authorities in the fields of mental health, sociology, and social psychology. Goodlad[57] and others urge a redress in the balance of curriculum directions, and they predict that we will see a return to a "humanized" curriculum in the years ahead.

The education essential to each individual person includes learnings concerned with how human movement functions in his experience and in achieving common human goals. Physical education has long been viewed as the series of school programs concerned with the development and utilization of the individual's movement potential. Currently, physical educators attempting to realize the full potential of this area of human experience are seeking to extend concepts of physical education to the needs of learners of all ages in both school and non-institutional contexts. Physical education is increasingly viewed as personalized, self-directed learning, using selected movement learning media to achieve individual human goals. Physical education provides instruction and selected experiences in human movements which help the individual to learn more about himself as a fully integrated person and to increase his understanding of the meaning and significance of his life in the social milieu in which he lives.[87]

Social Involvement

As it is increasingly recognized that education is a continuing life activity, more professional educators are referring to institutionalized aspects of education as schooling, thus distinguishing the organized relatively formal phases of education which are the primary responsibility of teachers, from the limitless range of experiences which may properly be considered education. The focus of this chapter is upon schooling as contrasted with education and upon the place of school programs of physical education in total school programs.

Although there are many educators who plead for narrowing the scope of school responsibility and many legislators and taxpayers who are seeking limited and specific definitions of school accountability, it is a fact that the American public in the 1970's insists upon school involvement in broad social programs and the application of curricular attention to the more critical social problems of our times. People are demanding that school personnel find ways of assisting with the resolution of urban ills, ecological crises, and the continuing problems of those children and youth disadvantaged by our social system and its institutions.

Under the changing conditions of the present and the predictable future, man tends toward a vastly different type of life from that of the past. While it is true that man's advancement in civilization has brought a multitude of advantages to the human race, it has also produced many conditions of living which are fundamentally detrimental.

A large percentage of the people are crowded together in cities or in suburbs of tract and row houses which afford them little incentive or opportunity to lead the type of life that is normal for human beings. In the cities, lack of open space inhibits the normal, free play life of children and adults alike. One of the greatest dangers in fast-developing suburban areas is that cities, school districts, recreation districts, and counties will fail to acquire sufficient outdoor space for educational and recreational use while such areas are available, prior to becoming subdivisions or business zones.

Everywhere, mechanical means of transportation tend to make walking a lost art. Housework, chores, and errands often no longer involve any considerable amount of vigorous activity. The motion picture, radio, and television offer sedentary forms of entertainment and recreation, providing vicarious emotional experiences as substitutes for the active enjoyment and genuine emotional experiences derived from the more natural pursuits of hunting, fishing, play, games, and the like. Machines have replaced thousands of workers who previously performed routine tasks with human muscle power. The development of automation in industry has reduced the amount of physical energy supplied by human beings.

In industry, the trend toward a shorter work week, longer periods of paid vacation time, earlier retirement, larger retirement benefits, and similar changing conditions is providing millions of Americans with previously unheard-of amounts of leisure time. Still, many persons, particularly those in executive and leadership positions, are working long, strenuous hours under pressure and strain. Leaders in the professions and in business may work seventy or more hours per week, and at a fast pace. Others, who work a forty-hour week or less, seek a second job. Such individuals actually may work 60 to 80 hours per week at two jobs. In many cases, this extended strenuous effort results in deleterious physical and mental fatigue.

The labor market is changing rapidly and drastically. Current difficulties in career entry by high school graduates and frustrations of career progression and re-education for second and third occupations by mid-career adults, particularly women, demand solution. The complexity of our present-day social and economic order and the lack of predictability of particular job status and opportunity develop much insecurity and undesirable emotional tension, for which there are insufficient acceptable outlets.

A majority of our population now lives in or near polluted air in the form of "smog," a potentially hazardous phenomenon whose health dangers have been dramatically reported and about which dire predictions have been made. Likewise, many large bodies of water such as streams, lakes, and reservoirs have become polluted by the dumping of sewage, garbage, and industrial waste products into them. Waters which formerly were pure enough to drink, and, until recently, were safe for swimming, have had to be declared "off limits" as health hazards. Even portions of the Atlantic and Pacific oceans near the shoreline have been marked "off limits" because large cities now drain their sewage into the ocean at those points.

A large portion of the American public is on the move. Individuals and family units move to new areas for various reasons. Many of them make multiple moves over a period of several years. One of the school's greatest problems is to maintain a program of continuity for an individual child as he transfers from one school to another, in different cities and frequently in different states. This easy mobility in turn tends to foster less stable friendships and neighborhood life. Many people are lonely and depressed. A trend toward "dehumanization" has been identified by sociologists who have studied these present-day patterns of working and living conditions.

Humanistic Education

Most current educational philosophers, authors, journalists, and critics endorse greater humanism in education. While thinking persons are challenging the schools to take greater responsibility for the resolution of major practical social problems, they are concurrently urging a clearer, more sensitive focus on the individual. Humanistic education strives toward individual self-actualization. The goal of every learner is to become all that he is capable of becoming.

Humanistic education is concerned with two modes of knowledge. It seeks what Bronowski[24] describes as "the single identity of man" through scientific knowledge and self-knowledge. Scientific knowledge uses empirical tests to provide us with a thinking language. The self-knowledge which underlies the arts provides "a second language in which a man converses with himself." Scientific knowledge is single-valued while the knowledge of the arts is many-valued. The two modes of knowledge complement each other to create an ethic that unites respect for what is done with respect for what we are.

Humanistic education seeks individual identity through the development of those qualities and abilities which are characteristically human. Humanistic education focuses on the interests and ideals of people in contrast to technological efficiency or the maintenance of a social status system. Humanistic education places the integrity of persons above the structure of knowledge or the quality control of material objects. Humanistic education helps each learner to find personal meaning in the confluence of cognitive, affective, and motor experience.

Weinstein and Fantini,[122] reporting their findings in working with ghetto children, propose that the concept of "disadvantaged" be extended to include anyone who is denied what he needs for fulfillment of his human potential. They support the development of a "curriculum of affect," a model for teaching based on pupils' concerns and feelings rather than on purely cognitive goals.

Models for School Programs

Many models have been developed by those seeking to improve the processes of schooling or to increase its effectiveness. Proposed models run the gamut from traditional grade-placement models, through cybernetic-systems models, to "alternative schools." Joyce has popularized the notion of a variety of educational models appropriate to a spectrum of educational missions. He proposes a pluralistic world of education composed of programs designed in accordance with differing models to further a large number of educational missions.[70]

Many curriculum models of the 1960's have been designated "conceptual" models and have emphasized analyses of the bodies of knowledge of the various disciplines. Key concepts have been identified in mathematics, biology, physics, chemistry, social studies, health education, and in physical education; instructional units are then organized in terms of selected key concepts and subconcepts. Schools place great stress on acquiring knowledge of these concepts as the most efficient means for the human central nervous system to receive, collect, classify, store, retrieve, and utilize essential elements from a vast reservoir of rapidly increasing and changing human knowledge.

Systems analysis is currently being applied in educational management by many who believe that these techniques can help to create outcomes which dedicated professionals have sought for years. Kaufman* defines the *system approach* as:

> A process by which needs are identified, problems selected, requirements for problem solution are identified, solutions are chosen from alternatives, methods and means are obtained and implemented, results are evaluated, and required revisions to all or part of the system are made so that the needs are eliminated.

System planning requires description of predictable learner-oriented results, clarification of inputs as well as outputs, and the use of such tools as mission analysis, function analysis, task analysis, and methods-means analysis. Those who support a system approach to schooling argue that precision and planning can be our best assurance that learners are not forced into arbitrary molds through ignorance or lack of adequate instructional tools. Whether or not a system approach is humanizing depends upon the people using it and whether they use its tools appropriately for making education individually responsive.

The youth rebellion of the 60's forced education decision makers to realize that schooling had in fact been largely irrelevant for many and had "miserably failed the individual student in his search for self-

---

* Roger A. Kaufman, *Educational System Planning* (Englewood Cliffs, N.J.: Prentice-Hall, 1972), p. 2.

fulfillment."* New programs which lend new emphases to many subject fields, which can be relevant only if they are developed through
interdisciplinary approaches, which attack key human problems
through creative curriculum designs and innovative instructional arrangements, are being introduced in many schools. Programs in early
childhood education, parent and family life education, human sexual-
ity, family economics, consumer education, race relations, and drug
abuse are examples. School programs in ecology and the control of
pollution have reoriented many established offerings in the sciences
and suggested new models for laboratory experience and outdoor education. Emerging concepts in continuing and adult education have
provided new models for off-campus learning and school-community
cooperation and stimulated educational change in equivalency certifi-
cates, creative leisure activities, apprentice training, public affairs
education, "women's world," "schools without walls," "education
about education."

The Federal government has mounted a major effort in the 70's
to strengthen programs of career education in the nation's schools.[33]
The fundamental concept of career education is that all educational
experiences, curriculum, instruction, and counseling should be geared
to preparation for economic independence and an appreciation for
the dignity of work. It is designed to increase the relevance of school
by focusing on the learner's career choice.

> The main thrust of career education is to prepare all students
> for a successful life of work by increasing their options for occupa-
> tional choice, by eliminating barriers—real and imagined—to attaining
> job skills, and by enhancing learning achievement in all subject areas
> and at all levels of education.

Under the career education concept, the elementary school child
explores the world of work through a wide spectrum of occupational
"clusters"; in the middle grades he explores those in which he is most
interested. During the secondary school years, all students develop elementary job entry skills and have opportunities to enjoy actual work
through cooperative arrangements with business, industry, and public
institutions. The career education concept is being developed through
state-level curriculum laboratories and vocational research coordinating units. Presently, four career education models are being exam-

---

* Margaret Gill Hein, "Planning and Organizing for Improved Instruction,"
Curriculum Handbook for School Executives (Arlington, Va.: American Association
for School Administrators, 1973), p. 366.

ined under the direction of the Career Education Development Task Force of the National Institute of Education.[50]

Alternatives is a key word in contemporary writings about education. Some of the current models for alternative curricula and programs within today's schools have been identified in the preceding paragraphs. Other proposals and models have been offered as alternative schools. The concept of the private school which provides an option for the individual child or family not satisfied with the manner in which the public school meets individual needs is not new. But the interest in attending and supporting alternative schools has greatly increased in the current decade in the context of concern for individual freedom and the preservation of cultural pluralism; of criticism of state and Federal regulation of schools and of inflexible certification and curriculum requirements; and of disenchantment with local schools and the frustratingly slow pace of educational change. Today, some alternative schools are publicly supported within the system, offering these wider options to individual learners without the financial resources to attend private institutions. On the higher education level, the free university, the non-resident degree, and new alternative programs through state university extension divisions are expressions of the alternative school concept.

Accountability

The term accountability first appears in the *Education Index* in June, 1970. The entry reflects changing concepts of the responsibility of the school to its constituents and the accountability of school agents to external authorities. Proponents of behavioral accountability are urging that the effectiveness of schools be judged by results achieved, measured in terms of student accomplishments. In many instances, not only effectiveness, but also efficiency, in the form of relating dollars spent to student accomplishment, is required. A program of behavioral accountability provides for a systematic attempt to specify objectives in measurable terms, the control of educational outputs to coincide with these objectives, and an external program evaluation of the extent of achievement of objectives.[25] The techniques used include program evaluation and review technique (PERT), program planning and budgeting system (PPBS), and management by objectives (MBO). It is anticipated that the current pres-

sures on elementary and secondary schools for behavioral accountability will continue in the 70's. Responsible educators accept the
desirability of shifting the focus from teaching to learning. The real
challenge of the next decade, however, is to find a balance between
protection of the public interest and the maintenance of an educational environment conducive to creative teaching and the continuous
growth and development of learners as self-actualizing individuals.

Curriculum Change

Curriculum modifications have characterized American schools
since their beginnings. Actual study of the process of curriculum
improvement is a relatively modern feature, however. Curriculum
change is social change. Planned curriculum change is typically
viewed as a problem-solving process directed toward changes in people, changes in the structure of the school as a social institution, and
changes in human relationships within local groups.

The question of procedures for curriculum change has begun to
receive formal attention from social scientists since about 1960.[51]
Miles[88] proposes a comprehensive strategy which includes provision
for careful design of an innovation, development of local awareness
and interest, local evaluation, and local trial. Clark and Guba[35] have
developed a logical structure for examining roles in educational
change which identifies and analyzes the four processes of research,
development, diffusion, and adoption.

Although the teacher plays a key role in curriculum change,
teachers and administrators, and even school boards, actually have
less direct control and unfettered power to make their own curriculum
decisions than at any previous time. For twenty years or more, it has
been considered desirable for students, parents, and citizens' advisory
committees to offer recommendations; today these groups are playing
a more vocal role. There are many sources of pressures for curriculum
change which every teacher should recognize and learn to deal with.
It is an inescapable fact of life today that public school curricula are
under continuous *political* influence not only at the level of the local
school board and city but also through county, state, and federal
levels of government.

Other sources of power and influence are identified and
described by Nixon and Jewett.[93] Briefly, they include the National
Education Association and its many agencies and divisions, and affil-

iated organizations; the American Association for Health, Physical Education and Recreation; the many programs under the auspices of the National Institute of Education in the Department of Health, Education, and Welfare, and particularly the implications of large federal grant programs administered by that agency; the President's Council on Physical Fitness and Sports; the American Medical Association; state departments of public instruction; state legislatures; state boards of education operating under various delegated legal powers; traditional curriculum reform groups; private foundations; colleges and universities; business corporations having education-related projects; individual consultants from business and higher education; and county school officials. Undoubtedly this list can be supplemented further.

Recommended changes should be based on thorough evaluation and appraisal of the existing objectives of the curriculum, and of the extent to which these curricular objectives are being attained. It is not sufficient to change the objectives, or some of the activities, or certain teaching methods, or to modify testing procedures listed in the course of study, in order to accomplish fundamental curriculum development. By definition, the curriculum is changed only when the actual learning experiences of students are changed. Basic to all curriculum change is the fact that teachers and administrators must change their values and attitudes, and hence their behavior. Changing people is a complex process and usually demands considerable time and effort on the part of those who change and of the leaders who aspire to effect specific changes.

Definitions

Definitions which describe *curriculum* as consisting of all experiences conducted under school auspices became established in the 1930's and were not generally questioned until the 1960's.[51] In the 1970's genuine controversy exists concerning the definition of the term. The predominant view at present appears to accept curriculum as both "the operational statement of the school's goals" and "the operational consequence of the school's goals." Broadly defined, the school program includes the classroom and laboratory instruction during scheduled classes and also the bus ride to school in the morning, the lunch hour activities, the football game after school, and the conference with the school counselor. The physical education program comprises all experiences organized and directed by the physical education staff, including dressing for class, being measured for height and weight, taking a physical fitness test, practicing for varsity basketball, and taking a shower, along with the formal instructional experiences presented during the physical education class period.

It is important to understand, and to interpret to others, that the gymnasium floor, the dance studio, the tennis courts, the swimming pool, and all of the other areas where physical education classes and sports teams participate are *classrooms* and *laboratories* in the same sense as are other learning areas throughout the school. They are not just facilities available for recreation, play, or recess.

The subject matter of physical education consists of human movement phenomena; its learning media include such movement forms as individual, dual, and team games, sports and athletics, aquatic activities, various forms of dance, body mechanics activities, and self-testing events. Vigorous movement activities constitute the most conspicuous feature of the physical education program because overt physical responses occur. Out of these observable responses come the desired physical modifications of the individual, and the accompanying mental, emotional, and social responses which are significant for the development of character, personality, and intelligence. Obviously, the proper selection of learning experiences is of fundamental concern to the development of a sound physical education program. Equally important are the proper placement and sequence or progression of learning activities according to the growth and developmental needs and characteristics of the learners. This planning process typically is referred to as determining the *scope* and *sequence* of the curriculum.

The *Course of Study* or *Department Handbook* or *Teachers' Guide* are terms commonly applied to the materials assembled by teachers, supervisors, and administrators to guide the organization, administration, instruction, and evaluation of the learning experiences under the direction of the physical education department.

Properly speaking, *curriculum* should be distinguished from *instruction*. In other references, the authors have supported Macdonald's distinctions and defined *curriculum* as a plan for instructional action based on a set of decisions intended to be reflected in the behavior of learners. According to Macdonald.*

---

* James B. Macdonald, "Educational Models for Instruction—An Introduction," *Theories of Instruction* (Washington, D.C.: National Education Association, 1965), pp. 1-7.

... teaching is defined as the behavior of the teacher, learning as the change in learner behavior, instruction as the pupil-teacher interaction situation and curriculum as those planning endeavors which take place prior to instruction.

For purposes of this text, however, the following deals with all four of the inter-related systems.

PHYSICAL EDUCATION CURRICULUM DEVELOPMENT

The process of curriculum development is extremely complex. Curriculum specialists in any subject-matter field must begin by clarifying the total educational setting in which they work. The overall educational philosophy of the local school is a starting point; the philosophy of the physical education department must maintain consistency with the overall school philosophy. The objectives of the physical education program and the goals of students are expressed in consonance with this philosophy. The needs of individual students and of groups of learners must be studied and assessed through a variety of techniques in order to state program objectives directed toward optimal implementation of local educational philosophy. Given well-defined program objectives, the physical education curriculum specialist can then work with the total teaching staff, supported by administrative resources, in consultation with representative students, parents, and community leaders, to plan for (1) scope, (2) sequence, and (3) continuous evaluation of physical education programs.

Scope

The total scope of physical education extends to the development and utilization of the individual's movement potential throughout his life span. It includes movement activities and related learnings in non-school as well as school settings. The procedure of selecting activities and learning experiences for inclusion in school programs is generally referred to as designating the *scope* of the physical education curriculum.

What does the discipline of human movement have to offer in man's search for knowledge? What movement understandings and skills and which attitudes relating to movement behavior are essential in his pursuit of happiness? These are questions which must be answered in determining the scope of the physical education curriculum.

Voluntary movement is a significant function of man. Thus, the school is concerned with how movement functions in an individual's experience and in achieving common human goals. Human beings of all ages have the same fundamental purposes for moving. The child needs physical education which will aid him in becoming a fully functioning adult; the adult needs movement activities which will permit continuing self-actualization and more nearly complete individual-environment interaction. Physical education experiences fulfill the same key purposes for persons of all ages. Each individual *learns to move* to achieve these human purposes. Curriculum content in physical education must offer the individual movement experiences related to the common purposes of moving planned so that he learns how movement functions in his life.

Traditionally, scope is displayed in the form of charts, which list instructional units by activity, grade level, and, usually, by number and arrangement of days or weeks assigned to each activity. Other data can be included such as level of instruction (fundamental, elementary, intermediate, advanced, enrichment), basis of pupil grouping into classes, assignment of teachers, and other relevant factors.

The scope can be described in narrative form in any degree of detail deemed desirable to express the judgment of those charged with responsibility for making curriculum decisions. An outstanding example of such a narrative description of physical education curriculum scope is formulated by Project Broadfront* in the public schools of Ellensberg, Washington. This detailed explanation of the scope of their curriculum appears in two sections, one entitled "Physical Education and Human Movement," and the other called "The Evolving Ellensberg Physical Education Program." The scope and sequence found in Broadfront are conceived as the bases for insuring an articu-

---

* Project Broadfront is an exemplary and innovative program of school health, physical education, community-school programs, outdoor education, and special education. This Project was conducted under a grant awarded under Title III of the Elementary and Secondary Education Act of 1965, 1967 to 1970. Mr. Lloyd Rowley was Director of Project Broadfront.

lated program of physical education from kindergarten through grade twelve. It is used in all five schools in the district.

The procedure for determining scope which has been developed through the Curriculum Project of the Physical Education Division of the American Association for Health, Physical Education, and Recreation* provides for the selection of curriculum experiences in terms of three key purposes or human movement goals: (1) to fulfill personal developmental potential, (2) to develop movement skills utilized in adapting to and controlling the physical environment, and (3) to assist the individual in relating to other persons. Seven major purpose concepts for describing the scope of the physical education curriculum have been identified and defined as follows:

A. Physiological Efficiency: Man moves to develop and maintain his functional capabilities.

B. Psychic Equilibrium: Man moves to achieve personal integration.

C. Spatial Orientation: Man moves to relate himself in three-dimensional space.

D. Object Manipulation: Man moves to give impetus to and to absorb the force of objects.

E. Communication: Man moves to share ideas and feelings with others.

F. Group Interaction: Man moves to function in harmony with others.

G. Cultural Involvement: Man moves to take part in movement activities which constitute an important part of his society.

These purpose concepts have been further subdivided into elements which serve as a starting point for local curriculum planners. Decisions concerning the relative emphasis to be given to particular purposes or elements are based on local educational philosophy and the needs and interests of the appropriate school population. The selection of specific movement activities or learning media depends upon the judgment of the professional staff and upon local conditions and resources.

Using this approach, programs in a community which is concerned about the physical fitness status of its young people will give

---

* Ann E. Jewett (ed.), *Curriculum Design: Purposes and Processes in Physical Education Teaching-Learning* (Washington, D.C.: American Association for Health, Physical Education and Recreation, 1974).

special emphasis to a greater proportion of physical fitness activities carefully selected in terms of the specific deficiencies or needs identified. If the local school philosophy lends strong support to the life-time sports concept, a popular emphasis in today's schools, curriculum planners will study the participation element of the cultural involvement purpose concept and will establish program goals in terms of variety of sports experience, types of essential "carry-over activity" experiences, and standards for desired proficiency. In instances in which a high priority is to be given to the competition element of the larger purpose of group interaction, the scope would reflect this choice in the predominance of skill development activities in the popular competitive sports and the availability of intensive practice opportunities in a wide range of sports to accommodate many students.

Sequence

Curriculum development also requires the organization of selected learning activities and the placement or ordering of planned experiences in designing educational programs for groups and individuals. These processes provide for *sequence* in a given curriculum. Repetition of a limited few activities from year to year, unthinking seasonal rotation of traditional sports units, and lack of sound sequence are criticisms frequently leveled at physical education.

The usual approach to providing sequence in physical education curricula in the past has been to assign particular activities to specific grade levels on the basis of age standards and the best available knowledge of typical developmental levels for comparable populations. This procedure does not lend itself to individualizing learning and is especially unsatisfactory in non-graded programs and appropriate placement schools. Conscientious physical educators have commonly analyzed sport, gymnastic, and dance activities in terms of complexity of the specific motor skills required, and established recommended "progressions." While this procedure permits broad classification into beginning, intermediate, and advanced activity units, and can be adapted to a continuous performance or phased curriculum, its limitation is that undue emphasis is placed on the subject matter as traditionally conceived in particular sports and games, thus discouraging the invention of new movement activities, modification of established activities, or the creative design of environments for individual learning.

It is suggested that sequence in physical education can best be facilitated by organizing curricular content in terms of desired movement process outcomes. Movement processes represent one large segment of human behavior. Process learnings are, therefore, essential physical education outcomes. Important learning opportunities include those concerned with the processes by which an individual *moves to learn,* the processes by which he learns to facilitate, extend, and utilize fully his unique movement capabilities.

The authors believe that the functions of movement in prolonging and enriching the quality of life can serve to define the scope of the physical education curriculum and that the processes of self-actualization through movement provide a basis for sequencing potential learning experiences in physical education. The movement classification scheme which follows conceptualizes seven movement process categories and offers a taxonomy for the selection and statement of educational objectives.*

1. *Perceiving:* Awareness of movement positions, postures, patterns, and skills. These awarenesses may be evidenced by motoric acts such as imitating a position or skill; they may be sensory in that the mover feels a posture when the limbs are manipulated; or they may be evidenced cognitively through identification, recognition, or distinction.
2. *Patterning:* Arrangement and use of body parts in successive and harmonious ways to achieve a movement pattern or skill. This level is dependent on recall and performance of a movement previously demonstrated or experienced.
3. *Adapting:* Modification of a patterned movement to meet externally imposed task demands. This would include modification of a particular movement to perform it under different conditions.
4. *Refining:* Acquisition of smooth, efficient control in performing a movement pattern or skill by mastery of spatial and temporal relations. This process deals with the achievement of precision in motor performance and habituation of performance under more complex conditions.
5. *Varying:* Invention or construction of unique or novel options in motor performance. These options are limited to different ways of performing specific movements; they are of an immediate situational nature and lack any predetermined goal or outcome which has been externally imposed on the mover.
6. *Improvising:* Extemporaneous origination or initiation of novel

---

* Ann E. Jewett (ed.), *Curriculum Design: Purposes and Processes in Physical Education Teaching-Learning* (Washington, D.C.: American Association for Health, Physical Education and Recreation, 1974).

movements or combinations of movements. The processes involved may be stimulated by a situation externally structured, but preplanning on the part of the performer is not usually required.

7. *Composing:* Combination of learned movements into unique motor designs or the creation of movements new to the performer. The performer creates his own motor response in terms of his own interpretation of a movement situation.

In practice, curriculum planners determine the scope of local physical education curricula as described above, making priority decisions concerning major emphases, identifying essential curriculum content, clarifying district-wide agreements, and establishing guidelines for planning within each school and within the various administrative units. Teachers develop instructional objectives, using elements of human movement as the content focus and movement processes to identify the level toward which instruction is directed. This procedure can be used to generate educational objectives for instructional groups in any learning environment, utilizing a wide variety of learning media encompassing traditional and popular games, stunts, sports and dance activities, innovative movement education challenges, and unfamiliar but potentially satisfying physical recreation opportunities. Even more important, it can be used to identify instructional objectives for individual learners and to guide personalized learning at different process levels for a number of individuals learning in a group environment, but not necessarily attempting to achieve the same goal at the same time.

Evaluation

An important aspect of curriculum development is continuous evaluation of the program as a basis for further improvement. At least once a year an overall appraisal of status is needed in order to review program objectives and modify short-term goals as necessary. In this phase of evaluation it is desirable to involve other members of the school teaching and administrative staff, district office personnel, interested parents, student representatives, and citizens' group representatives, in addition to all department staff members who should be involved in both formal and informal procedures to appraise the physical education program on a continuous basis. Consultation on particular aspects of educational evaluation may also be sought from District Curriculum Department personnel, the State Department of Education, professional associations, and nearby colleges and universities.

Day-to-day evaluation and appraisal of program strengths and weaknesses and the ongoing collection of specific assessment data are responsibilities of the local physical education staff, however. In program areas in which it is feasible to use specific performance objectives, these are developed by the teaching staff, who work directly with students. The concept of formative evaluation is gaining adherents because it permits organized and well-planned instruction to be modified immediately on the basis of information concerning student learning progress.

Certain important educational goals and accomplishments cannot be evaluated satisfactorily by means of specific performance objectives. Learning progress and relative program success in these areas should also be included in appraising the effectiveness and quality of physical education in the local schools. Assessment techniques available include interest preference scales, ratings, attitude inventories, interaction analysis, interviews, structured observation category systems, and audio- and videotape analysis. Evaluation is discussed in greater detail in Chapter 12.

ORGANIZATIONAL PATTERNS

The crucial curriculum decisions are those relating to scope, sequence, and evaluation. If these decisions are soundly based, many organizational patterns can be selected or developed to implement effective educational programs. Many local factors, including geographic and climatic conditions, available instructional areas, available equipment, nature of the total school schedule, class size, teacher loads, and time allotted to physical education, need consideration in planning for the administration and conduct of physical education programs. For purposes of discussion, these are considered in four categories: (1) grouping, (2) scheduling and staffing, (3) learning resources, and (4) individualization and personalization.

Current interest in innovative organizational patterns was stimulated in the 1960's by the work and publications of the National

Association of Secondary School Principals, particularly its Commission on the Experimental Study of the Utilization of the Staff in Secondary Schools and the more recent Model Schools Project directed by Trump.[115,116,117] Although the original impetus related to secondary schools, the key organizational concepts have also been extended to elementary school education. Physical educators have recognized the unique possibilities for similar approaches to improving instruction in their field. The Committee on Organizational Patterns for Physical Education and Recreation, chaired by Heitmann, studied organizational patterns across the nation and reported a variety of innovative patterns and practices. The report of this committee is recommended to all physical educators for helpful descriptions of ways to organize time, students, and staff to facilitate learning in physical education.[11]

Grouping

Since the function of student grouping is to facilitate learning, any plan for grouping should be flexible and pupils should be able to transfer from one group to another as appropriate. The group environment most conducive to learning will vary with student characteristics, teacher abilities, and learning tasks. Heitmann[60] has identified nine methods of student grouping in physical education: grade level, anthropometric, chronological, social ability, interest, achievement, physical capacity, temperament, and learning characteristics groupings.

Experience and accumulating evidence seem to argue that physical education classes should be grouped on the combined bases of interest and ability. Nixon and Jewett[93] suggest such a plan. There are secondary schools which have four or five such groupings, each of which has an appropriately different curriculum. These groupings can be achieved by selection of various criteria such as physical performance tests, specific skills tests, teachers' judgments of skills and interests, and pupil expression of interests on inventory forms, questionnaires and free-response instruments. Local staffs should select criteria for grouping after thoughtful consideration of program objectives.

The nongraded elementary school presents a unique challenge in grouping pupils for physical education. These schools give careful attention to the need for continuity in individual pupil progress. Students proceed through school at individual rates, operating within broad age level ranges. A variety of diagnostic procedures can be used for student placement. A particularly interesting plan used in the University Elementary School, UCLA, is reported by Cunningham.[42] In this situation pupil placement is determined by diagnostic tests in seven major areas of movement: locomotor skills, eye-hand skills, eye-foot skills, body coordination skills, balance skills, sensory motor skills, and rhythm and dance skills. Other procedures for student grouping in nongraded programs are reported by Curtis[43] and Burson.[32]

Prior to about 1930, there was a traditional feeling among professional leaders that boys and girls should be separated for purposes of physical education activities, starting in the fourth grade. This judgment was predicated upon physiological grounds, with particular reference to the safety of girls, and in consideration for the needs and capacities of both sexes. Social customs were a factor also.

Further study in recent years supports a philosophy that because boys and girls play and work together, not only in adolescence but throughout life, it is natural and logical that coeducational experiences should be given them in recreational activities throughout their public school years. Actually, the distinction commonly made of "girls' physical education" or "boys' physical education" is no more tenable than "boys' English" or "girls' arithmetic." In physical education we select some activities appropriate only for boys, and some appropriate only for girls, because of organic and structural differences, and still other activities which are appropriate for both sexes to participate in together. By definition, our physical education program provides selected learning experiences for all of the "students." The factor of sex is merely one of several considerations which determine the selection of activities in the physical education program.

There has been an ever-increasing trend to select more and more activities which boys and girls can engage in together. Many secondary school programs and most junior college and college and university programs are now predominantly coeducational. These activities have been labeled "coeducational" or "co-recreational." Actually, the term "coeducational activities" is more appropriate with reference to the physical education program, where the emphasis is primarily instructional in nature.

We realize now as never before that socialization is an important part of education, and that in physical education we have an excellent natural opportunity to contribute to this objective. From the experimentation and developments of the past thirty years in the field of coeducational activities the following suggestions are offered for the conduct of these activities.

1. The program of coeducational activities should be only one phase of the entire program. In enthusiastic consideration of the desirability of coeducational activities, it is possible to overemphasize them and to neglect certain other integral phases of a well-rounded program.

2. Participation in specific coeducational activities should be voluntary, not compulsory, although a general coeducational requirement is defensible. Some schools assign one day a week as coeducational activity day. Three or more different activities are offered, and each student selects the activity of his choice. An increasing number of schools now offer particular instructional units or modules in a variety of selected coeducational activities.

3. The opportunity for coeducational activity should be provided at a variety of times, so that all who are interested may be accommodated.

4. Activities should be adapted equally well to both sexes. This will eliminate games involving contact. It will also provide for an appreciation of abilities by both sexes. It implies, too, a modification of rules in certain games.

5. Importance must be attached to the selection of activities that can readily be organized and played in out-of-school hours; otherwise one of the purposes of coeducational activities is lost. Provision must also be made for the organization of these activities under competent leadership during the leisure time of students.

6. Costumes must be appropriate to the activity. What may be appropriate for classes of one sex will not necessarily fit the situation for coeducational activities.

7. Sex distribution according to growth, development, and social maturity is highly desirable. In social or square dancing, for example, sophomore girls and senior boys may be combined to form a successful social and instructional situation.

8. The teaching of coeducational activities is a cooperative undertaking. In the past, it has been largely the women who have undertaken the leadership. Today there is common agreement that men and women instructors should be involved equally. It is not necessary to assign arbitrarily a man and a woman instructor to each activity. The best arrangement involves, first, the assignment of teachers to activities they are most competent to instruct, and second, the assumption of approximately equal responsibility between the

men's and women's staffs for teaching assignments and loads. The program is more readily accepted by the boys if the male teachers demonstrate natural enthusiasm and interest in it through their active participation and leadership. The number of teachers assigned to a specified activity is primarily to be determined by class size and school policy on class size and teacher load.

9. The assistance of student leadership will be helpful. Secure the help of peer leaders, and the program will enjoy high status with a majority of pupils and will move along rapidly. The training of student leaders will also provide a source of leadership in recreation activities during out-of-school hours.

Scheduling and Staffing

Recent changes in physical education scheduling have been directed primarily to minimizing the rigidity which was characteristic until the past decade. Secondary school schedules, in particular, are opening up options within the physical education program. *Selective* programs, which permit students to select from among several alternative offerings within the requirement, are increasingly popular. Many schools now offer *elective* programs in which participation itself is optional. Requirements in physical education based on compulsory time spent in activity programs have become more difficult to support in light of the trend toward eliminating all specific subject requirements. Forward-looking physical educators are giving extra thought and attention to strengthening elective programs. Imaginative elective offerings at both secondary and college levels have attracted large enrollments. The physical education activity programs in junior colleges, colleges and universities are now largely elective.

Another innovation in scheduling is the intersession plan which permits intensive study of a particular subject for a brief period of time. Intersessions are usually scheduled during brief vacation periods or other times outside the typical academic calendar. Together with the year-round school concept, intersessions have increased options for student course selection. In physical education, special off-campus opportunities such as skiing, scuba diving, and mountain-climbing, are very popular.

Flexible group practices are more feasible now through various

(Courtesy of the Department of Physical Education and Athletics for Men, Stanford University.)

forms of modular scheduling which are computer generated. Groups of varying sizes are most appropriate to facilitate the purposes of a particular class on a given day. Although flexible group procedures can also be devised within traditional schedules, many schools are now using modular scheduling as well as flexible grouping arrangements.

Modular scheduling permits the more efficient use of school time to attain educational objectives. A unit of time is selected and the school schedule is built in combinations or multiples of one or more time modules for each subject. Although modules of many different time lengths have been used in the past few years, it appears that twenty-minute modules are in use by a majority. Usually they are scheduled for 21 to 24 modules per day.

Typically, the school schedule repeats itself weekly rather than daily. However, this is not an essential requirement. Other lengths of schedule cycle are possible. The modular schedule is generated by a computer; there are too many combinations and permutations to do it by hand.

Pupils are scheduled into formal classes for from 40 to 60 percent of the total school time available. This time normally includes both small group instruction in groups of 12 to 15 pupils and large group instruction in groups of up to 100 or more. The remaining unscheduled time is available for independent study and for participation in open laboratory work in various subjects, including physical education. Heitmann[60] has provided helpful descriptions of the use of large group instruction, small group instruction, independent study, and open laboratory practice in physical education, and excellent analyses of the advantages, purposes, suggested activities, and operational considerations for establishing each of these four phases of instruction.

Considerations of class size and teacher load have plagued physical educators for years. In 1961 the President's Council on Youth Fitness* recommended:

> Maximum class size not to exceed 35 pupils unless special organization and leadership makes possible the effective handling of larger groups.
> Teaching load not to exceed 200 pupils per day, with adjusted work load for those who direct extra-class and complementary programs.

While this was somewhat helpful, the proposed solution was based on an oversimplified view of the problem and did not have a significant impact on the instructional loads of most physical educators.

Heitmann** reviews four methods used in assigning the responsibility of teaching physical education to the primary grades.

> The one preferred by most authors on the subject is the employment of a physical education specialist to handle virtually all phases of the physical education program. The second preference is the employment of a rotating specialist, sometimes called a curriculum associate, to assist classroom teachers by team teaching with them at least once a week, and by providing leadership in program development, equipment and facility planning, and in-service assistance. A third approach is through the exchanging of assignments, whereby one teacher will teach physical education for another teacher, who in turn, will instruct in another subject. A different form of this pattern, called "team teach-

---

* President's Council on Youth Fitness, *Youth Fitness*. (Washington, D.C.: U.S. Government Printing Office, July, 1961), p. 11.
** Helen M. Heitmann. "Rationale for Change," *Organizational Patterns for Instruction in Physical Education*. (Washington, D.C.: American Association for Health, Physical Education and Recreation, 1971), pp. 30–31.

ing" by some, requires one teacher to learn and teach dance, for example, another tumbling, and a third ball skills. . . . The fourth and least effective approach is the self-contained classroom where the teacher assumes the complete responsibility without assistance from other teachers.

An unusual analysis of tasks performed by high school teachers of boys' physical education by Gilmore[54] throws light on a basic staff problem of major proportions. He identified 68 tasks which these teachers typically perform. He then developed sets of criteria by which each task was evaluated as being professional, semi-professional, or non-professional. A sample of teachers kept daily diaries concerning the amount of time they spent on the 68 tasks. Gilmore found that 46 percent of their time was devoted to professional tasks, 25 percent to semi-professional tasks, and 29 percent to non-professional tasks. If these figures accurately represent the status of male physical education teachers in high schools, there is cause for considerable concern.

The obvious basic principle of effective staff utilization is that credentialed teachers primarily should be assigned to perform professional duties. Personnel with varying kinds of preparation and experience should be employed to perform semi-professional and non-professional duties under the supervision of senior credentialed teachers. Accompanying this differentiation of duties would be a differentiated salary schedule.

Many physical education departments have realized this problem, and there are examples of schools now assisting teachers by using teacher aides, skill aides, community sports specialists, specialized resource people, volunteers, student teachers, interns, student leaders, community-school directors, custodians, matrons, secretaries, and clerks.

Trump popularized team teaching and differentiated staffing in the '60's.[114,115,117] His current recommendations for the nation-wide Model Schools Project sponsored by the National Association of Secondary School Principals are as follows:[116]

> For every 35 pupils enrolled in a school, the instructional staff should include: one teacher, 20 hours per week of instructional assistance and 5 hours per week of general aides.

He further recommends that the number of teachers assigned to health, physical education, and recreation be one-eighth of the total staff number.

The use of flexible scheduling does not guarantee improvement of instruction; it does permit varying groups and more efficient use of time. Heitmann* recommends the following steps in the process for effective utilization of flexible scheduling:

1. The school population must be analyzed to identify the students' needs. . . .
2. The learning tasks that would lead to the desired goal must be determined for each group identified. . . .
3. The most effective methods of presentation for each specific learning task and group must be determined. . . .
4. Determine effective ways to organize instruction. . . .
5. Class sizes appropriate for each learning group must be decided. . . .
6. Designations of time allotments compatible with the student's learning characteristics, planned teaching methods, and learning tasks must be made. . . .
7. Analyze staff requirements and existing staff strengths.

Learning Resources

Recent innovations involving the application of computers, television, and other sophisticated forms of technology to educational processes have changed instruction in most school subjects, including physical education. Individualizing each pupil's total program has now become a reality through the capabilities of the computer to generate a flexible or modular schedule. Complex "learning systems" now make it possible for a student to take an entire course on an individual study basis, in a foreign language or in basic biology, for example, with the assistance of a "learning console."

Computer-based instruction in physical education is still in its infancy, but a limited number of programs are in operation. Computers are being used in some schools and colleges to schedule pupils into physical education classes, and to schedule complex intramural sports programs. They are used extensively for recording registrations and grades. Some coaches use them to analyze opponents' strategies in football. Physical education researchers have been more active in utilizing the computer than any other segment of the profession.

The potential impact of educational and instructional television is as great in education as that of commercial television in society.[61]

---

* Heitmann, *op. cit.*, pp. 8–13.

Hixson notes that physical education has utilized television at every level of instruction.[61] Series of television lessons such as "Ready? Set ... Go!" produced by the National Instructional Television Center at Bloomington, Indiana, have been used to provide a major resource for physical education instruction in schools. Single programs have also been used to enrich or supplement instruction.

Instant playback portable television is becoming very popular in physical education and athletic programs. One of the earliest innovations was in teacher education at Stanford University where micro-teaching is employed as both a pre-service and in-service medium.[92,69] It is used to tape "micro-teaching" episodes by interns in the training program. The camera is transported to the physical education classes of the interns in nearby high schools during the school year. This instrument has proved to be a beneficial source of immediate, accurate "feedback" information, which contributes significantly to rapid progress in teacher preparation. The instant playback television camera also can be used to project models of excellent teaching, to serve as a selection procedure for the employment of a teacher, and to train student teachers and intern supervisors. The full possibilities of micro-teaching are still being developed; it seems a particularly promising technique for changing a teacher's perception of his own behavior. For a more detailed analysis of the potential and status of micro-teaching, the reader is referred to Jordan's[69] appraisal of the Stanford program.

Instant playback television is being used extensively as a teaching and coaching aid in physical education classes and with athletic teams. Teachers and coaches are enthusiastic in their support of this assistance. However, very few rigorous experimental research studies have been reported which cite evidence of the efficacy of this instructional instrument in comparison to standard methods of instruction without the camera.

Hixson has provided an excellent summary of the current status of television in physical education, including a list of thirteen additional ways in which television is now being used in physical education.[61] Of particular interest is the recent establishment by the American Association for Health, Physical Education and Recreation of a Resource Center on Media in Physical Education, located at Ohio State University. The Center maintains a small library of video and audiotapes and is able to provide modest storage, duplication, and distribution services.

Other forms of technology are finding their way into physical education and sports programs, such as automatic timing devices keyed to the starting signal and the finish line, the finish touch plate at the end of the swimming pool to record the order of finish and the time in hundredths of seconds, an electrical "blanket" placed under the turf of athletic fields, radiotelemetry to study physiological phenomena of athletes in action, use of 8- and 16mm motion pictures, use of tape recorders, and other forms of instructional technology too numerous to recount here.

Recent innovations in facilities make it possible to individualize instruction to a greater extent than previously. Restricted indoor space long has been a source of limitations on programs during inclement weather. Limited shelters[104] provide covered and sheltered space at fractions of the cost of typical gynasiums and multi-purpose rooms. The Educational Facilities Laboratory at Stanford University has pioneered a new standard school building construction unit.[101] It is a flexible building module of standard dimensions which can be erected on almost any site. By joining two or more of these building modules together, flexible gymnasium space can be provided at substantially reduced cost. Air-supported shelters are coming into increased use.[1] These are large plastic bubbles, supported by a forced-air generator, which are large enough to cover tennis courts, swimming pools, and outdoor play spaces, thus permitting year-round use of these facilities at low cost.

Astro-turf, Tartan, and other synthetic surface materials now cover indoor space and convert it for use for football, baseball, tennis, track, and numerous other activities. Elementary schools are covering activity room floors with these materials. Likewise, outdoor football fields, running tracks, and other sports areas are being covered by these products. They have proved to be highly successful and durable. In all of these ways the total physical education and sports programs are expanded and made available year-round to larger numbers of students.

School instructional areas can be used more efficiently where modular scheduling has been adopted. Modular time scheduling permits 90 to 100 percent utilization of available facilities because it allows one class to move into a teaching station almost as soon as the preceding class has left it, rather than to have a fifteen to twenty-minute period of non-use between classes, as is typical several times each day in traditional scheduling. As much as one and one-half hours of extra time thus is made available for use of physical education facilities each day.

Schools now are establishing physical education resource centers at all levels. These centers contain a wide selection of instructional aids and relevant literature of value to both pupils and teachers. Audio-visual equipment, bulletin boards, areas for poster display, and similar materials are provided. The center is program-oriented. Sometimes this center is part of the school library or instructional materials center; in other instances it has its own designated area. The latter arrangement is preferable.

Many schools are now using non-school facilities for physical education classes. There is increasing use of such off-campus facilities as community golf courses, driving ranges, bowling lanes, tennis courts, swimming pools, skating rinks, ski slopes, and public playground areas. The open campus concept or the "school-without-walls" suggests many avenues for bringing the community into the school and for extending physical education programs.

Individualization and Personalization

By far the biggest challenge facing American education today is to provide a quality program, while at the same time serving large numbers of students. The increasing application of technology to education has led many to express concern about the possibility of "dehumanizing" education. In truth, the many innovations in organization of physical education programs can serve the goals of humanistic education, provided they are used by teachers who are dedicated to the basic goal of meeting individual pupil needs, who interact in a genuinely supportive way with students, and who encourage positive self-concepts and a desire to learn. The primary purpose of contemporary grouping arrangements is to provide a better group environment for individual learning. The real benefits of modular scheduling and differentiated staffing lie in their success in making more possibilities available for personal achievement of different learners. Inventive resources are designed to maximize the learning progress of individual students.

The ascendance of humanism in education increases the concern for individualization in school experiences. Analysis of some of the difficulties resulting from widespread adoption of innovative organizational plans has led some to prefer the term "personalization" to "individualization." It is possible to individualize learning by adjusting the rate or sequence of planned activities or by isolating a single learner from the group setting. But learning is not necessarily personalized under these conditions. For the humanistic educator concerned with the self-actualization of learners, personalization is what makes learning experiences human.

Personalization in physical education should begin with a thorough medical examination before beginning participation in the program. Examinations, given by a family or school physician, are recommended for all students in grades one, four, seven, and ten, for all new pupils entering the district, and for pupils who have had extended absence from school due to severe injury or illness. Pupils for whom the typical physical activities offered are inappropriate should be accommodated in adapted physical education programs. Adapted programs should be provided for students having either permanent or temporary disabilities which prevent their normal participation in the regular program. The official statement of the American Association for Health, Physical Education, and Recreation should be the guideline followed by all schools.[38] Several states have passed special legislation to emphasize the importance of this program, to spell out the types of physical handicaps which are in need of special programs, and to authorize financial reimbursement so that these programs can be carried on without "excess cost" to the local district. California and Pennsylvania have exemplary laws on this subject, and provide for adequate state financial support to local districts, so that classes of limited size can be conducted by specially qualified teachers of "corrective" physical education.[45]

It is the belief of the authors, and of many other physical educators, that no student who is physically able to attend school regularly and carry a normal program of studies should be excused from the physical education requirement. A primary administrative goal in connection with any school program of physical education should be "100 percent participation," although we admit the difficulty of attaining the objective.

The physical education administrator should be concerned with having every student in his school engaged regularly in appropriate physical education activities. This ideal is difficult to achieve. However, the ideal can be approached in practically every school if individual medical examinations are administered to determine the specific types of activities in which the pupil should engage; if the program is varied enough to offer activities appropriate to the needs and conditions represented in the entire group of students; if the "why" of physical education is clarified for students and others involved; if the physical education department wins the confidence and cooperative interest of school administrators, officials, parents, medical examiners, and students through good communications; and if students are grouped, scheduled, and guided in ways which truly facilitate personalized learning.

Current thought is that by the end of the age of compulsory education all youth should be well-grounded in a broad, liberal education, and should have the motivation to continue it throughout life by assuming responsibility for maximum self-direction in learning, both in formal school situations and informally. Not only should the schools provide the broad, liberal education for all pupils, but by the time of high school graduation or school-leaving age, students should have begun specialized study along lines of their individual abilities and interests.

Individualized or personalized instruction in physical education is an aspiration in consonance with this challenge. Physical education has been slow to accept responsibility for helping pupils to develop self-responsibility and the skills of personal decision making. In general, teaching has been quite "authoritarian" in nature, and too often taught by what Mosston calls a "command style."[90]

Schools committed to this viewpoint now provide opportunities for pupil responsibility and decision-making experiences in several ways.

1. Each student assesses himself with respect to a physical education inventory at the beginning of each year. He tests and evaluates his present skills and knowledges in each activity which will comprise his physical education program that year.

2. He records the results of this assessment on a physical education profile form, which is a permanent record included in his physical education cumulative file.

3. At the start of each unit, the student sets his own personal goals in skill, knowledge, and attitude, toward which he will work purposefully. These pupil aspirations are recorded. The student checks his progress periodically throughout the unit, records it, and compares it with his goal.

4. Each pupil plans learning experiences and proposes practice routines and schedules which he will follow during the unit. He notes

these plans in his cumulative folder, which is available to him during his physical education class.

5. The pupil pursues his practice, participation, and evaluation plans. He obtains assistance from classmates and from teachers. He, in turn, helps his peers.

6. At the end of the unit, each learner participates in a terminal evaluation procedure, and he notes the results in his folder. He discusses his progress, his feelings, his remaining problems, and his hopes for the future with his teacher.

The role of the teacher under this concept of physical education is in marked contrast to the assumptions underlying the "mass instruction" methodology characteristic of traditional programs. The teacher is involved with all students in the procedures explained above. The teacher becomes primarily a diagnostician, a prescriber, a consultant, and a resource agent. He believes in the unique worth, the integrity, and the dignity of each pupil.

This type of individualized and personalized program can be observed in some American schools today. Hopefully, a humanistic philosophy of education will come to guide more physical education programs throughout the country.

PHYSICAL EDUCATION
CURRICULUM MODELS

Issues relating to national standards or exemplary models in education are difficult to resolve. For generations, physical educators have recognized uneven quality in local curricula. Many have sought models of ideal curricula to provide guides toward upgrading programs. A similar situation pertains to all subject-field areas. It is probably inevitable in a country in which the major curriculum decisions are made on the local district level, while important educational regulations are legislated at the state level, and federal grants and subsidies and affirmative action programs also have significant impact on certain aspects of local curriculum development. The problem of supporting high quality educational opportunities for all in a democratic society without unduly restricting local autonomy is exceedingly complex. When this problem is studied in the context of differing local and individual educational needs, the appropriate use of educational models becomes an important question.

Educational Models

A large number of educational models have been developed over the years. Probably the best recent analysis is that reported by Joyce, Weil, and Wald,[71] in which they state that educational models can be used in three ways: for the making of curriculum plans, as guidelines for teacher interaction with students, and as specifications for instructional materials. They classify 16 models of teaching by "family" and mission. The selection of an educational model from among those which have been developed depends upon one's view of man and his universe and the expression of one's view of reality as a philosophy of education. The choice of an educational model, in turn, determines the roles of teacher and learner, the function of subject matter, the selection of methodologies, and specifications for learning environments and instructional materials.

Models for physical education programs can be grouped into three broad families in terms of the prevailing orientation. Disciplinary models are subject-matter oriented; knowledge and understanding of human movement phenomena and development of fitness and movement skill are top priorities. The teacher is a performer, a model, an information dispenser, even a taskmaster; the learner's role is to receive instruction, to emulate the teacher's model, and to strive to master the knowledge and skill exemplified. The focus is on learning to move; subject matter is of primary importance.

Social-interaction models are society-oriented. They are concerned with environments which facilitate social processes. The teacher is the source of authority and a guide to the accumulated group wisdom, a facilitator of group activity and an environmental manager. The learner is viewed as an immature and relatively inexperienced group member whose goal is to become socialized into the prevailing customs, mores, and ideals of the group. Subject matter is regarded as the context for group interaction. The physical education class or the athletic contest is society in microcosm and the focus is on learning movement activities as a means of growth toward optimum contribution to social betterment.

Personalized models are learner-oriented. The teacher, as well as the pupil, is a learner; he is a stimulator, a reflector, a counselor, a resource. The learner is self-directed; he is responsible for identifying his own goals, for developing his own uniqueness, for directing his own learning. Subject content becomes the medium for fulfillment of individual human potential. The focus is on moving to learn and upon the processes of personal self-actualization.

These three broad families of physical education models are selectively adapted to filling academic, social, and personal missions of different educational programs. Many variations within each broad family as well as hybrid models combining elements of more than one basic model are in use. The individual physical educator chooses his role, his methodologies, and his instructional materials in accordance with the model best adapted to his educational philosophy and his professional competencies.

Physical Education Conceptual Frameworks

The use of any educational model presupposes that the curriculum planner is working within some framework which defines the scope of his operations. It is now generally accepted, in physical education as in other educational specializations, that any particular curriculum should be developed within some conceptual framework. Many professionals are concerned about the need for an adequate conceptual framework for physical education; a number of proposals have been offered.

LaPlante[79] has reviewed those frameworks which provide a conceptual network for curriculum development in physical education and evaluated them according to four criteria: (1) the important concepts of the body of knowledge are represented; (2) the concepts are revelant to man's total development; (3) the processes of knowledge acquisition receive attention; and (4) the framework is dynamic and flexible to reflect societal change and allow for the inclusion of new knowledge. She found that while many structures are used for organization of content she was able to identify only eight which qualified as demonstrating development from a conceptual framework.

The Stanley[107] and Tillotson[110] frameworks are each based on analysis of movement elements. The Stanley framework grows directly from Laban principles and is definitely suggestive of a movement education approach. The Tillotson framework was a result of the Title III Project ME conducted in Plattsburgh, New York, which developed an innovative elementary school program with a movement education focus. The Battle Creek[121] framework was also initiated as a

Title III project. It was developed for use in Battle Creek, Michigan, and was one of the first systematic approaches to planning a physical education curriculum emphasizing carefully selected scientific concepts.

The Mackenzie[83] framework offers guidelines for the development of the "kinesiology" curriculum from preschool through undergraduate professional education. This framework is distinctive in the breadth of purposes offered, the humanistic philosophical orientation, and its specific suggestions for organizing experiences at five stages of learning.

The Pye and Alexander[98] framework was developed as a teaching-learning guide for the college physical education program at the University of Florida. It is rooted in an overall philosophy that physical fitness is a way of life which is individually related to one's potential and performance.

The Austin[19] framework, the Brown and Cassidy[27,28] frameworks, and the Purpose Process Curriculum Framework[65] build on concepts of the role of movement in man's total development. The premise of the Austin framework is that physical activity is a unifying life force which makes operational the whole man by integrating and extending all of his resources as he moves in relation to other objects in various environments. The Brown and Cassidy frameworks describe man's movement behavior in terms of both individual and environmental variables and postulate three categories of movement possibilities, development, coping, and expression and communication. The Purpose Process Curriculum Framework originates from man's purposes for moving.

The Purpose Process Curriculum Framework is being developed under the auspices of the Curriculum Project of the Physical Education Division of AAHPER. The project is part of a large scale long term effort to clarify the theoretical structure of physical education, to generate curriculum theory appropriate to human movement knowledge, to apply theoretical insights to exemplary curricular practices, and to provide guidelines for improving physical education programs throughout the country.

The Purpose Process Curriculum Framework is based on the assumption that the primary concern of physical education is the individual human being moving in interaction with his environment. The functions of human movement in achieving the goals of man have been logically analyzed and organized as the three key concepts of individual development, environmental coping, and social interaction, encompassing seven major purposes which are used to define the scope of the physical education curriculum and to select program content. Instructional planning requires a second or process dimension in the model. The process dimension has been developed in the form of a classification scheme for identifying major types of movement operations, by describing seven processes by which a human being learns to move. The focus is on learning processes and the attempt has been to differentiate important learning operations in order to facilitate improvement of instruction. Summaries of both purpose concepts and process categories of the Purpose Process Curriculum Framework appear in earlier sections of this chapter.

The individual curriculum planner selects a conceptual framework within which to develop local physical education curricula. Using this framework to clarify educational objectives and a teaching model chosen in terms of his educational philosophy, he develops programs appropriate to societal conditions and goals and the personal needs and goals of learners.

Program Emphases

Although general guidelines can be helpful, local curricula must be developed in accordance with local considerations and with the participation of those persons who implement them in particular school programs. The suggestions for program emphases which follow reflect the orientation, experience, and convictions of the authors. Both authors have been involved in the development of the Purpose Process Curriculum Framework; the programs envisioned in the succeeding paragraphs illustrate curricular decision making using this framework.

Elementary School Programs. The youngest school learners should certainly have daily opportunities for movement experiences. Organized preschool educational programs are increasing rapidly; in the expansion of this important phase of organized education, it is vital that the role of physical education be recognized and that the priorities in learning in and through motor performance activities be established. Elementary school children may be programmed as classroom groups for some phases of physical education. However, some of the time allotted to physical education should be used to encourage the children to come to various movement learning centers individually or in small groups for self-directed individual learning projects, teacher-assisted supplementary practice of movement performance skills, or movement activities designed for groups of children from several different classrooms.

Much of the child's movement curriculum is organized to focus on "man in space." Curriculum content for the youngest school learners is designed to achieve purposes of body awareness, locomotion, object manipulation, and movement expression. Movement exploration techniques can be used to develop concepts of general body awareness, movement capabilities of various body parts, relationships of different body parts to each other, personal size relative to the external physical environment, and voluntary modification of individual body shape and size.

Basic locomotor patterns of walking, running, sliding, and jumping are the introductory content in the area of relocation and are learned, adapted, and refined through imitation, experimentation, solving movement tasks set by teachers, and performing such skills in self-testing, chasing, and rhythmic games. More complex locomotor patterns are introduced as the children demonstrate their readiness.

Ball and object handling activities involving throwing, catching, kicking, and striking also receive major attention. Primary children enjoy rolling, tossing, bouncing, and catching rubber balls, balloons, plastic balls, bean bags, beach balls, and yarn balls. They should participate in striking activities requiring *foot*-eye coordination as well as *hand*-eye coordination. They can develop object *reception* skills by catching parachutes or other objects dropped from a height; by intercepting rolled balls with feet, hands, or paddles; by striking tossed objects with or without implements.

The elementary schools now view communication as a legitimate core around which to plan the curriculum, so that the various areas of study may contribute to the child's ability to cope with his world on his own terms. Movement experiences in schools have come into their own in the last decade as educators have recognized the crucial role played by movement in self-expression and communication. Elementary learnings in using movement to relate to others are achieved through creative rhythms, folk dance, and games. Every child should have opportunities in physical education to express his personal ideas and feelings through self-directed movement.

Learning sequences appropriate for most seven-, eight-, and nine-year-olds emphasize body projection, spatial relationships, object manipulation, and teamwork. In addition to the more complex locomotor skills such as galloping, hopping, leaping, and skipping, the child learns more advanced forms of propulsion on hanging and climbing apparatus, on poles, ropes, ladders, and stegels. He develops more sophisticated concepts of directionality and spatial relationships and better control of his moving body in space through games emphasizing dodging, guarding stationary and moving objects, chasing, and tagging; and through stunts, tumbling, trampoline, and other kinds of gymnastic activities.

The teacher plans object-manipulation challenges using hoops, ropes, wands, batons, and many types of balls and striking implements. Games are selected and designed to provide practice in the particular movement skills already identified and to stimulate the development of elementary concepts of cooperation, competition, leadership, and the functioning of rules in group activities. Although concepts of body projection, spatial relationships, object manipulation, and teamwork generally determine learning progressions at this level, teachers are also alert to opportunities to emphasize self-knowledge, challenge, and movement expression.

Purposes emphasized at the intermediate level are those of physiological efficiency, spatial orientation, object manipulation, and group interaction. Together with continuing attention to increasing efficiency in skill performance, learning sequences are designed for progressive development of strength, balance, agility, flexibility, and circulo-respiratory endurance. Elementary concepts of effective body mechanics are included. Modified track and field events are popular with both girls and boys.

A major goal of the physical education program at this level is to help the student to integrate his learnings dealing with coping with his physical environment and to guide the development of more sophisticated concepts of "man in space." Gymnastics are stressed; skating and basic swimming instruction are recommended. Students learn to maneuver weight with simple combatives such as handwrestling and in a variety of weight training activities using circuit training designs. Object projection activities focus on more advanced ball and stick skills and on competitive throwing events.

Concepts of group interaction are stressed through group and team games, relays, and folk dance. Concepts of offense and defense and position play are introduced and the roles of partner, opponent, teammate, captain, squad leader, coach, official, and spectator are experienced and analyzed. Each child is encouraged to compete with himself to better his own performance as well as to vie with others to achieve group and individual goals.

Learning sequences are also structured to provide basic concepts and skills required for cultural involvement of pre-adolescents. For these purposes children learn rope-jumping, tether ball, hop-scotch, four-square, marbles, jacks, skating, swimming, kickball, dodgeball, prisoner's base, and other popular games. Many of these skills are learned and practiced by children in small groups as they select their own movement learning activities; often they learn these from classmates or older children rather than by formal teacher instruction.

Physical education experiences throughout the elementary school are designed to assist the individual child in self-mastery, through development of an acceptable body image and a positive concept of himself in movement settings. Each child should have ample opportunities for knowing personal joy in movement. Physical activities already discussed (movement exploration, fundamental locomotor movements, body management activities, ball and object handling practice, rhythms and dances, traditional and creative games) provide the learning media for reaching these goals.

Middle School Programs. The middle school offers a unique challenge to the physical educator. Middle schools are using modular scheduling, team teaching, ability grouping, large group instruction, small group instruction, and open laboratory plans effectively. The curriculum in middle school physical education should emphasize two major elements, expanding understanding of movement through refining personal skills, and greater depth of social understanding through experiences in movement activities of the student's own and other cultures.

Concepts of self-mastery are strengthened through achievement of higher levels of skill in familiar activities and successfully meeting the challenges of learning new skills. Venturesome activities requiring more personal courage should be included. Students should attain a growing understanding of movement principles in situations emphasizing modifications of environmental media. Aquatic experiences may comprise from 20 to 35 percent of individual programs. All students should learn principles of buoyancy and adaptations of biomechanics, balance, and breathing appropriate to propulsion in the water. Instruction can include specific water survival techniques, elementary forms of rescue, standard stroke patterns, diving, water stunts, and electives for those students qualified for more advanced aquatic activities.

Tumbling, gymnastics, and trampolining are emphasized to extend concepts of spatial awareness, relocation and balance and to encourage the development of body projection skills utilizing limited ground contact. Basic gymnastic skills acquired during elementary school years serve as a foundation for learning standard stunts required in competition on all pieces of apparatus. Capsule programs have been developed to assist students at a wide range of individual performance levels to work independently in large group instructional settings with minimum supervision. Creative exercise routines offer opportunities for fun and novelty as well as for the satisfaction of skill achievement.

Outdoor education should be stressed. Track and field activities may be continued, cross-country running added, skiing introduced. The student should be challenged to perform skillfully on land surfaces modified by sand, snow, or ice. Unique forms of body projection and locomotion, more advanced skills in object projection, and concepts associated with physical activity as recreation can be meaningfully experienced in such contexts.

Middle school organization offers unparalleled opportunities for socialization through the development of team sports and social dance skills. Skill development and team strategy are stressed in popular team games. Teamwork concepts are highlighted through instruction in soccer, touch football, basketball, volleyball, hockey, and softball. Group games which reflect the recreational interests of young people in other societies also should be introduced. Students from differing subcultures can share such aspects of their heritage with each other. Exchange students from other countries and local citizens or foreign visitors who have lived in regions where other games are popular can provide key resources. Social dance offerings may include traditional dances, American square dance, folk dances of many lands, and current popular dance forms. Opportunities for healthful competitive sport and for corecreational dance should be varied and extensive in middle school extraclass programs.

Secondary School Programs. The physical education curriculum in the modern American high school has been modified by changing concepts of education and schooling and by the introduction of more flexible graduation requirements, and more options in course offerings; wider use of modular scheduling, team teaching, flexible grouping, and open campus organization; more student responsibility, more open laboratory and independent study programs; increasing demands for accountability; and greater involvement of students in decision making. The major goals of high school physical education curricula should include understanding and appreciation of human movement, physical fitness, and life-time sports competence. Student assessment and program evaluation should be concerned with each of these areas; student learning progress should be guided in terms of demonstrated achievement in each of these areas.

Understanding and appreciation of human movement should include knowledge of principles of human movement and the ability to apply these principles in sound body mechanics in daily movements, in participation in physical recreation activities, and in learning new work or leisure skills. It encompasses abilities to use movement as an expressive and communicative medium. Secondary school students can develop these abilities through choreographic experiences in dance, water ballet, or free exercise, or through developing new games or movement forms. Student projects have included designing movement sequences for musical and theatrical productions, staging physical education demonstrations, programming movement for film or television showing, planning novelty events for local track and field days, archery meets, or aquatic fun nights.

Physical education learnings in movement understanding and appreciation should also include introduction to the role of human movement activities in society. Movement appreciation offerings can provide analysis of the historical role of sport in various cultures, explore the critical role of movement in child development, highlight basic concepts of sociology of sport and of sport psychology, and identify contemporary social problems relating to sport locally, nationally, and internationally. Student participation experiences in guiding movement activities of children, leading neighborhood activity programs, planning family recreation activities, or engaging in movement activities of other societies or particular subcultures are especially desirable.

The development of physical fitness is discussed in detail in Chapter 8. As a goal in the high school curriculum, it is reasonable that students demonstrate individually appropriate levels of muscular strength, circulo-respiratory endurance, and survival aquatics. Adequate assessment techniques are available and adapted programs should be provided for students with unusual needs in this area, in secondary school as at all other educational levels. The student should have several options for achieving desired levels of fitness, including participation in vigorous sports of his choice, as well as such fitness activities as weight training, jogging, circuit training, and developmental exercise programs.

More and more schools are adopting competence in lifetime sports as a physical education program requirement. Numbers, types, and participation levels for identifying "lifetime sports" goals must be determined at the local level. Competence standards should be practical tests of ability to participate at a personally satisfying level, since the intent is to provide instruction in procedures for planning personal activity programs and to encourage voluntary participation throughout life. The secondary school student should be free to select from among many elective sports offerings at beginning, intermediate or advanced levels.

College Programs. While physical educators are practically unanimous in their endorsement of a required program in elementary and secondary schools, there exists a wide variety of opinion regarding the requirement in colleges and universities. Probably all physical educators agree that it would be well to have every college student engaged in appropriate and enjoyable activities, but many are unwilling to support a compulsory program. Actual practices in colleges illustrate this diversity of opinion. Because of rapidly expanding enrollment on limited campus space, a decrease in specific requirements in higher education generally, and increasing pressures toward fiscal economy, the recent trend is toward reduction or elimination of physical education requirements.

Community colleges enrolling large numbers of youth for postsecondary education need to give particular attention to changing the focus of physical education programs from repetition of traditional secondary school courses to innovative programs designed to have genuine relevance for young adults. Four-year colleges and universities should give similar attention to "basic instruction" programs designed primarily for entering freshman students; their major contribution probably should be made through expanding elective programs open to all undergraduate and graduate students. Analysis of the college physical education curriculum using the Purpose Process Curriculum Framework suggests that the purposes which provide soundest direction are physiological efficiency, psychic equilibrium, communication, and cultural involvement, and that the processes to be emphasized are perceiving, refining, varying, improvising, and creating.

Many of today's college students are genuinely interested in personalized physical conditioning regimens. Designing program offerings attractive to the college student seeking to improve and maintain his or her functional capabilities would result in courses of instruction in aerobic training, weight training, and neuromuscular relaxation. It would provide the rationale for adding class sections in scuba diving, judo and orienteering. It would require laboratories equipped for student self-assessment of conditioning levels and individual self-directed exercise routines. It would support requests for jogging trails, bicycle traffic lanes, expanded swimming facilities, and all-season orienteering courses.

The college student who looks to the physical education department for opportunities to achieve psychic equilibrium or personal integration may be seeking joy of movement, self-knowledge, catharsis, challenge, or any combination of these. Some haven't experienced genuine pleasure in strenuous physical activity since early childhood and have forgotten the pure joy inherent in vigorous human motion. As young adults, one may find joy in simple running, another in dance, a third in springboard diving. Others prefer the sensations of movement characteristic of gymnastics, swimming, or physical combat sports.

Self-knowledge can be gained through basic movement instruction (often remedial in nature); but it can also be enhanced through participation in any one or several of a multitude of activities which permit the individual to determine what he, as a functioning organism, is capable of doing and becoming. Successful learning may increase his self-appreciation as he extends his own physical capabilities beyond limits he had previously accepted. College youth may experience catharsis in conditioning exercises, running, dance, skating, sailing, handball, tennis, wrestling, karate, volleyball, or softball. An individual may test his prowess and courage in a wide spectrum of activities; those which offer great challenge to many college-age individuals certainly include skiing, surfing, fencing, riding, mountain climbing, and sky diving.

The typical undergraduate of the seventies is preoccupied with the search for his own identity. He wants to answer his own questions concerning what he is and who he is. A wide variety of appropriate physical education experiences can be structured to support the human quest for personal integration or psychic equilibrium.

Communication is a fundamental human activity. It is a prime concern of this generation of college and university students. Most key social problems have at one time or another been attributed to communications breakdowns. It is often alleged that student isolation from the system and individual alienation from the larger society constitute a major factor in campus crisis and young adult illness and crime. It is not suggested that physical education can resolve the most significant current campus tensions nor provide antidotes for the most serious defects of the modern university. But physical education classes could become more nearly exemplary in providing an environment for healthful interpersonal communication, and extra-class programs could be conducted in ways which would facilitate for participants more open communications with student peers and faculty members. It is recommended that greater emphasis be given to opportunities within our programs for the development of personal movement communications skills. Words do not represent the only means of communication any more than they represent the only means of learning. Among common purposes of human movement, man moves to share ideas and feelings with others. College programs in dance and other forms of expressive movement should maximize opportunities for enhancing individual communicative movement skill.

A major contribution of physical education as a professional field to cultural involvement lies in man's desire for participation in the movement activities of his society. Sport is a cultural universal. The popularity of specific activities varies cross-culturally, but participation in sport is a phenomenon which exists in all societies. Physical recreation programs in college and university communities should provide opportunities for ethnic subgroups to enjoy and extend interest in movement activities which lend uniqueness to a particular cultural heritage. Instructional electives should provide for the development of advanced skills in these activities as well as for skill development in currently popular adult physical recreation activities.

College students all over the United States are interested in being able to participate in tennis, golf, bowling, handball, volleyball, and social dancing. Local interests and facilities determine whether students seek opportunities to learn sailing, judo, orienteering, mountain climbing, curling, fencing, ballet, casting, skiing, scuba, surfing, or white water canoeing. General college programs in physical education should be directed toward helping the young adult to become an educated and more appreciative observer of sports and expressive movement forms as well as a more skillful participant in his chosen activities. Full participation in his society includes both direct involvement in sport and dance and the intellectual, aesthetic, and emotional involvement of indirect participation in movement activities.

The scope of a college or university physical education curriculum is determined by the common purposes of human movement as they are sought by selected young adults in a particular campus environment. Important curricular decisions must also be made relative to the process orientation of teaching-learning opportunities. The most typical movement process needs of American college and university students are perceiving, refining, varying, improvising, and composing.

The movement process of perceiving is usually associated with preschool or elementary school learning. However, many freshmen still enter our colleges and universities without having experienced quality foundational elementary and secondary school physical education; as long as this circumstance continues, remedial instruction should be provided in basic movement, movement fundamentals, or foundations of human movement. Specialized laboratory offerings in posture, relaxation, object projection, and rhythmic training may also be needed. In addition to remedial work directed toward perceiving movement, college-level physical education should be concerned with increasing levels of sophistication in perceiving. Regardless of his level of physical performance skill, the college student can profit from greater kinesthetic awareness, keener sensitivity to his own perceptual-motor responses, deeper understanding of the integrated perceptual-motor act.

While the learning of new sports or physical activities selected by the college student necessitates learning and adapting movement patterns, the focus in much of our sports instruction should be on the ordinative processes of refining learned movement patterns. We need to offer more courses designed to help participants achieve intermediate or advanced levels of skill. Instruction should aim toward the acquisition of smooth, efficient control of performance through the elimination of extraneous movements, the mastery of spatial and temporal relations resulting in precision timing, and habitual skillful performance under more complex conditions.

It is generally agreed that our civilization must find better ways to encourage and nurture creativity. The very least physical educators can do is to permit freedom for the generation of possibilities and to offer guidance in the development of creative movement potential. Although many college students today have almost no prior physical education experience with creative movement processes, they can be encouraged to construct unique or novel options in performing movement patterns or skills. Variations in techniques for returning a badminton serve, putting a golf ball, negotiating a slalom course, or drawing a fencing opponent off balance may serve the individual's purpose more effectively than the "correct" style as his instructor learned it. Classes can be structured to maximize opportunities for extemporaneous origination or initiation of novel movements or combinations of movements and thus give students more experience and skill in improvising. Courses in choreography or composing movement can be designed to achieve advanced competency in dance, aquatic arts, or gymnastics. They can be planned as independent study options to challenge students capable of creating new games or movement forms, or as interdisciplinary courses integrating the creativity resources of more than one department.

CONCLUSION

The challenge still confronts all teachers and administrators of physical education to work for constant curriculum improvement, better selection of activities, development of new activities which can provide even more desirable learning experiences for students, improvement of instructional methods and organizational procedures, and more effective appraisal techniques.

Physical education, like all other curricular areas, seeks "frontier thinkers," leaders with vision who, through creative thought, are willing to experiment with new ideas in curriculum development. The authors argue that the greatest current challenge lies in clarification of the essentially human variables in physical education curricular decision making—the purposes and processes of human movement. What man achieves as a moving being will always depend upon human purposes. What meaning he finds in movement experiences will always be a function of how appropriate the processes are to his unique needs. The opportunities are unlimited.

Selected References

1. *Air Structures for School Sports.* New York: Educational Facilities Laboratory, 1966.
2. Alexander, William M. (ed.). *The Changing Secondary School Curriculum. Readings.* New York: Holt, Rinehart and Winston, Inc., 1967.
3. Allen, Dwight, and Ryan, Kevin. *Microteaching.* Reading, Mass.: Addison-Wesley Publishers, 1969.
4. American Association for Health, Physical Education and Recreation. *This is Physical Education.* Washington, D.C.: AAHPER, 1965.
5. American Association for Health, Physical Education and Recreation. *Knowledge and Understanding in Physical Education.* Washington, D.C.: AAHPER, 1969.
6. American Association for Health, Physical Education and Recreation. *Promising Practices in Elementary School Physical Education.* Washington, D.C.: AAHPER, 1969.
7. American Association for Health, Physical Education and Recreation. *Programmed Instruction in Health Education and Physical Education.* Washington, D.C.: AAHPER, 1970.
8. American Association for Health, Physical Education and Recreation. "Essentials of a Quality Elementary School Physical Education Program: A Position Paper," *J. Health-Phys. Educ.-Rec.,* 42:42-46 (April, 1971).
9. American Association for Health, Physical Education and Recreation. "Guide to Excellence for Physical Education in Colleges and Universities: A Position Paper," *J. Health-Phys. Educ.-Rec.,* 42:51-53 (April, 1971).
10. American Association for Health, Physical Education and Recreation. "Guidelines for Secondary School Physical Education: A Position Paper," *J. Health-Phys. Educ.-Rec.,* 42:47-50 (April, 1971).
11. American Association for Health, Physical Education and Recreation. *Organizational Patterns for Instruction in Physical Education,* Heitmann, Helen M. (ed.). Washington, D.C.: AAHPER, 1971.
12. American Educational Research Association. *Perspectives of Curriculum Evaluation.* Monograph Series on Curriculum Evaluation. Smith, B. Othanel (ed.). Chicago: Rand McNally & Co., 1967.
13. American Educational Research Association. "Curriculum," *Rev. of Ed. Res.,* 39:283-375 (June, 1969).
14. Arnheim, Daniel D., and Pestolesi, Robert A. *Developing Motor Behavior in Children.* St. Louis: C. V. Mosby Co., 1973.
15. Association for Supervision and Curriculum Development. *Perceiving, Behaving, Becoming.* Washington, D.C.: ASCD, 1962.
16. Association for Supervision and Curriculum Development. *Individualizing Instruction.* Washington, D.C.: ASCD, 1964.
17. Association for Supervision and Curriculum Development. *To Nurture Humaneness: Commitment for the '70's.* Washington, D.C.: ASCD, 1970.
18. Association for Supervision and Curriculum Development. *The Unstudied Curriculum.* Washington, D.C.: ASCD, 1971.

19. Austin, Patricia L. "A Conceptual Structure of Physical Education for the School Program," Unpublished doctoral dissertation, Michigan State University, 1965.
20. Bailey, Sherm, and Rowley, Lloyd. "A School for Today and Tomorrow at Mt. Stuart Elementary School, Ellensburg, Washington," *J. Health.-Phys. Educ.-Rec.,* 40:31-35, 1969.
21. Bennis, W. G., Benne, K. D., and Chin, Robert (eds.). *The Planning of Change.* New York: Holt, Rinehart and Winston, 2nd ed., 1969.
22. Berman, Louise, *New Priorities in the Curriculum.* Columbus, Ohio: Charles E. Merrill, 1968.
23. "Broadfront," *J. Health-Phys. Educ.-Rec.,* 38:10-12 (November-December, 1967).
24. Bronowski, J. *The Identity of Man.* Garden City, N.Y.: Natural History Press, 1971.
25. Browder, Lesley H., Jr. *Emerging Patterns of Administrative Accountability.* Berkeley: McCutchan Publishing Corporation, 1971.
26. Brown, B. Frank. *The Appropriate Placement School: A Sophisticated Nongraded Curriculum.* West Nyack, N.Y.: Parker Publishing Company, Inc., 1965.
27. Brown, Camille. "The Structure of Knowledge in Physical Education," *Quest* IX:53-67 (December, 1967).
28. Brown, Camille, and Cassidy, Rosalind. *Theory in Physical Education: A Guide to Program Change.* Philadelphia: Lea & Febiger, 1963.
29. Brown, George I. *Human Teaching for Human Learning: An Introduction to Confluent Education.* New York: The Viking Press, Inc., 1971.
30. Bruce, James. *Alternative Models of Elementary Education.* Waltham, Mass.: Blaisdell Publishing Co., 1969.
31. Bruner, Jerome S. *The Process of Education.* Cambridge: Harvard University Press, 1960.
32. Burson, Robert. "Nongraded Curriculum and Modular Scheduling." From Heitmann, Helen M. (ed.), *Organizational Patterns for Instruction in Physical Education and Recreation,* Washington, D.C.: American Association for Health, Physical Education and Recreation, 1971.
33. *Career Education.* U.S. Department of Health, Education, and Welfare Publication No. (OE) 72-39.
34. Carr, William G. *Values and the Curriculum: A Report of the Fourth International Curriculum Conference.* Washington, D.C.: NEA Center for the Study of Instruction, 1970.
35. Clark, David L., and Guba, Egon G. "An Examination of Potential Change Roles in Education," *Rational Planning in Curriculum and Instruction.* Washington, D.C.: National Education Association, 1967.
36. Clarke, H. Harrison. *Nature and Extent of Individual Differences and Their Significance for Physical Education and Athletics.* Eugene, Ore.: Oregon School Study Council, School of Education, University of Oregon, 1967.
37. Clarke, H. Harrison, and Clarke, David H. *Developmental and Adapted Physical Education.* Englewood Cliffs, N.J.: Prentice-Hall, Inc., 1963.
38. "Classification of Students for Physical Education." (Statement of the Committee on Exercise and Physical Fitness of the American Medical Association.) *J. Health-Phys. Educ.-Rec.,* 38: 16-18 (February, 1967).
39. Corbin, Charles B. *Becoming Physically Educated in the Elementary School.* Philadelphia: Lea & Febiger, 1969.
40. Cowell, Charles C., and France, Wellman L. *Philosophy and Principles of Physical Education.* Englewood Cliffs, N.J.: Prentice-Hall, Inc., 1963.
41. Cowell, Charles C., and Hazleton, Helen W. *Curriculum Designs in Physical Education.* Englewood Cliffs, N.J.: Prentice-Hall, Inc., (6th ed.), 1963.
42. Cunningham, Craig. "Movement Education at the University Elementary School." From Heitmann, Helen M. (ed.), *Organizational Patterns for Instruction in Physical Education.* Washington, D.C.: American Association for Health, Physical Education and Recreation, 1971.
43. Curtis, Delores M. "Bringing about Change in Organizational Patterns in Ele-

mentary Schools." From Heitmann, Helen M. (ed.), *Organizational Patterns for Instruction in Physical Education*. Washington, D.C.: American Association for Health, Physical Education and Recreation, 1971.

44. Daughtrey, Greyson. *Effective Teaching in Physical Education for Secondary Schools*. Philadelphia: W. B. Saunders Company, 1973.

45. "Education of the Physically Handicapped" in *State Legal Provisions in California Relating to Health Education, Physical Education and Recreation*, pp. 41-44. Burlingame, Calif.: California Association for Health, Physical Education and Recreation, 1962.

46. Educational Facilities Laboratories, Inc., and the Institute for Development of Educational Activities. *The Open School Plan: A Report of a National Seminar*. Melbourne, Florida: I.D.E.A., 1970.

47. Eyler, Marvin H. (ed.). "The Nature of a Discipline." Monograph. *Quest* IX. (National Association for Physical Education of College Women and National College Physical Education Association for Men.) (December, 1967).

48. Featherstone, Joseph. *Schools Where Children Learn*. New York: Liveright Pub. Corp., 1971.

49. Felshin, Janet. *Perspective and Principles for Physical Education*. New York: John Wiley & Sons, Inc., 1967.

50. *Forward Plan for Career Education Research and Development*. Career Education Development Task Force, National Institute of Education, Education Division, Department of Health, Education, and Welfare (April, 1973).

51. Foshay, Arthur W. "Curriculum." From Ebel, Robert L. (ed.), *Encyclopedia of Educational Research*. London: Macmillan, 4th ed., 1969.

52. Foshay, Arthur W. *Curriculum for the 70's: An Agenda for Invention*. Washington, D.C.: National Education Association, Center for the Study of Instruction, 1970.

53. Fraleigh, Warren P. "A Prologue to the Study of Theory Building in Physical Education," *Quest*, XII:26-33 (May, 1969).

54. Gilmore, John C. *The Professional Levels of Tasks of Teachers of Boys' Physical Education*. Unpublished Ed.D. dissertation. Stanford, Calif.: School of Education, Stanford University, 1967.

55. Goodlad, John I. *The Changing School Curriculum*. New York: Fund for the Advancement of Education, 1966.

56. Goodlad, John I. *The Development of a Conceptual System for Dealing with Problems of Curriculum and Instruction*. ERIC Report Resume ED# 010-064. Washington, D.C.: USOE, 1966.

57. Goodlad, John I. "Directions of Curriculum Change," *NEA Journal*, 56:33-36 (December, 1966).

58. Halsey, Elizabeth, and Porter, Lorena. *Physical Education for Children*. New York: Holt, Rinehart & Winston, Inc., rev. ed., 1963.

59. Hein, Margaret Gill. "Planning and Organizing for Improved Instruction," *Curriculum Handbook for School Executives*. Arlington, Va.: American Association for School Administrators, 1973.

60. Heitmann, Helen M. "Rationale for Change." From Heitmann, Helen M. (ed.). *Organizational Patterns for Instruction in Physical Education*. Washington, D.C.: American Association for Health, Physical Education and Recreation, 1971.

61. Hixson, Chalmer G. "Television in Physical Education," *Quest*, XV:58-66 (January, 1971).

62. Humphrey, James H. *Child Learning through Elementary School Physical Education*. Dubuque, Iowa: Wm. C. Brown and Co., 1966.

63. Jackson, Philip. *Life in Classrooms*. New York: Holt, Rinehart and Winston, 1968.

64. Jewett, Ann E. "Would-You-Believe Public Schools, 1975," *J. Health-Phys. Educ.-Rec.*, 42:41-44 (March, 1971).

65. Jewett, Ann E. (ed.). *Curriculum Design: Purposes and Processes of Physical*

Education Teaching-Learning. Washington, D.C.: American Association for Health, Physical Education and Recreation, 1974.

65a. Jewett, Ann E. "Physical Education." From Ellena, William J. (ed.), *Curriculum Handbook for School Executives.* Arlington, Virginia: American Association of School Administrators, 1973.

66. Jewett, Ann E., Jones, L. Sue, Luneke, Sheryl M., and Robinson, Sarah M. "Educational Change through A Taxonomy for Writing Physical Education Objectives," *Quest,* XV:32-38 (January, 1971).

67. Johnson, Perry B. and others. *Physical Education—A Problem-Solving Approach to Health and Fitness.* New York: Holt, Rinehart and Winston, 1966.

68. Jones, Richard. *Fantasy and Feeling in Education.* New York: New York University Press, 1968.

69. Jordan, T. C. "Micro-Teaching: A Reappraisal of Its Value in Teacher Education," *Quest,* XV:17-21 (January, 1971).

70. Joyce, Bruce R. *Alternative Models for Elementary Education.* Waltham, Mass.: Blaisdell Publishing Company, 1969.

71. Joyce, Bruce R., Weil, Marsha, and Wald, Rhoada. "The Training of Educators: A Structure for Pluralism," *Teachers College Record,* 73:371-391 (February, 1972).

72. Kaufman, Roger A. *Educational System Planning.* Englewood Cliffs, N.J.: Prentice-Hall, Inc., 1972.

73. King, Arthur R., and Brownell, John A. *The Curriculum and the Disciplines of Knowledge.* New York: John Wiley & Sons, Inc., 1966.

74. Kirchner, Glenn. *Physical Education for Elementary School Children.* Dubuque, Iowa: Wm. C. Brown Co., 2nd ed., 1970.

75. Klausmeier, Herbert J., and Harris, Chester W. *Analyses of Concept Learning.* New York: Academic Press, 1966.

76. Knapp, Clyde, and Leonhard, Patricia H. *Teaching Physical Education in Secondary Schools.* New York: McGraw-Hill Book Company, 1968.

77. Kohl, Herbert R. *The Open Classroom.* New York: Vintage Books, Inc., 1969.

78. Kozman, Hilda C., Cassidy, Rosalind, and Jackson, Chester O. *Methods in Physical Education.* Dubuque, Iowa: Wm. C. Brown and Co., 4th ed., 1967.

79. LaPlante, Marilyn. *Evaluation of a Selected List of Purposes of Physical Education Utilizing a Modified Delphi Technique.* Unpublished doctoral dissertation, University of Wisconsin, Madison, 1973.

80. Leonard, George B. *Education and Ecstasy.* New York: Dell Publishing Co., Inc., 1968.

81. *Lifetime Sports for Every Student.* Washington, D.C.: American Association for Health, Physical Education, and Recreation, 1967.

82. Macdonald, James B. "Educational Models for Instruction—An Introduction," *Theories of Instruction.* Washington, D.C.: National Education Association, 1965.

83. Mackenzie, Marlin M. *Toward A New Curriculum in Physical Education.* New York: McGraw-Hill Book Co., 1969.

84. Mager, Robert F. *Developing Attitude toward Learning.* Belmont, Calif.: Fearon Publishers, 1968.

85. Mager, Robert F., and Pipe, Peter. *Analyzing Performance Problems.* Belmont, Calif.: Fearon Publishers, 1970.

86. Maslow, Abraham H. *Toward a Psychology of Being.* Princeton, N.J. D. Van Nostrand Company, Inc., 2nd ed., 1968.

87. Metheny, Eleanor: *Connotations of Movement in Sport and Dance.* Dubuque, Iowa: Wm. C. Brown and Co., 1965.

88. Miles, Matthew B. (ed.). *Innovation in Education.* New York: Teachers College, Columbia University, 1964.

89. Mordy, Margaret A. (ed.). "Educational Change in the Teaching of Physical Education," Monograph. *Quest,* XV. (NAPECW and NCPEAM.) (January, 1971).

90. Mosston, Muska. *Teaching Physical Education: From Command to Discovery.* Columbus, Ohio: Charles E. Merrill Books, Inc., 1966.
91. NEA Center for the Study of Instruction. *Rational Planning in Curriculum and Instruction.* Washington, D.C.: National Education Association, 1967.
92. Nixon, John E. "Innovations in Teacher Education," *J. Health-Phys. Educ-Rec.,* 37:55-57 (September, 1966).
93. Nixon, John E., and Jewett, Ann E. *Physical Education Curriculum.* New York: The Ronald Press Company, 1964.
94. Oberteuffer, Delbert, and Ulrich, Celeste. *Physical Education.* New York: Harper & Row, Publishers, 4th ed., 1970.
95. Parker, J. Cecil, and Rubin, L. J. *Process as Content: Curriculum Design and the Application of Knowledge.* Chicago: Rand McNally and Co., 1966.
96. Phenix, Philip H. *Realms of Meaning.* New York: McGraw-Hill Book Co., 1964.
97. President's Council on Youth Fitness. *Youth Fitness.* Washington, D.C.: U.S. Government Printing Office, (July, 1961).
98. Pye, Ruby Lee, and Alexander, Ruth Hammock. *Physical Education Concepts: A Teaching-Learning Guide.* Middletown, Ky.: Maxwell Co., 1971.
99. Rogers, Carl R. *Freedom to Learn.* Columbus: Charles E. Merrill Publishing Company, 1969.
100. Schmuck, Richard A., and Miles, Matthew B. (eds.). *Organization Development in Schools.* Palo Alto, Calif.: National Press Books, 1971.
101. *School Construction Systems Development: The Project and the Schools.* New York: Educational Facilities Laboratories, Inc., 1967.
102. Schurr, Evelyn L. *Movement Experiences for Children: Curriculum and Methods for Elementary School Physical Education.* New York: Appleton-Century-Crofts, 1967.
103. Schwab, Joseph J. *The Practical: A Language for Curriculum.* Washington, D.C.: NEA Center for the Study of Instruction, 1970.
104. *Shelter for Physical Education.* College Station, Texas: Texas A. & M. College, Texas Engineering Experiment Station, 1961.
105. Silberman, Charles E. *Crisis in the Classroom: The Remaking of American Education.* New York: Random House, Inc., 1970.
106. Smith, B. Othanel. *Research in Teacher Education: A Symposium.* Englewood Cliffs, N.J.: Prentice-Hall, Inc., 1971.
107. Stanley, Sheila. *Physical Education: A Movement Orientation.* Toronto: McGraw-Hill Book Co., 1969.
108. Taba, Hilda. *Curriculum Development.* New York: Harcourt, Brace and World, Inc.. 1962.
109. Thelen, Herbert A., Peterson, Henry, Oppenheim, Alan, Hoock, William, Pearls, Steven, and Brody, Anne. *Classroom Grouping for Teachability.* New York: John Wiley and Sons, Inc., 1967.
110. Tillotson, Joan. *A Program of Movement Education for the Plattsburgh Elementary Schools.* Final report of Title III Elementary and Secondary Education Program, 1969.
111. *Today's Education.* "Institutional Technology." 59:8:33-40 (November, 1970).
112. *Today's Education.* "Accountability and the Classroom Teacher." 60:31:41-56 (March, 1971).
113. Travers, Robert M. W. (ed.). *Second Handbook of Research on Teaching.* Chicago: Rand McNally & Co., 1973.
114. Trump, J. Lloyd. *New Horizons for Secondary School Teachers.* Urbana, Ill.: Commission on the Experimental Study of the Utilization of the Staff in the Secondary School, 1957.
115. Trump, J. Lloyd. *Images of the Future.* Washington, D.C.: National Association of Secondary School Principals, 1961.
116. Trump, J. Lloyd. "The NASSP Model Schools Program for Health, Physical Education, Recreation." From Heitmann, Helen M. (ed.), *Organizational Patterns for Instruction in Physical Education.* Washington, D.C.: American Association for Health, Physical Education and Recreation, 1971.

117. Trump, J. Lloyd, and Baynham, Dorsey. *Focus on Change: Guide to Better Schools.* Chicago: Rand McNally & Co., 1961.
118. Tyler, Ralph W. *Basic Principles of Curriculum and Instruction.* Chicago: University of Chicago Press, 1950.
119. Vannier, Maryhelen, and Fait, Hollis F. *Teaching Physical Education in Secondary Schools.* Philadelphia: W. B. Saunders Company, 3rd ed., 1969.
120. Vannier, Maryhelen, Foster, Mildred, and Gallahue, David L. *Teaching Physical Education in Elementary Schools.* Philadelphia: W. B. Saunders Co., 1973.
121. Vogel, Paul. "Battle Creek Physical Education Project," *J. Health-Phys. Educ.-Rec.,* 40:25-29 (September, 1969).
122. Weinstein, Gerald, and Fantini, Mario D. *Toward Humanistic Education.* New York: Praeger Publishers, Inc., 1970.

(From Price, La Ferne E.: The Wonder of Motion: A Sense of Life for Woman. Grand Forks, North Dakota: University of North Dakota Press, 1972.)

Chapter Ten

COMPETITIVE SPORTS

SPORT IN TODAY'S WORLD

Sport permeates American life in a myriad of ways. Scholars and other interested observers have described and analyzed the purposes of sport, they have sought to capture the elusive definition of what Metheny[25] describes as this "thing" called sport, they have studied the individual's participation, the role of spectators, the place of sport in educational institutions, and the roles of sport in government at various levels, including the use of sport as an instrument of national policy and the alarming international trend of the "politicizing" of sport. Sport has been dissected from the viewpoint of psychiatric theory, it has been viewed from the frame of reference of the philosopher, and investigated by the physiologists and motor learning specialists seeking to understand the intricate neuromuscular mechanisms which underlie skilled motor patterning in sports performance. Sociologists, anthropologists, and sport historians long have studied play, games, and sport from societal, cultural, and cross-cultural perspectives. From the time of the earliest cave drawings man through history has recorded the deeds of his fellow man in sport activities through the artistic media of paint, clay, wood, and metal. Millions of pictures of sport have been recorded by photographs, motion pictures, and video tapes. Individual movements in sport are recognized as examples of aesthetic expression. Sport as one form of entertainment and commerce is self-evident. Physical recreation through sport is extremely widespread in America and in other countries. This list of sport involvement in the fabric of national life is incomplete. The many facets of sport that are subsumed under the major categories listed here cannot be made explicit in this chapter. The professional student should read and study broadly in the literature relevant to these topics. A basic recommended reading list is provided at the end of this chapter.

Definition

The term "sport" long has resisted attempts to define it with precision and there is still no generally agreed upon definition. It is a very complex phenomenon, hard to reduce to a few sentences, or even paragraphs. Three recent efforts are cited by way of example.

Metheny[25] and a group of advanced graduate students developed the following lengthy descriptive definition and even this statement was not entirely agreed to by all members who contributed to it after several hours of intensive study and discussion:

> As commonly used today, the term sport refers to a diverse set or category of *activities* or *organizations of human behavior* in which:
> One or more persons, designated as *performers,* move about in an *environmental setting,* which may be described in terms of *time, space,* and *terrain,* performing *actions* which are directed toward an attempt to induce or bring about a series of *observable changes* in the *location* and/or *configuration* of certain specified objects, animals, and/or persons.
> While the performers are pursuing this *objective,* their actions are governed by the provisions of a set of *man-made rules* or *personal agreements.* These rules also identify the *procedures* to be utilized in *evaluating* the achievement of the *objective* or the extent to which the objective was achieved by each performer or set of performers.
> Characteristically, after each series of attempts to achieve the objectives has been completed, all persons involved in that series of attempts *return* to their *initial location/configuration;* and all objects and animals utilized in that series of attempts are either *returned* to their *initial location/configuration* or *replaced* by similar objects/ animals before the next series of attempts is initiated.
> Characteristically, each *performance* of a sport or sport-type activity is conducted within the context of a specified *pattern* or *organization,* which is known to and accepted by all persons involved in that particular performance.
> Typically, some performances are organized by individual performers or sets of performers who plan, conduct, and evaluate the outcomes of that performance in accordance with the provisions of a

set of personal or mutual agreements about the objective and about the actions which may be performed during each attempt to achieve the objective. For purposes of classification, this *type* of performance may be identified as a *personally organized* or *individually organized performance.*

Further, many performances are organized as *contests* in which two or more performers or sets of performers openly *compete with each other* in their attempts to achieve a common objective. Such *contests* are usually governed by a commonly accepted set of operational rules, based on, but not necessarily identical with, some recognized set of standard or official rules.

Typical *contest patterns* may be classified as:

Individual performances in which each personal or individual performance is rated or judged by another person, who compares his conception of that performance with a conceptual model or standard.

Side-by-side performances in which the performers move either simultaneously or sequentially, and each individual performance yields objective evidence of the extent to which the performer has achieved the objective.

Comparative parallel performances in which all performers move simultaneously and in the same direction, attempting to outdistance each other.

Face-to-face oppositional performances in which two performers or two sets of performers attempt to move in opposing directions as they contend with each other in their attempts to achieve the objective.

Loy[22] uses fifteen pages to describe what he calls a "definitional effort" to explain the meaning of sport. One cannot accurately synthesize this statement, it must be read in its entirety. It is organized into four main considerations: (a) sport as a game occurrence, (b) sport as an institutionalized game, (c) sport as a social institution, and (d) sport as a social situation.

Sheehan[31] provides one of the most concise definitions of sport extant:

> . . . the act of vying physio-cognitive behavior against an obstacle in a competitively structured, institutionalized situation. This obstacle may take the form of another individual(s) possessive of physio-cognitive behavior, an inanimate obstacle, or an animated obstacle. This definition encompasses sport from fishing to football.

It is interesting to take a sport of one's choice and to analyze it in terms of the Metheny, or Loy, or Sheehan definition to see if the definition is comprehensive and accurate. If one can locate an activity which, by common usage of the term, is generally called a "sport" and determine that some aspect of it is *not* covered by the definition, then the definition still is faulty.

By and large, the terms "sport," "athletics," and "games" are used quite interchangeably and without great consequence or harm to anyone. However, attempts by the scholars to evolve accurate definitions and descriptions are valid and valuable contributions to the development of more intensive study and analysis of the nature of sport and its relationship to individuals and to society.

Organizational Classification

The term "sport" is widely applied in terms of programs which are organized and administered by a variety of public and private agencies. The criticism of sport is often overgeneralized when a critic takes a "pot shot" at some aspect he finds undesirable. Thus, it is contended that sport is becoming too "politicized," it has a "dehumanizing" effect on many participants, and so on. It is not defensible to attack "sport" in general in this manner. The originator of such a charge has the responsibility to identify the specific target at which his complaint is directed—a particular individual, a designated team, a certain league, or one specific country. Of course the evidence which presumably substantiates the charge must also be presented in accurate and clear form so that the interested person can come to his own independent judgment about the case.

Sport is organized and conducted by many diverse organizations and it is not practical to attempt to name them all in a limited space. However, it may be helpful to realize that sport is offered in many degrees and forms to men, women, and children of all ages, under the following auspices.

Schools, colleges, and universities, both public and private, provide a variety of sports programs such as intercollegiate or interscholastic, physical education class teams, either voluntary or required, intramural sport which is voluntary, voluntary sport clubs usually under student leadership, and recreational sport on the campus and also off-campus under the jurisdiction of special interest groups in the school. Finally, many campuses provide recreational sport areas where individuals and groups can gather informally to engage in a sport contest or in practice. Public agencies sponsor many forms of sport competition through recreation department leagues and instructional classes. Police Departments in some cities sponsor Boys' Clubs which offer valuable sport programs. Private and semi-private organizations sponsor sport teams and leagues in many activities on a local, regional, and even national and international basis. Some examples are Little League Baseball, Pop Warner Football, Age Group Swimming, Age Group Tennis, and many others. Professional leagues and teams in various sports are well known in most countries, with soccer being the most widely played sport in the world.

The philosophical line one might draw between the competing purposes of "sport" and "profit" is the subject of many controversies centering on the motives behind the professional sport scene. Olympic teams and other representative national teams, such as squads assembled in various sports to represent America in the Pan American Games, involve still another level of sport competition. The list could be extended to several pages by becoming more and more specific but perhaps the point has been established that to discuss and understand the personal-social dynamics of "sport" is probably an impossible assignment. Carefully identified entities must be pinpointed and then analyzed and studied by the rational modes of inquiry of the humanities and the sciences if we hope to build a reservoir of warranted concepts, a network of plausible theories, and a consistent philosophical frame of reference within which to continually advance the goal of legitimate sport opportunities for all and which will satisfy human motivations and needs in healthful, positive ways.

Sport and Culture

Sport constitutes a fundamental and extensive element of American culture. The same statement can be made for most other countries of the world. The interest of Americans in sport is evident in many ways. There seems to be a definite trend toward increased sport participation on a wide scale, at all age levels. The fear of "spectatoritis" diminishes if there is evidence that persons who are spectators at one event are themselves participants at other times.

A Gallup poll in early 1973 indicated that "interest in sport is gaining remarkable momentum (in America)," both in active participation and spectator attendance. In recent years there have been most rapid and persistent increases in participation in swimming, bowling, tennis and baseball (including softball), with volleyball, golf, horseback riding, skiing, and ice skating not far behind. Spectator attendance has shot up rapidly in soccer, football, boxing, hockey, and basketball, with football being the leader in total attendance. Interestingly enough, there has been a decline in the number of persons engaging in indoor and sedentary games such as bingo, pinochle, checkers, bridge, and cross-word puzzles. There has been a sharp increase in the number playing chess (perhaps encouraged by the publicity from the Fischer-Spassky chess duels) and in Monopoly in the past year or two.

Major reasons advanced for the increased interest in sport around the country are a general increase in leisure time available to many people, the recent medical stress on the values of exercise, increasingly higher family income, and a desire to find relief from crowded living conditions and a polluted environment. The staggering amounts of money spent on sport equipment, attendance at sporting events, admission to facilities, and related expenses such as travel cost, clothing and accessories, and food and beverage, seem almost to be beyond comprehension. Sport-related expenditures constitute one of the largest segments of the total American economy.

Boyle[8] provides a fascinating description of sport in American life, including interesting historical information about the role sport played in the development of American cultural and business life. Miller and Russell[26] have recently published an exhaustive inventory of examples, statistics, quotes, and views of sport in American life and culture which provides a unique, broad, complex perspective of the roles and functions of sport clearly depicting the extent to which sport has permeated most facets of our daily existence. Its total effect upon the reader is one of awe and wonderment that sport can indeed be such a pervasive, potent influence on the warp and woof of the pattern of our cultural existence.

One of the major problems associated with this rapid increase in the number of active participants is that of providing enough facilities to meet the demand. Federal, state, and local governmental agencies are becoming more alert to this pressing problem than ever before, and many steps are being taken to procure and set aside, "in inviolate perpetuity," all types of recreational areas and facilities—parks, forests, wilderness lands, golf courses, and water resources—for the use of future generations of Americans with this sports and recreational interest. The recreation and parks literature abounds with statistics about this problem and examples of attempts being made to provide suitable solutions.

It is also interesting to note briefly the extent to which national governments use sport as an instrument of national policy. In an ongoing study of this subject, one of the authors has found that one or more countries throughout the world use sport to achieve national goals such as world prestige, political propaganda, national income (through soccer lotteries), improved physical fitness of the citizens, international relations and good will, health, recreational objectives, improvement of the financial status of farmers (by conversion of farm land to recreational use through government subsidy and loans), armed forces morale, juvenile delinquency prevention and treatment, physical medicine rehabilitation, psychiatric treatment, and so on. The tremendous interest in sport, and the actual and potential influences of sport upon the lives of a great majority of people in America, as well as in other countries, cannot be denied.

We are just beginning to see the fruits of more sophisticated, formal research studies into the nature, function, and influences of sport in societal contexts. The relatively new field of specialization known as the Sociology of Sport is growing rapidly and many young people are electing to take doctoral programs in this area. Chapter 6 discusses the nature of their work and their recent findings in more detail.

Another development of recent years which has important implications for sport and for the competitor is the interest in and contributions of the American College of Sport Medicine, and the Federation Internationale de Médecine Sportive. These organizations are composed of physicians, coaches, trainers, physiologists, physical educators, and other professional personnel having a direct interest and competence related to the total care, training, injury, and recuperation of the athlete. Through research, experimentation, conferences, and publications, the world of athletics will surely advance to higher qualitative levels, as well as to improved performances per se, through the combined efforts and talents of representatives from these educational and medical disciplines. All physical educators should know about these organizations and their publications.

Whatever the particular course competition in sport and athletics may take in this country, it is vital to keep in mind the fact that man is competitive, that sport and athletics are the expression of fundamental human needs millions of years old, that the young will always play, that we have equally great opportunities through the medium of these expressions to inculcate in the young either valuable or undesir-

able social habits and attitudes, and that the point of view we as
teachers take toward this whole problem can contribute to the character of the social order of the future and the values on which it is based.

Politicizing of Sport

Although many countries have used sport as a vehicle to promote
the political aims of the party in control of the government, both
internally and in terms of world prestige and power, it has not been
until recent years that blatant, unethical uses of influence in sport
have been deliberately employed to enhance the popularity of the
country at home and in the estimation of selected friendly nations in
other parts of the world. This state of affairs has reached such extreme
proportions as to draw the wrath of critics both at home and abroad.

One of the most noteworthy examples of this trend toward the
politicizing of sport is well known to all readers, namely several
episodes which occurred in the 1972 XXth Olympic Games held in
Munich, West Germany. Several participating countries, large and
small alike, believed their competitors were unjustly victimized by
faulty judging in such events as gymnastics and boxing by a "power
block" of officials in those events from the central European countries.
The Americans point to a variety of incidents to support similar
claims, primarily in boxing, track and field, diving, and gymnastics.
The most notorious example was when the Secretary of the International Federation for Basketball directed the score keeper to reset the
clock for a replay of the last three seconds of the final Olympic
championship game between Russia and the United States with the
USA leading by one point. This decision is unprecedented in the
annals of international basketball as far as is known and is not provided for in the rules. The Americans lost in the replayed three
seconds on a rare and controversial play in which at least one and
possibly two rules violations by the Russians are clearly evident in the
motion pictures of the games.

The point here is not merely to recite these incidents and the
strange judgments and rulings that attended them, but to use these
examples to illustrate the trend toward the use of sport as a vehicle
to promote national prestige and pride at home and abroad. There are

legitimate, sportsmanlike ways to carry out this aim and there are other strategies which seem obviously to be unethical both in intent and in practice.

It is little wonder then that one now hears louder and more persistent outcries by sportsmen, public leaders, public media representatives, and idealistic young people everywhere against such policies and practices. Should the playing of the national anthem of the country represented by the winner of each Olympic event be eliminated along with the raising of the national flags of the first, second, and third place winners? Should other symbolic forms of reinforcing national identity and pride in victory be diminished or exempted from use in the Games of the future? What are the possibilities that the present governing structures of the Olympics and similar international sporting events can correct the glaring problems which have been allowed to proliferate in recent years so as to presage a return to the true Olympic spirit of friendly strife and competition? Some critics are highly skeptical that such corrections can, or will, be made in the future.

Some Eastern European countries use sport as one of their most important vehicles for aid to developing countries such as Africa and South America through financial aid and consulting services. Millions of dollars are spent on sport advisers, team coaches, the building of sport facilities, and the provision of sport supplies to the people of developing countries. It has been perceived that sport is a major area of human interest around the world and that such a concentration of financial support and technical leadership can be very influential in winning the gratitude and support of the countries being aided. The promotion of sport ranks right along with fundamental education, health care, and economic development as human activities to which farsighted consultant nations give priority.

So far, the United States has not seen fit to put so much emphasis on the development of sport programs in its projects to aid lesser developed countries. It has given some attention to this avenue of assistance in the Peace Corps program, and some high leaders of this program have testified in confidence that sport programs have been effective in achieving the goals of the Peace Corps. Yet these officials are hesitant to make this judgment public and to argue forcefully for funds to support sport work in the Peace Corps on a larger scale. The reasons for this reluctance are not clear but undoubtedly there is a fear that the Congress and other high governmental officials will not look favorably on such a high priority for funds for sport in international programs of assistance to other countries. One need only to talk with returning Peace Corps veterans who have conducted sport and recreational activities as part of their duties to hear virtually unanimous testimony as to the popularity and efficacy of these programs among the recipients of Peace Corps aid.

Our government makes other minor overtures to the success of sport as a vehicle for promoting our political aims in foreign countries. The State Department sends coaching and officiating "big names" on brief tours to hold clinics and workshops and to serve as advisors to the coaches and athletes on the national teams of other nations. The State Department also cooperates with the AAU, the NCAA, and the American Olympic Committee to send small representative teams, or selected individual athletes, to tour in other countries in order to compete there and to conduct sport clinics as a "good will" gesture from the United States.

Occasionally physical educators from this country receive Fulbright Lectureships in Physical Education and Sport with appointment to a representative Physical Education Institute or University in a host country to work with the sport leaders, the physical education teachers and students, the Sport Club coaches and athletes, and coaches and athletes on national sports teams, as well as with sport dignitaries in Ministries of Education and Ministries of Sport.

Likewise, sport leaders from other countries are invited by our government to spend a brief time, usually one to three months, visiting one or more universities in order to learn more about the organization, administration, and coaching of sport in the United States.

In concluding this very brief overview of an important, volatile issue which is a major concern now of many young people as well as established leaders in and out of sport, we assert our staunch belief in the positive values that sport programs potentially can buttress and reinforce. The key to the current problem is primarily that of the ethical *values* held by the decision makers, both in and out of sport, who have the power to make decisions as to how sport will be used in the future to foster international goodwill as well as to contribute optimally to the education, health, welfare, and enjoyment of the participating sportsman. Hopefully, ways will be found to emphasize the positive values and to deemphasize the negative ones although the road may be long and difficult.

Dehumanization of Sport

In recent years we have seen a spate of books, articles, and speeches decrying an alleged "dehumanization" of individual members of a sport team by coaches at the high school, college, university, and professional sport levels.[24,29,30] Several of these exposés have appeared in popularized paperback books authored by former professional athletes who became disenchanted with the ways in which they were treated by their coaches and team owners.

Some of the major charges are that the coach regards each player as a robot rather than as an individual; that little or no freedom of choice is permitted the players in any aspect in the practice, training, or conditions of playing in the game; that players are used and exploited to build the reputations of the coaches, the school, or the club owner; and that individuals are demeaned, sworn at in front of the other players, and embarrassed in public when they make a mistake in the game. In schools and colleges the players are made to feel that the *only* important activity going on in the institution is the sport team and the necessity to win at almost any cost. Players believe they are "used" to produce a winning team which, in turn, attracts large audiences and television contracts which will bring hundreds of thousands of dollars into the institution's treasury. Some players believe they are lied to about their prospects for playing now, or in the future, and that some of them serve only as "cannon fodder" in scrimmage for the stars.

The stringency of dress codes, rules concerning the maximum length hair, the type of clothing which must be worn on team trips, training rules, and similar personal conduct requirements are viewed as an infringement of personal rights and also indicate implicitly that the coach holds little or no faith in the player's ability to discipline himself and to be responsible for his own actions and decisions. He is treated almost like a child. The coach is regarded as an "authoritarian" who has not kept pace with the rapid changes in cultural values, particularly those relating to the so-called "youth culture." Other complaints could be added to this list but perhaps it is representative of some of the major charges which athletes, parents, friends, faculty members, newspaper writers, and other observers have brought against the sport scene in the past few years.

The fact that such situations as described above do exist cannot and should not be denied. The problem is that there is no way available now to assess the actual extent and degree to which these mal-practices exist on the campuses of the schools and colleges of this country. It may be that professional athletes can give a more accurate accounting of the situation, but so far the public information emanates mainly from the writings of a few disgruntled athletes who "blew the whistle."

Who knows? Perhaps a large majority of athletes are generally satisfied with the conditions which prevail on their teams and in their organizations. As in most areas of human affairs it is usually the dissi-dent who takes the time and makes the effort to publicize his dis-content and the reasons therefor. We do not hear the testimony of the many who are at least nominally satisfied with the program as it is. Sometimes there is rebuttal to the critics but usually it does not receive the same public attention as the critic. There may be literally thou-sands of male and female athletes, both past and present performers, on school and college sport teams who believe their experiences were among the highlights of their educational careers and that their coaches are outstanding individuals who make significant contributions to the personal growth and development of the athlete.

Coaches by and large have changed with the times, too. There are differences of opinion among them as to what are proper training rules and regulations, the extent to which players should participate in decisions about what plays will be used, which players will be on the starting team, who will call the signals, and similar instructional and morale problems. There will always be these differences. But when one looks at the tremendous voluntary participation which con-tinues to increase each year in more and more sports at both the school and college level of inter-school sport for men and women, there is considerable prima facie evidence that the clients of these programs, the students themselves, are sufficiently satisfied and motivated to want to be on these teams. The emotional fervor with which most par-ticipants engage in competitive sport is high compared with a major-ity of other school activities. This involvement and commitment pro-vides the coach with an unparalleled opportunity to exert leadership through the medium of sport which will help young people to develop values and attitudes which will benefit them in later life. Coaches can be, and often are, the most influential teachers the stu-dents have in their educational career. There is constant, abundant testimony to this judgment.

Of course it must be recognized that the unscrupulous coach can teach players to be unethical, or to be poor sports, to complain, and to be uncooperative. He can place winning above all other considerations and thus distort the real values of a bona fide educational sport experience. In the long run, the quality of the coach's personal character is the crucial factor in the success of the athletic programs under his direction in terms of the long range values, understandings, and personality traits he helps to instill in the young people under his charge.

So, because of the sensitive nature of the coach's role it behooves teacher education institutions to apply strict standards to the certification of young men and women who graduate from their programs to enter the coaching profession. Careful scrutiny of the candidate's personal fitness for coaching is as important as the assessment of his technical sport skills and coaching methods. Likewise, the administrator for whom the coach works should evaluate his competences and behaviors relative to his assignment on a regular basis the same as for all other professional education personnel. If the coach shows he is unfit for his assignment he should be moved to other duties or relieved from this position.

Racism in Sport

Another charge against sport which has gained currency in recent years is that of "racism." The particular allegation was first made prominent by Harry Edwards through speeches and a book.[14] This controversy has become nationwide and still appears in the news. Manifestations of the discontent with the way members of minority groups have allegedly been treated on sport teams are strikes by players who have stayed away from practice or who have voluntarily resigned from teams in mid-season, protests by Black Student Union groups on behalf of their athletic members, sitting down or not standing at attention when the national anthem is played at sports events, and raising the arm and fist in a "black power" salute to call attention to grievances.

It is frequently pointed out that blacks and chicanos seldom are assigned to key leadership positions such as quarterback, that they must play less desirable positions, that they are "stacked" on the team roster so that one of them is the substitute for another minority group member, that they are treated unequally on trips with respect to lodging facilities and sometimes are discriminated against in other ways. Many coaching staffs do not have representatives from various ethnic groups in proportion to the number of athletes on the team from the minorities. Few blacks or chicanos are head coaches or athletic directors or game officials. Few are elected to high office in athletic associations, and few are selected for honors bestowed by the coaching fraternity through its professional associations. Promises of work-aid and adequate on- or off-campus living accommodations made by the school's recruiters sometimes fail to materialize, seemingly more often than in the case of the white prospects. Aptitude tests required for admission to some colleges are culturally biased against members of minority races yet are crucial to selection for admission. There are other charges of racism which could be added to this list.

Undoubtedly, many of the charges which have been made are valid. Bringing them to public light has had salutary effects in some schools and colleges around the country. Injustices still prevail and should be remedied as quickly as possible. On the other hand, the coach, the institution, and the athletes should have fair protection and full access to all information relevant to any such charges so that an accurate assessment of the situation can be made in fairness to all concerned. Some charges may not be substantiated. There may be reasonable grounds for doubt about other allegations. A legal and humane mechanism should be established by the institution wherein the full rights of all parties involved are fairly heard and duly arbitrated.

Full opportunity to participate freely in sport should be made equally available to all persons regardless of color, race, or creed. Sport should be an arena which provides for the democratic participation of all without overtones of racism, prejudice, or inequality.

COMPETITION AND COOPERATION

Competition and cooperation both are fundamental elements in the American cultural pattern. The political and economic systems of American democracy are rooted in the concept of competition. The schools, and many homes, use competition as a motive to influence children's behavior. However, regulation of competition now exists in many governmental as well as private agencies, in order that "unfair advantage" will not be attained by the unscrupulous and dishonest competitor. Also, there are many groups, agencies, and individuals who believe strongly that cooperation is the basis of successful democratic action. The relative merits of competition and cooperation are argued in educational systems, each having its vocal advocates. Many school practices are influenced by the weight of authority held by the proponents of one view or the other.

Perhaps the entire question should not be decided on the basis of a dichotomy of choice—either competition or cooperation—but should be considered through an understanding of the essential interrelationship of both concepts. Sport and athletics, under proper leadership, provide an excellent medium for the development of acceptable attitudes toward both cooperation and competition which are believed to have lifelong application. In order to clarify the nature of the cooperation–competition problem, and the role of sport and athletics in attitude and value development in these areas, the following analysis of human nature may be helpful.

Six characteristic behaviors of man may be described in these categories of basic tendencies:

1. Man is gregarious; he has a need to live in social groups.

2. Man is competitive at times and cooperative at other times.

3. Play is spontaneous; play of children is a natural response to organic needs; all sports and athletics have this same natural basis.

4. Man tends to repeat and learn behavior—mental, emotional, social, or physical—which brings him satisfaction.

5. Man does not inherit codes or standards of moral or ethical conduct; he must learn them. Thus, he is socialized in early childhood in those cooperative and competitive behaviors which his society values.

6. Man is imitative; he tends to adopt responses suggested by other persons whom he regards as prestigious or influential.

These six categories of behavior provide a partial answer to fundamental questions and problems which arise in connection with the promotion and control of competitive sport and athletics. Conversely, if we fail to take these categories sufficiently into account, we may never arrive at satisfactory solutions. They indicate why group activity in physical education is of such great educational significance. They tell us why the ideals and behavior of the teacher or "coach" are of such great importance; why some teams or individuals display good sportsmanship and others bad. They suggest the causes for and the answers to problems of overemphasis, commercialism, exploitation of the athlete, and others. They point the way to the essential characteristics of a desirable program of competitive sport and athletics.

The Function of Group Competitive Activity

If the human being were an organism sufficient unto himself, with no need for or inclination toward group living, education would not be concerned with group activity. If man were a strictly cooperative organism, education would have no place for competitive activity. Man is both competitive and gregarious in most cultures. The American social order is based primarily upon these characteristics, so organized education is concerned with the need to give the young opportunity for practicing fundamental behaviors which will promote both individual and group welfare.

The research available to date tells us little about the long range, generalized effects of training children in "desirable" competitive and cooperative behaviors in formal educational settings. Virtually no warranted conclusions have yet been derived from research in sport activities. Thus, what can be taught in schools, particularly in sport, about desirable long range competitive-cooperative behaviors is highly uncertain. Many variables confound the studies in this area such as age, dependent variables used to exemplify cooperative or competitive behaviors, and the criterion measures of independent variables from which an inference can be drawn that some demonstrable, desirable change in behavior has in fact occurred.

It is interesting to note that we try to teach and emphasize cooperation in American families, schools, and many social organizations, yet much of what we *do* and require of children is competitive, and usually is assessed by a traditional, highly competitive grading system. Teachers unconsciously transmit their own value systems as they deliberately attempt to teach subject matter. Thus, these teachers, and most particularly, physical education teachers and athletic coaches, apply implicit and explicit reinforcements to competitive behaviors. Many teachers are from the middle class strata of American society and almost inevitably they transmit one of the strong traditional values they have learned in a lifetime, the value of "competition."

Nor can the physical educator learn much from studies done with children in other classrooms. Klausmeier and Ripple[20] reported that competition as motivation did not result in superior performances compared with cooperation. They do suggest that a cooperative learning environment has a proven advantage in reducing the threat of failure and frustration for students with learning difficulties. Therefore, schools should diminish emphasis on competition in regular classroom situations.

In summary, man behaves cooperatively under certain conditions and competitively under others. Therefore the prime educational function of group competitive activity is the promotion of cooperative types of behaviors and the proper modification of competitive responses, so that both may contribute ultimately to individual and group welfare.

This important function is often overlooked. It is common to think of football and basketball largely in terms of their contributions to physical and mental development, whereas it is in the social elements of these activities that their distinctive significance lies. Football players, when asked how they benefit from participation in their sport, frequently cite the social relationships with teammates and coaches, and the opportunities to become acquainted with players and coaches of other teams, as being the most important outcomes of the experience.

Physical education recognizes group activity as the chief source of learning which will promote better group living. Also, group activity may be considered as contributing to individual welfare by providing opportunity for the expression of human tendencies and emotions which cannot be exercised successfully in any other way. In fact, it is partly through conflict that the nature of cooperation becomes better understood by children.

Research seems to indicate that there is a positive correlation between cooperative and competitive response in children. The more cooperative students are also at times the more competitive individuals, whereas pupils who are not highly competitive are also not very cooperative. Schools should not eliminate competition, but should help students to learn to compete properly, with acceptable attitudes, in friendly situations.

Williams[36] makes the important point that competitive activities, properly conducted in physical education, emphasize that "struggle" and effort are of utmost importance in personality development, as struggle to improve oneself and to realize one's potentialities more fully gives fiber to personal development. Thus, in sport as well as in business or other competitive situations, excellence should be the aim, rather than privilege, and performance should be valued, rather than unfair advantage.

Dangers of Competitive Sport and Athletics

The points we have been discussing are important in the considerations which lead the physical educator to attach such educational importance to dual and team competitive sport. Properly organized and controlled, not only do these activities meet the needs of youth for physical, mental, and emotional self-expression, but they involve so deeply most of the emotions of human beings that they are of significance in molding ethical, moral, and social habits and attitudes. The perceptive educator realizes that the modifications brought about in individuals through these experiences may be socially undesirable. In sport and athletics, it is just as possible for the individual to learn ruthless selfishness as to learn considerate cooperation, or to learn dishonesty rather than honesty. Some of the other potential dangers in a program of sport that is not properly controlled should be explained.

Physical and Emotional Stresses. A program not properly directed may also endanger the physical welfare of many players. The intense emphasis upon the competitive element may lead individuals to sacrifice their physical well-being. The administration of drugs to "pep" up the player, or of a "shot" to reduce pain in a sprained ankle, is an example. Some teachers or coaches may condone or encourage such needless sacrifices. The glories heaped upon the "winner" and the unjustifiably deep feeling of defeat and futility cultivated in the "loser" have unfortunate effects upon personality and upset the sense of values. An undue emotional strain in competitive athletics is unhealthy, and not conducive to a normal emotional life.

Overemphasis. Some institutions are guilty of what their critics call "overemphasis on athletics." The intense and long-continued concentration upon one interest and one type of activity may interfere with other important and legitimate interests and activities, and can lead to a narrow spirit of professionalism not compatible with worthy living. The intense spirit of competition communicated to the student body and other interested persons tends to upset their sense of values, with resultant development of commercialism, "stadiumitis," and shady forms of proselyting. And, finally, undue emphasis upon competition and winning tends to cause the leadership to devote its attention largely or exclusively to the highly skilled group, with resultant neglect of the interests and welfare of the greater number. Many examples can be cited of schools and colleges which have allotted human and financial resources to the men's varsity sport program to the detriment of well rounded physical education instructional programs, intramural sport, sport clubs, and girls' and women's sport, all of which serve the vast majority of the student body.

Psychiatric View. We cannot close this discussion without reference to the possible psychiatric dangers in the teaching of competition. Davidson[11] offers the observation that for many persons the need for, and fear of, competition can affect the personality adversely. Competition puts all persons on guard. Hostilities and aggressions may arise from improperly motivated competitive situations. Teachers and coaches should develop techniques of teaching whereby students are motivated by internal satisfactions, such as the feeling of having performed well, of having mastered the learning task, and of having solved the problem, rather than by pride in having "defeated" the opponent, having won the gold cup, or having received the silver watch. After all, the most compelling motivation of the participants, in sport competition at any level, should be to "play for the fun of it."

CHARACTERISTICS OF A DESIRABLE PROGRAM

The desirable program of sport and athletics has at least four general characteristics.

Provision of a Place for All Students

1. A variety of sports and athletics, appropriate to various interests, degrees of physical power, and stages of development, experience, and skill, should be provided.

2. There should be adequate equipment and facilities for all.

3. There should be qualified and interested leadership for the entire program, not for the superior group of performers alone.

4. The superior students should not be exploited in such a way as to submerge interest in the ordinary performer.

5. Competition should be equalized so as to maintain the interest of players of all degrees of proficiency.

Promotion of Physical Well-being

1. A medical examination should be required, and a physician should approve the student for participation as a member of an athletic team, an intramural team, or a physical education class.

2. Every precaution to prevent accidental physical injury should be exercised and provision should be made to obtain prompt emergency service in the event of a serious injury at practice or in a game at any time of day or night.

3. No contestant should be permitted or encouraged to sacrifice his physical well-being, either in competition or in training.

4. The rules of healthful living should be taught in connection with activities.

5. Coaches and teachers should be models of the exemplary behavior they espouse to their students.

Direction of the Competitive Spirit toward Educational Goals

1. The coach, the individual athlete, and the team should make every legitimate effort to win their games. They practice with purpose and train with dedication. They play with intensity and desire according to the rules and ethics of healthy sport competition. They play to win, but not at all cost. When the contest is over, they accept the victory or the defeat with natural emotional reactions, but they do not regard the world as "coming to an end" if they lose. Neither do they gloat over opponents whom they have defeated.

2. The idea that trying fairly and wholeheartedly to win is more important than winning at all cost should be developed.

3. Recreational values should be maintained. Players should enjoy participation in the practices and in the games. Basically, sport should be "fun."

4. Respect for academic and other worthwhile interests should be cultivated. Participation in sport should be scheduled and engaged in with respect to a reasonable personal time and energy commitment in relation to the academic and social programs and responsibilities of each student.

Emphasis on Social Development

1. The individual should be helped to find satisfaction in socially desirable behavior and dissatisfaction in poor sportsmanship.

2. Trickery or shady dealing in the promotion, management, teaching, or conduct of sport and athletics should not be tolerated.

3. Respect for and friendliness toward the opponent should be encouraged.

4. Emotional control should be stressed.

5. Leadership which sets good examples in habits, attitudes, and conduct should be provided.

6. The group should be protected from the necessity of competing against unsportsmanlike opponents.

7. Material rewards of significant monetary value should not be offered for winning or participating.

8. The contestant should be helped to see similarities in desirable conduct in athletic contests and in other phases of life.

All of these points are important enough to deserve treatment in detail, which space does not permit. We shall attempt only to point out in which of these respects American school programs of competitive sport and athletics approach or fall short of the ideal, together with brief comments on improvements to be made.

COMPETITIVE SPORT FOR ALL

Almost everyone is familiar with the fact that, in past years in secondary schools and colleges, there has been a strong tendency generally to concentrate upon competitive athletics for the superior group of male students. This superior group composes the teams which engage in interschool competition. In order to provide more boys with the opportunity to engage in competitive athletics, many colleges and universities have increased in number and types of athletic teams in recent years in such sports as rugby, crew, and gymnastics. Many community colleges and high schools likewise are expanding athletic programs by having teams in a wider variety of sports, such as cross country, water polo, gymnastics, wrestling, soccer, fencing, and softball. Also, more schools are organizing junior varsity, lightweight, and reserve teams in many sports, so that boys of lesser ability will have opportunities to compete against boys of similar skill from other schools. The broadening scope of the program is indicated by the fact that in at least one state more than thirty sports are sanctioned for high school competition. Also, in recent years, girls' and women's inter-school sport programs have expanded rapidly in many sections of the country, providing additional opportunities for sport competition by a significant percentage of pupils in the total student body. This trend is discussed in a later section of this chapter.

Many schools and colleges have also attempted to provide wholesome athletic and recreational participation for a majority of students, regardless of skill, by providing comprehensive intramural programs. Good intramural programs offer a wide variety of activities in an attempt to suit the needs and interests of all the students. They equalize the competition by excluding the superior groups who are members of school teams. In the main, they promote a sense of responsibility in the participants and an interest in wholesome competition marked by fine sportsmanship. The part of the student body engaged in these activities ranges to almost 100 percent in some schools.

The physical education department should provide interested staff leadership for the promotion, organization, and conduct of the intramural program.[23] The intramural director should be assigned sufficient time in his staff "load" to perform his duties properly. Many intramural programs fall short of perfection because the participants are given little assistance in acquiring greater skill, slight attention is given to the matter of physical conditioning, and not enough thought is devoted to methods of stimulating more general participation. Many intramural programs have expanded their activities to include those suitable for both boys and girls. Also, some programs include not only athletic activities, but non-athletic recreational activities.

Another method of extending opportunity for athletic competition to more students has developed in recent years under the name of the "extramural" program. In many cases it is an extension of the intramural program. For example, at the end of the intramural season in a particular sport, one or more of the intramural teams from school A will travel to a nearby school for contests against similar intramural teams from that school. In some instances a school will select an all-star team from its own intramural leagues to play the all-star team of another school. It is believed that the most beneficial results are against teams from other schools. Another form of extramural program is found in many elementary schools, where an entire sixth grade is transported to a neighborhood school and all members of both sixth grades, boys and girls, are placed on one of several teams in two or three sports, thus affording all children an opportunity to compete in friendly games with pupils from other schools without regard to selection by playing ability.

In recent years there has been a rapid increase in sport clubs on college and university campuses across the country. To a lesser extent this movement is also taking place in high schools and community colleges. The clubs are organized around sports which are not in the formal institutional sport program. Examples are sailing, karate, judo, skiing, mountain climbing, cycling, lacrosse, volleyball, bowling, fencing, and others. The leadership is provided mainly by interested students, staff, and faculty members. Physical education and athletic departments usually cooperate by making available ground and building space not already committed to existing programs in those departments. Sometimes at least partial funding is provided by the school but most of the expense of operation is borne by the students in the clubs. Many of these clubs use facilities off campus such as bowling lanes, ice rinks, ski slopes, and so forth.

One cannot help noticing and admiring the rapid rise in popularity of these sport clubs. Students are to be congratulated and encouraged for the quality of their enthusiastic leadership to extend opportunities for sport participation to ever larger numbers of students and staff on a voluntary basis. There is every indication that this promising trend will continue and broaden its scope and influence in the years ahead.

The responsibility of the school to provide wholesome athletic experiences for all students is well stated in an important publication of the Educational Policies Commission of the National Education Association and the American Association of School Administrators, which says, in part, "We believe that the experience of playing athletic games should be a part of the education of all children and youth who attend school in the United States."[28]

Boys' and Men's Athletics

The school program of competitive sport for men had its beginings and early development in the time span of 1852 to 1875. Up to that time, schools and colleges were under the control of administrators who attributed little significance to play, except to consider it more or less a necessary evil. They did not envision it as an educational activity. Play and sport always have been of intrinsic interest to young Americans, even in the early days of the settlers who lived under the influence of the "Puritan work ethic." College boys in the 1800's likewise organized and enjoyed informal sport activities among themselves on and off campus. It was inevitable that sooner or later a group of students from one college would issue a challenge to students in a nearby college.

In 1852, the first intercollegiate athletic competition took place in the form of a boat race between Harvard and Yale. Regattas were a popular form of athletic competition between colleges on an expanding basis through 1875. Gradually, the students organized contests with other schools in additional sports. The enthusiasm and popularity of these sport programs became more intense and widespread. Also, spectators became more numerous, and publicity was developed to "spread the word."

Gradually, athletically inclined alumni began to interest themselves in the athletic fortunes of their alma maters, and as the management of affairs became too complicated for the ever-shifting student control, the graduate manager system developed in American colleges. Soon thereafter the position of the professional coach made its appearance.

This developing program was not under the direct control of the college administration, but intense, widespread student interest, coupled with obvious abuses and unpleasant complications which reflected negatively upon the institutions, made it necessary for college administrations to take over control of athletics.

At the present time, a vast majority of the schools and colleges of this country officially conduct sport programs as a legitimate educational function. They employ well-trained, competent instructors and coaches, many of whom hold traditional academic rank as regular faculty members. With few exceptions, these programs are responsible to the president and the faculty of the institution. In some cases the program still is operated and administered under delegated powers held by associated students' organizations.

Thus, the schools and colleges of the United States provide a broad base for sport participation by millions of boys and girls in a long list of sanctioned activities, involving many millions of dollars worth of facilities, and conducted by thousands of qualified instructors, coaches, trainers, athletic directors, and physical education administrators. It is this broad concept of school-based athletics which in part has accounted for America's international successes in sport competition.

It is interesting to note that this expansion of athletic opportunity and increased participation has occurred simultaneously with the intensification in recent years of the so-called "academic" program, which involves most students in more "solid" courses which require longer hours of homework than previously at higher levels of competence.

Secondary Schools. Some high schools report the participation of 60 percent or more of the total number of boys in the student body on one or more of the interscholastic athletic teams. Thousands of high school youth have demonstrated that they can compete successfully in athletics and at the same time meet the increased challenge in their academic work. The control and administration of high school athletics has been vastly improved in recent years, through the work of State High School Athletic Associations and the coordinating efforts of the National Federation of State High School Athletic Associations. Also, national educational associations have held national conferences on athletic programs and administration, and have adopted and published official policy statements of athletic standards. In recent years there has been a concerted movement to upgrade the quality of junior and senior high school athletic coaching. Some states have passed legislation requiring each coach to be certificated for coaching by completing an approved coaching minor in a four year institution. Of course traditional physical education major and minor teaching credentials still qualify a teacher to coach an inter-school team. More colleges and universities are offering a coaching minor program. The AAHPER and other professional organizations are adopting official statements of standards to apply to the coaching minor credential.

All of these forces have had significant impact on the strengthening of high school athletic programs, and on the reduction of certain intolerable practices developed over the years by overzealous coaches, administrators, and townspeople. Finally, the role of the athletic program in the total educational context of the high school frequently has been described by coaches and athletic directors with keen insight, although few persons have realized the extent of the influence upon the students in the schools as it was revealed in the analysis of sport in high schools by Coleman.[9]

Community Colleges. A majority of community colleges sponsor a wide-ranging athletic program. These programs attract large numbers of students and hold wide community appeal. Athletic performances usually are of high caliber. Many athletes transfer to four-year colleges, where they enjoy continued success. Coaching at this level is excellent, and many colleges have athletic facilities which rival or exceed those of numerous four-year colleges.

The community college athletic program must be recognized for its extensive, high quality contributions to the sport experiences of thousands of students throughout the country. The high school graduate with limited funds can find enjoyment and success in these programs, usually in his local area. In many ways, employment at this level is extremely desirable. The physical education profession recognizes the roles and potentials of these institutions. They are regarded as equal educational partners with elementary schools, junior high schools, high schools, and four-year colleges and universities in the athletic continuum.

Colleges and Universities.   At the college and university level, similar strides have been taken in recent years to broaden the base of intercollegiate athletic competition and to effect better control and administration of these programs. Sports such as soccer, lacrosse, bowling, and water polo have been sponsored by more and more colleges.

One ominous threat has arisen for many four-year institutions in the past two or three years, namely, inflation and the rapid increase in the cost of conducting intercollegiate athletic programs. Some institutions have had to eliminate one or more sports from their intercollegiate program. Several major schools are now operating on a deficit budget because profits from gate receipts no longer cover the expenses of the total intercollegiate sport program. General fund allocations are required to make up these deficits or sports attracting few spectators are being eliminated. Whether or not this trend has long term significance can only be speculated about at this time. Private institutions may face the gravest dangers because of the high cost of athletic grants-in-aid mainly due to significantly higher tuition coverage required. One further new factor is that with the long overdue recognition of the equal rights and opportunities for women to engage in intercollegiate sport the funds formerly allotted to men's departments are now being used to pay for women's team expenses as well.

College athletes must meet higher entrance requirements than ever before. In some colleges, research indicates that varsity athletic award winners maintain a grade point average higher than the average of all men in the schools, and that the percentage of athletes who graduate from college is greater than the percentage of men in the total student body who graduate. As at the high school level, thousands of fine young male athletes have demonstrated that they can do an excellent job academically, and at the same time perform at high levels of ability in comprehensive sport programs.

Control of Amateur Athletics. The control and administration of college sport is more diverse than in high schools. Some colleges are "independent" in athletics; that is, they do not belong to any athletic conference. A majority of colleges in the United States do belong to some type of athletic conference. Two national bodies provide overall guidance and control: the National Collegiate Athletic Association (NCAA), and the National Association of Intercollegiate Athletics (NAIA). Most larger schools are under the jurisdiction of the NCAA, while more than four hundred smaller schools are affiliated with the NAIA. This division of control is controversial. Many athletic authorities think that all college athletics should be under the control of one organization, in order to provide greater coordination and consistency of policy and practice.

Because all high school, community college, and college athletes who are declared eligible for competition by their school and league are presumed to be amateurs, the matter of the approval of the individual athlete for international competition rests with the Amateur Athletic Union of the United States (AAU). Also, the AAU exercises control over both men and women athletes who wish to compete as amateurs within the United States, under affiliations not school connected, such as sport clubs, or when competing "unattached," as individuals.

In recent years, there has been heated strife between organizations over the jurisdiction over amateur athletes and their selection and approval for international competition.[15] In an attempt to remedy the situation, United States federations have been formed by authorities representing sports such as track and field and gymnastics. In recent years the controversy became so heated that Presidents Kennedy and Johnson appointed federal mediators to work with the opposing factions in an attempt to arbitrate the differences between them.

To date, the AAU and the NCAA have failed to accept mutually the proposals of the federal mediator and the committee. It is difficult to predict when a satisfactory solution will be reached by these two organizations. Some observers believe that the longer the stalemate exists, the greater the possibility that the United States Congress will lose its patience and will enact binding legislation to institute the first significant degree of federal control over sports in this country. This action would be unfortunate, in the view of most sportsmen who believe that schools, colleges, and independent voluntary organizations should administer local, regional, national, and international competitions involving American athletes.

In the interim, the amateur athletes suffer from legal uncertainties, implied and explicit threats, and a general atmosphere of distrust and narrow jurisdictional loyalty. Genuine concern for the general welfare of the United States sport programs and for the specific welfare of thousands of American athletes who compete voluntarily "for the love of the sport" should be the overriding criterion for settlement of the dispute.

All is not yet serene in college and post-college athletic control. Large problems remain to be solved. Students of physical education should acquaint themselves thoroughly with the issues involved, and the steps being taken in the amelioration of these difficulties.

Girls' and Women's Sport

Important differences exist in sport competition in American schools and colleges between current programs for girls and women and those for men and boys. The differences between the two programs are in large measure due to sharp contrasts in historical development.

Several factors have influenced, and continue to influence, the development of intercollegiate sport competition for women. Among the more notable influences are changing cultural roles of women in American society, evolving national and international conditions, the women's liberation movement, publicity and mass communications media, professional leadership, medical judgments and biological research evidence, and public interest and acceptance of women in sport.

Oberlin College was the first institution to admit women (in 1833). By 1880, more than half of the liberal arts colleges in the country admitted both men and women. Social customs, then as now, influenced the extent and type of participation by women in physical education and competitive sport.

Intercollegiate competition developed in the latter half of the nineteenth century. Dr. James Naismith invented basketball for men in 1891. A committee was appointed to investigate basketball rules for women in 1899. In 1901, the first basketball rules guide was published by the American Sports Publishing Company. A standing committee for women's basketball rules became a reality in 1905. As women's sport expanded, student athletic associations were formed to meet the growing interest. The first association was formed in 1891 at Bryn Mawr to suport a tennis program.

Sport days, as well as regularly scheduled games with other colleges, were held. Often women's basketball games were played as preliminaries to men's games. Officiating and coaching frequently were done by men. Generally, women physical educators did not approve of this development.

In the early 1900's, intercollegiate competition for women suffered from lack of support from women physical education leaders. In fact, from 1920 to 1930 there was a reduction in the number of institutions having such a program. Programs which remained were very limited in scope.

Despite this negative picture, a positive force toward eventual development of women's programs occurred when women were authorized to compete in the Olympic Games in swimming in their own division (1912), in fencing (1924), and in track and field (1928). The Amateur Athletic Union (AAU) was founded in 1888 to control sport outside colleges and schools. When women were made eligible to compete in the Olympic Games, the AAU was involved in the coaching and selection of women for the American team. AAU influence on women's sport has been continuous since that time, although there have been conflicts with other groups concerned with girls' and women's sport, chiefly because of differences concerning standards.

Much of the leadership in the development of sport for American girls and women has come from the Division of Girls' and Women's Sports of the American Association for Health, Physical Education, and Recreation. DGWS traces its history to 1917, when the American Physical Education Association established a Committee on Women's Athletics to develop standards and formulate rules for girls' and women's sports. This committee went through a series of name changes over the years and emerged as the National Section on Women's Athletics in 1932. The section achieved division status in 1958 and voted to become an Association in the 1974 reorganization of AAHPER.

A parallel development occurred in the early years of the organization of the Athletic and Recreation Federation of College Women in 1917. This group was formed to further programs of Women's Athletic Associations and to promote greater sport participation by women. Throughout its history, it has been essentially an organization of student leaders. Since 1962, it has been affiliated with DGWS and received the services of a consultant employed by AAHPER. It is now called the College Women in Sports group (CWS).

During World War II, in the early 1940's, there was a nation-wide concern for physical fitness for men and women. Competition for women was curtailed by wartime conditions. Interest in "carry-over sports" increased in schools and colleges; a national intercol-legiate golf tournament for women was initiated in the early 1940's. National competition in tennis followed soon afterward. Telegraphic and postal meets and "extramural" contests (defined as all types of competition except "varsity type" athletics) increased during the forties and fifties.

GAA and WRA sport programs continued to expand into the 1950's. But by the late fifties, these programs were evidencing con-siderable change in emphasis. The student organizations were giving more attention to the "carry-over sports" and co-recreational activi-ties, and the team sport competitions were being sponsored more often by other groups. This trend was probably accelerated by the development of active student union programs on many college cam-puses; a number of these programs competed with traditional WAA tournaments for student participation. School and college programs in the 1950's reflected the increasing international exchange in expan-sion of educational gymnastics programs.

In the 1960's, a new concern was expressed from several quar-ters relative to the restricted opportunities for competition by girls and women with high levels of sports ability. There was impetus to improve America's performances by women athletes in the Olympic Games. It was felt that the sound way to build high competence was to expand opportunities for all girls and women in the secondary schools and colleges. In a joint effort to strengthen girls' and women's sport at the national level, the United States Olympic Development Committee, Women's Division, and the DGWS of the AAHPER spon-sored a series of National Institutes for girls' sports, beginning in 1963. Changes also resulted from the influence of the presidents of some of the major universities who, through their conference commis-sioners and institutional athletic representatives, stimulated their departments of physical education for women to reevaluate the sport program for women and to upgrade it in terms of high-level competition.

To guide the new emphasis on national-level sport competition for women, a Commission on Intercollegiate Athletics for Women was formed by DGWS in 1966. The Commission "sanctioned" the First Annual U.S. Intercollegiate Archery Meet and a national swimming meet, both in 1967, and a gymnastics championship in 1968. One of the notable results of the work of this Commission was the approval of a policy which provided for National Intercollegiate Championships for Women in gymnastics and track and field in 1969, and in swimming, badminton, and volleyball in 1970. The Commission became functionally independent of DGWS as the Association for Intercollegiate Athletics for Women in 1972. Its stated purpose is to provide leadership and initiate and maintain standards of excellence in intercollegiate competition for all college women. In 1973 AIAW National Championships were conducted in volleyball, badminton, swimming and diving, basketball, gymnastics, track and field, and golf. The first AIAW National Junior/Community College Basketball Championship was also held in 1973. DGWS continues to work closely with AIAW and to expand its activities in support of sport programs for girls and women.

Over the years substantial controversy has persisted with regard to whether there are biological limitations which restrict participation in sport by girls and women. The gradual resolution of this issue has supported the trend toward increasing opportunities for competitive sport participation by girls and women. Considerable research evidence and medical judgment has been accumulated in recent years. This evidence indicates that participation in most events by normal, healthy women is not harmful. Studies have been made concerning menstruation, pregnancy, masculinization, and emotional stress. The general conclusion is that girls need not be barred from competitive sport because of any innate biological or psychological characteristics.

Another traditional concern has been the "feminine image" and sport competition. Because of a long history of conflict concerning the female role in America, society has tended to restrict or not support girls' participation in highly competitive sport. Although a social rejection attitude still prevails in some instances, the double standard is being overcome. Girls in schools and colleges enjoy vigorous sport participation. They find that it is not incompatible with female values and interests, and it has become socially acceptable.

Not surprisingly, the recent drive for equal opportunity for women has extended to sport. In the 1970's it is recognized that discrimination against females in athletics exists and that this discrimination should be abolished. Although many professional educators still object to the participation of women on athletic teams established primarily for men, there is increasing support for the principle that qualified athletes should not be excluded from participation in sport because of sex. In practice this has meant participation of girls and women on boys' and men's teams in instances in which separate teams were not provided, and in other instances in which they could demonstrate a level of skill superior to that of male candidates. Both DGWS and the American Academy of Physical Education have recently published written statements supporting the principle of equality in athletics, including certain options for students to participate on mixed teams.

Renewed concern regarding financial aid for athletes has also resulted from questions raised by women's affirmative action groups. It has been traditional policy to prohibit the awarding of athletic scholarships to women, based on the belief that financial aid for athletes tends to create abuses detrimental to the participants themselves. It is now clear that it is legally untenable to deny financial aid to women athletes when men in the same institution are receiving athletic grants-in-aid. DGWS and AIAW are revising regulations relating to recruitment and financial aid for athletes in order to prevent interpretations which are discriminatory against girls and women.

One consequence of this movement toward increased competition for girls and women is that there are not enough women instructors who are highly experienced and qualified to coach women at advanced levels of proficiency. Some professional preparation institutions are developing specializations in coaching for women in an effort to meet this need. DGWS is now sponsoring national coaching conferences to provide opportunity for coaches to examine current trends and issues in girls' and women's sport and to share ideas in conducting athletic competition. It is now recognized that qualified women are also needed as athletic trainers. DGWS is sponsoring athletic training workshops and it is likely that more women will be enrolling in college and university programs designed to prepare

trainers. Secondary schools, colleges, and universities are now opening positions to women, not only in coaching and athletic training,
but also as athletic directors and assistant directors.

Many of the same problems men have faced over the years are
now subjects for resolution by women instructors and directors. Qualified leadership, certification of officials, eligibility rules, athletic scholarships, scheduling, monetary costs, and governing bodies to control
the change of rules are areas of crucial concern.

Sport for Young Children

One of the most vexing problems facing the physical education
profession concerns the desirable nature and extent of athletic competition for young children. Questions such as the following are
constant sources of debate when school and recreation agency policies
are established, are discussed frequently in popular and professional
literature, and in general are of tremendous interest to parents,
educators, children, and the public. At what age should intense athletic competition begin for boys and girls? What is the best age at
which to begin athletic competition in each of the sports? How should
sport competition be organized for young children—on an informal
interschool basis, on an interschool formal league basis, on a play-day
and sports-day basis, or on other plans? What are the beneficial and
harmful effects of intense participation in sport competition for
young children? What qualifications should the adult leaders of these
programs possess? To what extent should schools, community recreation agencies, and outside groups which sponsor sport competition
for young children work together to coordinate their programs, make
optimal use of facilities, provide the most highly qualified leadership,
and provide maximal opportunity for participation?

For several years now, these and similar problems have been the
subject of many research studies, conferences, workshops, organizational policy statements and platforms, and articles in newspapers and
magazines. This is all part of a serious effort on the part of interested
individuals and groups to advance knowledge in this vital area of
youth experience, so that young people will best be served through
desirable programs of athletics.

It is not posible within the space limitations of this book to
discuss the many ramifications of this problem and to cite the argu-

ments and evidence, pro and con, on the many aspects of the situation. Professional leaders in the areas of health, physical education, and recreation should join forces with other individuals and groups now involved in programs of athletic competition for young children, with a view to providing the best available professional advice and guidance for the continuing improvement of the conditions under which such athletics are administered and conducted. In the meantime, the profession has a serious obligation to seek all possible research evidence upon which to make more effective judgments and decisions concerning these programs and their ultimate effects upon children.

The quality of the adult leadership seems to be the key to successful and properly conducted sport programs for young children. Most governing boards of organizations which conduct these sports are aware of this major problem, and are taking steps to improve the situation. The Athletic Institute sponsored a national conference on this problem and published a booklet containing sound recommendations of policies and practices which should apply to the "volunteer coach–leader."[35]

The present-day scope of participation by young boys and girls in a wide variety of athletic competitions is vast throughout the United States, and is constantly enlarging at a very rapid rate. One of the reasons for this expansion is that over the years, physical education and community recreation programs have not done the job of fully meeting the needs and interests of elementary age children in sport activities. Thus a large gap has developed, into which have moved the private groups and sponsors who are motivated to serve youth's insatiable desire for wholesome activity and fun through sport. The Little League Baseball program, with over one million participants throughout the United States and with organizations in several other countries, is one of the most extensive sport programs ever organized under one auspice. Approximately four million youths participate in the various baseball programs sponsored by nonschool agencies.

International Sport

The Summer and Winter Olympic Games, televised around the world to millions of sport fans, are the premier events which are representative of a wide variety of international sports competitions continually being carried on between teams of many of the countries of the world. These competitions are common both in amateur and in professional categories and include men and women alike.

History does not accurately record when and where the first such international sport contest was held. However, it is speculated that the 77th ancient Olympiad, held in Olympia, Greece, in 468 B.C. was the original event. Competitors came from many of the countries stretched along the shores of the Mediterranean Sea. In one form or another, international sport has persisted from that time, with occasional interruptions during periods of warfare.

Administration and Control. The International Olympic Committee (IOC) exercises policy control over the rules and regulations which govern the quadrennial Winter and Summer Olympic Games. The Committee selects Games sites, establishes rules concerning amateur status, and generally sets forth the program of sports to be scheduled and conducted. It also rules on appeals presented during the Games.

At the international level, there is an international sport federation for each sport officially included in the Games. These federations control the conduct of their respective sports around the world. With some exceptions which occur mainly in the United States, each country has a national federation for each sport responsible to the international federation. Most countries also have regional and zone sport federations which provide for local control and operation under the aegis of the respective national federations.

In addition, each country has a National Olympic Committee which coordinates the efforts of all the national sport federations with respect to participation in the Olympic Games.

The United States has fewer national sports federations than most other countries in such sports as track and field, wrestling, gymnastics, and tennis. For reasons of historical accident the official sanctioning and selection body for American athletes in the Olympic Games is the Amateur Athletic Union (AAU), which is recognized by the IOC.

International sport is sponsored under other auspices as well— the list is far too long to recount here. Harvey* and Vendien and

---

* Charles Harvey, ed. *Sport International,* 1960. New York: A. S. Barnes and Company, Inc.

Nixon* provide detailed descriptions of a variety of sporting events held around the world.

In most countries the national government directly controls sport participation both by the policies it sets forth and by direct subsidy of federal funds. This control usually is vested in a Ministry of Education or a separate Ministry of Sport, although there are other organizational patterns. The United States does not conform to this procedure. Although many federal laws and regulations do exist concerning sport, there is no centralized control of sport in schools and colleges as a matter of mandated educational policy. Education is a state function, under powers delegated by the Constitution of the United States. Non-school sport likewise is not highly controlled or directed by the federal government. There is a President's Council on Physical Fitness and Sports, located in the Department of Health, Education, and Welfare which works to promote the values of sport and fitness activities for all Americans throughout the country through a program of public relations, sport clinics, professional publications, and other public media. The federal government does not appropriate the funds required to pay the costs of sending our teams to the Olympic Games as is the case in most other countries. The American people are requested to make voluntary contributions to the United States Olympic Committee to pay for the training, transportation, and lodging of our teams at the Olympics.

So far, the Olympic Games have been restricted to amateur athletes. There is agitation to remove the distinction between amateur and professional athletes in order that the most gifted performers from each country may participate in the various sports in the Games. One cannot foretell when this proposal may become effective, if ever.

Countries use international sport contests as an arena for political action at times by boycotting a particular event in order to show solidarity with a particular cause in which they believe. For example, some African nations have withdrawn from international events in which they have been entered when they learned that South Africa, which still practices apartheid, was entering a team. Thus, a sporting event can become an international arena upon which the spotlight of political and national power can be directed in order to publicize a

---

* Vendien, Lynn C., and Nixon, John E., *The World Today in Health, Physical Education, and Recreation*, 1968. Englewood Cliffs, New Jersey: Prentice-Hall, Inc.

strongly held policy and to enlist the sympathy of other nations. Further discussion about the "politicizing" of sport is contained elsewhere in this chapter.

Purposes of International Sport. Why has international sport always been so noteworthy? Why have national governments provided support for teams to participate around the world? Why are vast sums of money expended to create the facilities and to conduct the activities of international competitions large and small in all parts of the world? Briefly, the following major purposes of international sport competitions have been identified by one of the authors of this book.

International goodwill and understanding between nations is often cited as perhaps the most common aim of sport contests among nations. Perhaps the athletes, and the officials, who have had the opportunity to participate in these events will provide general testimony to support this claim albeit there are isolated examples of unfortunate occurrences which dim the prospects implied by this noble purpose.

Using international sport for the purpose of national political propaganda is also high on the list although one is not likely to find a public pronouncement couched in quite these explicit terms in the government news release or on the national television broadcast of the event at home or abroad. National prestige can be highlighted through the crowning championship exploits of international champions, individuals and teams alike. People admire a "winner." They like to extoll his virtues which led to his superior performance. The news media are willing messengers of these feats, whether they are in the public service or operate in the private sector, as anyone who reads the sports section well knows. Of course television coverage through the eyes and voices of the Howard Cosells and the Jim Simpsons also carries this same message to millions of homes.

Sport provides an avenue for international communication, both verbal and non-verbal, during the competition, and also at other times before and after. One man can learn about a friendly competitor from another country by how he acts, how he practices, how he reacts to stress and to competition. One can infer cultural values which motivate the actions of a citizen of another country if the acquaintance is sufficiently long term and close, as it often becomes among athletes.

Other purposes can briefly be stated. Cultural exchange is facilitated by the sending of representative sport teams, officials, and coaches on goodwill tours to other countries, and by inviting similar groups to come to one's own country. Internal propaganda can be developed from the achievements of world class athletes by publicizing their performances in the newspapers, on the radio, and on television. People take pride in the highest achievements of their fellow citizens in sport, the arts, music, science, and other fields of human endeavor. It is claimed that more Americans read the sport page than any other page in the newspaper, so they become well acquainted with the performances of their athletes when on tour in foreign countries. Finally, well known athletes are held up as models for youth to emulate, both for improved sport performance per se, and for other purposes such as good health. Note the influence of young teen-age swimmers and tennis players of world class, such as Shane Gould and Chris Everett, and of remarkable young athletes such as Mark Spitz and Frank Shorter.

Upon reflection, it is little wonder that international sport is so popular, that nations give it high priority in a political sense, and that interested fans and spectators around the world follow the exploits of their national heroes so ardently through the press and the television. This interest is also manifested in the vast number and variety of publications of all types available in bookstores and libraries on many aspects of international sport.

Selected References

0a. AAHPER, *AIAW Handbook*. Washington, D. C.: American Association for Health, Physical Education, and Recreation, 1973.
1. AAHPER, *DGWS Research Reports: Women in Sports*. Washington, D. C.: American Association for Health, Physical Education, and Recreation, 1971.
1a. AAHPER, *DGWS Research Reports II*. Washington, D.C.: American Association for Health, Physical Education, and Recreation, 1973.
2. AAHPER, *Philosophy and Standards for Girls' and Women's Sports*. Washington, D. C.: American Association for Health, Physical Education, and Recreation, 1973.
3. Anthony, D. W. J.: "The Role of Sport in Development." *International Development Review*, 10, 11. Dec., 1969.
4. Ashton, S.: "Athlete's Changing Perspective." *J. Health. Phys. Educ.-Rec.*, 43:46 (April, 1972).
5. "Athletics as Academic Motivation for the Inner City Boy." *J. Health, Phys. Educ.-Rec.*, 43:40, 41 (Feb., 1972).
6. Baitsch, Helmut, Bock, Hans-Erhard, Bolte, Martin, Bokler, Willy, Grupe, Ommo, Heidland, Hans-Wolfgang, and Lotz, Franz: *The Scientific View of Sport*. Berlin: Springer-Verlag, 1972.

7. Barnes, Samuel Edward: "Sport Clubs." *J. Health, Phys. Educ.-Rec.*, 42:23, 24 (March, 1971).

8. Boyle, Robert H.: *Sport—Mirror of American Life.* Boston: Little, Brown and Company, 1963.

9. Coleman, James S.: *The Adolescent Society.* New York: The Free Press of Glencoe, Illinois, 1971.

10. "Competitive Athletics for Children of Elementary School Age." (Joint Statement of American Academy of Pediatrics, AMA Committee on the Medical Aspects of Sports, and the American Association for Health, Physical Education, and Recreation, and the Society of State Directors of Health, Physical Education, and Recreation). *Pediatrics*, 42:703, Oct., 1968.

11. Davidson, Henry A.: "Competition, the Cradle of Anxiety." *Education*, 76:162-166 (November, 1955).

12. Davies, Gomer: "Single Physical Education Departments and Equality for Women." *J. Health, Phys. Educ.-Rec.*, 44:62-63 (April, 1973).

13. Dowling, Tom: *Coach: A Season With Lombardi.* New York: W. W. Norton and Company, Inc., 1970.

14. Edwards, Harry: *The Revolt of the Black Athlete.* New York: Free Press, 1969.

15. Flath, Arnold W.: *A History of Relations Between the National Collegiate Athletic Association and the Amateur Athletic Union of the United States.* Champaign, Ill.: Stipes Publishing Company, 1964.

16. Gehrke, Delbert, and Slebos, Warren: "Guys and Gals Intramurals." *J. Health, Phys. Educ. and Rec.*, 43:75 (Jan., 1972).

17. Gendel, Evalyn S.: "Fitness and Fatigue in the Female." *J. Health, Phys. Educ. and Rec.*, 42:53,54 (Oct., 1971).

18. Gerber, Ellen W.: "Changing Female Image: A Brief Commentary on Sport Competition for Women." *J. Health, Phys. Educ.-Rec.*, 42:59-61 (Oct., 1971).

18a. Gilbert, Bil, and Williamson, Nancy. "Women in Sport." *Sports Illustrated*, 38: 88-98 (May 28, 1973), 44-55 (June 4, 1973), and 60-73 (June 11, 1973).

18b. Hart, Marie M. (ed.). *Sport in the Socio-Cultural Process.* Dubuque: William C. Brown, 1972.

19. Klafs, Carl E., and Lyon, M. Joan. *The Female Athlete: Conditioning, Competition, and Culture.* St. Louis: The C. V. Mosby Company, 1973.

20. Klausmeier, H. J., and Ripple, Richard E.: *Learning and Human Abilities: Educational Psychology.* New York: Harper and Row Publishers, Inc., 3rd ed., 1971.

21. Lowman, Charles: "Some Thoughts by an Orthopedist." *The Physical Educator*, 28:34 (March, 1971).

22. Loy, John W.: "The Nature of Sport: A Definitional Effort." *Quest*, X:1-15. (May, 1968).

23. Means, Louis E.: *Intramurals: Their Organization and Administration.* Englewood Cliffs, N. J.: Prentice-Hall, Inc., 2nd ed., 1972.

24. Meggyesey, Dave: *Out of Their League.* San Francisco: Ramparts Press, 1971.

25. Metheny, Eleanor: "This 'Thing' Called Sport." *J. Health, Phys. Educ.-Rec.*, 40:59,60. (March, 1969).

26. Miller, Donna Mae and Russell, Kathryn R. E.: *Sport: A Contemporary View.* Philadelphia: Lea & Febiger, 1971.

27. "Perspective for Sport." *Quest*, XIX:1-76 (Jan., 1973).

27a. Poindexter, Hally B. W., and Mushier, Carole L. *Coaching Competitive Team Sports for Girls and Women.* Philadelphia: W. B. Saunders Company, 1973.

28. *School Athletics, Problems and Policies:* Educational Policies Commission report. Washington, D. C.: National Education Association and the American Association of School Administrators, 1954.

29. Scott, Jack: *The Athletic Revolution.* New York: Free Press, 1971.

30. Shecter, Leonard: "The Coming Revolt of the Athletes." *Look Magazine*, July 28, 1970.

31. Sheehan, Thomas J.: "Sport: The Focal Point of Physical Education." *Quest*, X: 59-67 (May, 1968).

32. Shepard, George E., and Jamerson, Richard E.: *Interscholastic Athletics.* New York: McGraw-Hill Book Company, Inc., 1953.
33. Stern, Barry E.: "Cultural Crisis in American Sports." *J. Health, Phys. Educ.-Rec.,* 43:42-44 (April, 1972).
33a. Ulrich, Celeste. "'She Can Play as Good as Any Boy.'" *Phi Delta Kappan,* LV:113-117 (October, 1973).
34. Vander Zwaag, Harold J.: *Toward a Philosophy of Sport.* Reading, Mass.: Addison Wesley Publishing Company, 1972.
35. *Volunteer—Coach Leader.* Chicago: The Athletic Institute, 1961.
36. Williams, Jesse F.: *The Principles of Physical Education.* Philadelphia: W. B. Saunders Company, 8th ed., 1964.
37. *Women and Sport, Proceedings of the National Research Conference.* University Park, Pa.: Pennsylvania State University, 1972.

(Courtesy of the Department of Physical Education and Athletics for Men,
Stanford University.)

Chapter Eleven

LEISURE AND PHYSICAL EDUCATION

Within the United States—and throughout the larger international community—is emerging a new leisure ethic. In the words of George T. Wilson: [27]

> The community education movement is on the threshold of unprecedented and exciting developments, largely as a part of the emergence of a new leisure ethic. Evolving out of old traditions, the new leisure ethic is one expression of the many profound changes occurring in our society today. But, it is one that may be recorded by history as being as significant as the Industrial Revolution or the forty-hour work week. . . . The new leisure ethic can emerge to be expressed in the human values of a harmonious life style in which work, recreation, education, and creature comforts blend into a conscious existence more compatible with human nature than any plan so far designed by the mind of man. . . . An understandable philosophy suggested here is that community education should assist people of all ages and circumstances to make worthwhile, enjoyable, and creative use of time.

In recent decades sociologists, urban planners, and recreation professionals have frequently expressed the need to deal with the fact of increasing amounts of leisure time for the average citizen. A panel of manpower experts participating in a study of prediction of leisure patterns for the 1980's[21] confirmed previous projections. A majority of these panelists expected the average work week to be reduced to a distribution of five days per week, seven hours per day prior to 1975. They foresaw not only a considerable increase in leisure time available but also a much more highly educated populace having this leisure, and a greatly expanded government interest in all aspects of manpower planning. The Commission on Goals for American Recreation[9] has emphasized:

> Much of work in our industrialized and mechanized society is highly specialized, monotonous, boring, repetitive, and noncreative. Millions of workers live fractionalized lives while on the job because their work provides no exercise for the body, no challenge to the mind, no appeal to the emotions. Furthermore, as industry and business grow in size and complexity, the more unimportant becomes the individual and the more remote his opportunity to gain recognition and a sense of personal worth through superior performance.
>
> The industrial–technological–spatial advances of this era in the United States mark with unprecedented materialism a society which, in general, lives comfortably, spends excessively, travels restlessly, and devotes much leisure to superficial and aimless recreation. Increasing automation has magnified the unemployment problem and will necessitate continuous retraining of vast segments of the population, the development of new concepts and practices in education, and the resettlement of mobile Americans.*

Modern man's scope of freedom has been greatly narrowed and is likely to be more so in the future. This seems an inevitable result of the complexity and interrelatedness of living in a modern society. Economically he is less and less a free agent. As a businessman, he conforms to accepted methods and competition if he hopes to succeed; as a working man, he is subject to control and manipulation by his union organization. In politics, especially on a national or statewide basis, he is left with the inner conviction that his one small voice or vote is not so vital. This state of affairs makes it even more important that man channel his development of the exercising of liberty into those areas of his life where he still has freedom of choice— at least, to a far greater degree. Man's leisure time represents his great reservoir of freedom, and what he does with that part of his life provides his best opportunity to exercise individual initiative. It thus becomes the responsibility of all educational agencies to assist him in the development of a high degree of discrimination and choice.

Leisure has been variously defined. In its simplest terms, it is "discretionary time," unobligated time, time free from work, or time not used for meeting the exigencies of life. Leisure is not really a simple concept, however. In a highly provocative analysis, Paul Weiss[26] concludes:

---

* P. 33.

Leisure, then, is the time when men can be at their best, making it possible for them to make the rest of their day as excellent as possible—not by enabling them to work with more zest or efficiency, but by enabling them to give a new value and perhaps a new objective to whatever is done. The good life is a life in which a rich leisure gives direction and meaning to all else we do.*

In June 1970 a Charter for Leisure[2] was agreed upon at the European Recreation Congress. The document grew out of a symposium convened by the International Recreation Association in Geneva in 1967, in which some sixteen organizations operating internationally in the field of play, recreation, and leisure participated. Three existing documents, the Colmar Charter, the United Nations Declaration of Rights of the Child, and the United Nations Universal Declaration of Human Rights, served as a base. The final document has been translated into five languages; its preface reads as follows:[2]

Leisure time is that period of time at the complete disposal of an individual, after he has completed his work and fulfilled his other obligations. The uses of this time are of vital importance.

Leisure and recreation create a basis for compensating for many of the demands placed upon man by today's way of life. More important, they present a possibility for enriching life through participation in physical relaxation and sports, through an enjoyment of art, science, and nature. Leisure is important in all spheres of life, both urban and rural. Leisure pursuits offer man the chance of activating his essential gifts (a free development of the will, intelligence, sense of responsibility and creative faculty). Leisure hours are a period of freedom, when man is able to enhance his value as a human being and as a productive member of his society.

Recreation and leisure activities play an important part in establishing good relations between peoples and nations of the world.

LEISURE AND EDUCATION

In a world in which leisure time for many exceeds working time, in which leisure may become the center of life for the majority of individuals, education for leisure is of prime importance. The "gospel of work" is obsolete for conditions of modern living. Alexander Reid Martin[19] urges educators to consider a holistic approach to man's nature, which would transcend our present conception of a workaday

---

* P. 7.

world and provide a new frame of reference in which work and leisure would in no sense oppose each other. "To gain a clear notion of leisure, we must begin by understanding and setting aside our prejudices that come for overvaluing the world of work . . . make men more fit for leisure, with the firm belief that only those fit for work and leisure will survive as creative individuals."*

Recreation for All

Recreation activities have one outstanding purpose—to enrich the lives of people by contributing to their fulfillment as individuals and as effectively functioning members of a democratic society.[9] By definition, recreation must be entirely voluntary and genuinely satisfying to the individual. Consequently, a free people must provide education for leisure for all.

One of the difficulties in educating for leisure is that the needs vary so greatly in different segments of the population. Those with the most money and personal resources to invest in leisure have the least amount of time. The average executive probably works about a sixty-hour week, while his unionized employee may be working as few as 25 hours per week, for a work week as short as four days. The unemployed and the marginally employed have plenty of time, but they are dependent upon inadequate, non-profit, public recreation services; without imaginative educational approaches they are likely to find most attractive the pathological types of leisure activity which tend to be more available to them.

Education for leisure is also complicated by the need to provide a foundation during the school years for satisfying use of leisure throughout life. People of all ages need meaningful recreation experience. But the most enjoyable recreational activities for youth may not provide satisfying leisure for those same individuals in their older years. All people, even the aging, can develop new skills and interests, but it is also true that older adults are more likely to participate in activities with which they have had previous experience than in those in which they have no skill. Consequently, young people need guidance in developing some interests and skills upon which they can build meaningful leisure pursuits in later life.

---

* P. 35.

Everything possible should be done to increase the value the community obtains from its school buildings and equipment. Schools should provide a place where young and old may come together and take part in activities that interest both. When new school buildings are planned, they should be designed to meet recreational and educational needs of the community in addition to the ordinary classroom requirements. Historically there are many obstacles to making the schools an integral part of the total educational and recreational life of the community, but none that could not be overcome by willing and intelligent planning.

Coordinated planning for school and community facilities indicates the value of such concepts as exemplified in the "park-school." This is conceived as a facility which combines a park, a school, and a playground or playfield, and which functions as an integrated unit to serve the educational and recreational needs of the community. Such cooperative planning solicits and utilizes the ideas of each organized agency within the community whose needs and interests might be involved. The professional training and technical competence of engineers, architects, landscape architects, and sociologists, in addition to education and recreation specialists, should be available for planning such facilities.[23]

One obligation, in relation to education for leisure, which seems to have been rather neglected consists of appropriate training for the intelligent use of the great forms of commercial recreation: the newspaper and periodical press, radio, motion pictures, and television. Too often the school has existed as an island apart from the mainstream of community life and has presented the strange paradox of youth being trained on this island to live on the mainland.

Scope of Leisure

Max Kaplan summarizes the new view of leisure as (1) holistic in conception and function, (2) dynamic and developmental in its methods, and (3) futuristic and policy-oriented in its intent.[12] The variety of leisure-time activities in which it is possible for human beings to engage is infinite. A leisure interest is highly personal and freely chosen by the individual. Because a person's interests are limited by his experiences, it is the responsibility of public education to widen horizons through enriching the recreational environment.

Weiss[26] takes the position that one ought to engage, during leisure time, in activities that are good in themselves and good for what is good in itself. Among the goods he identifies health, knowledge, self-expression, character formation, personality, and self-adjustment. He extends this concept to describe the scope of leisure-time activities, including sports, intellectual activities, the arts, adventurous challenges, or contests with nature or another person, social activities, and communal activities including those based on shared religious beliefs and ideologies.

Particular extensions of the scope of leisure are identified by two selected articles from the Charter for Leisure.[2]

> Article 1: Every man has a right to leisure time. This comprises reasonable working hours, regular paid vacations, favourable travelling conditions and suitable social planning, including reasonable access to leisure facilities, areas and equipment in order to enhance the advantage of leisure time.

> Article 4: Every man has a right to participate in and be introduced to all types of recreation during leisure time, such as sports and games, open-air living, travel, theatre, dancing, pictorial art, music, science and handicrafts irrespective of age, sex, or level of education.

ROLE OF THE SCHOOL

For our future society, an education which prepares an individual for his work will be only half an education. The first function of our schools and colleges is to provide an education that makes a person; vocational or professional education is of secondary importance.[5] In fulfilling its responsibility to educate for leisure, the school should provide the following:

1. Encouragement and instruction leading to the development and maintenance of the organic systems of the body to a sufficient degree that the individual is *capable* of participation.

2. Introduction and basic instruction in a variety of activities with the potential for development of life-long leisure interests, including intellectual, social, artistic, physical, and service activities.

3. Opportunities and encouragement to develop skills which will prove satisfying and useful both during his time as a student and when he leaves school.

4. Stimulation of original thought and creative self-expression and guidance of creative energies toward individual self-fulfillment.

(Courtesy of the Department of Physical Education and Athletics for Men, Stanford University.)

5. Encouragement of the development of socially acceptable standards of conduct which make the student a desirable companion, competitor, and humanitarian.

6. Encouragement of desirable attitudes toward play, recreation, leisure, activity, rest, and relaxation.

7. Some appreciation and understanding of the role of leisure and of particular leisure-time activities in his own and other cultures, including the role of sports and outdoor recreation in the cultures of all peoples everywhere.

The responsibility of the school and its role in the total spectrum of education for leisure is well summarized by the following articles of the Charter for Leisure.[2]

> Article 6: Every man has a right to the opportunity for learning how to enjoy his leisure time in the most sensible fashion. In schools, classes, and courses of instruction, children, adolescents, and adults must be given the opportunity to develop the skills, attitudes, and understandings essential for leisure literacy.

Article 7: The responsibility for education for leisure is still divided among a large number of disciplines and institutions. In the interests of everyone and in order to utilize purposefully all the funds and assistance available in the various administrative levels this responsibility should be fully coordinated among all public and private bodies concerned with leisure. The goal should be for a community of leisure.

Appreciation of Leisure

Growing evidence supports the prediction that leisure activities will replace work as the central life-interest in future societies. Many feel today that the amount and quality of leisure constitute a better measure of wealth than possessions, and that the school's primary obligation is the development of skills, appreciations, and interests basic to the effective and satisfying use of leisure. Basic to this goal are the understanding and appreciation of leisure broadly defined.

It is essential that we revise our concepts of the relationships between work and play. Milton R. Stern tells us that "what is becoming obvious in the combination of growth of population and increased sophistication of machines is that we must focus on what we presently call leisure rather than on work as the major source of meaning in life."* John S. Diekhoff[5] recently observed:

> Most Americans, unfortunately, think work is good in itself, and we have guilty consciences when we are not working. Work for us is not only useful and necessary, but is in itself honorable whatever its object, and we think of the occupations of leisure as mere pastimes, self-indulgences. The occupations of leisure, however, include not only play, but also worship, the duties of a citizen, a neighbor, and a parent, enjoyment of the arts, and study.

The school should help young people to understand the vital role which leisure plays for people of all ages in all cultures, emphasizing its importance in individual self-fulfillment in their own society. During the school years, opportunities should be provided for worthwhile leisure activities in the school environment and encouragement to engage in other appropriate activities outside the school setting. Children and youth should also receive education basic to the development of leisure-time activities which will be suitable in later life.

---

* Milton R. Stern: "The Neanderthal Space Man," in *Proceedings of the Sixth Annual Seminar on Leadership in University Adult Education.* East Lansing: Michigan State University, 1963, p. 19.

A third appreciation which the school should promote begins with a recognition of the need for varied leisure interests. Each individual will find different activities satisfying. But, in addition, each individual should develop leisure interests of different types. If he is to live life fully, he needs interests which he can find satisfying alone, as well as some which he can share with others; he needs some in which he is physically active, as well as some which are relatively sedentary; he needs esthetic experiences and intellectual challenges, as well as the satisfactions of community service.

Outdoor Education

Human beings lose much when they are out of contact with nature. Some of the most meaningful recreation is experienced in contending against the elements, testing one's own physical, emotional, and spiritual resources in the natural environment. Countless human beings have gained insight and inspiration in viewing landscapes, studying the stars, listening to brooks or the calls of birds, and learning about different forms of plant and animal life. With 80 percent of our population living in cities, and significant numbers of people existing under ghetto conditions, many persons will have no opportunity for these experiences unless the school offers outdoor education and outdoor recreation programs.

Julian Smith,[24] Director of the AAHPER Outdoor Education Project, has defined outdoor education as follows:

> Outdoor education, as we see it, is a means of curriculum enrichment through experiences *in* and *for* the outdoors. It is not another discipline with prescribed objectives like science and mathematics; it is simply a learning climate which offers opportunities for direct laboratory experiences in identifying and resolving real-life problems, for acquiring skills with which to enjoy a lifetime of creative living, for attaining concepts and insights about human and natural resources, and for getting us back in touch with these aspects of living where our roots were once firmly established.

Donaldson and Donaldson[7] predict a promising future for outdoor education:

> After steady but unspectacular growth through the 1940s and 1950s, outdoor education experienced a surge of quantitative and

qualitative growth in the 1960s. Powerfully urged on by an increasing ecological awareness as well as by a variety of federal activities, it gained a whole new thrust. Especially, impetus was given by Titles I and III of the Elementary and Secondary Education Act of 1965. . . .

An important breakthrough of the 1960s was the beginning of outdoor education for inner-city children and youth. Title I of ESEA provided the new money which funded a dozen or more of these programs. In terms of the pupil personnel served, this move into urban centers where, in the view of many educators, outdoor education is most needed, is probably the most significant gain of the last decade.

. . . Indeed, variety may be said to be the watchword of outdoor education activities in the United States over the last 25 years. Every section of the country has become involved; no state is without some kind of program. It is this variety and geographical spread which bolster the promise of outdoor education in the 70s.

Intelligent use of the outdoors for better living requires certain skills, knowledges, attitudes, and appreciations. The schools must accept some of the responsibility for these learnings. Outdoor education laboratories are available in the immediate school site, parks, camps, farms, forests, gardens, and many other community resources. Among outdoor activities in which people can participate as they choose for the greatest part of their lives, some of the most popular are camping, fishing, boating, hunting, archery, skiing, and skating. Other skills worthy of consideration include hiking, bicycling, survival skills, use of a compass, mountain climbing, lapidary activities, woodsmanship, and many others. Outward Bound programs, which are just beginning to receive recognition in this country, have tremendous potential for education. Great expansion is taking place in all types of camping. Reynold E. Carlson predicts that ". . . by the year 2000 A.D. there will be more than 15 million children in summer camps in the United States and that schools will be providing an outdoor education experience for 3 or 4 million children during school time."*

Donaldson and Donaldson[7] make nine predictions concerning the expanding role and significance of outdoor learning:

1. Outdoor education experiences will become available to more people.
2. Outdoor education will employ a rich variety of environments.
3. Community involvement in outdoor education will increase markedly.

---

* Reynold E. Carlson: "Camping in the Year 2000." In Jay B. Nash: *Recreation: Pertinent Readings.* Dubuque, Iowa: Wm. C. Brown & Co., 1965, pp. 222–224.

4. Governments will increasingly come to cherish the contributions of outdoor education.
5. Staff development for outdoor education will be an important commitment of schools.
6. Outdoor education will seek a balance among cognitive, affective, and psychomotor learning.
7. Outdoor education will contribute to significant action and understanding of environmental problems.
8. Outdoor education research will focus on what educators need to know about the field.
9. Education of teachers for outdoor instruction will grow both quantitatively and qualitatively.

Environmental Education

The quality of leisure time experiences in the outdoors is inextricably bound to the environment in which we live.[20] Overcrowding and pollution menace our urban areas; pollution has disfigured our countryside. National parklands are insufficient to accommodate our people. Existing outdoor areas and facilities are deteriorating.

President Nixon, in his first Message on the Environment, in 1970, said, "No longer is it enough to conserve what we have; we must also restore what we have lost." The Council on Environmental Quality has been established to provide overview and advise the President on the whole spectrum of environmental matters from closing the energy gap to bringing parks to people. All federal agencies are stepping up activities to restore or preserve the quality of the environment.[20]

Environmental education is clearly a school priority. Environmental education is interdisciplinary and should involve the entire school.[10] Awareness stimulated through school programs should bring students into action in community and school projects; student involvement can spur the total community to determined action.

The relationships between environmental education and outdoor education are sometimes controversial. Outdoor education has been a part of the educational scene for a quarter century and it is entirely possible that a share of the nation's ecological awareness is traceable to the influence of these early outdoor education ventures.[7] It is important that professionals in both these fields work toward cooperation and accommodation in the 70s. As environmental educators work toward developing the knowledges, attitudes, and skills needed to solve environmental problems, environmental learnings in the affective domain should continue to be a major contribution of outdoor education.[7]

Creative Expression

In today's world there is a crucial need for self-expression and for creative experience. Jay B. Nash[22] viewed creative participation as the best of all possible uses of leisure time. In his final contribution to the professional literature, he offered the following definition of recreation:

> As work becomes mechanized and routinized and ceases to be an outlet for creativity, recreation is those activities which form an outlet to creativity, both in a physical and a spiritual sense.*

Too often the school environment has discouraged the development of creative expression, rather than nourishing the creativity which is inherent in each human individual. The creative instinct is fostered in childhood education, but, quite illogically, many have not considered this equally important in secondary school education. The Commission on Goals for American Recreation[9] has chosen to highlight creative expression as one of Democracy's top priorities.

> There must be a way to discover and teach activities that are constructive, have creative possibilities, and carry continuing challenge. Education for leisure must be concerned with creative environments that can have diverse meanings to different personalities, environments only partly interpreted and prepared. In stimulating settings, the goal is to help people to find themselves.**

Esthetic Appreciation

Few individuals have great talents in many media. But life is enriched through the personal interpretation of the creative artist.

---

* P. 8.
** P. 36.

(From Price, La Ferne E.: The Wonder of Motion: A Sense of Life for Woman. Grand Forks, North Dakota: University of North Dakota Press, 1972.)

Thus it is desirable that education for leisure help the individual to discover and develop his own creative talents, and, in addition, provide opportunities for increasing his appreciation of the creative expression of others. Listening to a great concert, viewing a fine painting, seeing a good drama, or witnessing a superior athletic performance may provide a degree of emotional participation and life enrichment for the appreciative person.

Much emphasis has been placed on creative participation in educating for leisure. Direct personal participation is a goal to be sought in art, music, drama, outdoor recreation, crafts, dance, and sports. But there is also value for individual self-realization in esthetic appreciation, provided the "participant" is a knowledgeable and truly appreciative observer. This too requires education, and is encompassed in the school's total responsibility.

Spectator sports are currently being placed in their proper perspective by the more thoughtful members of the physical education profession. Teachers are ever-conscious of their role in encouraging and stimulating wider participation in pleasurable physical activities.[13]

CONTRIBUTIONS OF PHYSICAL EDUCATION

If we believe that such considerations as have been set forth justify efforts to cultivate interest in physical education activities for leisure time, we ought to consider carefully how the school program may best contribute to this purpose. What leisure-time activities should physical education undertake to teach? What factors determine sequence of leisure-time activities in the physical education curriculum? How may we most effectively educate for leisure?

Selection of Activities

It is a mistake to assume that leisure-time activities are to be used only by the individual when he becomes an adult. Children of all ages have their leisure time, and it is important that they be engaged

in worthy activities. This fact makes it necessary from the very beginning of the child's physical education that we teach activities which
have an intrinsic value for the child at the particular stage of his
development, so that these activities will carry over into his immediate
life as leisure-time activities.

It is sometimes assumed by physical educators that the function
of the program in the elementary and intermediate school is to cause
the student to exercise, so as to realize the developmental effect of
muscular activity. This is a primary function, but it is a serious mistake to overlook certain principles. To be satisfactory, the program
of activities in physical education for young children should be of
such a type that the children will be inclined to engage in these
activities in out-of-school hours. There is no question that the normal
child will be engaged in some form of physical activity during those
periods when he is out of the control of the school, and one of the
best contributions the school can make to acceptable child life is that
of creating a carry-over interest in worthy and enjoyable activities.

No artificial scheme of exercise or even of games will serve this
important purpose. The activities taught must be selected, not only
with their developmental values in mind but also with careful consideration of the interests of the child at the moment. At the same
time, a different consideration must also receive due attention: the
child's changing interest in activities necessitates anticipation of later
needs and preparation to meet these needs. For instance, the child
may be interested for the time being in tag games and activities on a
similar level, and therefore we teach him skills in such activities with
some assurance that he will utilize them in out-of-school hours; but at
the same time we are aware that in two or three years his interest in
these activities will wane and will turn strongly to team games of high
organization. With this fact in mind, the intelligent teacher paves the
way for future successful and satisfying participation by introducing
instruction in the skills which will be needed later in these games.

In the selection of activities for secondary school and college
physical education curricula, it is important to plan for a wide variety
of activities in order to develop at least basic skills in many activities
from which the individual might reasonably select particular sports
or physical recreation activities which he chooses to pursue as life-
long interests. Organization of the program to permit some election
of activities, particularly at the senior high school and college levels,
will also further this goal. Program development should also ensure

inclusion of activities which have particular potential for creative self-expression, such as dance, aquatics, and gymnastics. The physical education program should include a full complement of activities which lend themselves to outdoor recreation. Every local school district should take full advantage of regional climate and terrain and unique local facilities for imaginative programs in outdoor physical education.

Sequence

In a certain sense, leisure-time activities should be taught throughout the child's school life, although in the early elementary school program the level is child's play and not adult's. From the point of view of future adult activities, we are concerned only with the child's learning to play, with his deriving great satisfaction from play, and with his development of as great a degree as possible of skill in fundamental bodily movements, such as are involved in running, climbing, balancing, jumping, and rhythmic movements.

In the intermediate grades, the concern, from the point of view of adult activities, is further development of play interest, of fundamental skills, including swimming, and in a measure of progress in the higher forms of skill which involve the use of such implements as balls, bats, rackets, and clubs, which will be used in adult activities. The play is still child's play and not yet adult's.

In the middle school, we begin to devote attention to direct adult carry-over activities. We do not make this a major objective, but if our program is satisfactory, it provides that every student be introduced at this period to certain activities, such as tennis, swimming, volleyball, golf, and other adult interests. Increasing attention should be devoted to this consideration in the secondary school. The carry-over element would probably be evaluated as one of the most important objectives of the college program.

The school and college programs of physical education have often failed to achieve carry-over of activities into adult life, because they have emphasized activities which are not compatible with adult interest, or because they have allowed the student to devote himself almost exclusively to forms of sports and athletics which are not appropriate for adults in ordinary life. The high school and college programs have sometimes not only allowed but encouraged male students to devote their time and attention exclusively to football, track and field athletics, basketball, baseball, wrestling, and similar activities. No student of physical education denies the social and developmental values of such sports and athletics. In view of the character of modern life in America, however, it is difficult to see how schools and colleges can avoid the responsibility to give to every student a reasonable measure of experience and instruction in suitable adult leisure-time activities, such as golf, swimming, tennis, and handball.

Organization of Learning Opportunities

If the school is to interest the student in activities which it is hoped he will find interesting and valuable as an adult, it must give consideration to the idea of a favorable introduction to them. Individuals tend to pursue types of activity in which they feel a genuine interest, and from which they derive satisfaction or pleasure. Every effort to promote the carry-over forms of activity from school life into adult life must be consistent with this psychological principle.

An attempt should also be made to introduce students to a number of such activities, for individual differences make it impossible to predict just what activities will ultimately make the greatest appeal in any given case. The student must be encouraged to acquire *skill* in the activities. Failure to acquire skill will very frequently consign the individual to the "dub" class, and in spite of arguments to the effect that the dub frequently derives more satisfaction from a sport than the expert, the fact remains that great numbers of persons abandon all such interests for no other reason than the discouragement attendant upon lack of progress or skill.

If physical education is to provide education for worthy use of leisure, it is imperative that democratic human relations provide the guidelines for the conduct of classes and cocurricular activities. Physical educators must ask themselves if students are truly treated as persons. Does the social interaction provide psychological support and pleasure for the members of the class? Do practice and contest procedures respect the dignity of individual team members and strengthen their commitment of individual responsibility to each other?

To make our potential contribution toward education for individual self-realization, teachers must reexamine physical education curricula, to determine whether activities are designed to permit and encourage a maximum of creative expression by the participant. Do we stimulate students to express themselves creatively? Do we allow as much flexibility as possible in student responses to learning opportunities offered? Or do we only give lip service to our concern for personal fulfillment?

To what extent can physical education contribute to esthetic appreciation? Opinions vary, but many persons in the profession believe that one of the purposes of physical education is to learn to recognize the art and artistry of human movement. It is generally agreed that sports appreciation is a desirable and realistic goal.

A good program should provide opportunity for students to observe top quality performance and to come in contact with the best in sports literature. It should lead to increased participation, more knowledgeable spectators, more appreciative readers, and better conversationalists in the field of sports. Such programs in sports appreciation should result in greater enjoyment and more complete living for many.

SPORTS—A CULTURAL HERITAGE

The exercise of physical skill, mental acumen, and spiritual courage in the field of sports and games is as old and as integral a part of the cultures of mankind as the expression of these same human capacities in the fields of music and art. The rich and colorful heritage in this area of human experience is as much a part of the birthright of the students in the schools as the songs that have been sung and the pictures that have been painted.[3]

In its efforts to educate for leisure time, the school should attempt to give the student a clear perception of the modern world and the relationship of work and play in that world; to make him aware of the scope, range, and variety of skills available to those who will make the effort to acquire them; to learn to protect his free time with courage and firmness against triviality and commercial exploitation; and to realize that it is essential to develop freely chosen, spontaneously enjoyed skills that will bring happiness and enrichment to his life.

(Courtesy of the Los Angeles City Board of Education.)

"Withal, the quality of life in America is on a steady rise toward higher and higher goals, which in a leisure society is reflected in the recreation of the people. Our country achieves greatness as it pleases the eye, nurtures the intellect, inspires the soul, and banishes the commonplace in the recreation of its people."[9]*

Selected References

1. Brightbill, Charles K. *Man and Leisure: Philosophy of Recreation.* Englewood Cliffs, N.J.: Prentice-Hall, Inc., 1961.
2. "Charter for Leisure." *J. Health-Phys. Educ.-Rec.,* 43:48-49, 56 (March, 1972).
3. Cozens, Frederick W., and Stumpf, Florence S. *Sports in American Life.* Chicago: University of Chicago Press, 1953.
4. deGrazia, Sebastian. *Of Time, Work, and Leisure.* New York: Twentieth Century Fund, 1962.
5. Diekhoff, John. "Adam, Automation, and the American College." *Quest,* V:59-66 (December, 1965).
6. *Directory of Environmental Information Sources, 1972.* Cahners Books, 89 Franklin Street, Boston, Massachusetts.
7. Donaldson, George W., and Donaldson, Alan D. "Outdoor Education: Its Promising Future." *J. Health-Phys. Educ.-Rec.,* 43:23-28 (April, 1972).
8. *Environmental Quality Magazine.* Environmental Awareness Associates, Inc., 6464 Canoga Avenue, Woodland Hills, California.
9. *Goals for American Recreation.* Washington, D.C.: American Association for Health, Physical Education and Recreation, 1966.
10. Goldstein, Judith. "Environmental Education for Teachers." *J. Health-Phys. Educ.-Rec.,* 44:38-40 (January, 1973).
11. *Journal of Environmental Education.* Dunbar Educational Research Services, Inc., Box 1605, Madison, Wisconsin.
12. Kaplan, Max. "New Concepts of Leisure Today." *J. Health-Phys. Educ.-Rec.,* 43:43-46 (March, 1972).
13. *Leisure and the Schools.* Washington, D.C.: American Association for Health, Physical Education and Recreation, 1961.
14. "The Leisure Enigma." *Quest,* V:1-74 (December, 1965).
15. "Leisure Today: Introduction." *J. Health-Phys. Educ.-Rec.,* 43:33-56 (March, 1972).
16. "Leisure Today: Leisure and the Environment." *J. Health-Phys. Educ.-Rec.,* 44:35-68 (January, 1973).
17. "Leisure Today: Major Aspects of Organized Recreation Service." *J. Health-Phys. Educ.-Rec.,* 44:24-40 (June, 1973).
18. "Leisure Today: Research and Thought about Children's Play." *J. Health-Phys. Educ.-Rec.,* 43:25-53 (June, 1972).
19. Martin, Alexander Reid. "Man's Leisure and His Health." *Quest,* V:26-36 (December, 1965).
20. Morton, Rogers C. B. "Leisure and the Environment." *J. Health-Phys. Educ.-Rec.,* 44:36-37 (January, 1973).
21. Nanus, Burt, and Adelman, Harvey. "Forecast for Leisure." *J. Health-Phys. Educ.-Rec.,* 44:61 (January, 1973).
22. Nash, Jay B. *Recreation: Pertinent Readings.* Dubuque, Iowa: William C. Brown and Co., 1964.

* P. 46.

23. *Planning Areas and Facilities for Health, Physical Education, and Recreation.* Chicago: The Athletic Institute, rev. ed., 1965.
24. Smith, Julian. "Outdoor Education—A National Venture." *Recreation,* LIV:26-28 (October, 1961).
25. Smith, Julian W., Carlson, Reynold E., Donaldson, George W., and Masters, Hugh B. *Outdoor Education.* Englewood Cliffs, N.J.: Prentice-Hall, Inc., 1963.
26. Weiss, Paul. "A Philosophical Definition of Leisure." *Quest,* V:1-7 (December, 1965).
27. Wilson, George T. "The New Leisure Ethic." *J. Health-Phys. Educ.-Rec.,* 44:64 (January, 1973).

(Courtesy of the Glenbrook North High School, Northbrook, Illinois.)

Chapter Twelve

EVALUATION AND RESEARCH

EVALUATION IN PHYSICAL EDUCATION

The term "evaluation" refers to one of the central components of the educational enterprise. Although many definitions have been ascribed to this word over the years, there is general agreement that it means the totality of the processes deliberately employed to assess the extent to which objectives have been attained in the areas of pupil behavioral changes, curriculum efficiency, and teacher effectiveness. Informally, evaluation probably is occurring most of the time, particularly in the teacher's mind, even though she may not necessarily be following a formal plan in collecting her observations and judgments. Formal stages of overtly planned evaluation programs take place at scheduled intervals such as the administration of a physical fitness test, taking the height and weight measurements of each pupil, and making out the final course grade for each student. Teachers informally observe their pupils in action every day and gain impressions about their behaviors, their physical skills, and their attitudes toward the program, toward other pupils, and toward the teacher. Of course students also are making a large number of similar covert evaluations throughout the course of time spent in the physical education class.

"Measurement" refers to that phase of evaluation which is concrete, identifiable, quantifiable, and capable of accurate assessment through the use of valid, reliable measuring instruments with the results being recorded in our numerical system. Thus, physical educa-

355

tion teachers can measure the time a student takes to swim fifty yards with the crawl stroke, how far he can put the 8 pound shot, and the score he can attain in a Columbia round of archery competition.

There are other areas of pupil progress toward objectives which are not yet measurable by such objective tests. In these areas, the teacher must render a subjective judgment, which should be based on many observations of samples of pupil behavior in the area of concern. Subjective judgment is required to assess sportsmanship, leadership, cooperation, and similar behaviors. Tests are available to assess student interests, attitudes, personality, sociometric relationships, values, and similar components of human behavior. These tests to date have achieved varying degrees of validity and reliability. In general, they cannot be regarded as having high validity and objectivity, so they must be used and interpreted with caution. However, they may provide valuable insights and "leads" for the perceptive teacher to attain a greater understanding of the members of his classes. Modern measurement and evaluation books in physical education describe these tests and cite the degree of validity, reliability, and objectivity of each.[2,7,20,33] The teacher who desires to do a thorough task of test selection, administration, and interpretation should study this evaluation literature as a valuable guide to one of teaching's most fundamental functions. Most physical education major programs now require a course in measurement and evaluation in physical education. In order to make intelligent selection of and use of tests, teachers must have a basic knowledge of statistics. The typical measurement and evaluation course in physical education starts with an introductory section on statistics most commonly used by teachers. The teacher who has not had such a course should enroll in one as soon as possible, for it is inconceivable that he can be an effective teacher if he lacks the knowledge to select, administer, interpret, and evaluate tests and test results, and to develop a valid grading plan.

Another reason for a thorough knowledge of measurement and evaluation is that the physical educator must have the competence to construct his own tests. This admonition applies particularly to the preparation of knowledge tests. It is virtually impossible to use a state or national standard knowledge test at the end of a teaching unit, because each teacher has taught the course in his own unique way, and has planned the content and instructional methodology without reference to how the test maker would have performed these tasks. Obviously, these tests should accurately cover the knowledge taught in the unit. There is a trend across the country for teachers to build and administer their own objective knowledge tests at the end of instructional units. It is possible to construct a departmental test of knowledge if two or more teachers work together on its preparation, and if they come to close agreement in planning and teaching the unit to several classes of pupils.

It is also recommended that the physical educator take at least one course in basic computer science. There are many ways in which the capabilities of the computer can be employed to expedite the work of the teacher in test scoring, analysis of data, reporting, and performing research. School districts are using computers in a variety of helpful ways.

Formative and Summative Evaluation

In recent years Benjamin S. Bloom[3] and others have popularized a distinction between two types of evaluation, namely, formative and summative. *Summative evaluation* is the traditional type which has existed in education for many years. It is based on the theory of the curve of normal distribution of test scores involving a large number of pupils taking the test. Typically, the well-known letter grades, A, B, C, D, and F, are assigned to students based on their relative placement on the test in relation to the normal distribution of test scores of similar students who have taken the same test in the past. Thus, this type of evaluation is *norm* referenced. Each student is competing for a score, and a grade, in competition with the scores made by others taking the test, or who have previously taken the test. Typically, this type of evaluation is made at the end of an instructional unit or at the termination of a course. Occasionally it is used at mid-term or with periodic quizzes over material covered in a class at certain time intervals. In each case the individual's score is compared with the table of norms composed of all of the scores of the students included in the norming group.

It is apparent that such information about pupil performance, and progress, frequently becomes available too late to be useful in helping the pupil to adjust his study habits or to diagnose his specific learning problems so that he can make a satisfactory adjustment while the course is still in progress. Summative evaluation is utilized to determine final course grades and pupil numerical ranking in a class or school, as a minimum prerequisite point for admission into a course of higher level of difficulty; to assess skills and abilities of specific types required for satisfactory performance in a specific occupational role; to provide information to the student as to the comparative level of his performance so that he may assess his status and have specific information upon which to predicate a plan and build a motivation for further development and success; and, finally, to compare the progress of two or more groups of students who have been exposed to differing pedagogical treatments or curricular arrangements.

Formative evaluation is a more recent concept which emphasizes the guidance function of test scores and other evaluative techniques concerning student performance and learning. This type of evaluation is *criterion-referenced*. Specific behavioral descriptions of desirable student behaviors are spelled out. These behavioral, or performance, objectives become the criteria which the pupils strive to "master." The concept of "mastery learning" is basic to the understanding of formative evaluation. The interested student should study the publications of Bloom,* Mayo** and others in detail for a fuller understanding of the nature of mastery learning.

Assessment of pupil progress can be made at any time during the instructional sequence—from the first day when "entering behavior" may be determined to as many times as the teacher deems useful throughout the course. The pupil's test result is compared with the *criterion* measure which was previously stated. When he has achieved the criterion at the specified level he has mastered that objective and is ready to move to the next higher level of behavioral objective. Hence, formative evaluation is *criterion-referenced*. Each student's performance at any given time is compared only with his past achievement so that the degree of progress since the previous test administration becomes evident. The student is not compared competitively with the other students in his class or in the norm group as in the case of summative evaluation. The pupil is given prompt feedback about his performance with respect to specific learning objectives.

---

* Benjamin S. Bloom, J. Thomas Hastings, and George F. Madaus. *Handbook on Formative and Summative Evaluation of Student Learning*, Chapter 3, "Learning for Mastery." New York: McGraw-Hill Book Company, 1971, pp. 43-57.
** S. T. Mayo. "Mastery Learning and Mastery Testing," *Measurement in Education*, I, No. 3:1-4 (1970).

Thus, he and the teacher will be accurately informed as to his present level of performance, the difficulties he is facing, and the successes he is achieving. Based on this information the pupil's study program can be adjusted and revised each time any formative evaluation is made so that his progress can be maximized. This concept promotes the individualization of both learning and instruction. It is also evident that when the threat and fear of being graded competitively and comparatively in relation to the other students, as in the summative evaluation model, is removed, an important psychological benefit accrues for the students, particularly those who typically score at the lower end of summative test norms. Each pupil can receive the advantages of diagnosis and of subsequent prescription of learning opportunities which will optimize his possibilities for achieving mastery of the behavioral objectives which have been set for him. Of course the objectives themselves can be modified in light of the evidence provided by the formative evaluation. The emphasis in formative evaluation is shifted from a final assessment of a student's capabilities to that of information to be used through guidance procedures to promote optimal learning conditions.

Bloom says that the main purpose of formative evaluation is to indicate the extent to which mastery learning has occurred and to enable the teacher and the pupil to know precisely where the pupil is not mastering the task. Also, data provided by formative evaluation to teachers facilitate revisions in teaching procedures and strategies, both group and individual, and reveal deficiencies. The teacher can use the results of formative evaluations from previous years in comparison with the present to determine areas wherein she can improve her own instructional competence. She can find clues as to ways to improve the amount of learning and the rapidity with which the pupils achieve the performance objectives. Bloom calls this purpose the "quality control" of instruction. Frequent formative evaluation throughout the course provides an opportunity to assess many more of the major units in the instructional sequence than does periodic summative evaluation which, at best, usually only samples a small proportion of those units offered throughout the course.

Finally, there is some evidence to indicate that formative evaluation data may be correlated positively with summative test scores. If so, final, summative test results can be predicted with some accuracy from on-going formative evaluation data. If the prediction at a given time in mid-course is that the end of course test results will be inferior the teacher is forewarned and can attempt to take appropriate remedial steps to improve the instruction in the desired directions.

Lack of space prevents other than the mere introduction of the important concepts about formative and summative evaluation. The discussion about marking in physical education, at the end of this chapter, will allude to these concepts again.

Physical education evaluation literature contains scant information and examples about formative evaluation. Undoubtedly many teachers and coaches are utilizing it and developing new methods and tests along these lines but it is too early for these efforts to appear in the professional literature. Margaret J. Safrit* is one of the first physical educators to make this attempt. Her book, *Evaluation in Physical Education,* discusses the concepts of summative and formative evaluation in the context of physical education instructional programs and provides concrete illustrations of how to teach and evaluate through the proper applications of these concepts and principles. All teachers and coaches interested in improving their evaluation techniques are referred to this excellent source.

What we have said in the preceding paragraphs gives some indication of the ramifications of the term *evaluation.* In summary, the total combination of all of the possible types of measurements, the observational data and inferences drawn from them, and the educational implications and conclusions which can be drawn therefrom, represent the highly complex art of evaluation.

As evaluative data are generated, teachers direct their thoughts to the program objectives. These objectives are revised, reformulated, and readjusted to the realities and needs revealed by the evaluation. So, it is a continuous process, circular in nature, in which teachers, department staffs, and school faculties engage to formulate objectives, to conduct programs designed to assist pupils to accomplish those objectives, to evaluate the degree and extent of pupil achievement with respect to the stated objectives, and in turn, to review, restate, and revise the original objectives. The cycle is never-ending. The program can be assured of steady improvement if this philosophy of evaluation is accepted wholeheartedly by the teachers in concept and in action.

Bovard and Cozens, pioneer leaders in physical education evalu-

---

* Margaret J. Safrit, *Evaluation in Physical Education.* Englewood Cliffs, New Jersey: Prentice-Hall, Inc., 1973.

ation, provided an apt, concise summary of the processes described above.

> The process of evaluation involves three steps. The *first step* is to define and appraise objectives. Evaluation presupposes an understanding of the specific goals or objectives of a given educational experience, a basic principle of evaluation being: *evaluation is done in terms of the objectives sought.* It further presupposes worth of the objectives. Merely to have objectives is not enough; the worth of the objectives must first be assured. The *second step* is to collect data. The process of evaluation utilizes all procedures, both quantitative and qualitative, which may be used to collect data necessary to appraise the extent to which the educational objectives have been achieved. The *third step* is to judge the educational significance, in light of the objectives sought, of the information and data collected.*

Purposes

Evaluation serves five major purposes: diagnosis and guidance, motivation, classification of pupils, appraisal of knowledge, and efficiency of instruction. In addition, tests in themselves can provide one form of practice in the skills being taught. Finally, data generated from tests can be employed in research designs which are developed to provide new knowledge or to seek new solutions to current physical education problems.

Diagnosis and Guidance. The starting point in physical education evaluation is to determine what are the specific needs of each pupil. What can we do in our program to minister to these physical education needs?

One of the greatest challenges facing the physical education teacher today is how to *individualize* the program so as to assist each pupil in making optimal progress toward the important objectives of this field. Typically, physical education teachers instruct five periods per day and have pupil contacts numbering between 200 and 250 students per day. By its very nature, physical education has the most complex logistical problem of any subject in the curriculum. Large numbers of students must be instructed every period of the day, in

---

* John F. Bovard, Frederick W. Cozens, and E. Patricia Hagman: *Tests and Measurements in Physical Education.* Philadelphia: W. B. Saunders Company, 3rd ed., 1949, pp. 4–5.

many kinds of facilities, employing diverse types of equipment and supplies. It is little wonder, under these conditions, that the need to individualize the program for each pupil stands out as a current major problem and challenge.

Encouraging progress is being made to solve this dilemma through such innovations as modular scheduling, the open laboratory concept, the phased or sequential curriculum, which relates to each pupil's ability to improve along a predetermined learning continuum, more imaginative methods of grouping pupils in direct relationship to the instructional objectives of the day, and more thoughtful procedures for assessing and recording pupil behavioral changes.

From the above statement, one can readily envision the significance of evaluation as one of the keys to the achievement of all of these new directions. And the starting point, to repeat for emphasis, is an accurate assessment of the present status and the individual needs of each pupil called the "entry behavior." Based on this accurate individual assessment, the physical education staff then is in position to provide maximal guidance to each pupil in his physical education experience.

Motivation.   While many of these tests mentioned in other categories can be and are used for the purposes of motivation, physical education literature describes several tests designed primarily to inform students of their individual standing in relation to a group, and to offer scoring scales by which students can keep accurate account of their improvement and can make performance comparisons in various activities. Students are not always conscious of their weaknesses in particular phases of an activity, and objective scales offer a means of encouraging effort and practice. Motivation may thus go on indefinitely.

One of the most promising trends in recent years in some schools is the intensive use of a cumulative Pupil Physical Education Profile Record. Under this concept, the pupil has a major role in testing himself and his peers in the basic elements of the activities which will comprise his semester's or year's program of physical education. He is then responsible for noting his status at the time of testing on his own Profile Record form. The form is designed not only to display his own performances. Each test is also scored in percentiles based on test scores of hundreds of similar pupils in his school or district. Of course state or national percentile norms can be included on the form. Thus, at all times the pupil knows exactly how he stands in relation to his peers and to the norm tables. An important aspect is that his confidence is respected. He does not have to display his results to others if he does not want to, thus avoiding the embarrassment which was present under the old system of posting the test results of all members of a class for everyone to see.

The Profile Record for each pupil is available at the time and place of his physical education class meeting on evaluation days. Each student has the personal responsibility for maintaining his file. Teachers counsel students individually about their status and their progress and offer suggestions as to how the pupil can work to improve himself. The Omaha Public Schools program of individualized instruction in physical education is a particularly noteworthy example of intensive student evaluation of self and of peers.

Schools which have adopted similar plans uniformly report an increased interest in physical education and a high degree of enthusiasm and morale among the students. Discipline problems decline or disappear and learning results seem to be produced more rapidly. Empirical experience and observation attest to the motivational purposes of evaluation not only with respect to the Profile Record plan but in other ways indicated in this section.

Classification. Classification, as a function of evaluation, is the arrangement of pupils into groups according to appropriate criteria which in turn relate to specific educational purposes.

If one is to examine the classification methods used in several schools in his area, it is likely that he will discover a wide variety of plans in use. One of the authors has made a detailed study of various pupil grouping plans in physical education in junior and senior high schools, and so far he has identified at least 18 different methods. These results would seem to indicate that there is little agreement within the profession as to the "best" grouping procedures.

The following classification plans seem to be most prominent: by grade in school, by age-height-weight scale, by physical fitness or physical performance test, by specific sports skills tests or teacher subjective judgment of sports skills, and by student interest. There are variations of these plans, and there are other systems not in general use. Also, there are embellishments involving elaborate point systems for a variety of positive and negative behaviors which can be observed or measured in the class time, usually with respect to physical fitness.

Schools which have adopted programs based on the principles

of individualized instruction have broken tradition with the long standing concept of moving groups of students through an instructional block, or a semester, of physical education as members of an intact "squad." Despite our knowledge that individuals enter such squads with varying achievement records, and that each pupil learns at his own distinctive rate, we have too long permitted the squad tradition to hamper efficient learning opportunities. Individualized physical education programs are based on the premise that each student should learn at his own rate and in a variety of ways most appropriate for him. Each pupil is frequently evaluated concerning his progress in relation to individual learning goals which he helps formulate. Formative evaluation is preeminent in this system. In fact, one could say that pupils really are no longer "grouped" in the old sense of the term. It behooves each physical educator to give careful thought to the implicit as well as the explicit assumptions which underlie his grouping practices.[9]

In concluding this section, the authors assert their professional judgment that on occasion when grouping is appropriate it is best accomplished by a consideration of both *pupil interest and pupil ability* in physical education. We believe there should be several curricula, for various groupings of boys and girls, based primarily on interest and ability factors, and that it is the responsibility and challenge of each teacher to capitalize on the unique interests, abilities, and personality of each pupil to assist him to make maximal progress toward the goals he holds with respect to his physical education experiences.

Appraisal of Knowledge. As was noted earlier, this phase of evaluation has expanded rapidly in physical education programs at all educational levels throughout the country. The American Association for Health, Physical Education, and Recreation recently has contributed to this endeavor with its excellent project to develop physical education knowledge and understanding tests. The resources of the Research Council of the Association are being employed in this massive study, which will upgrade physical education knowledge testing throughout the nation. In addition, another recent AAHPER project has resulted in the publication and dissemination of an instructional manual entitled *Knowledge and Understanding in Physical Education* which contains facts and understandings about physical education that students can be expected to learn through participation in physical activity. Three examinations on this material are available for upper elementary grades, junior high school, and senior high school, with two forms available for each test. The Educational Testing Service of Princeton, New Jersey, is the source and publisher.

Teachers must master the techniques and the statistical assumptions of knowledge test construction, because a majority of the tests they use will be constructed by themselves or by local committees. Knowledge tests may cover an individual activity, and contain questions about terminology, history, leaders, equipment, scoring, rules, strategy, etiquette, court dimensions, mechanical skill principles, and similar relevant factors. Knowledge tests may also concern basic knowledge related to physiological phenomena associated with training and conditioning, or to psychological principles governing learning, motivation, and personality development. Likewise, kinesiological principles of movement are suitable topics for knowledge tests. There is a considerable trend throughout the country to test for these kinds of knowledges in consonance with the new philosophy of emphasizing the teaching of the "why" of physical education as well as the "how." With the development of the concept curriculum approach in physical education, as explained in an earlier chapter, we may safely forecast increased importance for knowledge type testing in physical education in the future.

Efficiency of Instruction. In the school system of a large city, it is often desirable for the administration to make a careful check on the efficiency of the instruction in the various schools of the district. Evaluation is a valuable aid in such a survey, but it must be used with caution. If tests are used as a basis for the determination of pupil progress, thus reflecting the efficiency of instruction as a comparative measure, good judgment must be exercised in equalizing all outside factors which may have a bearing on the situation. These factors may include the experience of the teachers concerned, the experience and ability of the pupils, the type of community and heritage of the pupils, working conditions in the physical education facility, and the work given the pupils from the standpoint of the content of the course of study.

Test results provide the teacher with valuable information about his own strengths and weaknesses. They also indicate areas in the instructional unit where more emphasis should have been placed and spots where less attention is required. Likewise, the teacher can determine the range of performance by the pupils in his class, and with this knowledge he can better prepare his instructional strategies to meet the individual needs thus revealed. It is believed that most experienced teachers will admit that they learn as much about themselves as they do about their pupils as they review the results of tests they administer.

TEACHER ACCOUNTABILITY

As a result of widespread increasing dissatisfaction with the performance of public school systems in this country in recent years several state legislatures have passed laws requiring that schools become strictly "accountable" for their educational endeavors. This model of "accountability" has been adapted from industry by business and professional men and women who compose local school boards and state legislatures. There is a voluminous literature[12,25] available which explains the various "systems" which have been imposed on educators under the accountability rubric. The central point here is that *teacher effectiveness* is the focus of concern by the critics of public education. Most of the state laws recently enacted on this subject require that the effectiveness of each teacher be evaluated by assessing the changes (improvement, hopefully) in learning in her classroom on the part of the students under her direction over the course of a semester or a school year. The process starts with teachers preparing behavioral objectives which can serve as criteria of pupil learning. At the beginning of the school year the teacher and principal confer and "negotiate" until agreement has been reached upon the suitability of the proposed performance objectives for each of the teacher's classes. The pupils are then given a pre-test. At some designated point in time prior to the end of the semester or year the pupils are administered a post-test. The differences in pupil scores indicate the degree of effectiveness the teacher demonstrated in the intervening time period.

There are many important assumptions underlying this model of teacher evaluation and a myriad of details about its organization and implementation which all teachers should study. Obviously, this process is highly controversial and vigorous debate is going on across the country in many circles about it. We can only say that it behooves all teachers to educate themselves to a high degree of sophistication about the latest techniques, statistical analyses, principles of test construction, and other aspects of evaluation which apply to their subject matter field and to the teaching and learning responsibilities they carry.

MARKING IN PHYSICAL EDUCATION

Evaluation in physical education is quite closely identified with the entire problem of credit, marking, and promotion. The legitimacy and value of assigning grades in any school subject may be a debatable point, but at present it is a function of the school, and, as such, must be properly accomplished.

In most schools and colleges, credit toward graduation is given for the successful completion of courses in physical education. Because some form of evaluation of the student's progress in every school activity is made, it appears not only administratively desirable, but necessary, for teachers of physical education to give careful consideration to the manner in which their evaluation is made.

Though many proposals have been advanced concerning the problem of marking in physical education, no national standardized procedure has ever been adopted. The probability is that teachers of physical education will continue to use their own plans, just as teachers do in other fields. There need be no quarrel with any plan which is based on sound philosophy and in which a conscientious effort is made to evaluate subjectively and objectively the attainment of objectives set up for the course in question.

If we were to consider the acquisition of skills in selected movement activities as the sole objective of the program, it would not be difficult to evaluate the student's attainment and to mark him accordingly. But if we adhere consistently to our belief that the possession of desirable habits and attitudes, the acquisition of certain types of information, and the development of organic power and vigor are also important considerations, then we are forced to take these considerations into account in marking the student. When viewed in this light, the marking problem appears to be particularly difficult, especially because of the lack of valid measuring devices.

In some schools, the position is taken that the physical education

mark should be based entirely upon the degree of skill displayed by the student in the activities making up the instructional program, and that the factors of habit, attitude, physical vigor, and others should be taken into account in assigning to the student a general mark in "citizenship." Those who take this position are motivated by the fact that more progress has been made in the measurement of skills than in the measurement of social and psychological qualities, and that the mark is bound to be largely a matter of subjective judgment.

Grading, like grouping, is a highly controversial subject among physical educators. There is little uniformity or agreement in practice. The system any teacher uses ultimately depends upon his philosophy of education, the way in which he perceives each student in his class, and his own personal value system. Some schools or colleges will put "pressure" on individual teachers to persuade them to join in a common grading system, even though a teacher might not agree with certain underlying assumptions. Other institutions will give the teacher great freedom to derive his own grading system. Generally,

368

some over-all faculty consensus is desirable about the purposes of grading in a school and the spread of grades to be awarded, without restricting the teacher to a formula which must be followed.

It is pertinent to state our own beliefs and assumptions which underlie our grading philosophy.

First, we must have complete faith in the integrity and individuality of each and every pupil, whatever his strengths and weaknesses. We must work with each child where he is today, and build on that base to make optimal educational growth through physical education experiences toward worthwhile objectives and pupil goals. Grades should be viewed as positive educational tools to facilitate growth, development, and desirable educational behavioral changes. In too many cases in physical education, grades are used to attain teacher purposes, such as to control discipline and even to punish errant pupil behavior. Likewise, they are used too often as an external motivating force to encourage hoped for learning. There is considerable evidence to indicate that grades in schools are not a strong motivational influence to stimulate learning. Threatening a student with a low grade for failure to comply with certain teacher expectations may not be very effective. In some cases it may even be detrimental. It is a negative reinforcer of dubious value.

The main question each teacher should be concerned about for each student can be stated as follows: "Is Johnny actually learning at the optimal rate of which he is capable?" This perception of grades is much more crucial than using them to compare Johnny's performance with that of Bill, Joe, and all the other students in his class. Johnny's test scores, his teacher's judgmental observations, and his grades should reflect his strengths and weaknesses as accurately as possible. The main purpose of the grade is to indicate the extent to which Johnny is growing, developing, and learning at a rate which is appropriate for him.

It is probable that highly competitive, publicly announced letter grading is more harmful to many children than has been realized in the past. Many physical education teachers have been guilty of subjecting pupils at the low end of test scoring results to public ridicule and embarrassment by posting these grades on a bulletin board, or by making them the overt basis for formulating groupings or teams. We are indeed fearful that we have done severe damage to the self-concept and self-confidence of many pupils who score at the low end of the scale by this public exposure.

It is also desirable, where possible, to utilize the observations and judgments of more than one teacher in grading each pupil. We believe that parent–teacher and parent–teacher–pupil conferences are the most effective methods for reporting and discussing pupil progress, particularly at the elementary school level.

More and more schools and colleges are changing their grading systems to increase student options and to decrease, or in some cases, to eliminate the possibility of recording on the official transcript any indication that the pupil has failed a course. Such plans can involve "pass-fail," or A, B, C, and Pass (with no record of any kind appearing on a transcript in the event a pupil does not complete the requirements of a course), and "plus" replacing a traditional letter grade as an indication that the student has fulfilled his obligations in the course but that no judgment of the quality of his work is implied other than satisfactory completion. Some institutions are supplementing these systems with teacher written comments and evaluations about their students for the official record. We generally favor this idea but realize it places a heavy burden of time and effort on the teacher, so the system must be tempered with the realities of time and energy limitations involved on the part of the instructional staff. A major complaint against these new trends is that transcripts contain less definitive information for reviewers in other institutions who have to depend on them for decisions such as admission to programs and departments, and even into classes of varying levels of ability.

Physical educators are facing the same influences and arguments that other teachers are concerning these new models of student evaluation. Predictably, the reaction is varied between teachers and among faculties. Younger teachers are now likely to be sympathetic to the new systems; in fact, most of them have already been evaluated by these systems in their high schools or colleges.

One discouraging development which is reported in a few schools and states is that a school board regulation or a state law has recently been approved which only requires each high school student to "enroll in a course in physical education" each semester he is registered as a full time student. The loophole is that the pupil who chooses not to do so need not work to achieve a "passing grade" in physical education. He can enroll in a class and then do little or nothing about meeting the normal expectations of the class. He can actually "flunk" the course but still meet the letter of the regulation or law which required him to "enroll" in the class. Ludicrous as this situation is, it is a reality in some locations. We can only hope the light of reason will beam on these situations soon and repeal such unwarranted legislation.

We wonder if perhaps the traditional letter grading system has outlived its usefulness in physical education. If we mainly are concerned about each pupil, if we really believe that our promise is to educate self-directing, self-responsible youths who have a wide repertoire of movement experiences, who participate skillfully in physical activities of their choice, who are highly motivated to participate in voluntary movement abilities on a regular basis throughout life, and who know and understand why, then perhaps our former concern for letter grades passes into insignificance. Particularly may this statement apply to pupils who, by most grading systems, are doomed to receiving C, D, and even F grades, by the assumptions inherent in the construction of that particular system. If we sincerely want to help each pupil to be as "physically educated" as possible, and to have a voluntary attitude toward physical education participation for a lifetime, as an outcome of his high school or college program, then we will eliminate the negative influences which impede such development.

Perhaps a pass–no credit system, accompanied by an individual profile of fitness achievement, sports achievement, knowledge achievement, and teacher judgment of social efficiency, constitutes the most desirable form of record keeping, pupil counseling, pupil motivation, and course reporting in physical education.

The other "great debate" in physical education grading concerns the identification of factors which should be considered in awarding the grade, whatever system of symbols is used. We believe the teacher should identify factors basic to the accomplishment of the objectives established for the lesson, the unit, and the course of physical education. The factors are assessable by measurement and by teacher judgment. They can be grouped in three major categories, with examples as follows:

1. Physical, or motor, factors. Skills in activities; fitness status; motor ability; postures; game performance.

2. Mental, or cognitive, factors. Knowledges and understanding of rules, strategy, performance, techniques, history, physiological and kinesiological principles, learning principles, health, safety, equipment.

3. Social, and affective, factors. Social behaviors in the physical

education environment; attitude; appreciation; sportsmanship; cooperation; citizenship; leadership; social relationships.

The teacher would have to decide arbitrarily which of these and similar factors to include in the total grade, and then would have to arrive at a relative "weighting" of them, based on his view of their priority of importance and the proportional time which had been devoted to their development in the instructional program. Thus, a total course grade can be evolved.

The controversy lies in the belief of many teachers that other factors besides the ones listed above should enter into the determination of the physical education grade, including attendance, uniform cleanliness, absences, tardiness, use of swear words, failure to take showers, and similar behaviors.

We believe these factors are inappropriate in a grading system. We regard them as matters of departmental policy, not as grading criteria. Hygienic practices and guidelines for controlling student conduct are important; we do not downgrade their significance, nor the role the physical educator can and should take in promoting desirable behaviors in these regards. However, we believe they are in the province of school administrative *policies,* and that violations should be handled through established school guidance and disciplinary channels. If grades are affected by these factors, they become confusing to students, parents, and administrators alike. It is not intended that the physical education grade serve the role of reward for good, or expected, normal behavior. Good teachers can manage these disciplinary and control problems without having to resort to the threat of lowering the grade.[5,14]

All instructors in the department should agree that normal behaviors with regard to dress, showering, conduct, language, promptness, and diligence are to be expected. It is assumed and expected that all pupils will behave in this manner. The authors know of physical education teachers who teach in this way and whose classes react accordingly, as expected.

In the case of persistent defiant behavior by a pupil which the teacher cannot correct or control, referral to the counselor, the dean of students, or the principal is in order. In such circumstances, the odds are high that this student has a generalized history of uncooperative behavior in and out of school. A case study should be made about this pupil and the sources of his difficulties. The school should take the lead in mobilizing the resources required to determine the exact nature of the problem and to assist with corrective action, through medical, educational, and social services of available community agencies.

TEST SELECTION

This extended discussion of the major purposes of physical education evaluation and pupil marking leads to the obvious conclusion that teachers must be familiar with many types of tests and evaluative instruments. Clarke* provides a summary statement to guide the physical educators' selection of relevant tests:

1. If individual physical fitness needs are to be met, tests measuring essential elements of physical fitness are necessary, in order to select those with such needs, to follow their progress, and to know when their needs have been met.
2. If maintenance of physical fitness on the part of all students is desired, again tests measuring essential elements of this quality are needed as a periodic check on fitness status.
3. If nutritional status or physiological efficiency of pupils are to be given special attention, appropriate tests in these areas should be selected.
4. If pupils with postural defects are to be selected for remedial classes, a test of this quality is obviously necessary.
5. If homogeneous grouping of pupils for the physical education program is considered desirable for pedagogical purposes and to provide a desirable setting for the development of social efficiency, general motor ability tests might well be selected.
6. If pupils with tendencies toward social maladjustments are to be discovered, personality and character tests and rating scales are essential.
7. If emphasis is to be placed upon the general development of athletic ability, tests of general motor capacity and ability will be found most useful.
8. If homogeneous grouping by specific skill ability is desired, appropriate skill tests and achievement scales are necessary.
9. If skill and understanding of specific physical education activities are sought, skill tests, knowledge tests, and attitude scales would be selected.
10. If reports of pupil progress are to be prepared for administrators, boards of education, and the public, the most essential physical and social growth factors should be measured.

It is now recognized that the systematic utilization of evaluation is one of the hallmarks of the professions which serve humanity.

---

* H. Harrison Clarke: *Application of Measurement to Health and Physical Education.* Englewood Cliffs, New Jersey: Prentice-Hall, Inc., 4th ed., 1967, p. 21.

RESEARCH IN PHYSICAL EDUCATION

Physical education is a relatively young field in the family of scholarly disciplines. By nature and tradition it has been an activity-oriented field. Young people basically enter this profession because of their desire to work with boys and girls through the medium of sports, dance, and fitness activities. They want to be teachers and coaches of youth. In the early days of the profession, very few physical educators dedicated their efforts to a research role. Some of these early research leaders were medical doctors who had been placed in positions of administration in college and university physical education programs. They developed anthropometric measurements, strength tests, and posture tests. They published their results and they altered their physical education programs in the directions indicated by research findings. They established the first physical education research laboratories, primarily in universities.

Gradually, the number of physical educators interested in research increased. Persons with basic graduate preparation in related fields such as psychology, child growth and development, physiology, and kinesiology became faculty members in physical education departments and fostered research relevant to their specialized interests.

As the number of young men and women entering the field expanded rapidly in this country, the percentage who selected a career in research remained very small. It became obvious that the way to increase the number of qualified research experts in physical education was to develop an interest in research among young, active teachers, coaches, and administrators. In effect, they had to be recruited and retrained with a research emphasis at the advanced graduate level. In some respects, this system for attracting qualified researchers into physical education differs from that of most other fields of knowledge, especially those which have held a place in the university curriculum for a long period of time. In many other fields, undergraduates decide that they want to become researchers, and they pursue an undergraduate and a graduate program which prepares them for this type of career, often under the tutelage of senior research professors. They continue in graduate education immediately upon receiving the bachelor's degree and remain in master's and doctoral programs until they receive their advanced degrees.

The physical educator typically has entered the field of teaching and coaching either at the end of the bachelor's degree work or after one graduate year of preparation leading to a master's degree or a teaching credential. Prior to World War II, a small number of these teachers and coaches did return to graduate school in order to complete doctoral degrees in physical education. Some of these persons prepared themselves for positions in research, while others turned to teacher preparation and departmental administration roles.

Since World War II, there has been a boom in enrollment in physical education preparation at all levels in hundreds of colleges and universities. More and more institutions are establishing physical education research laboratories. Interdepartmental research programs are being developed. Young people are learning about research opportunities in their undergraduate programs, and more physical educators are electing a career in research at an early age. Physical educators are obtaining funds to sponsor their research from governmental agencies and private foundations.

The scope and variety of inquiries and investigations being made on physical education topics broaden each year. It is astounding to peruse the table of contents of recent issues of the *Research Quarterly,* and the topical index provided in the yearly report, *Completed Research in Health, Physical Education, and Recreation,* published by the AAHPER, and to note the great diversity of subjects covered in the research literature of physical education. Research reports by physical educators also appear in the scholarly journals of many other fields.

In a recent unique book Clarke and Clarke[7] have clearly described the current status of research endeavors by physical educators. One cannot help being highly impressed, if not slightly overawed, by the broad scope of the investigations reported and the variety of research methodologies employed. A review of this book clearly fortifies the somewhat self-evident assertion that today physical education can be regarded as a multi-disciplinary field of broad scope. It relies on the foundational fields of knowledge for much of the theoretical formulations and scientific and philosophical underpinnings upon which its understandings and practices are based. Physical educators are now receiving advanced research preparation in doctoral and post-doctoral programs across the country, not only in physical education itself but frequently in Ph.D. major and minor programs in several other disciplines as well. Likewise, interested scholars and researchers from related fields study various phenomena central to the body of knowledge of physical education and make significant contributions to it.

A brief review indicates that physical education research today delves into many diverse topics in areas such as philosophical inquiry; history and historiography; child growth and development (maturation, body types, growth patterns); psychological foundations (motor learning, behavior modification, motivation, concept foundation, attitudes, non-verbal communication, personality, self-concept and body image); exercise physiology (physiological control systems which adapt the organism to exercise stress under various environmental influences); biomechanics of human movement (gravity, resistance, air pressure, leverage, flexibility, stability, acceleration); neurological foundations (motor learning, reaction and movement time, kinesthesis, memory, retention, transfer, mental practice, specificity of motor skills); sociology (socialization, norms, social stratification and mobility, sport in institutions, religion, economy, mass communications, leisure, work, social problems); nutrition (diets for athletes); anthropology (competition, cooperation, acculturation); political science (sports as an instrument of national policy, international goodwill, propaganda, health, rehabilitation, ritual and ceremony); economics (spectator sports, leisure time expenditures, newspapers and magazines, motion pictures and television); and, indeed, other disciplines could, with justifiable reason, be added to this list. Of course the examples in parentheses above are not all-inclusive; space prohibits a more exhaustive listing.

Two of the persistent problems which have faced physical education over the years are pointed up by the above observations. First, physical education has never been clearly identified and described as a scholarly discipline with its own body of knowledge and central concerns.[17] Several professional organizations have studied this problem in recent years, and progress is being made toward identifying and describing a theoretical framework of physical education as an area of scholarly study and research.[21] Individuals[6,17] and university faculties also are contributing significantly to solutions to this problem. Let it suffice to indicate here that one reason these efforts are so essential to the progress of physical education is that a theoretical framework of a field of study is essential to the formulation of hypotheses which guide the work of the researchers of that field, and which give relevance and priority to their endeavors. Arriving at a common acceptance of the nature and scope of the body of knowledge which is unique to physical education will enhance the mobilization of our resources on significant research and further advancement of knowledge in this field. Likewise, practical applications of basic research to the solution of educational problems, through applied and field research, will improve the quality of educational decisions being made every day by teachers, coaches, supervisors, administrators, and teacher educators.

Because of the diversity of phenomena which physical education researchers investigate, we are entering an era of research specialization. Doctoral candidates interested in a career in research now choose a concentration in areas such as exercise physiology, neurological bases of human movement, history of physical education, sociology of sport, philosophy of physical education, anthropological foundations of physical education, curriculum, teacher education and other relevant specializations. Several doctoral programs now are highly interdisciplinary in content. A student may take as much as one-third to one-half of his total program in one or more departments outside of physical education, such as in physiology, psychology, neurology, sociology, history, philosophy, or anthropology.

In summary, research in physical education today is much more highly sophisticated than formerly in conceptualizing significant problems and approaches to their investigation, in research design, methodology, and instrumentation, and in analysis of data and the formulation of conclusions and recommendations.

Research is a fascinating and challenging career in physical education. Young people entering the profession should become aware of its potentialities as one possible career goal. Many teacher education programs now are providing research experience to undergraduate students, so there is more opportunity to become acquainted with this type of professional activity.

Another major problem in research is that of acquainting teachers, coaches, and administrators with recent research findings of significance for school practices. Practitioners in physical education should know the major sources of research publications. They should have enough training and experience in studying and interpreting research results that they can make appropriate applications to the modifications of their teaching and administration practices for the purpose of improving the program offered to boys and girls. Most graduate programs attempt to help solve this problem by offering some type of course in research review, critique, and analysis. Unfortunately, these offerings are not an entirely satisfactory solution to this problem. The profession needs to extend its best effort and thought to the question of how to bridge the gap between research findings and school practices. Practitioners need to be convinced of the value of devoting some of their time to keeping up with selected recent research and of applying the most relevant and best validated findings to the improvement of on-going programs. Researchers must find meaningful ways to communicate their results to practitioners.

Professor Lawrence F. Locke,[19] and others, believe that very little progress will be made in bridging the gap between the knowledge produced by the researchers and improved curriculum and instruction activities by teachers until a third type of specialist becomes available, namely, an interpreter of research. This role requires specialized preparation, a talent for understanding the results of significant research and its implications for practice, plus an unusual ability to translate these findings into written and oral prose which communicates clearly to practitioners precisely how these research results can be incorporated into teaching and coaching practices. Few such experts exist at the moment. Hopefully, they will become more numerous in the near future so that we may take full advantage of their expertise to improve our instructional programs in all phases of physical education.

Two excellent examples of publications which exemplify this proposal are the *Physical Fitness News Letter,* published by Dr. H. Harrison Clarke of the University of Oregon, and the *Learning and Physical Education Newsletter,* by John N. Drowatzky.

Not only does the physical educator have an obligation to keep himself informed of selected research findings from the literature within his own profession, but he should keep up with recent information from highly related fields which have been mentioned previously. Actually, this approach has long existed in our traditional teacher education programs, particularly at the undergraduate level, through the courses in "foundations" or "principles" which virtually every major student has taken at one time or another. These courses use well-known texts which propose desirable "principles" of physical education[1] which are based on knowledge from "foundation"[23] fields. "Principles" are guides to action which, if followed by the teacher, coach, and administrator, presumably enable them to perform more effectively.

Physical education principles[4] generally are evolved from validated "generalizations" produced by scholars and researchers in related fields and in physical education. The enormity of the challenge to the physical educator to attempt to keep up-to-date with these principles and generalizations is strikingly evident upon perusal of even one principles book. A recent approach to this dilemma is the *Foundations of Physical Education* series,* which consists of books written by physical education scholars who also are noted authorities in one related field of knowledge. These authors have selected recent "relevant generalizations" from their respective fields of knowledge and have described them for the physical educator. The physical educator in turn can formulate his own principles and desirable practices, based on the validated generalizations. This series is another attempt to bridge the gap between research and practice.

Commendable progress indeed is being made throughout the United States and many other countries of the world in physical education research. There still remain many unanswered questions and unsolved problems to occupy the time, energies, intelligence, and talents of interested and qualified students. An acceptable notion of the unlimited possibilities available in physical education research can be obtained by reviewing such publications as: (1) *Research Quarterly* of the American Association for Health, Physical Education, and Recreation; (2) *Completed Research in Health, Physical Education, and Recreation* (yearly), published by the American Association for Health, Physical Education, and Recreation; (3) *Journal of Sports Medicine and Physical Fitness*; (4) *Microfilm Bulletin,* School of Physical Education, University of Oregon; (5) *Education Index*; and (6) *Bridging the Gap,* Department of Physical Education, City University of New York.

Let us remember a principle that is axiomatic in many other fields—the lifeblood of practical progress is uninhibited basic research.

Selected References

1. Barrow, Harold M.: *Man and His Movement: Principles of Physical Education.* Philadelphia: Lea & Febiger, 1971.
2. Barrow, Harold M., and McGee, Rosemary: *A Practical Approach to Measurement in Physical Education.* Philadelphia: Lea & Febiger, 2nd ed., 1971.
3. Bloom, Benjamin S., Hastings, J. Thomas, and Madaus, George F.: *Handbook on Formative and Summative Evaluation of Student Learning.* New York: McGraw-Hill Book Company, Inc., 1971.

---

* *Foundations of Physical Education* series, John E. Nixon, editor. Englewood Cliffs, N.J.: Prentice-Hall, Inc., 1968.

4. Bookwalter, Karl W., and Vander Zwaag, Harold J.: *Foundations and Principles of Physical Education*. Philadelphia: W. B. Saunders Company, 1969.
5. Broer, Marion R.: "Are Our Physical Education Grades Fair?" *J. Health, Phys. Educ.-Rec.*, 30:27 (October, 1959).
6. Brown, Camille, and Cassidy, Rosalind: *Theory in Physical Education: A Guide to Program Change*. Philadelphia: Lea & Febiger, 1963.
7. Clarke, David H., and Clarke, H. Harrison: *Research Processses in Physical Education, Recreation, and Health*. Englewood Cliffs, N. J.: Prentice-Hall, Inc., 1970.
8. Clarke, H. Harrison: *Application of Measurement to Health and Physical Education*. Englewood Cliffs, N. J.: Prentice-Hall, Inc., 4th ed., 1966.
9. "Classification of Students for Physical Education." (Statement of the Committee on Exercise and Physical Fitness of the American Medical Association). *J. Health, Phys. Educ. and Rec.*, 38:16-18 (February, 1967).
10. *Completed Research in Health, Physical Education and Recreation.* 1967 (Vol. IX), 1968 (Vol. X), 1969 (Vol. XI), 1970 (Vol. XII), 1971 (Vol. XIII), 1972 (Vol. XIV), 1973 (Vol. V), Washington, D. C.: American Association for Health, Physical Education, and Recreation.
11. Franks, B. Don, and Deutsch, Helga: *Evaluating Performance in Physical Education*. New York: Academic Press, 1973.
12. Glass, Gene V.: "The Many Faces of 'Educational Accountability'." *Phi Delta Kappan,* 636-639. June, 1972.
13. Golder, Philip: "A New Physical Education Report Card." *The Physical Educator*, 26:162-164 Dec., 1969.
14. Gustafson, William F.: "A Look at Evaluative Criteria in Physical Education." *The Physical Educator,* 20:172-173 (December, 1963).
15. Hart, Thomas A., and Whitfield, Melvin: "Physical Education and Athletics in Western Africa." *J. Health, Phys. Educ.-Rec.*, 33:19-21 (March, 1962).
16. Haskins, Mary Jane: *Evaluation in Physical Education*. Dubuque, Iowa: William C. Brown and Company, 1971.
17. Henry, Franklin M.: "Physical Education, an Academic Discipline." *J. Health, Phys. Educ.-Rec.*, 35:32-33, 69 (September, 1964).
18. Johnson, Barry L., and Nelson, Jack K.: *Practical Measurements for Evaluation in Physical Education*. Minneapolis: Burgess Publishing Company, 1969.
19. Locke, Lawrence Fred: *Research in Physical Education: A Critical View*. New York City: Teachers College, Columbia University, 1969.
20. Mathews, Donald K.: *Measurement in Physical Education*. Philadelphia: W. B. Saunders Company, 4th ed., 1973.
21. Metheny, Eleanor: "The 'Design' Conference," *J. Health, Phys. Educ.-Rec.*, 37:6 (May, 1966).
22. Neilson, N. P., and Jensen, Clayne R.: *Measurements and Statistics in Physical Education*. Belmont, Calif.: Wadsworth Publishing Company, 1972.
23. Oberteuffer, Delbert, and Ulrich, Celeste: *Physical Education*. New York: Harper & Row, Publishers, Inc., 4th ed., 1970.
24. *Research Methods in Health, Physical Education, and Recreation.* Washington, D. C.: American Association for Health, Physical Education, and Recreation, 1973.
25. Rosenshine, Barak, and McGaw, Barry: "Issues in Assessing Teacher Accountability in Public Education." *Phi Delta Kappan,* 53:640-643. June, 1972.
26. Safrit, Margaret J.: *Evaluation in Physical Education: Assessing Motor Behavior*. Englewood Cliffs, N. J.: Prentice-Hall, Inc., 1973.
27. Shea, John B.: "The Pass-Fail Option and Physical Education." *J. Health, Phys. Educ.-Rec.*, 42:19, 20. May, 1971.
28. Sheehan, Thomas J.: *An Introduction to the Evaluation of Measurement Data in Physical Education*. Reading, Mass.: Addison-Wesley Publishing Company, Inc., 1971.

29. Smith, Bryan C., and Lerch, Harold A.: "Contract Grading." *The Physical Educator,* 29:80-82 (May, 1972).
30. Thomas, G. Patience: "Skill Testing." *The Physical Educator,* 26:122-123. October, 1969.
30a. Ulrich, Celeste, and Nixon, John E.: *Tones of Theory—A Tentative Perspective.* Washington, D.C.: Physical Education Division, American Association for Health, Physical Education and Recreation, 1972.
31. Van Hoven, James B.: "Reporting Pupil Progress: A Broad Rationale for New Practices." *Phi Delta Kappan,* 53: February, 1972.
32. Weber, Jerome C., and Lamb, David R.: *Statistics and Research in Physical Education.* St. Louis: The C. V. Mosby Company, 1970.
33. Willgoose, Carl E.: *Evaluation in Health Education and Physical Education.* New York: McGraw-Hill Book Company, Inc., 1961.
34. Zeigler, Earle F., Howell, Maxwell, and Trekell, Marianna. *Research in the History, Philosophy, and Comparative Aspects of Physical Education and Sport: Bibliographies and Techniques.* Champaign: Stipes Publishing Company, 1971.

INDEX

208988